I0004233

How Safe Is Safe Enough?

Measuring and Predicting Autonomous Vehicle Safety

Philip Koopman, Ph.D.

Carnegie Mellon University

For Cindy, Moira, Brynn, and Ben.

First Edition, 2022. (Version 1.0.01)

Copyright © 2022 by Philip Koopman
All rights reserved.
ISBN: 9798846251243   Trade Paperback
ISBN: 9798848273397   Hardcover

No part of this publication may be reproduced or transmitted in any form or by any means, including photocopy, scanning, recording, or any information storage and retrieval system, without permission in writing from the copyright holder.

INFORMATION IN THIS BOOK IS PROVIDED *"AS IS"* AND ANY EXPRESS OR IMPLIED WARRANTIES ARE DISCLAIMED. IN NO EVENT SHALL THE AUTHOR OR PUBLISHER BE LIABLE FOR ANY DIRECT, INDIRECT, INCIDENTAL, SPECIAL, EXEMPLARY, CONSEQUENTIAL, OR OTHER DAMAGES, EVEN IF ADVISED OF THE POSSIBILITY OF SUCH DAMAGES. THE INFORMATION IN THIS BOOK IS INTENDED TO ONLY PARTIALLY SUPPORT SAFETY PRACTICES, AND MORE IS REQUIRED TO ACHIEVE ACCEPTABLE SAFETY. YOU ARE RESPONSIBLE FOR THE SAFETY OF THE SYSTEMS YOU DESIGN AND OPERATE REGARDLESS OF THE CONTENT OF THIS BOOK. THE AUTHOR IS NOT A LAWYER AND NOTHING IN THIS BOOK SHOULD BE CONSIDERED AS LEGAL ADVICE. BY OPENING THIS BOOK, THE READER AGREES TO THESE TERMS AND ACCEPTS SOLE RESPONSIBILITY FOR ANY AND ALL DIRECT AND INDIRECT USES OF ITS CONTENTS.

Contents

Preface

The promise of autonomous vehicles

The promise of fully autonomous cars that drive themselves has beckoned for decades. It is typical for an American to spend an hour a day in a car, with much of that time spent in a relatively unpleasant commute to work rather than enjoying the idyllic lure of an open road adventure that is so baked into the culture. Wouldn't it be nice if we could watch a movie, take a nap, or otherwise relax instead of jockeying for position with all the other commuters? Or maybe we could go to sleep in our garage and wake up in another city, our personal luxury transportation pod having let us sleep away the boring hours of an all-night drive to the next business meeting.

Other potential applications for autonomous vehicle (AV) technology abound. They include a potential major restructuring of long-haul trucking, parcel delivery, public transportation, and in particular, dramatically increased access to transportation for those who cannot drive. There are tradeoffs involved, and it remains to be seen how things will play out. But with tens of billions of dollars pouring into investments in the technology, expectations are set high.

A salient AV promise is dramatically improving road safety. Indeed, the lead selling point has come to be that deploying the technology is urgent because every year it is delayed means more people die on our roadways.

However, the topic of safety is far more complicated than the facile talking points usually involved, such as "computers won't drive drunk so of course they will be safer than human drivers."[1] On the other hand, it is unreasonable to expect AVs to be perfectly safe. Rather, AVs should be acceptably safe, achieving some balance between the benefits they provide and the risk they impose on society.

A common notion is that AVs will be safe enough if they are better than human drivers. While intuitively appealing, that simple criterion is unlikely to work in practice. First, "safer than a human driver" is much more complicated than it might seem if you need to address which driver, operating where, and under what conditions. Second, other considerations need to be addressed such as how much redistribution of risk is permissible. Is it OK to kill twice as many pedestrians if the total fatalities including passengers decreases? And third, the technology is so immature that predicting the safety of an AV before it is deployed is a major challenge.

In reality, nobody yet knows if AVs will be as safe as human drivers when deployed at scale. We hope that will be the case, but it might not even be possible with our current technical abilities beyond a small number of benign environments with highly constrained capabilities. Or we might just be another few billion dollars of investment and a year away from self-driving

---

[1] This particular fallacy is debunked in section 4.8.2.

utopia.[2] Regardless, we would like to do better than deploy with insufficient evidence that the technology is safe and just see how it turns out.

Being able to know that an AV is safe enough before we have experience with at-scale deployment is no easy problem. But if we cut corners on being able to ensure acceptable safety, it seems likely that high-profile crashes are inevitable. A pattern of such crashes – or even one especially horrific event – might cause society to reject the technology, setting back progress a decade or more.[3]

AVs have been the technology of the future for decades. Maybe this will be the time the technology really deploys at scale. Certainly I'd welcome improved road safety and the ability to relax instead of having to concentrate on drives I find boring. But this technology will not be viable if the public does not find it acceptably safe. To get there we need to understand not only what acceptably safe means, but also how we might measure whether we are there or not. That is the scope of this book.

An important scope disclaimer is in order. This book does not address the significant challenges involved in taking a machine learning-based technology and making it safe. That topic is crucially important, but is an entirely different area that is still in flux. So this is not about telling anyone how to design a safe AV. Rather it is about how to structure a way to evaluate whether the designers have actually achieved their goal of being safe enough.

Why should I listen to this guy?

I started working on AV safety in the mid-1990s as a member of the Carnegie Mellon University Navlab team as part of the Automated Highway Systems (AHS) project run by US DOT Federal Highways.[4] That was years before the DARPA grand challenges. The work culminated in a 1997 demo on a closed highway in San Diego.[5] At the AHS demo, Carnegie Mellon demonstrated camera-based lane following technology on not only cars, but also a pair of city buses. Berkeley PATH demonstrated platooned cars guided by magnets embedded in the roadway. A number of other organizations also produced useful technology and engineering analysis[6] but in the end there was no planned path forward, and the idea went dormant in the public eye for almost a decade before DARPA picked up the topic.

---

[2] Unlikely to happen. More likely, it will be many years and many more tens of billions of dollars before this technology can deploy at scale.

[3] While different in many ways, the history of the nuclear power industry is an important cautionary tale for what happens when high-profile loss events occur after society has been assured that a technology is safe.

[4] See this AHS status report by Lay et al. from 1996:
https://rosap.ntl.bts.gov/view/dot/38381

[5] See Thorpe, Jochem & Pomerleau, 1997:
https://www.ri.cmu.edu/pub_files/pub2/thorpe_charles_1997_1/thorpe_charles_1997_1.pdf

[6] See Bishop, Dopart & Shladover 1997:
https://path.berkeley.edu/sites/default/files/demo97foravs17v6.pdf

I was not part of the DARPA Grand Challenges, but I was involved in other ground robotics safety and robustness via work with a team at the National Robotics Engineering Center (NREC) at Carnegie Mellon University.[7] NREC and its parent Robotics Institute have produced many of the key players in the AV industry today. However, I'm not a "robo-grad" as they are called. Rather, I have worked at the engineering school with a concentration on dependability and safety. During the initial AHS project and later the decade or so I spent working with NREC, I learned about autonomous vehicles and spent a lot of time thinking about safety.

I also have considerable experience with non-autonomous embedded system software design practices and safety in a number of other industries. I've had research funding, industry experience, and hundreds of consulting engagements covering conventional automotive, railway, chemical process, aviation, factory automation, building automation, vertical transportation, electrical power, consumer goods, combat systems, chip design, and even medical applications. I have also dealt with safety standards across those fields. Additionally, I have up-close and personal lived experience with applied safety practices from my time as a US Navy submarine officer, where so many things must be done perfectly if you and your shipmates want to avoid having a very bad day. Finally, I have seen the inside of a courtroom and other legal processes while working as an expert witness.[8]

More recently I have become involved in safety standards specific to AVs and processes that are creating AV regulations. Sensing a reluctance of the industry to commit to AV-specific standards, I spearheaded an effort to create ANSI/UL 4600, which is aimed at ensuring that an AV is acceptably safe.[9] As I write this, ANSI/UL 4600 is well on its way to being updated to a third edition to fully encompass not only light vehicles, but also heavy trucks.[10] I am also active on several other industry standards committees that deal with conventional and autonomous vehicle safety.

After those experiences and more, I feel that I have as much visibility and insight into the problems with AV safety as anyone can have in such a fast-moving and secretive world. I hope that this book makes it easier for others to understand the various challenges and potential solutions I've seen along the way.

Audience

This book is intended to be useful for a wide range of stakeholders who are interested in ensuring that AV technology is deployed safely. That includes engineers, regulators, legislative technical staff, government affairs

---

[7] See: https://www.nrec.ri.cmu.edu/

[8] For a one-hour lecture on what I learned in one such case, see:
https://youtu.be/DKHa7rxkvK8

[9] See Koopman et al. 2019:
https://users.ece.cmu.edu/~koopman/pubs/Koopman19_WAISE_UL4600.pdf

[10] For a simple starting page for ANSI/UL 4600 information, see:
https://users.ece.cmu.edu/~koopman/ul4600/index.html

staff, insurers, technical journalists, students, mobility experts, and technology enthusiasts. Rather than attempting to write for a single uniform audience, each section is written in a way that is as accessible as I can manage while still not holding back on detail relevant to deeper understanding of the core issues for specialists.

Depending on the reader's background some sections will be more accessible than others. I've provided summaries for second and some third-level headings to follow the main flow for those who might find some sections less relevant to their needs. If you find your eyes glazing over at some point, feel free to skip ahead to the next summary paragraph to get a change of topic. If you are relatively new to the area of AV safety in general, you might want to start with my free video short course on AV safety to get up to speed before diving into the details in this book.[11]

Book Organization

The chapters of the book are organized as follows:

- Chapter 1 provides a light introduction and whirlwind tour of the material in the book.

- Chapter 2 goes over terminology, vehicle automation modes, and key safety challenges that need to be addressed to be able to say an AV is acceptably safe.

- Chapter 3 covers risk acceptance frameworks. It turns out there is more than one way to frame the question of what risk might be acceptable.

- Chapter 4 covers what people mean by "safe." This chapter is a result of having been in too many discussions where people were talking past each other meaning completely different things by the word "safe."[12] It also includes a list of misleading industry-promoted talking points that are harmful to productive discussion about acceptable safety.

- Chapter 5 discusses how to set an acceptably safe goal, including setting a comparative safety baseline and accounting for things beyond simply total number of fatalities involved in crashes.

- Chapter 6 discusses how to measure and predict safety in more detail. It is not enough to count up the losses after the fact. There needs to be a way to build confidence before deploying.

- Chapter 7 covers safety cases and how Safety Performance Indicators (SPIs) can be integrated into safety cases to provide safety metrics supporting a "safe enough" decision-making process. I believe the concept of SPIs as presented will be a key to deploying AVs safely at scale.

---

[11] Short course lectures are hosted with open access both on YouTube and Archive.org, including both video lectures and slides:
https://users.ece.cmu.edu/~koopman/lectures/index.html#av

[12] Too often, I myself have been a participant in the talking-past exercise. This chapter is in part a reflection to help me get better at not doing that. More importantly, if we don't even know what we mean by "safe" we cannot have an intelligent discussion about "how safe."

- Chapter 8 deals with how to identify, monitor, and respond to SPI-based metrics. Coming up with an actionable and measurable safety case is the hard part. This book frames the situation, but is not a deep dive into the nuances of safety case construction itself.
- Chapter 9 (finally!) outlines how to decide when it is ethically responsible to deploy an AV despite inevitable uncertainty. It also covers how to ensure acceptably safe road testing, which is more difficult to do safely than simply putting a driver in the vehicle and telling them not to crash.
- Chapter 10 discusses some ethical issues relevant to AV safety that will need to be addressed before the technology can be deployed at scale, including regulatory considerations. Spoiler: the infamous Trolley Problem is not what we should be spending time talking about.
- Chapter 11 wraps up, presenting pointers to resources readers might find helpful.

Writing Practicalities

This book is more of a discussion and not an academic review paper. It is light on references not directly relevant to the discussion, and even has a bit of snark to lighten things up at times.[13] You will not find an exhaustive literature survey here, but rather mentions of things that have caught my eye as being especially relevant. There is a bit of redundancy across some sections because some topics interact with multiple other topics. I've tried to cross-reference and shorten overlapping discussions, but there is no perfect solution for this. If you think I really missed the boat on something let me know.[14]

Part of the informality is that many references are to information on the Web, with an emphasis on finding as many open access sources as possible rather than paywalled material. Rather than spend time on tedious (and often elusive) formal citations, I've added URLs. If a URL goes stale, readers are encouraged to look up the history of the URL via the Wayback Machine at: https://archive.org/ to recover the relevant content. All URLs listed have been checked as being active as of July 2022.

Some footnotes refer to Wikipedia and other non-authoritative sources. These references are made because the particular material cited seems like a reasonable starting point for those who want to understand more about a topic. They are not meant as a definitive justification for a point being made. Readers are cautioned that material on Wikipedia might not always be accurate.

I've used footnotes to try to avoid derailing the main discussion with parentheticals and to provide references to resources that are freely

---

[13] Safety of life-critical systems is in fact serious business. But education without at least a little humor is ineffective, even if the topic is serious.

[14] We also use the "royal we" in subsequent chapters. It is really just me talking.

accessible to the maximum degree practical. Rather than typing in all the URLs you can find a web page with clickable links here:

https://users.ece.cmu.edu/~koopman/SafeEnough/

Some of the contents of this book have appeared in various forms in blog entries, web pages, and the like. However, the new material is substantial, and even existing material has been edited or even rewritten for this book. This book is definitely not just a rehash of blog posts – not by a long shot.

Finally, examples use English and Metric units more or less at random in an attempt to appeal to users of both systems.[15] Discussions of regulatory matters emphasize what is happening in the US. Regulatory challenges outside the US differ in the details, but those differences are not central to the message of this book.

Acknowledgments

While the book has been written recently, the path has been long and winding. I thank the following with special recognition for their contributions both direct and indirect on this path: Michael Barr, Michelle Bayouth, Ensar Becic, Sagar Behere, Jen Black, Simon Burton, Missy Cummings, Rami Debouk, Wes Doonan, Jackie Erickson, Uma Ferrell, Frank Fratrik, Tom Fuhrman, Mallory Graydon, Glen Haydon, Mahmood Hikmet, Daniel Hinkle, Yoav Hollander, Michael Holloway, Casidhe Hutchison, Rolf Johansson, Aaron Kane, Tim Kelly, John Knight, Katina Michael, Joe Miller, Beth Osyk, Brendon Ouimette, Fred Perkins, Jens Pollmer, Deborah Prince, Justin Ray, Paula Ranallo, Heather Sakellariou, Steve Shladover, Dan Siewiorek, Don Slavik, Zhongxin Sun, Chuck Thorpe, Kim Wasson, Jack Weast, Chuck Weinstock, William Widen, Marilyn Wolf, Junko Yoshida, David Zipper, Membership of IFIP WG 10.4, and Contributors to ANSI/UL 4600. Also, after the first printing, I received helpful comments that informed revisions from: Patricia Herdman, Tom Fleischmann.

Everyone can improve, and I'm no exception. If you see something in this book that you disagree with, something exceptionally relevant I did not cover or, worse, an outright mistake, please let me know via an e-mail to: AVSafety@Koopman.us

Philip Koopman
Pittsburgh, PA, September 2022.

---

[15] That is my story, and I'm sticking to it. Consider it trying to be fair to readers of both systems.

1.   Introduction

Just make sure the autonomous vehicle is at least as safe as a human driver. Really, how hard can it be to figure that out?

The fact that you are reading an entire book on the topic of "safe enough" should be a hint that this problem gets more complex the deeper you go. Find a comfy reading place and let's dig in.

This book attempts to find answers to a question that seems simple on its face: how will we know when Autonomous Vehicles (AVs) are safe enough to deploy?

To answer that question we touch upon terminology, why AV safety is difficult, the nature of safety vs. risk, what "enough" might mean for safety, dealing with uncertainty, metrics, decision criteria, regulations, and accompanying ethical issues. While we go through those topics, do not forget that the point of all this is to be able to answer the question: "Is this AV safe enough to deploy on public roads?" We seek answers based on knowledge and engineering rigor rather than hope, faith, bluster or willful ignorance.

1.1. Scope

The scope of this book is a discussion of how to determine that an AV is safe enough to deploy. While there is an overview of many of the technical challenges to creating an AV, the emphasis is more about how to measure whether the result is acceptably safe. That includes defining a risk framework as well as metrics that can both predict safety and provide a traceable path to the AV design and validation.

Later chapters have a fair amount of detail on the use of Safety Performance Indicators (SPIs) as they are conceived in the ANSI/UL 4600 safety standard.[16] While there might be other ways to accurately predict AV safety before deployment, an SPI-based approach is the way we think will work best.

Topics in scope tend to be in the areas of safety engineering, metrics, ethics, and regulatory approaches. This book encompasses topics relevant to company leadership, regulators, and other stakeholders having a way to know that any decision to deploy an AV or test it on public roads is being made in a responsible manner after considering relevant factors.

Topics out of scope for the book are details regarding machine learning validation, software safety, and technical details of suitable arguments that might be put into a safety case. Much of that can be found in ANSI/UL 4600, but it is not our emphasis here. What ANSI/UL 4600 puts out of scope is a

---

[16] See materials at: https://users.ece.cmu.edu/~koopman/ul4600/index.html

framework for deciding how safe is acceptably safe. That is what we do in this book.

1.2. A whirlwind tour

Here is a whirlwind tour of the contents of the book. Buckle your seat belts!

Chapter 2:

To understand how safe we need an autonomous vehicle (AV) to be, we first need to understand what we actually mean by "autonomous." We take that to mean a situation in which there is no natural person immediately responsible for safety regarding the "self-driving" part of the vehicle. While it is traditional to use the infamous SAE levels in this discussion, we believe the Levels hurt more than help for discussions regarding safety with the general public and regulators. We propose an alternate categorization of: driver assistance, supervised automation, autonomous operation, and vehicle testing. Those categories revolve around the role of the driver rather than the technical approach used to implement automation.

Make sure that you know that an ODD (Operational Design Domain) is the set of conditions for which an AV is designed to operate, and that articles describing the SAE Levels typically get Level 3 wrong in some way that is relevant to safety.

Autonomous vehicles have key safety challenges at every stage of what is often called an "autonomy pipeline" that runs from sensors through computations to vehicle outputs. Traditional safety-critical software approaches make convenient assumptions such as the external world is perfectly understood and there is one uniquely correct response to every stimulus. Moreover, software safety typically assumes someone can look at the software and determine if it is in fact correct. None of that really works out for the perception and "AI" parts of AV technology. And there is the matter of unknown unknowns – things we do not realize we do not know that might nonetheless cause a fatality while driving. It's a can of worms.[17]

Chapter 3:

A variety of different risk acceptance frameworks might be used. Frameworks vary by whether acceptable risk is some value relative to natural phenomena or is in comparison to some alternative system. Do you want to compare to the risk of death by lightning? Or the risk of death from a human-driven car instead of an AV? While comparing to the risk of human-driven cars is a popular starting point, it is only a starting point.

---

[17] If it were easy everyone would already have an AV in their garage. We are not even close to that now.

Chapter 4:

Whenever someone says an AV is "safe" you might be astounded by the range of things that can mean. Indeed, if you ask someone what they mean by safe you might get a tangled up set of answers instead of a clean definition. We break the possible meanings of "safe" down into categories including: comparison to human driver, good roadmanship, lots of testing, lots of simulation, followed safety standards, is insured, is a product of a company that says safety is #1, and cannot be as bad as a human driver because it uses a computer instead.

The thing is, maybe safety is most of those definitions all at once. We propose a hierarchy of safety needs to organize all the definitions.[18] We also tear into more than a dozen myths, talking points, and outright propaganda themes that tend to be used to confuse the topic of what safety might be and why we should believe AVs will improve safety on public roads.

Chapter 5:

The current default for "safe enough" in most discussions is at least as safe as a human driver. Understanding what that means requires knowing what kinds of harm we are comparing (fatality, injuries), on what types of roads, in which states, in which operational conditions, and for which drivers. By the way, 60-something year old drivers are the safest.[19]

The difficult part is that just being exactly as good as a human driver will not be enough because of consumer attitudes and the tendency of AV crashes to get more press. A simplistic utilitarian argument is that if an AV is just 10% safer overall than human drivers it should be deployed because it will save lives. However, stakeholders expect computers to be much better than human drivers, and engineering margin needs to be included to handle inevitable uncertainty about safety predictions. In reality, AVs might need to have a predicted safety of 10 to 100 times better than humans when initially deployed to be viable. Anything less risks a loss of trust and backlash when the crashes start happening in the real world.

Chapter 6:

You cannot measure safety without putting numbers on things. Lagging metrics tend to measure outcomes, whereas leading metrics try to predict how safety will turn out later. However, the leading vs. lagging thing is relative to other metrics on a spectrum rather than a clear-cut distinction.

There are all sorts of metrics that might be useful, including measuring different stages of autonomy pipeline performance, engineering rigor, and even road miles. Disengagements are probably not that helpful in predicting

---

[18] Maslow comes into play. Who said freshman psychology was a waste of time?

[19] Bet younger readers did not see that one coming! For older readers keep this in mind the next time someone tries to age-shame you on social media about AV safety. It has certainly come in handy for us.

safety.[20] A good leading metric needs to be predictive of safety rather than just correlative or it is prone to being gamed. We like ANSI/UL 4600-style Safety Performance Indicators (SPIs) because they are linked to a safety case (see next chapter).

Metrics need a pass/fail threshold criterion or they cannot be used to answer the "safe enough" question. The numbers we need are not "more is better" but rather "is this number good enough to meet the safety goal?" The average probably is not what matters for most metrics. Safety is not about the 99,999,999 miles where there was no fatal crash – it is about the 1 mile where there was a fatal crash. That means safety metrics need to be especially good at measuring and predicting very infrequent but high consequence events. Safety is about other harms too, but fatalities tend to be the headline issue.

Chapter 7:

Safety cases provide a structured argument based on evidence that a particular claim for safety is true. Once we have defined what we mean by "safe enough" we should build a safety case to convince stakeholders that a claim of "safe enough" is true based on a reasonable argument backed up by evidence. A Safety Performance Indicator (SPI) is a metric that is directly attached to a claim that can monitor if the claim is falsified (disproven). If your claim is that you never get too close to a pedestrian, the SPI metric looks at how often that happens,[21] and raises an alarm if the claim is invalidated too often.[22]

Another issue with safety cases in the real world is that the safety case will have omissions, because it is impossible to guarantee you have fully analyzed an open world operational environment. There is always some safety issue that you have not thought of, or that will not even exist until after you deploy. This means safety cases are only somewhat about mathematically deductive proof, because they need to grapple with the

---

[20] Disengagements might have seemed like a good idea at the time, and kudos to California for trying to promote data transparency for AV testing. But it's time to move on to something that reflects testing safety outcomes. On the other, hand crash descriptions are proving a lot more useful as an impetus for safety transparency.
See: https://www.dmv.ca.gov/portal/vehicle-industry-services/autonomous-vehicles/autonomous-vehicle-collision-reports/

[21] Remember the part where safety is about very low probability events? The threshold might be once every million hours. But most thresholds will not be zero because no system is perfect. Safety does not quite require perfection, but it can get extremely close to that, so we need SPI thresholds that can cope with very low probabilities.

[22] Wait – if a claim is only a little false is that OK? The difference between a mathematically pure safety case and the real world is right here staring you in the face. A claim that is *almost* never false can be good enough. Whether the "almost never" is built into the claim or into the metric associated claim is a design choice. This is a slippery point, so we spend time on this in the chapter.

inevitability of unknown unknowns. More important are robustly supported claims that are true – as far as we know.[23]

Chapter 8:

Now we get into applying SPIs with numerous examples of the types of things that might be measured. We revisit a baseline safety metric target with more detail, and warn that SPIs need to directly match up with claims in the safety case to be useful. Any metric that does not directly trace to a claim in the safety case might be interesting, but is of questionable prediction validity.

Leading SPIs can be defined at the system level (did the vehicle do something it is not supposed to – even if no crash resulted?), components (is your camera struggling to see things it should be able to see?), process (is your development team skipping required reviews, analysis, etc.?), and operations (are you skipping required maintenance?).

Monitoring SPIs can be a bit tricky. Even in an unsafe AV, safety SPIs will have violation budgets so low that many vehicles will never violate the SPI. This means you will need to aggregate data across vehicles to check SPI violation rates. Also, an SPI violation does not (necessarily) mean a vehicle is about to crash. Rather, it means your safety case has a defect. You need to fix that, but it is a much more indirect safety warning compared to "you are about to crash" type metrics.

It seems that everyone wants to "bootstrap" safety by doing a little testing, having no crashes, and then using that to argue they can operate safely even if the total amount of testing is inadequate for a confident safety prediction. The math is seductive, but the math does not answer the question that really matters. In practice, a typical bootstrap approach amounts to getting lucky rather than being safe. We give an alternative approach based on measuring SPI failure rates and safe failure fractions rather than bootstrapping based on lack of crashes.

Chapter 9:

Finally we get to figure out how to make a deployment decision. Beyond net risk (on average "safer than human") are the issues of risk distribution equity, whether best practices for other aspects of safety have been considered including safety standards, and how uncertainty regarding expected safety is being handled. Moreover, software updates need to be done in a way that does not undermine safety or security.

A special aspect of ensuring overall safety is being sure that road tests are safe. This is significantly different than deployment safety, because safe outcomes for public road testing are all about the human safety driver rather than autonomy computers.

---

[23] If you are getting concerned about how we can say that an incomplete safety case is good enough, look up "defeasible reasoning." If that helped, then great. If not, don't worry – we'll try to do better than Wikipedia when we get to that chapter.

Chapter 10:

Having discussed how to consider a deployment decision, we revisit themes from the book in the context of ethical concerns involved with AV safety, with an emphasis on the practical. The infamous Trolley Problem is not what you should be worrying about. Rather, the biggest issue is how people who have huge financial and professional incentives to deploy will handle a deployment safety decision – given that they are not going to be the ones in the vehicles when the crashes occur.

A laundry list of other ethical concerns must be addressed for any practical AV system to be deployed at scale. Many of them are not talked about often, but they will cause practical problems if not addressed.

Finally, we present a set of principles for ethical regulatory approaches that address safety, compensation, transparency, inclusion, and non-discrimination. Legislators in most US states are running roughshod over those concerns, but one can hope that will improve over time.

Chapter 11:

This final chapter describes other materials that might be useful, including free online videos we have recorded on topics relevant to this book.

1.3. Terminology and abbreviations

Here is a list of abbreviations and key terms used in the book for reference. More precise definitions for some terms are provided in the chapters. These are quick reference definitions to remind the reader of the essential part of the definition.

Abbreviations and terms

- **Acceptable safety** – A system is acceptably safe if it has a very small probability of substantive harm, follows best practices for safety engineering, and presents a risk vs. benefit tradeoff that accounts for all stakeholders who might suffer direct or indirect harm.
- **ADS** – Automated Driving System. The computer system that drives an autonomous vehicle.
- **AEB** - Automatic Emergency Braking. A computer-based function that automatically applies brakes to mitigate an impending collision.
- **AHS** – Automated Highway Systems. An AV technology demo project from the 1990s.

- **AI** – Artificial Intelligence. This is so messy we're not going to even attempt a definition.[24] When you hear "AI" in the context of AVs usually the term machine learning should have been used instead.
- **ALARP** – As Low As Reasonably Practicable. A risk framework approach requiring reduction of risk to the degree practicable. For our purposes this is reasonably equivalent to ALARA (As Low As Reasonably Achievable) and SFAIRP (So Far As Is Reasonably Practicable).
- **ALKS** – Automated Lane Keeping System, UNECE #157. A standard for implementing a traffic jam pilot automation feature.[25]
- **ANSI/UL 4600** – A safety standard to ensure that an AV safety case has considered everything it should.[26]
- **ASIL** – Automotive Safety Integrity Level. An automotive-specific variant of the concept of a SIL.
- **AUHD** – Average Unimpaired Human Driver. A potential baseline reference for driving safety.
- **Autonowashing** – Overstating the autonomy capability of a vehicle or technological approach.
- **AV** – Autonomous Vehicle. A vehicle operating without a requirement for continuous human safety supervision.
- **BRB** – Big Red Button. An emergency stop button or the like to trigger an urgent, but hopefully safe, shutdown of an automated system.
- **DDT** – Dynamic Driving Task. Normal driving, whether done by a person or a machine.
- **Defeasible reasoning** – an approach to argument that is rationally compelling but potentially falsifiable due to incomplete information.
- **DMV** – Department of Motor Vehicles. A state organization that licenses drivers and manages vehicle registrations.
- **DOT** – Department of Transportation. US state and federal organizations that regulate transportation safety.
- **Fallback** – Reacting to a vehicle failure, such as pulling to the side of the road.
- **Falsified** – a claim that was thought to be true has been proven false by observed data. Any claim in a sound safety case is believed to be true, but is potentially falsifiable in the face of yet-to-be-encountered unknowns.
- **FMVSS** – Federal Motor Vehicle Safety Standard(s). US test-based standards for specific minimum required safety functionality.

---

[24] Spoiler: an AV does not "think" like a person, even if we indulge in occasional anthropomorphizing descriptions.
[25] See: https://unece.org/transport/documents/2021/03/standards/un-regulation-no-157-automated-lane-keeping-systems-alks
[26] See: https://users.ece.cmu.edu/~koopman/ul4600/index.html

- **FN** – False Negative: an object is there, but the system fails to detect it.
- **FP** – False Positive: there is no object, but the system detects an object.
- **GAMAB** – "Globalement Au Moins Aussi Bon" which describes a risk framework in which one thing is overall at least as good as another comparable type of system. (See also: PRB)
- **Geofence** – An ODD limitation to specified locations and/or routes. ODDs typically address other operational limitations beyond just geofencing.
- **GSN** – Goal Structuring Notation. A defined notation for safety cases.
- **Harm** – Injury or fatality inflicted upon people. See also PDO.
- **IIHS** – Insurance Institute for Highway Safety. A US nonprofit funded by auto insurance companies.
- **ISO 21448** – An automotive standard for "safety of the intended function" (SOTIF) that encompasses driver assistance features and AVs.
- **ISO 26262** – An automotive functional safety standard that applies to conventional vehicles as well as AVs.
- **KPI** – Key Performance Indicator. A metric used to emphasize an important aspect of AV performance or some aspect of a company's process performance that might – or might not – be relevant to safety.
- **Lagging metrics** – Metrics that are gathered regarding safety outcomes from operating the AV.
- **Leading metrics** – Metrics that are gathered to predict safety before loss events occur.
- **Loss event** – An AV incident involving damage to property or harm. Used instead of the term "accident." A typical loss event involves a crash, but other types of loss events are possible.
- **MEM** – Minimum Endogenous Mortality. A risk framework based on determining whether the risk of a system is significantly higher than the background exposure to other risks of everyday life.
- **ML** – Machine Learning. An approach to computation based on using training by example to set up a computationally simulated neural network. This is a specific technology used by most AVs that is often what is being referred to as "AI" (see: artificial intelligence).
- **Moral Crumple Zone** – The practice of assigning responsibility and blame for an automated system failure to some conveniently available person, especially if that person could not reasonably have been expected to prevent a loss event. See section 10.2.2.
- **MRC** – Minimal Risk Condition. Stopping the vehicle after performing fallback. There is no actual requirement for the risk to be "minimal" in any sense as currently defined, but there is a requirement that it involves stopping the vehicle. This term is often used in regulations in a way that intends risk of harm while in an MRC to be acceptably low.

- **NHTSA** – National Highway Traffic Safety Administration. The US Department of Transportation administration responsible for vehicle safety and managing recalls.
- **NSC** – National Safety Council. A US nonprofit public service organization promoting health and safety.
- **OD** – Operational Domain. The portion of the real world that the AV operates in. The ODD is an approximate model of the OD.
- **ODD** – Operational Design Domain. The conditions under which an AV is intended to operate. This should be an acceptable model of the OD.
- **OEDR** – Object and Event Detection and Response. Detecting objects and other road situations, then changing own vehicle behavior in response. Example: steering to avoid collision with an object.
- **OEM** – Original Equipment Manufacturer. A company that integrates and sells cars. Contrast with automotive suppliers who provide components to the OEM.
- **PDO** – Property Damage Only. A crash severity category in which no harm was done to people, but some objects were damaged.
- **Permissiveness** – How aggressively an AV can move within its ODD without exceeding its safety limits.
- **PRA** – Probabilistic Risk Assessment. Assessing risk as a sum of probabilities times consequences.
- **PRB** – Positive Risk Balance. An AV should be no worse than a human driver.
- **RSS** – Responsibility Sensitive Safety. A strategy for attaining provably blame-free AV behavior based on a Newtonian physics approach.
- **SAE** – The organization formerly known as the Society of Automotive Engineers. Now SAE is just short for "SAE International."
- **SAE J3016** – A terminology standard for automated vehicles that is commonly mistaken for (but is most definitely NOT) a safety standard.
- **SAE J3018** – A standard covering human safety driver aspects of road testing safety.
- **SAE Levels** – A six-level categorization (Levels 0 to 5) designating the functionality assigned to automation equipment in a vehicle. The Levels are defined in SAE J3016.
- **Safety Case** – A structured argument, supported by evidence, that supports a claim that an AV is acceptably safe to deploy.
- **SIL** – Safety Integrity Level. Used to determine the engineering rigor to be applied to achieve acceptable risk mitigation for a safety-critical system or feature.
- **SMS** – Safety Management System. A system of metrics used to monitor for, identify, and correct safety issues.
- **SOTIF** – Safety Of The Intended Function. Associated with a methodology for identifying safety-related performance and requirement insufficiencies for driver assistance and AV technology. See ISO 21448.

- **SPI** – Safety Performance Indicator (pronounced S-P-I rather than "spy"). A metric tied to a claim in a safety case and associated with a threshold beyond which the claim has been falsified. An SPI violation occurs when the SPI's threshold has been exceeded by the metric value.
- **TN** – True Negative: there is no object and the system detects no object.
- **TP** – True Positive: an object is there and is recognized.
- **TTC** – Time To Collision. A risk metric for how long it would be until a collision if vehicles were not maneuvered to avoid that collision.
- **VMT** – Vehicle Miles Traveled, often in millions (e.g., 100M VMT is 100 million miles in total traveled by a set of vehicles).
- **VSSA** – Voluntary Safety Self-Assessment. A report to NHTSA submitted by some AV companies disclosing some information relevant to plans for safety.

Numerical conventions:

- "K" – kilo/thousand (1,000), e.g., 100K is 100,000
- kph – kilometers per hour
- "M" – million (1,000,000), e.g., 80M is 80,000,000
- mph – miles per hour

2.   Terminology and challenges

This chapter covers common terminology for the discussions in the rest of the book. We will also throw in a brief tour of the types of problems that make it so challenging to ensure that Automated Vehicles (AVs) are acceptably safe.

Discussions of AVs are awash with imprecise, potentially misleading terminology. For example, the term "self-driving" with associated misuse and abuse [27] has been common in efforts to make vehicle automation technology sound more capable than it really is – a practice known as autonowashing. [28]

Far too many discussions use terminology incorrectly, often in ways that increase confusion even if the writer is attempting to educate the reader. This is not necessarily the fault of the writer, because some definitions are more complex and muddled than they need to be. We attempt to provide some accessible definitions without making things even more confusing than they already are.

2.1. SAE J3016 key terms

Summary: SAE J3016 is the most often used terminology reference for vehicle automation technology. Those definitions can help when discussing the technology. Here we define ADS, DDT, OEDR, MRC, and other key concepts.

Discussing AVs accurately requires using some defined terms. The usual starting point for term definitions is SAE J3016:2021 Taxonomy and Definitions for Terms Related to Driving Automation Systems for On-Road Motor Vehicles (which we refer to as J3016 for short). [29] This is a no-cost standard for terminology widely used in the AV industry.

The definitions below are informal summaries of J3016 that are suitable for our purposes. [30] Official definitions can be found in the text of that standard.

- **Automated Driving System (ADS):** Hardware and software that drives the vehicle.

---

[27] For example, the term "Full Self Driving"

[28] Kudos to Liza Dixon for coining and promoting this concept as inspired by the term "greenwashing." See: https://lizadixon.com/Autonowashing

[29] See SAE 2021: https://www.sae.org/standards/content/j3016_202104/

[30] A 20 minute video lecture on SAE J3016 terminology by the author is available here: https://youtu.be/Kykb75_41hY

- o *Example:* The "software driver" (and associated computer hardware) installed in a vehicle.
- **Dynamic Driving Task (DDT):** A person and/or computer performing normal driving.
    - o The DDT includes two important sub-tasks: vehicle movement (acceleration, braking, steering), and OEDR (defined below). It excludes short-acting driver assistance features such as Automatic Emergency Braking.
    - o *Example:* Driving for several minutes on a highway while staying on the road, observing the actions of other road users, and maneuvering to avoid crashes.
- **Fallback:** A response to operate the vehicle when something goes wrong, such as bringing it to an MRC (defined below).
    - o By definition, Fallback is not included in the normal DDT.
    - o Depending on the system and situation, either a human driver or the ADS performs Fallback.
    - o *Example:* The ADS notices something has gone wrong and performs a Fallback.
- **Minimal Risk Condition (MRC):** A Fallback operation results in an MRC, eventually stopping the vehicle.
    - o The MRC is a "stable, stopped" condition that is presumed to be less risky than continuing operation. However, per J3016 there is no guarantee that it is the least risky possible condition for the situation, nor is there a guarantee that any risk reduction by an ADS is comparable to risk reduction that a human driver might have attained in a similar situation.
    - o *Example:* Stopping on the shoulder of a road after an equipment failure.
    - o *Example:* Stopping in the middle of a travel lane.
- **Object and Event Detection and Response (OEDR):** Monitoring the driving environment including other road user actions to recognize the need for a response, and then commanding the vehicle to respond.
    - o OEDR is a part of the DDT.
    - o *Example:* Noticing a pedestrian walking into a roadway, then planning and ordering the vehicle to maneuver to avoid a collision.
- **Operational Design Domain (ODD):** Conditions the ADS is designed to handle.
    - o Exiting the ODD means the vehicle is operating in conditions it was not designed to handle, and is one reason to initiate a Fallback.
    - o *Example:* Paved dry roads in daylight on a specific preselected route that has good lane marking paint condition, no significant

potholes, and for which high-definition maps are available and up to date.

Putting all the pieces together, in an AV an ADS computer system performs the DDT, which includes both OEDR and controlling vehicle motion. If something happens that makes the ADS unable to continue driving, such as an equipment failure or impending exit from the ODD, a Fallback response is initiated to bring the vehicle to an MRC. The AV is intended to be acceptably safe when operating within its defined ODD.

We use the term "AV" to refer to a vehicle equipped with an ADS that is capable of performing the DDT without continuous human supervision of driving safety. The reader is welcome to translate our use of the term "AV" into "Autonomous Vehicle," "Highly Automated Vehicle (HAV)," or "ADS-equipped Vehicle" as desired. Beyond the scope of some of the nuanced points in this chapter, the difference will be immaterial.

J3016 identifies some terms as undesirable, including:

- Automated Vehicle; Autonomous Vehicle
    - o *Preferred:* ADS-equipped vehicle
- Autonomous
    - o *Preferred:* Automated
- Robotic; robotic taxi; and presumably robotaxi
    - o Do not use
- Driverless vehicle
    - o "Driverless operation" is acceptable
- Self-driving
    - o Do not use

Having listed those deprecated terms,[31] in this book we commit the minor sin of referring to "autonomous" rather than "highly automated" vehicles when referring to a vehicle for which there is no human driver continuously and directly responsible for driving safety. This usage of "autonomous" is in keeping with terminology in the ANSI/UL 4600 standard which refers to the entire scope of vehicle safety that goes well beyond the limited scope of the DDT and Fallback tasks relevant to SAE J3016. That expanded scope for "autonomous" operation includes other aspects of operational and lifecycle safety such as selection of safe routes, occupant safety, maintenance, and post-crash behaviors.

Some other terms we will use are:

- **SAE:** A professional organization that creates standards and runs other activities for the automotive industry as well as some aspects of the aviation industry. They were formerly known as the Society of Automotive Engineers, but they have rebranded as SAE International.[32]

---

[31] And with apologies to Dr. Steve Shladover.

[32] In other words, SAE now officially stands for SAE. They also do aviation standards work in addition to automotive standards.

- **Geofence:** The notion of limiting an AV to a specific geographic area to constrain the ODD. Sometimes geofences are a compact geographic footprint such as particular sections of a city. Other geofence examples are a set of specific pre-mapped highway segments or a fixed route on city streets. It is important to note that a geofence is just one possible limitation that defines an ODD.

2.2. SAE Levels and safety

Summary: The SAE vehicle automation Levels have little to do with safety, and some choices made in the SAE Level definitions might even enable deploying unsafe vehicles. While the SAE Levels seem ubiquitous, we suggest they be avoided for non-engineering purposes.

It seems that no discussion of vehicle automation technology is complete without a walk-through of the SAE Levels from J3016. We will do that here as well, pointing out a few common misconceptions that can be relevant to safety.[33]

The SAE Levels divide different automated driving operational modes according to which driving functions are performed by the vehicle versus a human driver. We will keep it brief, but still fairly precise, and identify the key attributes of each defined level first with a simple version, then with a more nuanced version that traces to a careful reading of the standard.

2.2.1. A simplified version of J3016 Levels

- Level 0: "No driving automation"
  - o An ordinary vehicle. The human driver handles all driving tasks.
- Level 1: "Driver Assistance"
  - o Typically this is adaptive cruise control that varies speed to maintain a constant following interval to a leading vehicle. Steering is still done by a human driver.
- Level 2: "Partial Driving Automation"
  - o This is both automated steering and speed control, but with limited OEDR capability. The driver must continuously pay attention to avoid crashing even if the vehicle behaves as if it can handle all the driving.
- Level 3: "Conditional Driving Automation"
  - o The ADS handles the entire DDT including OEDR, but a human driver is responsible for noticing at least some equipment failures and performing Fallback if necessary.

---

[33] For a more detailed user guide to J3016 including a number of myths emphasizing issues with the SAE Levels, see: https://users.ece.cmu.edu/~koopman/j3016/

o Contrary to common misconceptions, J3016 does not say this is "eyes off road" nor does it guarantee 10 seconds of warning from the ADS – or any ADS warning at all – if something goes wrong.

o Contrary to a common misconception, the driver has no obligation to maintain awareness of what is happening on the road, and is not responsible for supervising the correctness of driving behavior within the ODD.

- Level 4: "High Driving Automation"
  o The ADS handles both DDT and Fallback within a limited ODD. Human driver involvement is not required.
  o Contrary to a common misconception, such a vehicle might have manual controls for manual driving outside the ODD.
- Level 5: "Full Driving Automation"
  o Level 4 with an "unlimited" ODD that approximates a competent human driver's full range of driving abilities.
  o Contrary to a common misconception, such a vehicle might still have manual driving controls.

2.2.2. A nuanced description of J3016 Levels

Misinterpretations and over-simplifications of J3016 abound, along with a wide variety of myths.[34] For example, J3016 does not say that Level 3 means "eyes off road" anywhere, even though that has been stated many times in so many various discussions. Here is a more rigorous explanation of the levels for those on a quixotic quest for nuance.

We loosely use the term "Level X vehicle" or "Level X system" to mean "a vehicle equipped with a feature operating at Level X" as is commonly done in regulatory text.[35]

The various levels are depicted in Figure 2.1:

---

[34] The previous section is definitely simplified compared to the complexity of J3016. However, we hope it was both useful and not misleading.

[35] Per strict J3016 terminology only a feature can be at a level, with many vehicles having multiple features. That means a single vehicle might have features that let it operate at Levels 0, 1, 2, 3, or 4 depending on which feature has been turned on. We consider a "Level X system" to be a vehicle with a feature that operates at Level X, and a Level X vehicle as a vehicle that has at least one feature operable at Level X.

Level	J3016 Level Name	Steering & Speed	Objects & Environment	Detect DDT Failures	Detect Vehicle Faults	Perform Fallback	ODD Scope	Other Safety
0	No Driving Automation	Driver	Driver	Driver	Driver	Driver	n/a	Driver
1	Driver Assistance	Split	Driver	Driver	Driver	Driver	Limited	Driver
2	Partial Driving Automation	ADS	Driver	Driver	Driver	Driver	Limited	Driver
3	Conditional Driving Automation	ADS	ADS	ADS	Driver	Driver	Limited	Driver
4	High Driving Automation	ADS	ADS	ADS	ADS	ADS	Limited	Driver
5	Full Driving Automation	ADS	ADS	ADS	ADS	ADS	"Unlimited"	Driver

Figure 2.1. J3016 levels.

- Level 0: "No driving automation"
  - The human driver performs the entire DDT.
  - This is an ordinary vehicle in which the human driver handles all driving tasks.
  - The vehicle might have driver assistance features such as Automatic Emergency Braking (AEB) that only temporarily take over some aspects of vehicle operation.[36] These do not count as "automation" if they only temporarily control vehicle motion.
  - The vehicle might have automation that does not respond to external events, such as conventional cruise control.[37] These do not count as "automation" because they do not alter their behavior directly in response to other road actors.
- Level 1: "Driver Assistance"
  - Partial performance of vehicle motion portion of the DDT (either speed or steering, but not both) within a defined ODD.
  - Typically this is adaptive cruise control that responds to other vehicle behavior to avoid rear-end collisions, with a human driver doing the steering. In principle it could be automated steering with a human driver controlling only speed.[38]
  - A human driver intervenes to take over full control if automation fails to operate properly.

---

[36] J3016 §3.28 Note 2

[37] J3016 §3.28 Note 3

[38] Speed-only control might make sense for a trolley-type vehicle that follows painted "track" lines on a roadway rather than rails, with the driver controlling speed but not steering.

- o   Because a human driver is performing a continuous control task (typically steering), it is anticipated that the driver remains alert and able to perform OEDR tasks.
- Level 2: "Partial Driving Automation" (vehicle automation performs motion control portion of DDT, but not full OEDR)
  - o   Sustained operation of the motion control portion of the DDT, but limited OEDR capability within a defined ODD. That means that speed, steering, and potentially braking are automated, but ability to react to external events is limited.
  - o   The human driver needs to notice and react to at least some external events and conditions within the ODD by taking over vehicle control manually. There might be very long periods of time in which no intervention is required if the operational environment is benign.
  - o   The human driver is expected to take over in case of an equipment failure.
  - o   Driver monitoring is said to be "useful" for Level 2 but is not required.[39]
- Level 3: "Conditional Driving Automation" (ADS performs full DDT)
  - o   Sustained performance of the whole DDT, but not Fallback, within a defined ODD. This includes motion control and the entirety of OEDR. The human driver is _not_ responsible for monitoring driving safety. That means that mishandled OEDR in the absence of an equipment failure is the fault of the automation, not the human driver.
  - o   Driving is automated, but human driver Fallback is required if the driver detects that something has gone wrong or a Fallback is requested by the ADS.
  - o   The ADS might be able to perform the Fallback itself sometimes, but not always. [40] If the vehicle is capable of executing an MRC in every circumstance without driver intervention, that is a Level 4 system, not Level 3.
  - o   The ADS sometimes (but not always) notifies the human driver that Fallback intervention is required. Technically when in automated operation the "driver" is called a "fallback ready user."
  - o   The ADS sometimes (but not always) gives the human driver "at least several seconds" to resume manual driving if Fallback intervention is required.

---

[39] J3016 §3.18.1 Note 2. Lack of robust driver monitoring for Levels 2 and 3 as defined in J3016 can reasonably be expected to result in an unsafe system. This is just noting that J3016 does not require such monitoring.
[40] J3016 §3.12 note 2

- o Driver monitoring is said to be "useful" for Level 3 but is not required.[41]
- o The standard does **not** say that this is "eyes off road" even though the driver is not responsible for behavioral defects in a fully operational ADS. The human driver is responsible for instant response to some types of vehicle failures, especially involving failures to mechanical systems such as steering. As a practical matter, safe Fallback responses will require paying attention to the road at higher speeds to maintain situational awareness even though the standard does not say this explicitly.[42]

- Level 4: "High Driving Automation" (ADS performs DDT, OEDR, and Fallback)
  - o Sustained performance of the entire DDT and entire Fallback within a defined ODD.
  - o Once you engage Level 4, the car drives itself without any need for human intervention, and with no need for human safety supervision of DDT and Fallback. This includes handling any driving problems that might occur.
  - o A human driver might be able to take over operation while driving (this is optional), but the vehicle cannot take safety credit for a human driver performing DDT or Fallback. If the vehicle exits the ODD, the ADS is responsible for automatically performing an MRC if a driver does not take over operation.
  - o There need not be any human driver involved at all, for example during cargo delivery operations.
  - o There is no expectation for a human safety supervisor to initiate a Fallback operation when necessary. If any human occupant or safety supervisor can be blamed for a crash due to inaction or not intervening quickly enough to prevent a crash while driving, that is a Level 3 system, not a Level 4 system.

- Level 5: "Full Driving Automation" (ADS performs DDT, OEDR, Fallback)
  - o Sustained performance of the whole DDT and Fallback within an "unlimited" ODD. ("Unlimited" is loosely constrained as

---

[41] J3019 §3.18.1 Note 2

[42] If this seems weirdly at odds with the concept that the driver should not held be responsible for ADS malfunctions, congratulations – you have been paying attention. In reality, the definition of Level 3 is a bit of a mess from the point of view of driver responsibility and practical driver oversight expectations, even though the definitions are precisely stated in the standard. That is because the standard covers what functions are performed by the automation, which turns out to be a different perspective than building a simple-to-understand model of what functions are the responsibility of the human driver.

generally comparable to what a human driver might be able to handle.)

o   This is the same as Level 4, but with an ODD that is "unlimited" subject to some fine print.

o   In the real world, Level 5 is more aspirational than practical.

The J3016 Levels are not defined primarily in terms of how the driver perceives vehicle operation, but rather in terms of which functions have been assigned to the ADS in terms of the operations of DDT, OEDR, and Fallback as well as the scope of the ODD.

A core issue that complicates Level 3 when considering safety is that it differentiates an internal ADS electronics failure from a vehicle failure such as a broken mechanical steering component. ADS failures must be annunciated to a human driver explicitly, while that same human driver is supposed to just notice other equipment failures even if the ADS does not announce there is a problem. Not every human driver can be expected to have the sophistication to diagnose and mitigate unannounced vehicle equipment failures that occur while the ADS still indicates it is driving.

The Level 3 failure distinctions make the job of designing an ADS simpler. But from a driver's point of view, the net result is that the ADS only signals there is a problem sometimes, and other problems the driver is supposed to notice and react to with no warning. That seems likely to make the job of supervising a Level 3 ADS more complex and perhaps less safe if there is no robust driver monitoring feature.

2.2.3. Clearing up SAE J3016 misconceptions

Several common myths and surprises show up time and again in discussions of the J3016 standard. Here are some statements that address common misunderstandings about the standard:

- **J3016 is not a safety standard.** It is a terminology standard that happens to define some combinations of behaviors as Levels without taking into account whether the result will be safe in practice. In particular, Levels 2 and 3 present significant safety issues if implemented as defined with nothing extra, because they put humans in charge of supervising automation without also requiring effective driver monitoring. Additionally, Level 2 does not enforce ODD restrictions, resulting in likely automation misuse or abuse.[43] Legislators and regulators that say they are using an "SAE Safety Standard" to check the safety box for new regulations via incorporating J3016 are making grossly misleading statements.

---

[43] For example, if a Level 2 feature is only intended to work on certain roads, it is the driver's job to enforce that. Any Level 2 system that restricts operation to designated roads is likely to be safer in practice, but is going above and beyond J3016 requirements.

- **Level 3 does not guarantee that the ADS will always notify the human driver** of a problem. The driver is supposed to notice "evident" vehicle failures and intervene even though the ADS does not initiate a human driver takeover process. Neither does Level 3 guarantee that the ADS will ensure safety of the vehicle while the human driver establishes situational awareness and starts operating the vehicle after a takeover. In practice, it will be difficult if not impossible for a safe Level 3 system to be "eyes off road" in a general-purpose ODD unless much more is done beyond what is strictly required by J3016 Level 3.

- **ODDs are more than just geofences.** Limiting the ODD to a certain city or geographic region does not mean that the vehicle will be able to drive safely at all times in that limited area due to potentially unusual weather, road conditions, infrastructure failures, and so on.

- **Vehicles that support Level 4 might still have steering wheels.** While talk of robotaxis dominates many Level 4 discussions, it is also possible to have a Level 4 feature in a conventional car. Consider, for example, a Level 4 feature that completely automates driving on highways, and even comes with a comfy reclining seat plus head pillow for naps. However, the ODD is only on highways, and excludes both local streets and on/off ramps. A human driver would use conventional controls to get onto a highway and then engage Level 4. Then Level 4 would drive until it is time to exit the highway. That feature would need to confirm driver re-engagement before exiting the freeway. If the driver does not wake up from a nap in time to retake control for an off-ramp, the feature must find a safe place to park while waiting for the driver to assume responsibility for driving. After that point, the driver might use conventional vehicle controls to complete the local portion of the trip.

- **The Levels are easily gamed.** Companies that are testing full automation capabilities can designate their vehicles as Level 4 even though a full-time safety driver is required if they claim they have Level 4 "design intent." In effect, what might otherwise be a Level 2 vehicle can be called Level 4 simply by saying it is Level 4.[44] By the same token, a company can attempt to claim that what is in reality a Level 4 test platform is Level 2 simply by saying that their "design intent" is Level 2. (We call this the "Level 2 Loophole."[45]) Additionally, a manufacturer could build a feature that performs at Level 4 except for some strategically inserted weakness that keeps it technically at Level 2 to evade regulations that only apply to Levels 3-5.[46] The ease of gaming the

---

[44] SAE J3016 §8.2

[45] Widen & Koopman, 2022:
https://papers.ssrn.com/sol3/papers.cfm?abstract_id=3969214

[46] As a hypothetical example, consider an ADS that has intentionally poor performance at detecting and avoiding elephants, but is essentially perfect at all other aspects of driving. That would be Level 2 on a technical basis if circus parades on public streets were declared to be within the ODD. For such a vehicle the OEDR

Levels arguably makes them unsuitable for use as a regulatory classification because of potential incentives that reward gaming.

We do not reproduce the commonly seen SAE Levels chart graphic produced by SAE because it contains a potentially very misleading description of Level 3.[47] That description indicates that the ADS notifies the human driver to take over. That only happens <u>sometimes</u>, and not all the time. Moreover, even if a takeover notification is given, it need only give "several" seconds of warning, with no consideration as to whether the driver can safely take control of the vehicle in the allotted time. There is no requirement that the vehicle ensures the driver is able to, or actually does take effective vehicle control when requested.

All this having been said, it is important to emphasize that these concerns are with regard to the standard itself. The concerns are not necessarily with any particular vehicle that is advertised at a particular level. Vehicles hopefully exceed the minimum requirements for a particular level.

The use of fractional level terminology such as "Level 2+" is commonly said to convey some notion of additional features.[48] But in practice that is just marketing puffery that has no real meaning. Fractional and "+" terminology applied to levels is explicitly prohibited by SAE J3016 §8.3.

The points made above re-emphasize that the J3016 standard provides useful terminology definitions such as ADS and ODD. The Levels, on the other hand, define somewhat arbitrary technology choices that if followed to the letter are unlikely to result in acceptably safe vehicles. The standard does not prevent AV makers from adding additional capabilities to make their vehicles safe, but does not provide a clear way to communicate if and how that has been done.

For better or worse, SAE J3016 Levels are the current way that people talk about vehicle automation technology. Moreover, that standard and its Levels have been baked into multiple State regulations and Federal policy documents. It behooves anyone who is doing serious work that involves using that terminology, especially in the area of setting policies, to understand the nuances and the safety pitfalls involved with uncritical acceptance of that standard for regulatory purposes.

---

capability would be incomplete due to lack of ability to handle elephants. Even if it has been decades since the circus actually came to town.

[47] The 2021 version of the graphic says of SAE Level 3: "When the feature requests / you must drive." But as we have noted there are equipment failure situations in which the "feature" itself does not request takeover. Rather, that driver is supposed to be "receptive" to "evident" failures (whatever that means) and notice such failures, without the ADS itself ever having issued a takeover request.

The graphic being discussed is here: https://www.sae.org/blog/sae-j3016-update

[48] In a perplexing turn of events, even though SAE standard J3016 bans the use of the term "Level 2+" SAE itself has apparently endorsed using "Level 2+" with this article: https://www.sae.org/news/2020/12/rise-of-sae-level-2

2.2.4. J3016 Levels augmented for safety

As just discussed, SAE J3016 Level 2 and Level 3 do not define safe automation features. Nor are they intended to, because J3016 does not claim to be a safety standard.

This is not to say that a vehicle that has Level 2 or Level 3 automation features is necessarily unsafe. Rather, it is that J3016 sets the bar too low for those Levels to ensure safety. Doing only what is required by J3016 is unlikely to result in a safe automation feature in practice. More is required.

While more detail follows, the general idea for ensuring safety for Level 2 and Level 3 features is simple. If you are counting on a human driver to support safety, the vehicle needs to ensure that the driver is alert and situationally aware so as to be able to respond to problems in a timely manner. Counting on a driver to display super-human alertness and responsiveness when monitoring automation is both unreasonable and a recipe for catastrophic loss events.

2.2.4.1. Safe Level 2 features need effective driver monitoring

SAE Level 2 says that "the driver completes the OEDR subtask." This means that the vehicle automation capability might do some, or almost all OEDR – but the human driver still needs to fill whatever gaps there might be in that functionality. The driving automation might or might not see some objects, and might or might not respond properly, thus requiring continuous driver vigilance. That vigilance is expected even if the automation handles 99.99% (or other similarly high fraction) of the OEDR responsibilities.

The problem is that human drivers do poorly at supervising automation. Paradoxically, the better the automation is, the worse the humans do. Something needs to be done to ensure that drivers are paying adequate attention to the driving to avoid automation complacency. Driver monitoring is said to be "useful" in SAE J3016, but is completely optional according to that standard. In reality, effective driver monitoring is a must for safety.

This is a complex topic, but if you want to deploy a safe Level 2 system you need to have effective driver monitoring. Effective driver monitoring means that the driver monitoring can be quantitatively shown to ensure the driver is paying enough attention when supervising the specific automation technology in use.

Steering wheel torque monitoring is clearly insufficient to ensure driver attentiveness on its own. [49] Perhaps eye tracking and facial expression

---

[49] It is a foregone conclusion that some set of drivers will use illicit defeat devices to fool steering wheel monitors. Whether the manufacturer should have to take responsibility for designing to be safe even when such devices are used is an interesting question. In the end, if crashes are too high due to the use of such devices it will be a problem for the manufacturer regardless of whether "blame" is assigned to drivers for using these devices. As an example, there is a continual arms race between Tesla and drivers regarding ways to defeat their steering wheel-based monitoring capability.

monitoring will be effective enough at driver monitoring to deploy Level 2 systems that are acceptably safe across a wide range of driver abilities and experience. But the jury is still out on real-world deployment at scale.[50] We will have to see.

In short, safe Level 2 vehicle automation features must include effective driver monitoring that ensures the net automation+human driver combination is acceptably safe. This monitoring needs to take into account the inevitability of automation complacency that reduces the driver's ability to monitor and intervene when automation fails.

2.2.4.2. Safe Level 3 features also need effective driver monitoring

SAE Level 3 puts the human driver in charge of Fallback operations.[51] If there is some sort of software or equipment failure the driver needs to bring the vehicle to a minimal risk condition (MRC), such as pulling over to a safe place at the side of the road. The ADS might help or even execute an MRC in most cases, but it is not required to do so in all cases.[52]

As previously mentioned, a crucial nuance in Level 3 is that the ADS is not required to notify the driver of all possible faults, and is not required to control the vehicle for long enough for the human driver to be able to resume control. For an ADS failure the requirement is only to give "several" seconds warning. However, in the event of an "evident" vehicle failure, there might be no warning at all from the ADS, and no grace period to regain control. The UNECE #157 Automated Lane Keeping System (ALKS) standard provides 10 seconds rather than just "several" seconds.[53] This might be sufficient for some low-speed traffic jam operations as envisioned by the ALKS standard, but will be insufficient for higher vehicle speeds. Regardless, that 10 second number is not in the J3016 standard.

See: https://www.consumerreports.org/autonomous-driving/cr-engineers-show-tesla-will-drive-with-no-one-in-drivers-seat/

[50] A possible problem for camera eye-tracking monitors more or less amounts to a situation in which "the lights are on but nobody's home" with a zoned out driver who has been inadvertently trained with biofeedback from the driving monitor to daydream with eyes open and facing forward. More sophisticated eye tracking looks for appropriate eye motion scanning the road and so on. It is not a simple task to infer mental state from facial expressions and eye tracking, but that is what must be done for driver monitoring to succeed. Here is a study that found drivers can crash when supervising automation even while looking at the crash obstacle:
Victor et al. 2018: https://journals.sagepub.com/doi/full/10.1177/0018720818788164

[51] It is a common misconception that for Level 3 the driver also needs to complete the OEDR by looking for unusual road events, but if that is true then the automation feature is Level 2, not Level 3.

[52] If the ADS guarantees it will handle Fallback in all situations, that is by definition a Level 4 feature.

[53] See: https://unece.org/transport/documents/2021/03/standards/un-regulation-no-157-automated-lane-keeping-systems-alks

Telling human fallback drivers on the one hand that the vehicle drives itself, but on the other hand that there are some failures that they need to react to instantly is a recipe for tragic loss events.

One issue is that a failure that is "evident" to an automotive engineer or professional driver might be meaningless to a civilian driver.[54] Expecting a driver to notice a suspension steering linkage failure due to a vehicle noise, thump, or change in ride feel while a vehicle is under automatic control and the driver is engrossed in watching a movie on the car center console is asking too much.[55]

Additionally, even if a human driver does feel the thump from a wheel falling off, consider that happening in dense, high-speed rush-hour traffic with the driver holding a messy sandwich in one hand and hot coffee in the other – while watching a movie. How long until the driver can grab to regain control of steering a car that is probably severely yawing, regain situational awareness, and react without hitting anything if their vehicle is suddenly missing an entire wheel?[56] Almost certainly regaining control will take longer than it takes to hit the first nearby vehicle, road barrier, or tree. To be sure, J3016 does not prevent the ADS from trying to do better, but it does not require it. J3016 does not prevent the manufacturer from warning the driver that they must pay attention to the road, but any such admonition goes beyond what is in J3016. That means that a vehicle feature that says "SAE Level 3" on the nameplate, but does no more than that, is problematic from a safety point of view.

There are several ways to improve this situation.

The first approach is to make sure that the driver is paying attention well enough to react to vehicle failures, just as with Level 2. Except with Level 3 the vehicle is even more capable, and the driver has even less to do. That means driver monitoring will be even more challenging than for Level 2. Driver monitoring will need to ensure that the driver has enough situational awareness and is alert enough to react instantly to a catastrophic vehicle failure despite potentially tens or even hundreds of hours of no engagement with the driving task.

A variant on the monitoring-only strategy is if the ADS always warns the driver of any possible failure (including "evident" vehicle failures). This simplifies driver monitoring to be a requirement for making sure the driver will detect an explicit ADS alert and have enough situational awareness to re-establish safe control in a timely manner. However, it will still be

---

[54] Have you ever seen a car driving with an obvious issue such as billowing smoke pouring out the back from an engine burning itself up, a tire so low on air it is pulling the car to one side, or even a completely flat tire – but the driver is oblivious? We have.

[55] The presumption of this failure mode as defined by J3016 is that the ADS has not detected the failure and therefore does not request a takeover. The burden is entirely on the driver to notice an "evident" failure with no defined criteria for what might be considered "evident" and to whom.

[56] Don't forget the hot coffee being spilled all over the driver while this happens.

important that the ADS can maintain vehicle control and do something reasonable approximating a Fallback operation to give the driver time to re-engage with the driving task. This can easily stretch much longer than 10 seconds depending on the driver and the complexity of the traffic situation.[57]

2.2.4.3. Safe Level 3 features via restricted ODD

A different strategy for Level 3 safety is to operate in an operational design domain (ODD) so constrained that an in-lane stop is likely to be safe enough if it does not happen too often, and then require the vehicle to always be capable of doing at least an in-lane stop.

By splitting hairs on wording you can align this with Level 3 by designating the MRC as pull to the side of the road if it can, and if it cannot do that, execute an in-lane stop. If the in-lane stop is called a "failure mitigation strategy" rather than an MRC maneuver this meets the definition of Level 3.[58] This seems to be more or less the strategy taken for UNECE #157 ALKS, which is intended to operate in slow-speed highway traffic jams. Adopting this approach would require arguing that an in-lane stop might be safe enough in a traffic jam due to low speed of other vehicles in the jam.

In-lane stops still do not deal with the issue of vehicle failures undetected by the ADS, nor of catastrophic ADS failures. Both of these are dumped on the driver by J3016. So to be safe, the vehicle would additionally need to be sure to do something (MRC or in-lane stop) in response to all vehicle failures relevant to safe driving – even if the driver has fallen asleep. ALKS is currently intended for lower-speed operation. Nonetheless, rear-ending a leading car at the 60 kph ALKS speed limit because a driver dozed off does not seem like a good idea for safety.

Combining these thoughts, a strategy for safe Level 3 might be ensuring that an in-lane stop can be done entirely by the vehicle regardless of failure and even without driver attentiveness. The only thing that stops this from being Level 4 is if the manufacturer chooses to say, quite legitimately, that an in-lane stop is not a proper MRC in some circumstances.

2.2.5. Public road testing

Public road testing of vehicle automation features brings with it safety concerns beyond those that apply to production vehicles.

Testing is an especially squishy topic in SAE J3016 because it categorizes vehicles based on "design intent" rather than vehicle capability when being

---

[57] One study shows that takeover time ranged up to 26 seconds in a driving simulator. It would be no surprise if a full demographic spread of all licensed drivers needed even longer than that. With that amount of time to work with the AV could have simply done an in-lane stop maneuver to a (potentially unsafe) MRC, technically making it a low-capability Level 4 vehicle rather than Level 3. See: https://www.southampton.ac.uk/news/2017/01/driverless-cars.page

[58] See SAE J3016 Figure 14.

tested. For example, J3016 permits a feature that requires constant human driver intervention to be classified as "Level 4" so long as the manufacturer intends for the testing program to culminate in a Level 4 feature. One of the many problems with this approach is that regulators have typically used the SAE Levels in drafting regulations that apply to test vehicles, resulting in much confusion and opportunities for testers to game the regulatory system.

The point of testing is to double-check that there are no defects in requirements, design, or implementation before release. By its very nature, technology that is being tested has the potential to misbehave. There might be a defect in the automation. Or there might be a defect that causes failsafes intended to ensure safety to work improperly, or not work at all when they are needed most. And so on. For example, vehicle automation should never cause the vehicle to swerve into oncoming traffic. But part of testing is to see if such swerves do happen due to design defects, with testers intervening as required to prevent collisions with other road users.

Because one goal of testing is to attempt to provoke dangerous misbehaviors of automated driving functions to see if safety functions work properly, it is inherently risky. That risk must be mitigated by using exceptionally well-qualified testers who follow test plans that are specifically designed to ensure that the net risk presented to the public is not unreasonable.

In other words, public road testing is not operation of automated vehicles. Rather, it is the potentially risky performance of tests on unproven technology that requires special efforts to reduce risks to acceptable levels. These issues are not dealt with by J3016 beyond permitting testers to claim higher automation levels, even if a safety driver is there to prevent crashes. This creates loopholes, such as J3016 not even mentioning driver monitoring in the context of Level 4 systems. In normal operation driver monitoring for Level 4 might not be required at all – but for testing it is likely to be essential for safety.

There are accepted practices for managing testing risk discussed in a different standard: SAE J3018. Testers should at the very least follow that standard regardless of the "design intent" of the feature they are developing. This topic is discussed in more detail in section 9.5.

2.3. Vehicle automation modes

Summary: A different vehicle automation classification system is proposed which is based on the driver's role in ensuring safety and whether the vehicle is a test platform vs. a production vehicle. The categories are: driver assistance, supervised automation, autonomous operation, and vehicle testing.

The SAE J3016 Levels might be useful for engineers who want to describe various features. But experience has shown that they are difficult for non-specialists to understand – including non-specialist engineers. In fact, at times using the Levels might do more harm than good, especially in regulatory situations where there is business incentive to game them. The issue is that an engineering-centric approach (how the functionality is built) is a poor fit for human-centric situations (how people interact with the functionality).

We propose a different categorization approach: one that emphasizes how drivers and organizations will deploy these vehicles rather than the underlying technology used to build vehicle automation functions. This is not a replacement for the engineering use of SAE Levels, but rather a complementary tool for public discussions and regulatory approaches for the technology that emphasizes the practical aspects of the driver's role in vehicle operation.

If you doubt that another set of terminology is needed, consider the common informal use of the term "Level 2+," which is undefined by the underlying SAE J3016 standard that sets the SAE Levels. Consider also the fact that different companies mean significantly different things when they say "Level 3." In some cases, Level 3 follows the minimum requirements set by SAE J3016, meaning that the driver is responsible for monitoring vehicle operation and being ready to jump in — even without any notice at all — to take over if something goes wrong. In other cases, vehicles described as Level 3 are expected to bring themselves to a reasonably safe stop even if the driver does not notice a problem, but somehow are not quite Level 4. That would be something more like a "Level 3+" concept.[59] The issue here is that the SAE Levels are arbitrary points in a large space of possibilities that do not support discussions about possible variations. They also implicitly lead one to believe that higher numbers are somehow better.[60]

Even more importantly, the SAE Levels say nothing about all the safety-relevant tasks that a human driver does beyond actual driving. For example, someone must make sure that the kids are buckled into their car seats. To deploy AVs we need to cover the whole picture. Driving task safety is critical, but only a piece of the safety puzzle.

We start with the premise that for practical purposes all new vehicles will have some sort of active safety system such as Automated Emergency Braking (AEB), and so skip a category specifically for vehicles with no active safety support for driving at all.[61] We also include a distinct category for testing. There is no mapping to the SAE Levels because that would import baggage into the discussion that could ultimately compromise safety.

---

[59] Using the term Level 3+ is also a sin. Please excuse us while we scrub our keyboarding fingers with soap and sanitizer for having written it. We truly hope that term does not take on a zombie life of its own!

[60] J3016 and its proponents are quite clear that higher levels are not "better" in any sense. And yet the industry sells to consumers based on higher numbers being better.

[61] You could add a "No Assistance" mode to the scheme below if desired, but in practice it will just introduce clutter to graphics and terminology summaries.

2.3.1. The four operational modes

In creating a driver-centric description of capabilities, the most important thing is not the details of the technology, but rather what role and responsibility the driver is assigned in overall vehicle operation.

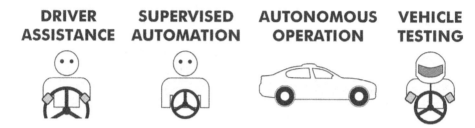

| DRIVER ASSISTANCE | SUPERVISED AUTOMATION | AUTONOMOUS OPERATION | VEHICLE TESTING |

Figure 2.2. Four operational modes for vehicle automation.

We propose four categories of vehicle operation: Driver Assistance, Supervised Automation, Autonomous Operation, and Vehicle Testing. See figure 2.2.

2.3.1.1. Driver Assistance

- Driver Assistance: A licensed human driver drives, and the vehicle assists.
- Human Role: Licensed driver performs driving task
- Vehicle Role: Active Safety, Driver Support, Driving Convenience

In this operational mode the technology's job is to help the driver do better by improving the vehicle's ability to execute the driver's commands and trying to mitigate potential harm from some types of impending crashes. Convenience features might also be provided, excluding sustained automated steering.[62]

Capabilities included as driver assistance might include anti-lock brakes, stability control, cruise control for speed, adaptive cruise control for speed, and automatic emergency braking. The driver always remains in the steering loop, exerting at least some form of sustained control over lane keeping and turns to ensure active engagement and situational awareness.

Momentary intervention by active safety and driver support functions in the steering function, such as a steering wheel bump at lane boundaries, is considered driver support rather than steering automation. Active safety might momentarily intervene in steering and/or braking in response to a specific situation but should not permit itself to be used in lieu of continuous driver control of steering.

---

[62] We choose to make sustained automated steering the difference between driver assistance and supervised automation here as a matter of practicality. Automating speed control is simpler than automating steering for general-purpose road vehicles.

Some collision avoidance active safety features such as Automatic Emergency Braking (AEB) might be active regardless of the current automation mode. The distinction between these and driving automation features is that active safety features engage momentarily to avoid a high risk of collision rather than maneuvering the vehicle in normal driving situations.

2.3.1.2. Supervised Automation

- Supervised Automation: The vehicle controls speed and lane keeping. A human driver handles things the system is not designed to address.
- Human Role: Licensed driver keeps eyes on road, monitors for and intervenes in situations the vehicle is not designed to handle, and executes turns and other tasks beyond ordinary lane-keeping.[63]
- Vehicle Role: Provides steady cruise functions of lane-keeping and speed control.

Technology normally provides a speed and lane-keeping capability when the feature is activated. A licensed human driver is responsible for continuous monitoring of driving and intervening when a situation is encountered that is beyond the design scope of the system. A human driver is responsible for situations outside the stated design capabilities of the system. The design capabilities exclude turning at intersections and other scenarios beyond continuing to drive on the current roadway. Automation might not be capable of handling situations outside its stated capability, which the driver is aware of and accounts for in supervision.[64] The human driver takes control whenever necessary.

An effective driver monitoring system is required to ensure the driver remains situationally aware and is capable of taking over when needed for safety. This does not necessarily mean hands on the wheel. Keeping hands on the wheel might be required for testing, and might help a bit with reaction time during normal operation. But the requirement for Supervised Automation is simply that the driver must be able to respond when needed within reasonable limits of human capabilities, and it is up to the feature developer to determine how to accomplish that in an effective manner. In practice, with current technology this is likely to mean a camera-based

---

[63] We choose to limit supervised automation to lane keeping and not include executing more complex behavior. This is based on the likely impracticality of expecting ordinary drivers to supervise partially capable automation for complex operations such as unprotected left turns in chaotic urban environments. Any expansion of capabilities beyond lane following on highways and the like should be based on compelling evidence of practical safety across a broad range of driver demographics.

[64] Automation modes should be diligent at refusing to operate outside primary ODD constraints to ensure the driver is aware of and respects major limitations. For example, a highway-only feature should not permit activation when not on a highway.

Driver Monitoring System (DMS) that can do at least eye tracking for all ODD conditions.[65]

Supervised automation should make it reasonable to expect a civilian driver without specialized training to achieve at least as good a safety record as would be the case without steering automation, given comparable other vehicle capabilities and operational conditions. This means that any vehicle less safe than a conventional human-driven vehicle (including not only crashes, but also violating traffic laws or exhibiting reckless driving at an elevated rate) should be considered to have a defective design. The scope of design relevant to safety is not just the car, but also the human/driver interface.

As a practical matter, we expect safe use of such a mode to be limited to highway and straight road-following cruise-control-style applications where the vehicle does both lane keeping and speed/separation control. Lane changing at the command of and under the immediate supervision of a driver might be included in such a feature, pending data showing acceptable safety in practice.

If the vehicle can make turns at intersections, that provides an indication that the vehicle is for practical purposes a test vehicle for autonomous operation. Perhaps this constraint will be controversial to some readers, but it is our best assessment of what it will take to keep such systems safe at scale on public roads for the foreseeable future.

2.3.1.3. Autonomous Operation

- Autonomous Operation: The whole vehicle is completely capable of operation with no human monitoring.
- Human Role: No human driver; steering wheel optional depending on operational concept.
- Vehicle Role: Responsible for all aspects of driving and driving-related safety.

The vehicle can complete an entire driving mission without human attention required to monitor safety. The vehicle is responsible for safely handling any exit from the ODD that might occur.

If something goes wrong, the vehicle is entirely responsible for alerting people that it needs assistance, and for operating safely until that assistance is available. Things that might go wrong include not only encountering unforeseen situations and technology failures, but also road mishaps including flat tires, a battery fire, being hit by another vehicle, or all of these things at once. People in the vehicle, if there are any, might not be licensed

---

[65] If night driving or other dark situations such as tunnels are within the ODD, that will likely require active infrared illumination of the driver's face for the DMS camera.

drivers, and might not be capable of assuming the role of "captain of the ship" as is the responsibility of a human driver in a conventional vehicle.[66]

Examples of Autonomous vehicles might include uncrewed robotaxis, driverless last mile delivery vehicles, and heavy trucks in which an otherwise qualified human driver is permitted to be resting in a sleeper berth. A vehicle that received remote assistance would still be in Autonomous Operation mode if (a) the vehicle requests assistance whenever needed without any person being responsible for proactively noticing there is a problem, and (b) the vehicle retains direct responsibility for safety even when it is receiving assistance.[67] In some cases, autonomous operation might change mode to remotely supervised operation if a remote operator becomes responsible for safety.

Achieving safety will depend on the autonomous vehicle being able to handle everything it encounters, for example in conformance with the ANSI/UL 4600 safety standard with additional conformance to ISO 26262 and ISO 21448.

2.3.1.4. Vehicle Testing

- Vehicle Testing: A trained safety driver supervises the operation of an automation testing platform.
- Human Role: Trained safety driver mitigates dangerous behaviors, and at times might intervene to perform driving.
- Vehicle Role: Automation being tested is expected to exhibit dangerous behaviors.

The vehicle is a test bed for vehicle automation features.[68] Because automation in test is not yet ready for release, the driver must have specialized training and operating procedures to ensure public safety, for example according to the SAE J3018 road testing operator safety standard in accordance with a suitable Safety Management System (SMS).[69]

Any vehicle that might exhibit dangerous behavior beyond the mitigation capability of an ordinary driver is an automation test platform. An "ordinary" driver must include all licensed drivers encompassing the full driver demographic span. Moreover, any vehicle that requires special qualification

---

[66] In commercial transport this likely also includes various forms of passenger distress, such as dealing with the safety of drunk passengers who pass out in the back seat during a ride home. As a practical matter, passenger cabin hygiene will also be relevant, including detecting the need for cleanup of any messes before the next passenger enters.

[67] As an example, an AV asking a remote support person if an object it senses should be classified as a traffic cone would remain responsible for operational safety, regardless of the answer it receives from that remote support.

[68] The design intent for the automation is far less significant to classification than the fact that automation is being tested and therefore must be presumed to be potentially defective, presenting risk to other road users.

[69] See section 9.5 for a discussion of public road testing safety.

or an elevated level of care for operations in which the driver compensates for design defects or behavioral anomalies is an automation test platform. Anyone operating such a test platform is performing vehicle testing regardless of whether the automation feature has been purposefully activated.[70]

Testing of a Supervised mode feature is properly said to be Vehicle Testing mode operation. From an external point of view, a human driver operating a vehicle in Supervised mode seems indistinguishable from a driver acting as a test driver for a Supervised mode test platform. In both cases, the human driver is there to intervene if necessary. However, what is going on both inside the vehicle technology and inside the driver's mind is quite different.

In a production vehicle operating in Supervised mode, the driver expects that the vehicle will behave in a consistently safe way, but perhaps not be able to deal with environments that are obviously unusual or chaotic to the driver. Or the vehicle might be fooled by some other situation that the driver recognizes as unusual. To be usable, the types of failures in a production Supervised mode system should be things that are easily understandable to the human driver to be out of scope for the automation. Moreover, any failure situation should give ample opportunity for the smooth transfer of control from automation back to a human driver without a crash occurring. In other words, the human+automation combination should be designed so that it does not present unreasonable risk in practical operation even though the driver has no special training. Moreover, the driver cannot be expected to have driving skills and response times better than other drivers.[71]

On the other hand, in Vehicle Testing mode it is possible that intended vehicle behaviors will malfunction in ways that an ordinary driver would not expect.[72] Additional skill and vigilance are required for a test driver to react to surprise dangerous failures compared to normal driving in Supervised mode.

2.3.1.5. Driver liability

An advantage of this classification approach is that it provides a straightforward way to address driver liability:

* Driver Assistance: As with conventional vehicles.

---

[70] One possible software defect in a test platform is incorrectly turning on automation when it is not supposed to be on. There is no truly safe driving mode for a test platform without qualified test driver supervision.

[71] In practice, if any licensed driver cannot drive a Supervised mode vehicle without more than a cursory familiarization, it is probably not safe to deploy unless it is re-labeled as a Vehicle Testing platform. Any required driver qualification such as a safety score requirement should be considered strong evidence that the feature in question is a Vehicle Testing mode.

[72] As an example, a Supervised mode feature should not panic brake for no apparent reason while driving on a high-speed road, but in Vehicle Testing that might happen due to a software defect.

- Supervised Automation: Absent vehicle defects, the driver is responsible for safe operation. Vehicle defects are activated when the automation does not perform as described to the driver, including incorrect responses to scenarios said to be handled automatically. Defects also encompass any failure to respond to a situation the driver has been told is covered automatically. As an example, automation that suddenly swerves a vehicle into oncoming traffic while performing lane keeping is likely to have defective automation (or really be a test platform with immature automation technology), even if the manufacturer tells the driver that attention is required to mitigate such defective behavior.
- Autonomous Operation: The vehicle automation is responsible for safety. If a human can be blamed for a crash due to not noticing a dangerous situation or failing to take actions to avoid a crash, it is not autonomous operation.
- Vehicle Testing: The organization performing testing is responsible for safety in accordance with a Safety Management System that includes driver qualification, driver training, and testing safety protocols.

2.3.1.6. Other safety considerations

A single vehicle can operate in multiple modes during a single trip. For example, a single trip can start in Driver Assistance mode on local roads, switch to Supervised Automation on a limited access highway, and then switch to Autonomous Operation on suitable portions of roads as is compatible with its design restrictions.

All modes must have provisions for mitigating risk from foreseeable misuse and abuse. That includes ensuring operation of modes only within any applicable operational restrictions (e.g., enforcing the J3016 concept of an Operational Design Domain (ODD)).

Mode changes must be done safely. The principle should be that a human driver can take control in a situation for which that can be safely done, but a human driver can never be forced to assume control involuntarily. This implies, for example, that in Autonomous Operation the vehicle must perform any safety stop entirely on its own in a reasonable safe location if it is unable to continue a mission without demanding human driver takeover.[73] A human driver, if present, might elect to assume control, but human driver takeover cannot be required to ensure safety.

Automation must make a best effort to ensure the highest level of safety it is capable of even without human intervention. The one exception is Vehicle

---

[73] This is related to the concept of an MRC. The important thing for safety is not whether stopping is safer than continuing. Rather, what matters is that the entire fleet of vehicles will experience a reasonable net safety outcome, taking into account how often they fail and the risks presented by each failure. A good starting point would be that after any significant equipment failure the vehicle should do at least as well as a human driver in seeking a safe place to park the vehicle. Sometimes in-lane stop might be unavoidable, but if a human driver would have made it to a road shoulder, or even better protected area, the ADS should be able to do that too.

Testing mode, which cannot be counted on to provide any automation safely beyond ensuring that the mechanism for a human test driver to assert control has high integrity. The automation must be designed to follow human safety driver control commands even if there are software defects in the version being tested.

Mode confusion is a critical issue for safety with any complex system. In mode confusion the human driver and the automation have a difference of opinion as to what the current automation state is. [74] There must be an effective scheme for ensuring that any driver is aware of the current vehicle mode. Changes between modes must also be safe. Mode changes should not be permitted without unambiguous determination that any human driver that might be involved has shifted their mental model of current mode to match the actual vehicle mode in effect after the transition – and that the responsible person is capable of fulfilling the expected human driver mode for that role.

2.3.2. Active safety systems

One school of thought is that Supervised modes should not be built due to the difficulty of ensuring effective driver monitoring. Instead, the thinking goes, drivers should always be driving, but be backed up by extremely capable active safety systems.

In principle, the ultimate active safety feature would make a car notionally crash-proof regardless of human driver error. [75] In other words, in such a system a person drives in a responsible manner, but the automation provides significant help in avoiding crashes. In practice such a system would not be perfectly crash-proof, but the idea is that highly capable active safety systems might prevent a very large fraction of crashes. The evolving capabilities of Automatic Emergency Braking (AEB) are taking steps along that path.

Active safety approaches have the appeal of playing to the strengths of humans (ability to handle novel, unstructured situations as the driver) and the strengths of computers (ability to prevent clear human driver mistakes in common situations, even if a few rare cases are not covered).

The emphasis of this book is autonomous vehicles, so a more thorough exploration of active safety is beyond our scope. However, it is important to consider the possibility that, in practice, active safety approaches might

---

[74] Calling this "mode confusion" is an indirect way of blaming human operators for what might better be characterized as a poorly designed human/computer interaction interface. Nonetheless, this is the standard term used, especially in aviation. For example, see: https://en.wikipedia.org/wiki/Mode_(user_interface)#Mode_errors

[75] A perfectly crash-proof car might be a mistake. Foreseeable misuse could reduce driving to a video game-like experience, where the driver's foot commands full acceleration at all times, and steering is vaguely in the correct direction. The computer takes care of not hitting things. What would amount to bumper cars for real roads is not what most people envision as a safe driving experience. While an effectively crash-proof car is a worthy safety goal, some thought would need to be given to the user interface to avoid such an outcome.

ultimately prove to be safer than Supervised mode operation – or even fully autonomous operation – due to their more natural fit to human strengths and computer weaknesses.

An additional implication of evolving active safety technology capabilities is that they continuously raise the bar for Autonomous operation safety. While it is common to talk about the safety of AVs vs. conventional human vehicles, such an approach is a straw man argument. The safety of an AV should be at least as good as for a human-driven vehicle equipped with a representative set of active safety technology of a comparable model year. Anything less might not be even as safe as what we would see from human-driven vehicles in the real world.

2.3.3. Which mode is safest?

A common misconception about the SAE J3016 Levels is that higher levels are somehow safer. A higher J3016 Level implies that the automation has more responsibility for vehicle operation, but it does not necessarily mean that the net result will be safer.

There is no inherent safety advantage to any one of the Automation Modes. Each has different strengths and weaknesses, and each can be expected to have different safety outcomes depending upon the deployment strategy and ODD.

One can hope that in the long term autonomous vehicles will be safer than human-driven vehicles for significant deployments. However, we are not there yet.

The right question is not which mode is safest. The question that matters is whether a particular mode is both acceptably safe and economically viable for deployment for a particular operational concept and business case.

2.4. Key safety challenges

Summary: AV designers face a number of key technical safety challenges. Many of these challenges revolve around the issue of building an accurate model of the external world that correctly represents other road users and forms a reasonable basis for predicting what is likely to happen next while dealing with inevitable issues of uncertainty.

Whichever terminology you prefer (SAE Levels or Vehicle Automation Modes), the remainder of this book deals with safety for a vehicle in which a human driver is not being held responsible for driving safety. That includes SAE Level 3 (other than for Fallback situations), SAE Level 4, SAE Level 5, and Autonomous mode operation. With a few exceptions related to public road testing we do not delve into the significant complexities involved with combined human driver plus machine automation safety.[76]

For our purposes the key attribute of AV safety is that any blame attributable in a crash is the vehicle's fault rather than the fault of a human driver or safety supervisor.[77]

Given that there is no human driver tasked with ensuring safety, there are significant challenges presented to make an AV acceptably safe. We review them here as context for a discussion in subsequent chapters of how safe is safe enough.

2.4.1. Sense-Plan-Act and more

A traditional framing of robot operation is the Sense-Plan-Act model and later elaborations on that theme.[78] That approach is still used as a starting point in many situations to describe how an autonomous system operates, but we expand it a bit here to give a more granular domain-specific framework for describing AV operation.

An AV must sense the world around it, make a model of the external world, predict how that world will change over time, plan its actions based on the predicted future, act according to its plan, and monitor how the actions it takes in the real world diverge from predictions. The action part mainly involves physical movements within the sensed external world. Once the action has been performed, the new world situation is sensed, and the cycle repeats.

To better understand AV safety, we can elaborate Sense-Plan-Act into a somewhat more detailed set of steps that an AV has to perform to operate safely in the real world. Then we can discuss some of the safety challenges that arise in each step.

- **Sense.** Multiple sensors of different types collect data from the external world. These sensors typically provide camera data, radar data, and lidar data. Other data such as infrared imaging might be available as well.

---

[76] The complexities of human/machine interaction for mode transition are especially problematic, as are issues involved with teleoperation lag and situational awareness. We are largely going to make those someone else's problems for the purposes of this book.

[77] "Blame" is not a particularly useful concept for ensuring safety, and can easily be used to deflect attention away from improving safety. However, the point here is that the autonomous features of the vehicle are solely in charge of safety. Human responsibility does come into play in terms of engineering, operations, and maintenance. But there is no responsibility assigned to a driver nor a safety supervisor to ensure safety in the types of systems we emphasize in this book. Regarding issues with blame culture, see this interview with Jessie Singer: https://usa.streetsblog.org/2022/02/15/the-brake-why-theres-no-such-thing-as-a-car-accident/ Her book is also a worthwhile read.

[78] See: https://en.wikipedia.org/wiki/Sense_Plan_Act

- **Fuse.** Sensor data is converted into objects. For example, a cluster of laser pulses returned from slightly different angles is detected by a lidar and determined to be different measurement points reflected from the same object. At the same time a cluster of different pixels in a camera image differs in color and intensity significantly from the overall background and is determined to be an object. If the camera pixels and lidar pulses are in the same direction and estimated distance from the AV space, they are likely to be from the same object and are "fused" to give more information for later stages. Data from multiple sensing modes give many different views of pieces of the external world.[79]

- **Classify.** Each object is classified into a type of object (pedestrian, vehicle, tree, building, ...), typically using machine learning-based techniques.[80] AV technology has been enabled by the relatively recent – and technically impressive – achievement of classifying objects with 90%+ accuracy. However, seeing only 9 out of 10 pedestrians in a crosswalk (or even 999 out of 1000) is insufficient for acceptable safety, so this remains an area of significant research effort.[81]

- **Model.** The AV builds a model of the external world that includes various objects it has detected and the space it believes to be unoccupied. A localization process establishes where the AV is relative to all the objects in the environment, often supported by a high-definition map. Each object is associated with a position and orientation, which is called the object's pose. It is also useful to annotate each object with its current motion. The result is a snapshot of where everything is along with each object's current motion. A robust world model should account for unknown parts of the environment, such as the possibility of an unseen pedestrian occluded by a bus, or cross traffic at an intersection not yet visible due to visual obstructions.

- **Predict.** Once a world model has been built, the AV needs to predict what happens next. It is not enough to drive where the road is clear right now. The AV needs to predict where the road is going to be clear of obstacles and other road users when it gets there. Moreover, the AV should not encroach on safety buffers surrounding other road users and

---

[79] Some systems convert sensor data into objects and then do fusion of objects rather than fusing low-level sensor data. Early vs. late fusion is an architectural tradeoff choice that does not make a substantial difference for our discussion.

[80] We are not going to try to teach machine learning in this book. Suffice it to say that a computer system looks at a lot of examples and builds statistical models in a training phase. When an AV encounters something on the road later, those models determine how to classify that newly encountered thing in terms of which training data might be statistically similar.

[81] For specialists, performance metrics beyond accuracy matter a great deal, but are beyond the level of detail needed for this discussion. If you want to dig deeper look up precision vs. recall and other topics such as:
https://en.wikipedia.org/wiki/Receiver_operating_characteristic
and https://en.wikipedia.org/wiki/F-score

objects. Prediction complexity can vary from trivial (it is a good bet that a building shown on a map will not suddenly jump out into the road), to moderately simple (a truck can only stop and turn so fast, so on very short time scales it will mostly keep going the direction it is going), to complex (people do in fact jump into the road from time to time). For objects with complex behaviors such as people, a prediction might be less of a single expected path and more of a probability cloud of potential next positions. That probability cloud might be weighted toward the most likely action given the context, person's body posture, crosswalk control device status, and other contextual information.[82]

- **Plan.** Given a model of where everything is and a prediction of what happens next, the AV plans what action it needs to take to make progress on its driving mission while not doing anything unsafe. The AV creates a trajectory for future motion that it expects will keep it acceptably safe as it drives down the roadway.

- **Act.** The trajectory is executed as vehicle motion commands to steering, propulsion, braking, signaling, and other vehicle equipment.

- **React.** Things frequently do not go quite as expected. Sensors have trouble seeing everything. Sensor fusion sometimes gets it wrong. The model might be incorrect or incomplete. Predictions might be incorrect, especially if pedestrians change their minds mid-step. Plans might not be executed exactly as intended due to unexpectedly slippery road surfaces or wind pushing the vehicle off track. Other road users will react to the AV's plan and change their behaviors. In general, the real world will seldom conform to the plan exactly. The AV partly addresses this by executing the Sense-Plan-Act multiple times per second to react to changes. It also might need to take a safety action such as executing a panic stop if an object suddenly appears in front of it or other events present unexpected risk.

- **Monitor.** The AV needs to continually monitor its own internal equipment health and performance. This includes potentially triggering a

---

[82] We don't have the illustration budget to attempt a convincing picture of a pedestrian probability cloud. Think of it as a 3-d picture of the likely positions the pedestrian will be occupying a short time later. There are high probabilities for standing still and walking forward. Lower probabilities for turning to change walking direction. Still lower probabilities for sliding sideways and backward. Also the possibility of jumping or falling. There is not one single direction guaranteed, but rather a set of possible next positions, with some positions more likely than others. A picture of these possibilities would look like a cloud surrounding the person, with the cloud fog-thick where probabilities are high, and whisper-thin in unlikely directions. The term "probability cloud" is used here in an attempt to evoke mental models of the sort used to illustrate atomic orbitals. At the risk of stretching the analogy too far, the situational context, body posture, and so on are analogous to selecting an energy state that selects a different probability cloud pattern depending on the situation. See: https://en.wikipedia.org/wiki/Atomic_orbital

Fallback operation due to an equipment malfunction, detecting when the AV needs to return to a depot for servicing, and recording information needed for engineering analysis. A critical monitoring task for the AV is detecting an ODD exit due to, for example, adverse weather conditions, and triggering a Fallback response to ensure safety when the ODD has been exited.[83]

- **Sustain.** While an AV driving down the street is literally where the rubber meets the road, there is more to safety than just driving. The AV needs to be fueled/charged, maintained, repaired, have software updates applied, and so on. Maps need to be updated as well. In addition, any procedural components that affect safety such as pre-mission inspections need to be monitored and have associated procedures updated. If any of these things is done improperly it can compromise safety, so safety-critical sustaining activities extend throughout the AV's lifecycle.

As involved as all that is, the above level of detail is dramatically simplified and is not necessarily the precise grouping and order of operations that will occur. Nonetheless, it provides a framework for thinking about the various challenges that arise in making an AV safe in real-world operation, each of which must be accounted for when determining if an AV is acceptably safe.

2.4.2. Sensor limitations

Each sensor type has strengths and weaknesses in terms of what and how accurately it can sense. For example, cameras are especially important because of their ability to interpret infrastructure meant for human eyes such as road signs. Lidar is better at three dimensional geometry. For example, lidar depth information can help distinguish between a real object or a flat picture of an object on a billboard that might confuse a camera. Radar penetrates fog and smoke, and is especially good at measuring speed of an object away from or toward the sensor.

However, each sensor has weaknesses. Cameras struggle with low contrast scenes such as a white truck against a hazy white sky. Automotive-grade radar can have poor vertical resolution, causing it to mistake overhead highway signs for road obstacles. In particular, radar might require disregarding many stationary objects to avoid false alarm stops for road signs and metal bridge expansion joints embedded in the road pavement. High-resolution lidar gives very useful information, but is more expensive than a

---

[83] It is important to realize that because an ODD involves more than just a geofence, the AV might have little or no warning that an ODD exit will occur in some cases. In other words, the AV might be forcibly ejected from its ODD before it has time to react. A simple example is a fog bank not seen until the last second coming around a curve. Any safety argument that the AV will initiate a Fallback to revert to a safe state before ODD departure is likely to be too simplistic. Safety must be ensured even if an involuntary ODD departure occurs during operation.

camera and is not able to detect purely visual information such as instructions on illuminated variable speed limit signs.

All sensors are vulnerable to at least some of dust, dirt, impact with road debris, fly splats, and temperature fluctuations, as well as drifting out of calibration due to vibration during the drive cycle. Sensors are also vulnerable to interference from active emission sources including emitters on other vehicles. A sensor that works perfectly at the start of the day probably will not work as well over time unless it is cleaned and maintained. And even a perfectly maintained and calibrated sensor will work imperfectly due to inevitable interference in some situations.

Most importantly, no sensor produces 100% accurate detection results. All sensors have a tradeoff between false positives (claiming a pedestrian is there when the road is empty) and false negatives (not detecting a pedestrian who is there).[84] A moderate rate of detection mistakes is not necessarily a sensor defect, but rather an inevitable consequence of using electronic devices to sense the real world. This limitation means that the model of the world being built by the AV is necessarily imperfect to some degree. For safety it is important that the model be good enough despite such sensor mistakes. This is a significant part of the challenge of safe perception.

2.4.3. Sensor fusion and classification challenges

Converting sensor data to objects and classifying those objects is typically done using Machine Learning-based (ML) approaches. ML approaches use statistical techniques to "train" an ML system to identify pedestrians, vehicles, traffic signs, and other aspects of the external world.[85]

It is important to note that it is common for ML training to occur as a batch process during development, with a frozen snapshot of the result of the training process used for each deployed software update. It is typically not the case that an individual AV is "learning" from its experience while it is driving. One would expect that unusual situations are sent back to the design team to help with the next batch training session, but that might take days to months and be incorporated into a software update rather than directly

---

[84]When considering the detection of an object there are four possibilities in a 2x2 confusion matrix. Using a pedestrian detection example they are: (1) true positive – pedestrian is there; pedestrian correctly detected, (2) false positive – no pedestrian really there; pedestrian incorrectly detected anyway, (3) true negative – no pedestrian really there; no pedestrian detected, and (4) false negative – pedestrian is there; pedestrian is incorrectly said to be absent. For safety it is often the false negatives that are the most problematic – failing to detect a pedestrian who is really there. We revisit this topic in section 6.3.2. A rather complex description is given here: https://en.wikipedia.org/wiki/Confusion_matrix

[85] ML can be used in ways other than perception, but we concentrate on its use in perception in our discussion. See: https://en.wikipedia.org/wiki/Machine_learning

training the vehicle that experienced the event. ML training for production AVs is not instantaneous.[86]

The ML training process is prone to suffering from any biases that might be present in the training data, even if completely unintentional. A special concern is that under-represented road objects might be poorly recognized due to insufficient training data. As a simple example, if wheelchair riders are only 1 out of 1000 people seen in a particular set of training data, a classification system could easily be 99% accurate even though it misses every single wheelchair rider.

Sometimes biases in training data can be surprising as well as hazardous. Training on images of people with light colored skin and then struggling on images of people of color is a famous bias. But we have also seen biases based on clothing color in the form of problems identifying construction workers in high visibility clothing as pedestrians. In essence, high visibility clothing is camouflage to a vision system that has not seen enough bright yellow and similar hi-viz clothing in its training data. One hopes that production systems have identified and fixed this problem that was found in an open source vision system. However, there are likely to be numerous other issues in the same vein that need to be resolved to achieve acceptable safety.

A principal reason for fusing multiple sensors is that if one sensing mode struggles, another can pick up the slack. If a road construction worker is not recognized by a camera, a lidar system might at least detect there is something in the road. So long as the "something" is not classified as a floating piece of plastic or falling leaves, the AV can avoid hitting it even if the classification is not entirely accurate.

However, a high rate of false positives (objects detected that are not there) might result in an AV that is basically afraid of its own shadow.[87] This might be worked around by having sensor fusion weigh different sensor inputs and decide which combination of inputs to trust when building the world model. The fusion algorithm will not get this 100% right, but it needs to do well enough that the world model constructed by the AV is close enough to representing the real world to result in safe operation.

2.4.4. World model limitations

Building a world model requires more than a list of generic objects and poses. Supporting the next step of prediction can require a fairly fine-grain classification approach based on sensor data.

---

[86] If you have watched a video in which a driver gives a vehicle automation feature several chances to try something difficult and then proclaims "see, it learned!" when the car eventually does the desired thing, that reflects a fundamentally mistaken interpretation of what is really just inconsistent automation behavior. Drivers who misapprehend the technology that fundamentally should not test on public roads.

[87] This might literally be the case if a camera-based sensor classifies shadows as road objects. Patterns made by repaired cracks in asphalt pavement can also be an issue.

For example, consider an object on a sidewalk right at the edge of the roadway. While it is helpful to know that an object is at the side of the road, the model needs to have a predefined set of classification bins for different types of objects to better support prediction. Some examples of that might be relevant and need to be classified in some reasonable way include:

- A bush, trash barrel, or other stationary object
- Parked car (might have a door that will open into traffic area)
- Deer (likely to dart out into road at last second[88])
- Construction worker (might be directing traffic)
- Bicyclist walking a bike (unlikely to move as quickly as a mounted cyclist[89])
- Light mobility scooter rider (superficially looks like a pedestrian standing still, but can move much more quickly)
- Child pedestrians
- Adult pedestrian about to run out into the road to catch a bus nearing a bus stop at the other side of the street
- Police officer directing traffic with hand signals
- School crossing guard trying to stop traffic
- And more…

Omitted relevant classification categories can cause a problem. If the world model does not know about school crossing guards because it uses data from summer months when school was not in session, that will become a problem the first week of school when crossing guards suddenly appear. Or perhaps the world model is not able to represent relevant combinations of characteristics such as a child acting as a crossing guard,[90] or a person leaning against a trash barrel vs. a person carrying a trash barrel.

A particular concern is the number of infrequent but important object classifications that will be required to support acceptably safe prediction. Many different objects or situations might each be individually rare compared to the general population, but still important to handle. Some simple examples might include children in Halloween costumes, runners in an annual marathon, large wild animals wandering on streets in urban

---

[88] Unless it is a stuffed deer outside a taxidermy shop. Or at another level of indirection, it might be an image of a deer on a deer crossing sign which is both not a real deer, but also a clue that deer might suddenly appear without much warning. Red circular sticker on the nose of the sign's deer optional. (Yes, that is a thing.)

[89] Unless the bicyclist has one foot supporting the person's weight on a pedal and the other foot pushing even though technically dismounted – a classic workaround to the "no bike riding allowed on school grounds" rule when late for class, at least in our experience.

[90] Yes, this is a thing.

See AAA: https://exchange.aaa.com/safety/aaa-school-safety-patrol/

centers,[91] collapsed bridges,[92] bus-eating sinkholes,[93] cattle spills,[94] road slickness due to eel slime,[95] and flash floods.

Each special case might occur very rarely, but still be important because the sum of risks from all the special cases remains unacceptably high. A so-called "heavy tail" distribution [96] is especially problematic because a significant fraction of all risk is spread across a very large number of rare cases. Each rare case might be low risk and indeed might never be seen in the entire operating life of a single vehicle. But with a huge number of such risks at least some of them will happen, even if it is impossible to predict which ones in advance, or perhaps even imagine what they might be. Nonetheless, because of the inevitability of some rare risk from a huge population of potential risks occurring, a heavy tail situation means that many of these rare risks have to be dealt with in some way that preserves safety.[97]

Training based on examples is the heart of an ML-based approach, so heavy tail environments present an existential risk to the success of such systems. ML-based approaches work by relating current observations to what they have already learned. If a heavy tail situation has never been seen before and has not been taught to the ML-based system, the ML-based system is in essence just guessing when it encounters one in the wild. If you need to be able to handle rare events, but you do not have enough examples of rare events to train on, how can you handle them? Approaches such as producing training data using simulators can help – but only if someone has realized the need to program the heavy tail rare event into the simulator. This topic remains a significant challenge to creating safe AVs.[98]

In the end, the ability of the AV to interpret the real world will be constrained by the limits of whatever modeling capability it has. Gaps in the ability to build an accurate real-world model will present safety challenges.

---

[91] Also a thing. See the story of Buzzwinkle the inebriated urban moose, Sinnott 2021: https://www.adn.com/voices/article/recalling-alaskas-most-notorious-drunken-moose-street-smart-buzzwinkle/2013/09/10/

[92] Such as the bridge collapse that happened within two miles of the author's home. See NTSB, 2022: https://www.ntsb.gov/investigations/Pages/HWY22MH003.aspx

[93] See Andrew 2019: https://www.cnn.com/2019/10/28/us/bus-sinkhole-pittsburgh-trnd/index.html

[94] See USA Today 2012:
https://www.usatoday.com/videos/news/nation/2012/12/20/1782791/

[95] Come on, now he's just making stuff up! Nope, we swear we are not making this up. If you are not squeamish, see Russo 2017:
https://www.huffpost.com/entry/oregon-slime-eels-truck-crash_n_596845e1e4b03389bb164e65

[96] See: https://en.wikipedia.org/wiki/Heavy-tailed_distribution

[97] See: https://youtu.be/VZpdUL5p4a4

[98] We revisit this challenge more generically in the context of unknown unknowns in section 2.4.12.

2.4.5. Prediction challenges

Different AVs vary in their need for sophisticated prediction. A slow-moving low-speed shuttle might need essentially no prediction at all if it can instantly stop without injuring passengers when something gets too close to it. This can make sense if the stopping distance is short compared to the detection range that activates the stop – and other moving objects in the environment can stop quickly as well.[99]

A next level of sophistication is projecting the future position of each object based on current movement, often called target tracking after the use of that term in military applications that pioneered this type of analysis. The laws of physics dictate that a detected object moving in a certain direction at a certain speed can only change direction and speed so much in a fraction of a second based on its mass and ability to maneuver. At least some AV design teams are taking this approach, relying on fast computer-speed reaction times to respond to an object that changes its behavior. This can be appropriate in some operational contexts, especially when predicting speed changes for vehicles and other heavy objects that have a lot of inertia and a limited ability to change both speed and direction quickly.

Human drivers not only predict by extrapolating current object trajectories, but also anticipate likely changes in behavior. Any experienced rural driver will know that a deer standing perfectly still at the edge of a road is not likely to stay that way. Rather, you expect a deer to wait until the very last moment and then jump into the road, seemingly bent on being hit on purpose. A prudent driver slows down to reduce the chance of a catastrophic collision with deer anywhere near the roadway regardless of the current motion of that deer. A prudent driver also speculates that other deer might suddenly appear even if they can only see one at the moment.

It is currently an open question whether AVs will need to parallel such anticipatory behavior prediction abilities to achieve acceptable safety, or whether superhuman response times will be enough. It seems likely anticipation will be required, if for no other reason than to avoid having the AV blamed for suffering crashes that a human driver would have likely avoided.

This type of anticipation of behavioral changes will require far more than tracking somewhat generic objects. Specific categories of wildlife will need to be identified based on likely threat to safety and the potential for sudden high-risk movements. Pedestrian intent will need to be estimated based on context, body posture, and perhaps facial expression. Light mobility users will need to be assessed for likely future behavior and the potential for rider falls throwing a rider into danger with no warning.

---

[99] Seat belts for passengers are also important, as illustrated by low-speed shuttle emergency stops that have resulted in passenger injuries. See Duncan 2020: https://www.washingtonpost.com/local/trafficandcommuting/a-traffic-incident-leads-to-robot-shuttles-being-ordered-to-stop-hauling-passengers/2020/02/29/db6bec64-5981-11ea-9b35-def5a027d470_story.html

It is impossible to predict behavioral changes and surprises perfectly. Nonetheless, driver education manuals teach human drivers that every ball rolling into the road near a playground predicts a child (seen or unseen) is likely to come chasing after it. AVs should at least achieve a comparable level of ability to predict impending risky situations from contextual hints that would be readily apparent to a human driver.

A related prediction problem has to do with occlusions, which are volumes of space within sensor fields of view that are hidden behind other objects. Prediction requires at least some ability to determine where significant occlusions might occur and to plan for hazards emerging from those occlusions. Common examples are inability to see a traffic light turning red when behind a tall truck on a city street, and inability to see a pedestrian about to emerge in front of a city bus after debarking to cross the street, even if that pedestrian is not supposed to be crossing at that time and place.

All prediction is probabilistic. In principle, every object has a probability cloud of potential next locations surrounding it. Similarly, cargo in vehicles has a probability of falling off and creating a sudden obstacle. [100] The prediction of the most dangerous place each object might move to in the near future does not have to be perfect. The question is whether an AV can predict what happens next well enough to match human driver safety and show reasonable care in avoiding unreasonable risk, especially in complex chaotic traffic situations.

Even after you know where all the objects are and have predictions of where they will be, there is an additional prediction piece remaining. You need to be able to predict environmental conditions and especially upcoming road surface conditions.

For example, an AV might decide that cross-traffic at an intersection where it has the right of way will finish crossing before it becomes a problem obstacle, and so continue at normal speed. But what if the crossing vehicle unexpectedly stops in the middle of the intersection and the AV cannot stop in time due to an ice patch right before the intersection? The AV might slide into the intersection and cause a collision because it was counting on a clean road surface.

Road surface variability can be accommodated to a degree by adding some safety margin. But driving as if all roads were covered by ice all the time will lead to unreasonably large following distances, degrading roadway throughput capacity most of the time. It will be important for AVs to anticipate changes in environmental conditions to adjust their safety margins. For example, recent precipitation in freezing temperatures should lead to caution, especially if the AV is about to drive over a bridge sporting a "bridge freezes before road" caution sign. Driving in hot summer weather might justifiably assume a lack of ice on normal upcoming roadways.

---

[100] Consider the last time you saw a car carrying a mattress poorly secured to the roof, flapping in the wind – and whether you were inclined to tailgate right behind it.

2.4.6. Planning challenges

Planning validation approaches typically rely upon creating a giant scenario catalog of all possible situations that can happen and ensuring that the AV has been trained on how to handle every single scenario.[101] Because the scenario catalog needs to address all combinations of own vehicle maneuver intentions, other road actor behaviors, environmental conditions, traffic rules, and other conditions, this can easily turn into a herculean effort. As a practical matter, significant simulation will be required to check all combinations, with additional road testing necessary to ensure that the simulation's predictions accurately reflect real-world outcomes.

Planning must also take into account uncertainty and the likelihood that the vehicle will not be able to follow the ordered trajectory exactly, both of which are discussed next.

2.4.7. Uncertainty

A significant challenge in safe AV driving is the requirement to deal with uncertainty. Sensors will create a model of the outside world that has uncertainty. Position and velocity estimates will be approximate. Classifications of objects will have some probability associated with them.[102] Predictions of movements over longer than the smallest fraction of a second will have substantial dispersion across a probability cloud surrounding that object. Environmental condition estimates can always hide a surprise slippery patch. Vehicle equipment such as brakes might be impaired or might even have failed completely mid-trip in a way that is not yet apparent until attempted use. And so on.

More generally, the AV planning challenge is that planning needs to occur despite a significant amount of uncertainty. Human drivers do amazingly well despite all this uncertainty, but are not perfect. AVs will need to approximately match this human ability to muddle through uncertainty to achieve acceptable safety.

An additional consideration is that the AV needs to always have a fallback plan in case of equipment failure. Stopping in a traffic lane if the AV fails to find a safe plan is better than crashing full speed into something. But in-lane

---

[101] A scenario is, to keep it simple, an operational situation in which the AV is trying to accomplish a specific motion or goal in the next few seconds, including all other relevant road users and objects. For example, a scenario might be the AV making an unprotected left turn across lanes that have oncoming traffic. The theory is that a complete scenario catalog will have entries that account for every possible operation of the AV in the real world.

[102] Consider an object in front of you is classified as 1% likely to be a child, and 99% likely to be a shadow. Maybe the AV decides to run over the thing that is 99% shadow. But what happens when, after a hundred or so times seeing such shadows, the AV encounters that one time it is really a child but runs over the it's-really-a-child-but-labeled-99%-shadow anyway? Odds that seem compelling in usual statistical discussions (99%) become problematic in life-critical systems.

stops can still leave the AV vulnerable to being hit by other vehicles on a busy high-speed road or in the middle of an unprotected left turn. Ensuring that the AV is capable of doing something reasonably safe in failure situations means that planning must be able to deal not only with normal driving, but also with planning despite loss of sensors, exiting the intended ODD into an environment it was not designed to handle, and other faults.

2.4.8. Motion challenges

Once there is a plan in place, the AV executes the planned trajectory. While following a defined plan is more straightforward than creating that plan, there are nonetheless safety issues to be addressed. Safe vehicle dynamic limits need to be enforced, and should have been taken into account in planning. [103] It is important to avoid a vehicle rollover due to a combination of an excessively fast tight turn, a gust of wind, and perhaps an unexpected road surface condition. In the real world, any vehicle will not perform quite as commanded. The motion controller will need to continually correct for deviations from the desired trajectory. If too big a deviation occurs the planner will need to re-plan to account for the new situation.

2.4.9. Reaction challenges

In the real world, nothing ever goes quite as expected in planning. For small differences, a quickly updated Sense-Plan-Act cycle can compensate for evolving situations on the fly. For large deviations from the plan, more urgent reactions might be required. However, those urgent reactions require a different type of what-if planning.

A classic example is if an object suddenly appears in front of the AV such as a large boulder or landslide, requiring a panic brake to avoid a collision. There might not be any collision-free path that can be planned, but the system should at least do what it can to reduce the collision speed.

A particularly challenging situation is a "cut-out" in which a leading vehicle changes lanes to avoid a road obstacle, suddenly revealing the obstacle that was previously occluded by that leading vehicle. While the AV might have been leaving a safe following distance to the moving lead vehicle in case of a panic brake, that following distance assumed the lead vehicle has limits on its ability to decelerate. A high-speed travel lane cut-out that reveals a disabled vehicle or boulder in the road might be worse than lead vehicle panic braking. Because the road obstruction is already stopped, no distance credit can be taken for limits to deceleration as was the case with a leading

---

[103] This set of steps is presented as more or less a start-to-end flow. However, upstream stages need to be aware of the limits imposed by downstream stages. For example, planning a path with a turn so sharp it will flip over the AV should be avoided by the path planner in the first place, even if the motion system would reject such a trajectory request for safety. That can avoid a situation in which there is no currently valid plan.

vehicle. Impact might be unavoidable if an immediate lane change cannot be executed safely.

Another factor in real-world road safety is that human drivers often compensate for other driver mistakes. If a car runs a stop sign or stops mid-turn while executing an unprotected turn across oncoming traffic, other drivers usually notice and give way to avoid a collision (potentially shouting some choice words [104]) even though the other vehicle is breaking traffic regulations. AVs will need to accommodate mistakes made by other road users as well. Hurling invective is optional.

Another consideration is that vehicle motion is an implicit communication channel between the AV and other road users as well as a risk modulation mechanism. Slight movement to break deadlock tie situations at 4-way stops, pulling into a bike lane (where legal and appropriate) to make a right turn intention more obvious, nudging across the centerline (when the opposing lane is clear and it is otherwise appropriate) to give a disabled vehicle or crash scene more room, and other subtle motions are an important part of driving and have real-world effects on safety outcomes as well as the behavior of other road users. These considerations need to be negotiated within the AV's architecture one way or another.

There are also ethical issues that we consider in Chapter 10.

2.4.10. Monitoring and dependability challenges

Equipment failures can be expected for any vehicle, including electronic failures in the ADS itself. Because there is no human driver to notice something has broken or that the vehicle is not behaving properly, it will be up to the AV to detect and compensate for equipment failures. An equipment failure might trigger a Fallback maneuver, bringing the vehicle to a safe location. If there is no feasible alternative, perhaps an AV will need to perform an in-lane stop. On the other hand, an undetected equipment failure could lead to a catastrophic vehicle crash.

Some equipment failures are difficult to detect. In practice an even more difficult issue is choosing which components to trust if they disagree about what objects are on the road or what the AV's next planned movement should be.

It is essential to consider how the Fallback maneuver is performed. If the primary autonomy computer fails, the AV needs a backup computer to perform the Fallback maneuver. Similarly, if a single main lidar sensor fails, the AV either needs a different sensing strategy to safely perform a fallback maneuver, or it needs a backup main lidar. An important part of any Fallback maneuver will be the ability to sense own vehicle motion and position well enough to avoid colliding with objects even if sensors have failed, been severely degraded, or the car has compromised motion control (e.g., due to spinning after hitting a patch of ice). While human drivers are not perfect at

---

[104] In the Pittsburgh region "Jagoff" is a preferred term.
See: https://en.wikipedia.org/wiki/Jagoff

these things, they can be remarkably good at performing reasonable risk mitigation despite serious compromises of equipment and visibility.[105] AVs will need to do at least as well in the face of equipment failures.

2.4.11. Lifecycle challenges for sustained operation

There is more to ensuring an AV is safe than teaching it how to drive properly and ensuring that equipment failures are handled. The design process must consider which lifecycle operations are safety-critical.

Everyday annoyances for a human driver such as running out of windshield cleaning fluid could become life-critical. Consider an AV that suffers a large mud spray event that covers all its optical sensors. Perhaps the vehicle can perform Fallback with radar and inertial navigation alone. But if the safety case for the AV was made that optical sensors will be available because there is a cleaning system, replenishing the cleaning system (and ensuring that the fluid reservoir does not freeze in winter) has suddenly become a life-critical maintenance activity.

Without a human driver to handle problems on the road, at least some maintenance, inspection, and response to warning signals will become much more safety-critical than it is on current vehicles. If a human driver ignores a dashboard warning light, we might blame the driver if something goes wrong. If an AV computer fails to handle running out of wiper fluid gracefully and that results in a crash, whom do we blame?

It is likely that, at least for the near term, AV operations and maintenance will need to be handled in a way more similar to aircraft than conventional road vehicles. Inspections, maintenance, and fleet operations will need to follow procedures rigorously and be done by qualified personnel. Over time, AVs might have enough automated diagnostic capability that they can tell when they do not meet their minimum operational requirements and refuse to engage automation. But that level of self-diagnosis sophistication is an additional development effort on top of just getting AVs to drive safely in the first place.

Security is a crucial topic that also needs to be handled. While security is beyond the scope of this book, it is no exaggeration to say that an insecure car will be an unsafe car. Security interacts most closely with safety in that software updates needed for both security and safety improvements will need to be both vetted for safety (does the intended update make the AV unsafe?) and security of the update process itself (does the update capability enable malicious code that will make the AV unsafe?). Dependence on outside data sources introduces both safety and security concerns (what if vehicle-to-

---

[105] While our experiences might be unusual, catastrophic equipment failures that have happened to us personally while driving at highway speed include: loss of visibility due to being entirely covered by a payload tarp blown off a truck, loss of visibility due to a windshield shattered by ice falling from an overpass, and complete loss of main service brakes at highway speed in a heavy traffic situation (both hydraulic loops compromised due to a single point failure). No crashes resulted.

infrastructure communications provide incorrect data, regardless of whether due to malicious intent or a software defect in the remote sensor?).

2.4.12. Unknown unknowns

For conventional vehicles, designers maintain a useful fiction that they have thought of everything that can possibly go wrong, and they have designed for safety in light of that knowledge. It is a fiction because there is always something that has been missed, which is a reason we have safety recalls. But it is a useful fiction in that a conventional vehicle design team earnestly trying to achieve safety by following appropriate best practices can reach a defensible safety target for their intended operational use. To make this concrete: it is unlikely that a list of potential hazards is perfect. But the goal is to use best practices and lessons learned to make it near-perfect enough that overall safety is acceptable. That can result in a design close enough to perfect for practical safety purposes.

AVs add a major additional challenge. Conventional vehicle designers mainly have to worry about what can go wrong inside the car itself. Some features are intended to help the human driver deal with external conditions, such as anti-lock brakes helping with slippery roads. However, ultimately the human driver is responsible for dealing with novel situations and mitigating risks presented by hazardous external events.

With an AV there is no human driver. (That is the point of having an AV, right?) But without a human driver to mitigate problems caused by external conditions, AV designers have to pick up that slack to achieve system-level safety.

2.4.12.1. Unknowns are not addressed by the ODD

AVs must be able to deal with anything that goes wrong in the outside world, including completely unexpected surprises not considered by the design team. This presents, for practical purposes, an infinite set of edge case conditions that must be handled safely. AV designers must build a system that can deal with unknown unknowns – a substantial set of things that will inevitably go wrong in deployment that designers did not think about.

Machine learning-based systems are notorious for being overly confident and brittle when exposed to data that breaks implicit assumptions and biases in the training data set. [106] The machine learning community commonly discusses this as sensitivity to distributional shifts, although the concept of a distributional shift does not necessarily convey the deeper safety issues here.

It is in principle impossible to know all the unknown unknowns. But they will gradually reveal themselves over time in a large-scale deployment, and ignoring them will not make them go away. As a practical matter, it is important to build an AV so that it can tell when it is in an unexpected situation that it has not been trained for or otherwise designed to handle, which is by definition outside its ODD.

---

[106] For a practical illustration, see this short video: https://youtu.be/cOYRGZECuL0

Saying that an AV has to detect when it is outside its ODD is tricky at two levels. At a first level it might be that there are dimensions to the ODD that are difficult to measure. As a simple example, an ODD limitation excluding heavy rain requires some method of sensing that it is in fact raining heavily.

2.4.12.2. ODD model deficiencies

At a second level, detecting that an AV is outside its ODD in the face of an unknown can trickier. What if the ODD limitation is not something measurable such as rain, but rather an implicit assumption that pedestrians will have one of a limited number of hair color hues? What if the training data does not include samples of people on scooters, rollerblades, unicycles, stilts, and extreme pogo sticks?[107]

In many cases the unknown will be problematic because it has an attribute that matters for safety that is not included in the engineer's model of the ODD and not accounted for in the ML model. It might not even be something seen in the training data at all. Or ML might have trained on an accidental characteristic such as color rather than a characteristic a human driver would consider more important such as shape.

Consider a construction worker with a pole sign for traffic control: one side says "stop" while the other side says "slow." If an AV has not been trained on this and it is missing from scenarios as well as training data, the AV might well struggle to infer that this is a construction zone, or that the "slow" sign it sees might instantly transform into a stop sign. If it has trained on shape instead of wording, it might not realize that the sign has two possible meanings in this context because shape does not change when the sign is spun to the other side. It might also think that it can stop at the stop sign and then proceed, when in fact this use of a stop sign means something quite different: wait until you see the slow sign even if the roadway appears clear. The vehicle might not realize that construction traffic control signs are outside its ODD even though it understands what construction zones are in general and what a stop sign means in other contexts. In other words, the unique combination of hand-held pole with a two-faced stop/slow sign requires significantly different behavior than someone standing next to an ordinary fixed-pole "stop" sign.

As another example, an AV might have learned that a stop sign is octagonal and red. The fact that it has the word "STOP" on it might be

---

[107] We are not saying that enormous engineering effort should be spent optimizing prediction performance for every exotic means of light mobility transportation possible. But we are reminded of the nighttime drive with a safety case expert in which there was a person on a bicycle performing a trick at an intersection involving rearing the bike back up onto one wheel and spinning crazily in place. The correct driving response was not to pick the bike's next movement direction (effectively impossible if spinning should stop or the rider were to fall), but rather to slow down and proceed with caution, leaving significant clearance until past the intersection. Knowing that something is happening the system is unable to handle is what matters most. And yes, extreme pogo is a thing: https://en.wikipedia.org/wiki/Extreme_Pogo

irrelevant to the classification algorithm. And this might work fine – until the AV encounters a blue stop sign in a shopping center parking lot in Hawaii which is octagonal and has the word "STOP" – but is light blue instead of red.[108]

In both these examples there is a gap between what aspects of objects and events in the real world matter, the ODD model used by engineers to validate the system, and the attributes used by the AV to transform its sensor data from the external world into an actionable model of the real world.

Even though people are not perfect, human drivers have an impressive ability to realize something odd is going on and adopt a lower-risk driving posture until they can reason out the implications. Informally, people are good at thinking "What the heck is that? Better take it easy while I figure it out."

2.4.12.3. Knowing when the AV does not know

Regardless of the technical mitigation approaches taken, it is important for the AV to know when it does not know what is really going on. Once it realizes it is struggling to comprehend the situation, it needs to treat such situations as a departure from the ODD that is handled safely – even if it has no way to model why the ODD has been violated. The difficult part is it needs to be able to do this even if it has not been pre-trained in what the source of the uncertainty might be (because it is an unknown).

Overall, there are many challenges to creating a safe AV, and all these challenges must be addressed adequately to achieve acceptable safety in real-world operation. Many of the challenges discussed are well understood from decades of robotics and vehicle experience, and this is just a quick tour rather than an exhaustive list. Approaches to address these and other challenges are in many ways still works in progress.[109]

2.5. Conclusion

Nothing in this chapter should be interpreted to mean that acceptable AV safety cannot be achieved. Rather it is intended to be a start at an explanation for why AV deployments are taking longer than many had predicted.[110]

There are tens of billions of dollars betting that the AV industry can deploy safe vehicles. That kind of resource allocation might well be able to address issues well enough to achieve acceptable safety. Nonetheless, the safety issues are numerous and significant enough that we should not simply

---

[108] See Kohlstedt 2020: https://99percentinvisible.org/article/red-white-sometimes-blue-how-safety-shaped-the-octagonal-stop-sign/

[109] Obxkcd: https://xkcd.com/1838/

[110] It is common to hear claims that AVs are taking longer to deploy than anyone could have predicted. We can assure you they did not ask us, or many others in the safety engineering research community.

assume that an AV will be safe without some assurance that the engineering design, testing, and deployment plans address these challenges and more.

3.   Risk acceptance frameworks

While it is essential that systems be acceptably safe, there is no such thing as perfectly safe.[111] That means we need to establish a basis for evaluating the risk of deploying AVs.[112] That risk needs to be put into the context of what types and levels of safety are deemed acceptable by relevant stakeholders. Relevant stakeholders include all those exposed to risk from deployment and the consequences of any loss events. We call this concept having *acceptable safety*.

A system is acceptably safe if it has a very small probability of substantive harm, follows best practices for safety engineering, and presents a risk vs. benefit tradeoff that takes into account all stakeholders who might suffer direct or indirect harm.[113]

Before we dive into specific questions about how safe is safe enough to be "acceptable" safety for AVs, it is helpful to cover existing approaches to framing the "how safe is safe enough" question in a more general sense than just AVs. Most risks in everyday life do not occur in isolation, so it is common for this question in general to be framed as a comparison to some other type of risk. For example, it is common to hear someone comparing the risk of a particular activity to the risk of being struck by lightning.[114]

We do not attempt an analysis of the various legal concepts of risk acceptability such as absence of "unreasonable risk." However, in our experience the concepts usable in practice by engineers designing systems are generally analogous to one of the approaches in this chapter, typically combining a requirement to meet one or more meanings of the word "safe" discussed in the next chapter.

3.1. Survey of risk acceptance frameworks

Summary: Several risk acceptance frameworks exist with different approaches as to what risk should be compared against, how heavily to

---

[111] For life-critical systems acceptably safe is very close to perfectly safe. For an acceptably safe system there is typically some very small probability of a loss event that is greater than zero, and also there is typically a requirement to follow best practices for safety engineering.

[112] A dangerous and incorrect fallacy amounts to "since safety cannot be perfect, there is no point trying to improve it." Variations on this theme, sometimes quite subtle, are shockingly common in companies with poor safety culture.

[113] There will be some sort of negotiated outcome across stakeholder needs.

[114] The odds of a person being struck by lightning in the US are about 1 in 500,000 per year, with significant variation based on region, time of year, and activity. See CDC 2022: https://www.cdc.gov/disasters/lightning/victimdata.html

weigh the cost of reducing risk, and the degree to which various factors contributing to risk should be weighed in selecting mitigation approaches.

There are several different ways to frame risk acceptance.[115] The usual suspects[116] are:

- **ALARP:** As Low As Reasonably Practicable
- **NMAU:** "Nicht Mehr Als Unvermeidbar" (no more than unavoidable)
- **MEM:** Minimum Endogenous Mortality
- **MGS:** "Mindestens Gleiche Sicherheit" (at least the same safety)
- **GAMAB:** "Globalement Au Moins Aussi Bon" (overall at least as good)
- **Risk table:** A risk table identifies risk mitigation effort necessary based on a combination of the probability of a type of loss event and the degree of harm caused by such a loss event.

All these approaches are getting at the concept that risk should be reduced as much as it can be within some stated constraint. However, each concept approaches the problem of defining the required amount of risk reduction somewhat differently.

Legal considerations will apply to AVs in ways that are not quite the same as these principles. The legal concepts relevant to "safe enough" encompass concepts such as unreasonable risk, manufacturing defects, design defects, consumer warnings, feasible safer alternatives, cost effectiveness of risk mitigation, and compliance with regulatory requirements. Add to that variation across jurisdictions and things get quite complex. In this book we will limit ourselves to the technical aspects and leave the legal aspects to the lawyers.

3.1.1. ALARP/ALARA

ALARP is one of a set of related terms with some subtle distinctions that for our purposes end up in about the same place.[117] They are:

- ALARP: As Low As Reasonably Practicable
- ALARA: As Low As Reasonably Achievable
- SFARP: So Far As is Reasonably Practicable

For ALARP, risk must be reduced if it is possible to do so without a "gross disproportion" of cost compared to the risk reduction. This results in an approach that is not merely a simple return-on-investment calculation where risk reduction costs are compared to, say, reductions in expected

---

[115] It is important to note that risk and safety are related but different concepts. This is a topic we will revisit several times throughout the book.

[116] The material in this section was inspired by a number of informal sources and discussions. This paper was especially influential: Kron, On the Evaluation of Risk Acceptance Principles, 2003:
http://citeseerx.ist.psu.edu/viewdoc/download?doi=10.1.1.455.4506&rep=rep1&type=pdf

[117] See: https://en.wikipedia.org/wiki/ALARP

lawsuit outcomes. Rather, there is a presumption that risk must be reduced in every case unless it is exorbitantly expensive to do so.

While how expensive is "grossly disproportionate" is not fully settled, it is clear that spending $1.00 to mitigate a particular risk on a car costing tens of thousands of dollars would be required under ALARP if it can be done, even if insuring against losses caused by that risk would be a less expensive $0.90 per vehicle. In other words, ALARP is not simply a balance of cost against expected loss. Rather, it is a requirement to mitigate risk if it can be done within reason, even if it costs more to do so compared to accepting the risk and paying out damages to cover loss events.

The scope of ALARP also requires following standards and accepted practices even if the cost of doing so is moderately more expensive than exposure to the risk of not doing so. The argument here is that if most some designs in an industry already follow accepted practices, it is practicable[118] and economically within reach for other designs to do so.

For mature technologies, the overall risk of a well-designed system that follows best practices and industry standards might be deemed acceptable, with ALARP serving to ensure that practicable risk mitigations are applied to maintain that acceptability. As risk mitigation tools and techniques mature, new cost-effective approaches will become viable, potentially making ALARP a moving target of continually improving risk reduction that is relative to the state of the engineering art rather than a fixed value of expected losses.

A shortcoming of ALARP is that it deals with practicable mitigations and not the resultant overall risk. For an immature technology area such as AV development, it might be possible that nobody knows how to build a system that is acceptably safe without further maturation of the technology. In such a situation, ALARP might be the best that can be done, but might still not be acceptably safe to at least some stakeholders. In those cases it would be appropriate to require both ALARP and other criteria to be met as well.

In other cases, such as commercial space flight, it might be acknowledged that an activity is inherently risky. ALARP might be used to provide a structured way to make decisions about using the best available risk mitigation techniques even though the end result is still quite risky.

ALARP approaches are mandated in some portions of the world, with an origin in UK law.[119]

3.1.2. NMAU

A somewhat less stringent take on reducing safety based on cost and effort to implement mitigations is NMAU ("Nicht Mehr Als Unvermeidbar," or no more than unavoidable). With this approach, risk mitigations that have

---

[118] Readers new to reading regulatory, legal, and standards documents should be sure to notice the use of a very strong requirement word "practicable" (it is possible), rather than the much weaker word "practical" (does it seem sensible).

[119] See UK HSE: https://www.hse.gov.uk/managing/theory/alarpglance.htm

reasonable cost are put into place. This reasonable cost approach is somewhat less stringent than ALARP's grossly disproportionate cost criterion. However, NMAU does concede that in some cases it might be more expensive to mitigate a risk than the expected cost. So for NMAU it is still important to mitigate a risk, even if the risk mitigation cost is a little bit more expensive than the expected cost of accepting the risk.

NMAU is mainly applicable to a system for which there is a presumed public benefit that is compelling, and for which potentially elevated risks are deemed to be acceptable due to that public benefit.

Since the primary selling point of AVs to the public so far has been to improve safety compared to human drivers, NMAU does not seem like an appropriate risk framework because it might permit AVs to be more dangerous than human drivers. NMAU might, however, be appropriate for systems that provide a capability so unique that people are willing to agree to informed consent of an elevated risk. For example, early commercial aircraft flights were much riskier than they are today, but the public benefit of much faster transit than alternate modes available could have been seen as compelling.

3.1.3. MEM

Rather than looking at the cost of reducing risk, one can instead simply consider how big a risk is presented overall by a system. That approach sets a particular overall risk budget that must be met, whether doing so is essentially free or is incredibly costly.

With MEM (Minimum Endogenous Mortality), a technical system should not significantly increase the total risk of a person given that there are already other existing risks in the environment. In other words, if the risk from an AV is so small that it does not significantly increase someone's risk of death overall, then perhaps it can be considered as an inconsequential risk. An inconsequential risk might be one that is small compared to other risks of normal life, such as walking on sidewalks, riding in elevators, using staircases, breathing polluted city air, being hit by lightning, and so on.

When people talk about something being so safe that someone is more likely to be killed by a lightning strike, they are making a MEM-type argument. The US averages about 26 lightning deaths per year,[120] with conventional vehicles yielding a fatality rate well over 1000 times higher.

Considering a broader scope, motor vehicle traffic deaths account for just over 20% of all unintentional injury deaths in the US,[121] which is decidedly more than a negligible difference to the baseline fatality rate. Thus current US traffic deaths exceed a reasonable MEM contribution limit.

MEM is a more stringent safety goal than a comparison against human-driven vehicle safety. A MEM safety goal is the type of framework being

---

[120] See US NWS: https://www.weather.gov/safety/lightning-fatalities20
[121] See US CDC: https://www.cdc.gov/nchs/fastats/accidental-injury.htm

invoked by advocates for Vision Zero, [122] among others, who strive to eliminate all traffic fatalities and severe injuries. While getting to essentially zero traffic deaths is a worthy goal, AVs by themselves are unlikely to achieve that without significant improvements in other aspects of infrastructure and traffic policies.

3.1.4. MGS

Another comparative safety metric is MGS ("Mindestens Gleiche Sicherheit" or at least the same safety).

MGS generally relates to ensuring that a deviation from accepted practice does not reduce safety from normal levels. A deviation must be supported by an explicit safety argument showing at least the same level of safety. MGS is more about ensuring that waivers for deviations do not compromise safety, and less about whole-system evaluation.

For example, consider if a standard practice uses a certain type of component, but that component is unsuitable for use in a particular design or is unavailable due to a supply chain disruption. An MGS approach would argue that a substitute component could be used and be at least as safe.

An MGS-style approach is taken by NHTSA when they permit waivers to federal safety requirements on the basis of the overall safety level of an exempted vehicle being at least equal to the overall safety level of a nonexempt vehicle. In other words, even though a vehicle might fail a particular Federal Motor Vehicle Safety Standard (FMVSS), a waiver might be granted if a credible argument is made that overall safety will not be compromised for some reason. [123]

While MGS can be a reasonable approach, it is primarily intended to address small changes to existing systems that would otherwise be considered to meet safety requirements. MGS is not meant for assessing the safety of an entire system from scratch.

3.1.5. GAMAB

A GAMAB ("Globalement Au Moins Aussi Bon" or overall at least as good) approach holds that new technology should offer a level of risk at least as good as the risk offered by a comparable existing system. In other words, a new system should not be more dangerous than an existing system that offers similar functionality.

One way to apply GAMAB to an AV would be to look at a similar conventional vehicle use. According to GAMAB, one would expect a robotaxi operating in New York City to be as safe as a human cabbie. In contrast, long-haul automated trucking would have a different safety target

---

[122] See https://visionzeronetwork.org/
[123] There are other bases for exemptions that do not necessarily mean safety is maintained. This is just one basis for an FMVSS exemption.

corresponding not to cabbies, but rather to human truck driver safety on comparable routes.

The most common quantitative approaches to AV safety boil down to variations on the GAMAB risk framework, taking the general form of "an AV will be at least as safe as a human-driven vehicle."

It is important that a GAMAB approach use a credible risk baseline for comparison. That risk baseline should be for a comparable function being operated in a comparable way under comparable conditions. We will dig into that area in section 5.2 on setting a baseline for human-driven vehicle safety.

3.1.6. Risk table approaches

Another, somewhat different approach is to emphasize how much effort must be spent on mitigating the potential harm caused by each possible type of hazard or loss event. Typically this is done with a risk table that tabulates the probability and consequence of a loss event, assigning each intersection of that grid to a risk value. The higher the risk, the more engineering effort must be spent on mitigating the risk. In some, but not all, cases there is a numeric range associated with each acceptable risk after mitigation.

EXAMPLE RISK		Probability				
		Very High	High	Medium	Low	Very Low
Conse-quence	Very High	Very High	Very High	Very High	High	High
	High	Very High	High	High	Medium	Medium
	Medium	High	High	Medium	Medium	Low
	Low	High	Medium	Medium	Low	Very Low
	Very Low	Medium	Low	Low	Very Low	Very Low

Figure 3.1. An example risk table.

Figure 3.1 shows an example risk table.[124] Each column is a probability of some hazard being encountered that, if not mitigated, would result in a loss event. The probability varies according to the specific application, but tends to cover a large dynamic range in frequency. A hypothetical example corresponding to Figure 3.1 would be columns of: very high (every 6

---

[124] This video describes the use of a risk table in the context of evaluating the risk from specific hazards: https://youtu.be/N9Yq_K0Y9gk

minutes), high (every 10 hours), medium (every 1000 hours), low (every 100,000 hours), and very low (every 10,000,000 hours).

The consequence rows similarly cover a large dynamic range. A row of very high might be a multi-fatality loss event, with very low being considered reasonably normal wear and tear.

A risk table is typically used by determining the amount of mitigation effort required for each hazard based on its risk as identified by the row and column intersection assigned to that hazard. For example, with this table a hypothetical low probability (once every 100,000 hours) of a high consequence (serious injuries) presents only medium risk (the intersection of the low column with the high consequence row). The assignment of specific risk values to specific row/column intersections varies depending on the application. In general risk increases toward the upper left of a risk table set up this way. It is common to see consequence weighed a bit more heavily in risk determination compared to probability so that a high consequence event gets a relatively higher risk even if it is thought to be unlikely to happen.

3.1.6.1. RAPEX

The European Rapid Exchange of Information System (RAPEX) is a rapid alert system for dangerous consumer goods. RAPEX uses a risk assessment matrix based on the type of consumer, along with the severity and probability of various injury scenarios.[125]

The RAPEX risk table uses probability of a loss event happening during the life of the product as one of four severity levels, with Level 4 encompassing potential fatalities. Human-driven vehicles, if rated according to RAPEX, might do the computation as follows. A 15 year passenger life vehicle is driven approximately 350 hours per year at about 30 miles per hour, giving an operational lifetime for an average car of 210,000 miles.[126] To have "High" risk per RAPEX the probability of a fatality happening to any one car would need to be less than 1 in 10,000, or no more than one fatality every 1575M miles for an AV to be only High risk.[127]

For US human-driven cars the fatality rate is about one per 100M miles. That means that an AV would need to be approximately 16 times safer than a human-driven vehicle to avoid a "severe" risk classification of RAPEX – and at that would still present a "high" risk to consumers. (Medium risk would need to be about 160 times safer, and a low risk 1600 times safer.)

---

[125]   See: https://www.baua.de/EN/Topics/Safe-use-of-chemicals-and-products/Product-safety/Market-surveillance/Rapex.html
[126] Many cars last longer than 15 years, but many cars also crash and are retired before then. This is just an example calculation that seems to generally correspond to online sources weighing in on this topic.
[127] See: https://www.wolframalpha.com/input?i=15*350*30*10000

3.1.6.2. SIL approaches

A number of safety standards take a Safety Integrity Level (SIL) approach to defining acceptable safety.[128] The results of a risk table are used to select a SIL corresponding to the risk. A SIL represents three things at the same time: the risk presented by a hazard, the engineering rigor applied to mitigate that risk, and the desired residual probability after mitigation.[129]

A low risk is associated with a low SIL that has modest engineering process and mitigation mechanism requirements. A low SIL provides a modest reduction in the risk of a loss event due to a corresponding hazard, which might be sufficient if the loss has lower severity consequence and lower probability. Higher risks are associated with higher SILs that require much more rigorous engineering to mitigate potentially more problematic loss events.

Different standards have different specifics and different target thresholds for how often risks associated with each SIL can be expected to result in a loss event. For example, the safety standard IEC 61508 defines SIL 1 as the lowest level of integrity and SIL 4 as the highest. SIL 1 is associated with a post-mitigation failure rate of less than one failure every 100,000 hours of operation, while SIL 4 is associated with a post-mitigation failure rate of less than one failure every 100,000,000 hours of continuous operation.

The functional safety standard customized for automotive industry use is ISO 26262. That standard considers severity and exposure (an aspect of probability) as well as the potential for humans to control a malfunction that does occur. ASIL A is the lowest level of integrity of a safety feature, while ASIL D is the highest.[130] No failure rates are associated with ASILs in that standard, although there is a general understanding that the highest integrity level of ASIL D corresponds approximately to IEC 61508 SIL 3 rather than SIL 4.[131]

Some standards or interpretations of standards have a separate category for functions that are not safety-critical. In ISO 26262 that is "QM" (for quality management). In IEC 61508 functions that do not qualify for SIL 1 through 4 are often informally said to be SIL 0.

---

[128] For a comparative SIL chart across several standards see:
https://en.wikipedia.org/wiki/Automotive_Safety_Integrity_Level#Comparison_with_Other_Hazard_Level_Standards

[129] See two slides covered in this video starting at this time mark:
https://youtu.be/gDsolNq2sEk?t=332

[130] ISO 26262 ASIL integrity levels are assigned based on Severity, Exposure, and Controllability. See:
https://en.wikipedia.org/wiki/ISO_26262#Part_9:_Automotive_Safety_Integrity_Level_(ASIL)-oriented_and_safety-oriented_analysis

[131] Whether there should be an ASIL E that corresponds broadly to IEC 61508 SIL 4 when there is no human driver to exercise control is highly controversial, but can be an entertaining topic to broach if a standards committee meeting has gotten too dull and you like making trouble. Proceed at your own risk!

An important characteristic of all SIL-type safety standards is that they do not provide a causal linkage between the engineering efforts applied and the expected failure rates after mitigation. There is no proof we are aware of that using SIL 4 techniques will *necessarily* result in failure rates of less than one per hundred million hours of operation, and that is not actually the claim being made by the standard. Rather, the claim is that it is reasonable to take credit for a target failure rate corresponding to the SIL based on use of best practices associated with that target rate.

A reasonable way of looking at SIL-based approaches is that (a) they provide a way to associate a set of engineering rigor and other practices with a level of risk to achieve reasonable risk mitigation, and (b) they make a ballpark claim of expected residual failure rates without necessarily guaranteeing it will turn out that way for any particular system. The SIL sets a defensible expectation of reaching a certain level of safety based on having used industry standardized accepted practices.

From a risk framework point of view the important aspect of a SIL-based approach is that there is an implicit linkage between integrity levels and socially acceptable risk. For most safety standards this linkage is a predicted post-mitigation failure rate associated with each SIL, which would need to be compared against some acceptable risk goal.

In the case of ISO 26262, the industry has collectively decided that a certain amount of engineering rigor is adequate for particular ASILs, but does not tie that to quantitative outcomes such as permissible fatality rates. So the risk framework is essentially "use the ASIL methodology and risk will be acceptable" without any quantitative risk expectation beyond expert opinion of the automotive industry experts who created the standard. Given that ISO 26262 was developed for conventional non-AV applications, it is possible that the ASIL arrangement may need to change in the future to ensure acceptable mapping to stakeholder expectations for safety.[132]

3.2. GAMAB as the default AV risk framework

Summary: We expect that the AV industry will use a GAMAB-style risk framework that compares AV safety to that of a human driver, although additional approaches will be needed to both provide practical safety and meet stakeholder expectations.

Each risk acceptance framework has its uses. For AV safety, the framework most commonly invoked in technical discussions is GAMAB in

---

[132] To be clear, the ASIL approach is entirely appropriate for most parts of an AV and should be conformed to across the maximum number of functions practicable. The brakes still have to work, as well as the steering. The question is how to map an ASIL approach onto higher-level autonomy functions that potentially exert controllability over the more conventional functions such as the brakes and steering. Other standards cover that topic and should be used with ISO 26262.

the form of an AV being at least as safe as some baseline risk for a human-driven vehicle. This is not to reject the aspirational appeal of a MEM approach to dramatically improve traffic safety to near-zero harm. It is simply that the policy discussions for the AV industry are GAMAB-centric, and that does not seem likely to change any time soon.

GAMAB is generally used as a default risk framework for AVs because it arguably sets the safety target to the easiest-to-achieve level thought to be socially acceptable. In particular, it is easy to message that AVs will "save lives" if they can be in some sense "safer than a human driver."

A specific safety framework popular in Europe is known as Positive Risk Balance (PRB), which is a GAMAB approach that is generally interpreted as an AV being net better than a human-driven vehicle when considering injuries and deaths.[133]

We believe that additional considerations from other frameworks are likely to be required to supplement a pure GAMAB approach. Aspects of ALARP will likely come into play, especially if the AV industry finds that some types of risks are higher than for human-driven vehicles. We will discuss what might be needed beyond GAMAB in subsequent chapters.

3.3. Summary

Determining how safe is safe enough requires selecting a risk acceptance framework. There are a number of possible frameworks, but the most common one proposed for AVs is GAMAB in the form of requiring that an AV be at least as safe as a human driver in comparable circumstances.

In subsequent chapters we will discover that characterizing the safety of a human driver used as a basis for comparison is more complex than might be expected. Moreover, that criterion will not be enough due to concerns about uneven distributions in risks and a need to ensure safety despite uncertainty as to how safe the AV will be before deployment. In other words, GAMAB is just the starting point, not the destination.

While technical approaches to AV development tend to use a GAMAB framework, public messaging and regulatory strategies sometimes invoke other risk acceptance frameworks or ignore principled risk acceptance frameworks in favor of rhetorical approaches. That issue of what people might mean when they say an AV is "safe" is the subject of the next chapter.

---

[133] PRB is discussed further in sections 4.1.2 and 5.1, and is the default risk framework for many discussions throughout this book.

4.   What people mean by "safe"

Everyone involved in the Autonomous Vehicle industry says they want AVs to be safe. Indeed, a typical conversation advocating for creating and deploying AVs starts with an assertion that of course AVs will be safer than those oh-so-terrible human drivers. That is followed by an explanation of how important it is to get that safety deployed immediately – even if all the regulatory frameworks and red tape are not in order – so that the savings of lives can commence as soon as possible.

But when you stop to ask what people mean by "safe" and how they know that AVs will be safe, you find out that definitions and perspectives vary wildly. Sometimes "safe" means fewer road fatalities. Sometimes saying a company's vehicles will be "safe" is essentially nothing beyond wishful thinking and marketing hype, perhaps backed by a few demos during which no crashes happened to occur. Sometimes a conviction that AV technology will be safe to the point that no crashes will ever occur and nobody will need a driver's license in the near future borders on pure faith. But at other times "safe" might mean that a rigorous, thoughtful, and credible safety engineering approach has resulted in a justified belief that a particular AV will present an acceptable risk to the public, taking into account best engineering practices and considering risk exposure as it affects all stakeholders including other road users.[134]

This wide diversity of understood definitions for the term "safe" when used in a conversation presents a problem. Two people in a conversation can both be thinking they're talking about the same topic of "safety," but in fact have dramatically different definitions and expectations for what "safe" might mean.

Understanding what is being promised when someone says AV technology will be safe is essential to creating a level playing field in the race to autonomy and making justifiable deployment decisions. It can also help avoid public disillusionment when marketing hype uses of the word are revealed to be just that – hype. Avoiding hype can mitigate problems for stakeholders who are devoting substantial resources to the topic of AVs when disillusionment sets in after a hype cycle falls flat.

This chapter covers the span of different perspectives and ways of arguing that an AV might be acceptably safe. We will illustrate the points by presenting potential "claims" of safety along with relevant follow-up questions that need to be resolved when such a claim is made. We are intentionally using generic characterizations of positions we have seen rather than attributing specific statements to specific people or organizations. Nonetheless, this chapter is definitely a case of "if the shoe fits, wear it."

---

[134] This last definition is more boring to be sure. But it is the direction we need to go if we want to convert aspirational safety goals into real-world safety outcomes.

4.1. Safer than a human driver

Summary: A requirement of safer than a human driver needs to detail which driver, under what conditions, and with regard to which types of harms might be done to which road user populations. The variation in response to those factors is significant for human drivers used as a baseline for comparison.

An intuitive definition of "safe" is that an AV will be no worse than a human driver. Deciding what that means is more complicated than it might seem at first glance. You need to answer the questions of which driver, operating in what conditions, driving which vehicle, while considering that different crashes have different severities of harm.

4.1.1. Fewer crashes than human-driven vehicles

Potential claim: Our vehicles will have fewer crashes overall than human-driven vehicles.

- Are the crashes for comparable geographic areas and conditions?
- Are the crashes comparable in severity?
- Do the vehicles have comparable passive safety systems?
- Do the vehicles have comparable active safety systems?

The issues here revolve around making an apples-to-apples comparison with a human-driven vehicle fleet. Comparing AV crashes in benign operational environments to human-driven vehicles driven in adverse conditions is misleading. Also misleading is comparing harm in AV vehicles equipped with the very latest crash avoidance and safety technology to decade-old traditional vehicles that lack such equipment.

4.1.1.1. Comparable driving conditions

It is unfair to compare AV safety in a benign (warm, dry, sunny) ODD to human drivers driving through a blizzard at night.[135]

If a company says that its vehicles have a lower crash rate than human-driven vehicles, it is important to understand whether the comparison is under comparable conditions. For example, rural fatality rates per 100M VMT are approximately double that of urban fatalities.[136] Moreover, overall fatalities per mile vary by more than a factor of 3 across different US

---

[135] Variation of crash rates will be revisited in Section 5.2

[136] From DOT HS 813 060 page 7, urban fatalities are 0.86 per 100M VMT vs. rural fatalities of 1.65 for 2019 data. Other sources indicate rural fatalities are primarily on secondary roads, with restricted access highways being much safer. See:
https://www.automotivesafetycouncil.org/wp-content/uploads/2020/12/2019-Fatality-Report-Overview-of-Motor-Vehicle-Crashes-in-2019.pdf

states.[137] This means an AV that has the same crash rate as the national average might be significantly more dangerous (or safer) than human-driven vehicles prevalent in some particular location that is less (or more) dangerous than the US average.

Even within a single geographic region, if AVs only operate in fair weather, AV safety should be compared to human drivers in fair weather. That means excluding crashes for human drivers having to cope with icing conditions, blizzards, and thunderstorms. This idea can extend to all aspects of the ODD, weighting for how much operation is done in the riskier parts of the ODD.

Initial AV deployments quite reasonably tend to favor benign ODDs that present lower risk of a crash. Depending on the location that might be during fair weather or at times roads are clear of other traffic. If they can only do as well as the national average in such situations, they might in reality be more dangerous than other vehicles on the same roads operating in similarly benign conditions. At the very least, any safety data comparing AVs with human drivers need to be weighted according to ODD factors to ensure a fair comparison.[138]

Along the same lines, for vehicles that have AV functionality available only part of the time, comparisons should be solely on the portion of time the AV feature is active rather than total vehicle miles. This is especially true for AV features that are only active on the most benign portions of trips.

4.1.1.2. Crash severity distribution

The number of crashes does not tell the whole story. All crashes are not created equal: severity also matters.

A simple classification of crash severity that might be used is whether a crash results in fatality, life-altering injury, minor injury, or property damage only (PDO). It is common in human-driven vehicles to see far fewer crashes as severity of crash type increases. For example, 2020 US public road data reflects 38,824 fatalities, 2.28 million injuries, and 5.22 million overall non-fatal crashes (injury plus PDO crashes).[139] That presents a ratio of approximately one fatality per 134 crashes, and one fatality per 58.8 injuries. The takeaway from this data is that car crashes are reasonably survivable. That having been said, there is still a significant problem with 2.28 million injuries.

An additional consideration is that crash severity is related to the speed of travel. High-speed crashes are more likely to result in high severity harm

---

[137] IIHS/HDLI state-by-state fatality data as posted May 2022 covering calendar year 2020 data shows a high of 1.97 deaths per 100M VMT for South Carolina vs. a low of 0.63 for Massachusetts, a factor of 3.13 difference.
See: https://www.iihs.org/topics/fatality-statistics/detail/state-by-state%C2%A0
[138] Goodall 2021 (preprint) is an example of a methodology for compensating for different driving conditions when making comparisons.
See: https://engrxiv.org/preprint/view/1973/3986
[139] See page vi: https://crashstats.nhtsa.dot.gov/Api/Public/ViewPublication/813266

than urban fender benders.[140] This means the operational profile of the AV in terms of high-speed vs. low-speed operation matters as well. For example, including rural interstate highway fatalities per mile in a comparison with an urban center robotaxi is nonsensical. A robotaxi might well have more low consequence crashes, while an automated heavy truck on a rural highway might have far fewer crashes per mile but a much higher fraction of fatal crashes.

It is common to see AV safety discussed solely in terms of fatality rates compared to human drivers. To be sure, fatalities matter! However, a case could still be made for significant AV safety benefits if the fatality rate were unchanged, but life-altering injury rates were dramatically decreased. On the other hand, a slight decrease in fatalities might still be unacceptable if the number of life-altering injuries dramatically increases. This means any safety metric based on deaths and injuries will need a way to account for both.

It can be tempting to declare that an AV is safe because it has fewer low-severity crashes than human drivers, and therefore a lower crash rate in a given environment. Such an argument implicitly assumes that the ratio of high severity to low severity crashes will remain the same as for human drivers. However, there is no compelling reason to believe this will be true in practice.

What if AVs have a different severity distribution? There is already reason to believe AVs will have an elevated property damage crash rate that has more low severity crashes than human drivers. Indeed, prototype AVs seem to be prone to being hit from behind.[141] The hit-from-behind tendency is often attributed to the AV being a more cautious driver. Extra caution might, in turn, result in fewer severe crashes. But maybe it will not.

Computers in general, and machine learning-based systems in particular, are notorious for missing what, for lack of a better term, we will call common sense. What if an AV's lack of common sense means that fatal crashes are infrequent, but are prone to a mass casualty event when they do occur? Consider what would happen if an AV was not designed to handle a collapsed road bridge. What if AVs assume any bridge on a map will actually be there when it comes time to traverse that road segment? Most of the time it will be right. But when the day comes that it is wrong, how many AVs will plunge into the ravine before something figures out there is a problem?[142]

A collapsed bridge is simply an example to illustrate the point that rare catastrophic events exist that can cause severe harm for many vehicles all at once. Hopefully AV designers will include that in their system design even if

---

[140] In particular, the risk of pedestrian fatality rises dramatically above about 20 mph vehicle speed. See Schmitt 2016: https://usa.streetsblog.org/2016/05/31/3-graphs-that-explain-why-20-mph-should-be-the-limit-on-city-streets/

[141] See Stanescu 2018: https://www.wired.com/story/self-driving-car-crashes-rear-endings-why-charts-statistics/

[142] This could happen on many bridges simultaneously in a high-severity earthquake event. AVs might be designed to handle such a situation as safely possible under the circumstances. The question is whether they will be.

they have never seen a bridge collapse themselves during road testing. Moreover, there are number of other scenarios that can cause large multi-vehicle crashes such as driving into smoke, fog, snow, and sudden icing. All of these must be dealt with.

While human drivers are imperfect in rare event situations, they are reasonably good at realizing when something rare and unexpected happens and trying to compensate for it. While humans sometimes struggle with difficult conditions,[143] that is no excuse for AVs making the same potentially avoidable mistakes. It is important that AV designers can handle rare catastrophic events, and we should not simply assume that AVs will have the same ability to mostly avoid them as human drivers do. Performance on fender-benders is unlikely to be predictive of high severity harm events until the technology is much more mature than it is now.

Even if the crash severity ratios turn out to be similar for AVs, any reckoning of AV crashes should include both the number of crashes and the comparative harm severities before making claims of being better than human driver outcomes.

4.1.1.3. Passive safety systems

Another vehicle attribute that can significantly mitigate harm is the availability of passive safety features such as airbags and crumple zones. In recent years passive safety features have matured significantly, with newer cars having ever-more-sophisticated passive safety systems. A new AV should be expected to have passive safety features comparable to other new vehicles, which will provide significantly improved occupant protection compared to older vehicles.

In contrast, the average human-driven vehicle fleet includes both old and new vehicles. If an "average" vehicle is used as the basis for comparison, its passive safety systems will be, on average, less capable than the newest vehicles.

A typical light vehicle is designed for an economic operational life of about 15 years, but many vehicles can stay in operation for much longer. The average age of light vehicles in the US is 12.1 years as of 2021.[144] Of necessity, that means many vehicles are much older than 12.1 years. Most older vehicles have much less capable passive safety features than new vehicles. Also, passive safety features tend to be add-on optional equipment and/or only available on more expensive vehicles when introduced. That means that smaller, less expensive vehicles wait until later model years to incorporate passive safety capabilities even though they comprise a large fraction of deployed conventional vehicles. Moreover, older vehicles can be in poor repair, and perhaps more prone to collisions due to equipment failure.

---

[143] For an example of a multi-car pileup in snow and fog see Medina 2022: https://www.nytimes.com/2022/03/30/us/pennsylvania-crash-snow-squall.html
[144] Source: https://www.bts.gov/content/average-age-automobiles-and-trucks-operation-united-states

All this adds up to an "average" vehicle having much less capable passenger protection from passive safety features than a newer vehicle.

An AV maker claiming fewer fatalities than an average vehicle on the road is comparing its generally newer vehicles to a fleet of vehicles that on average has passive safety technology more than a decade older. It is normal to expect new high-end vehicles (which presumably the AV is) to have lower harm severity per crash than an older mix of both low-end and high-end vehicles, even if the AV driving is no better (or perhaps even slightly worse) than a human driver. It is not a fair comparison.

4.1.1.4. Comparable active safety systems

Another factor affecting the safety of human-driven vehicles is the emergence of active safety systems that reduce crash rates. The poster child for this type of equipment is Automatic Emergency Braking (AEB). AEB uses sensors to automatically apply brakes to avoid or reduce the severity of imminent frontal collisions.[145]

AEB has generally been credited with significant reductions in frontal vehicle crashes since its introduction. It is now becoming ubiquitous on new cars.[146] AEB performance in mitigating collisions with pedestrians and other road users still has significant room for improvement,[147] but is a topic of considerable interest.[148]

As an example, one study found that AEB reduced rear-end crashes (frontal collisions by a trailing vehicle) by over 40% for human-driven vehicles.[149] If an AV also equipped with AEB hypothetically claims a 30% improvement in frontal collisions compared to human drivers, that is not necessarily a case of the AV being 30% safer. Perhaps the AEB is delivering on its 40% promise, and the AV is net 10 percentage points more dangerous than a human driver for crashes AEB cannot prevent.

The baseline for comparison in vehicle equipment matters for counting collisions. Any comparison should take into account the effect of AV driving while holding constant the level of other active safety features. In other words, AV safety should be compared to vehicles with comparable active safety features used by human drivers. AV safety should not deny the

---

[145] A frontal collision for the vehicle with AEB is a rear-end collision from the point of view of the leading vehicle being hit.

[146] By the 2023 model year most new passenger vehicles sold in the US will have AEB. See NHTSA 2019: https://www.nhtsa.gov/press-releases/nhtsa-announces-update-historic-aeb-commitment-20-automakers

[147] See Barry, 2022: https://www.consumerreports.org/car-safety/automatic-emergency-braking-struggle-to-stop-for-pedestrians-a9924685047/

[148] For example, Euro NCAP tests for pedestrian and cyclist collisions: https://www.euroncap.com/en/vehicle-safety/the-ratings-explained/vulnerable-road-user-vru-protection/

[149] See IIHS 2020: https://www.iihs.org/news/detail/study-shows-front-crash-prevention-works-for-large-trucks-too

baseline human driver used for comparison the benefit of AEB and yet take credit for AEB in AV safety data.[150]

A related consideration is that the target for any AV that promises to have fewer crashes than a human driver steadily increases due to increased deployment of active safety features in human-driven vehicles. By the time AV fleets scale up, the human-driven vehicle fleet will have a much higher fraction of vehicles with effective active safety technology than it does today. AV safety targets should be set taking that into account.

4.1.2. Positive Risk Balance: better than human

Potential claim: Our vehicles will have "Positive Risk Balance"
- What is the baseline human population baseline being compared against?
- Does PRB apply to different demographic segments of potential victims?

Positive Risk Balance (PRB) is an articulation of the idea of having fewer crashes than human drivers.

The general idea of PRB is that an AV should be at least as safe as a human driver in that the risk from operation of an AV should compare favorably with a human-driven vehicle. Despite the use of the word "risk" instead of "safety," a PRB goal is commonly interpreted in terms of being at least slightly better than human driver fatality and significant injury rates.

In principle, PRB sounds like a reasonable starting point for an acceptable level of safety. Surely being worse than human drivers presents problems, so you want to be better.

However, defining "better" turns out to be complicated. In practice there are many factors that need to be considered. These include operational conditions, active safety systems, crash severity, and passive safety features that affect harm outcomes. Chapter 5 discusses this topic in detail.

4.1.2.1. Which human driver is the baseline?

When comparing to human drivers, the question arises of which human driver? Do you aspire to be no worse than a teenager driving home late at night from an illicit beer keg party? Hopefully your aspirations are set higher.

Human drivers have a range of capabilities. It is common to hear the message that older drivers are unsafe. However, the reality is that younger drivers have far higher fatality rates. It seems that the slower reaction times for older drivers are compensated for in older drivers by experience and judgment maturity. There is a reason that car rental companies are reluctant to rent to drivers under the age of 25! This is discussed in more detail in section 5.2.4.

It is important to realize that overall human driver performance includes all the impaired drivers, distracted drivers, and those who have crashes that

---

[150] Unfair AEB credit is taken indirectly when comparing a new car with automation features against average drivers, because most average cars driven by those average drivers do not have AEB installed. AEB would be in new, non-AV cars too.

are at least in part attributed to driving too fast for conditions. Subtracting those crashes would significantly improve the baseline performance of human drivers at any age.

Proponents love to say that AVs will not drive drunk, will not check their text messages, and learn from fleet experience. Therefore, one would hope that they drive at least as safely as an experienced, unimpaired, undistracted human driver. That is significantly better than the average across all drivers.

One could go further and compare the AV against a defined "expert" driver operating a comparably equipped human-driven vehicle.[151] This type of approach would require an AV to avoid any crash that a top-rated human driver would be able to avoid. It seems likely that an expert driver target would correspond more closely to public stakeholder expectations of automation by avoiding "driver error" caused crashes.

If safety is truly a priority for the industry, the standard of care for AV driving behavior should be that of an expert human driver, not a baseline population that includes the contributions of immature and impaired drivers.

4.1.2.2. Victim demographics

Another factor to consider in a PRB approach is who the victims of harm are. Not all victims are inside the vehicle. Increasing traffic fatalities are occurring to people outside vehicles, often called vulnerable road users.[152]

Even if a PRB approach projects fewer overall fatalities and serious injuries, it is likely to be unacceptable to redistribute harm to a different population segment, and especially one that does not benefit directly from riding in AVs. As an extreme hypothetical to make the point: what if total fatalities were cut in half, but every single fatality were a child pedestrian?[153] Despite an aggregate "fewer road deaths" claim being achieved, that hypothetical result is unlikely to go over well with the public.

Section 10.4.2 discusses the issue of risk transfer and demographic groups further. At this point suffice it to say that a PRB approach must pay attention not only to the total harm being done, but also to the distribution of harm across different types of victims.

---

[151] Such an approach is used in ISO-26262:2018 Part 12 regarding expert motorcycle operators.

[152] Internationally, more than half of road traffic deaths are vulnerable road users. See WHO: https://www.who.int/news-room/fact-sheets/detail/road-traffic-injuries

[153] Again, this is extreme to illustrate the point that if a demographic group bears a disproportionate burden of harm that will be a problem. How readily identifiable such a group has to be and how much slight excess harm might be acceptable (if any) are open questions. The industry should be mindful of the historical lesson from women and children suffering disproportionate harm from early airbags that did not take into account passenger size and position. See:
https://www.baltimoresun.com/news/bs-xpm-1996-11-07-1996312009-story.html

4.1.3. Enhanced personal safety

An important feature of a personally owned human-driven vehicle is having more control over personal safety. A locked private vehicle provides a measure of physical protection against potential threats to personal safety. In a single occupancy conventional vehicle the driver can make personal safety choices beyond the obvious one of not sharing a vehicle with a stranger as would be the case in a taxi or ride-share vehicle. [154] The availability of a single-occupancy AV might extend this safety benefit to those who cannot drive or do not have resources to own a private vehicle.

Example safety choices beyond just riding solo include debarking in an escort-provided portion of a parking lot, selecting routes that seem to present lower personal risk, and deciding not to exit the vehicle at a preselected destination location that turns out to look dangerous. To the degree that a single-occupant AV provides similar personal risk management features, riding solo in an AV might be safer than in a shared vehicle, including one with a human driver.

Personal safety is especially important to more vulnerable demographic segments, particularly when traveling alone, such as women, the elderly, and children. Also potentially at risk are identifiable minority groups in areas prone to abusive behavior based on race, gender, ethnicity, religion, or other factors. Beyond that, any AV user might have personal safety concerns, especially in areas with high crime rates.

Personal safety on shared AV mass transit vehicles will be an obvious concern as it is with crewed transit. On crewed mass transit the crew members can provide an additional measure of social supervision and deterrence. A potential move to smaller AV shared transit vehicles increases the opportunity for a passenger being isolated with a potential bad actor in a travel module, and complicates remote surveillance by multiplying the number of small passenger compartments being managed rather than fewer large compartments. Supervising dozens or hundreds of people on a single fully automated passenger train seems a more tractable problem (e.g., done with an on-train conductor) than remotely supervising dozens or hundreds of robotaxis shared by strangers.

Beyond the ride itself, there are also safety issues related to waiting for transport arrival and offloading. In particular, it will be important for vulnerable passengers to be able to change their destination at the end of the

---

[154] A popular meme goes something like this: Years ago we were told not to get into cars with strangers and not to talk to strangers on the Internet. Now we literally contact strangers via the Internet so we can get into their cars.

While ride-share companies recognize that personal safety is a key issue, and put effort into improving it, personal safety needs more work. See Marshall 2019: https://www.wired.com/story/criminologist-uber-crime-report-highly-alarming/

Also Saddiqui 2021:

https://www.washingtonpost.com/technology/2021/10/22/lyft-safety-report/

trip if local conditions at the destination seem too dangerous. Consider a city that requires using designated drop-off points of AV robotaxis. What should a passenger do if they do not like the looks of a group of people, potentially armed, waiting at the stop for them to get out?

A simple argument is to say that every automated low-speed shuttle will have an attendant. While attendants might be desirable and might prove necessary for a variety of reasons, requiring full-time staff on an automated vehicle that is smaller than a mass transit vehicle is largely at odds with the argument that AVs provide economic benefits due to not having to pay a person to be on board.

The question here is: will riding on an automated vehicle be as safe as riding in a vehicle with a human driver from a personal safety point of view?

4.2. Behaves safely on the road

Summary: Safe driving behavior spans multiple areas including following traffic laws, driving skills (roadmanship), and ensuring adequate buffers between the AV and other road users.

Another approach to claiming safety is saying that the AV in some sense is a good driver, or possibly even has been mathematically proven to have behavior that promotes safety. Having safe driver behavior is useful and can help build a more comprehensive picture of safety. But safe driver behavior is not sufficient on its own to provide a complete safety picture.

4.2.1. Following traffic laws

Potential claim: Our vehicles are safe because they follow traffic laws.
- Do the vehicles know how to interpret laws in response to exceptional situations in a safe way?
- Do the vehicles break traffic laws in a reckless manner?

The issues with traffic laws are both tricky and largely unaddressed. The main problem is that traffic laws are written for human drivers with an expectation that any bending or breaking of the rules will be done with a display of responsibility and common sense.

As a simple example, vehicles should not cross a centerline in a no-passing zone, typically marked with a double yellow centerline. However, if there is construction in a travel lane or other obstruction, traffic direction personnel can direct vehicles to break that rule. Moreover, on lightly traveled roads drivers can break that rule at their own discretion to, for example, permit extra clearance when passing slow-moving farm equipment that is partially blocking the travel lane, or to go around a fallen tree or other object obstructing the travel lane.

While this is not a legal analysis, in everyday situations the framework for breaking the rules involves whether there are exceptional circumstances not built into the rules (e.g., a huge tree blocking your travel lane), whether breaking rules is out of necessity or simply out of expediency, whether breaking the rules happens in a way that needlessly presents risk to other road users, and whether there was a reasonable alternative available that presented less risk or did not break the rules at all.

An AV that scrupulously follows every single rule might be painful to ride in. A typical point of discussion is obeying the speed limit when other traffic not only flouts the limit, but acts aggressively or worse toward vehicles that respect the limit. Another is whether so-called rolling stops at stop signs are OK.[155] These are cases of convenience or efficiency, not necessity. AVs should follow the laws when the only concern is convenience, marginally improved speed of travel, or potentially irritating other road users who are not following traffic rules. Rather than flouting laws that AV companies perceive as inconvenient, they should work with law enforcement and regulators to effect reasonable change if necessary.

An AV that breaks traffic laws due to an overwhelming loss of utility is a more complicated question. On the one hand an AV rider would be unhappy if stuck at a fallen tree for hours waiting for a road crew to eventually clear debris while other human-driven vehicles whip into the opposing lane to pass the scene on a mostly deserted road. On the other hand, driving in an opposing lane puts responsibility for making that decision squarely on the AV, with potential criminal liability for any resulting crash due to it involving breaking a law.[156] Until it is resolved who might bear criminal responsibility for breaking a traffic law in a reckless manner, AVs should not do so even if designers think that the functionality they are designing would be justified. This implies that safety drivers will need to be able to take control and responsibility for an AV stuck in a position that requires it to break a traffic law to make progress.

In some instances, mindless compliance with traffic laws can itself result in a public hazard. For example, pulling over in a roadway in a manner that still obstructs emergency vehicles might be technically and narrowly in compliance with a simplistic rule to pull over, but defeats the purpose of freeing up space for the emergency vehicle to make progress.[157] Sometimes minor violation of traffic rules might be advisable in the service of public safety. Sometimes a police officer or other official is there to direct a vehicle to deviate from normal traffic rules, but other times the situation is much

---

[155] The answer is that rolling stops are not OK. Tesla was forced to do a safety recall for that behavior: https://static.nhtsa.gov/odi/rcl/2022/RCLRPT-22V037-4462.PDF

[156] A Tesla driver faces criminal charges for running a red light, potentially with the Autopilot feature engaged. While this is a driver assistance system, it illustrates that the consequences of failing to comply with traffic laws can include criminal penalties. https://www.npr.org/2022/01/18/1073857310/tesla-autopilot-crash-charges

[157] As an example, a Cruise driverless test vehicle operating in San Francisco positioned itself in a way that left a fire truck unable to proceed. https://www.wired.com/story/cruise-fire-truck-block-san-francisco-autonomous-vehicles/

more ambiguous, requiring human judgment calls to do the right thing in a special situation.

While conforming to traffic laws almost all the time is required for safety, there are gray areas in which non-conformance is in practice permissible, and some instances in which limited non-conformance is in practice required for public safety. Saying that a vehicle conforms to traffic laws is for the most part a good thing, but it is not the full picture for real-world safety.

4.2.2. Good roadmanship

Potential claim: Our vehicles have the roadmanship skill of an expert human driver.

- How far is the planning horizon to avoid getting into risky situations?
- Does safety analysis include responding to design faults and system faults?
- Does safety analysis include responding to departures from the ODD?

The general idea of roadmanship as a safety metric for AVs was discussed in a 2018 research report by RAND Corporation that dealt with the thorny topic of how to measure AV safety.[158]

The concept of roadmanship is defined in that RAND report as "the ability to drive on the road safely without creating hazards and responding well (regardless of legality) to the hazards created by others." The general concept encompasses ideas such as maintaining prudent buffer areas from other road users, yielding right-of-way, and exercising caution when sensor limitations or road conditions present situations with elevated risk.

It is clear that good roadmanship is desirable for an AV. Having an AV that drives in a way that we would hope an experienced human driver does will add more forgiveness to road situations in which one or more traffic participants make an error in judgment or experiences a difficult-to-foresee perturbation to normal driving behaviors. Ideally an AV should drive at an expert level, such as including the skills taught at a high-quality advanced skill and defensive driving course.

One question to ask when assessing roadmanship is, in effect, how far the AV looks down the road when planning vehicle movement. One level of roadmanship is going slowly down a steep icy slope and leaving plenty of extra distance to other vehicles once you realize you are on it. Somewhat more sophisticated is not pulling up closely behind a manual transmission truck stopped going up an icy hill ahead of you because it is likely it will slide backward (and into you) when it tries to start going up the hill again. But still better is taking a longer route to avoid the steep hill entirely during icing conditions and not have to deal with any of that mess. More

---

[158] See Fraade-Blanar et al. 2018:
https://www.rand.org/pubs/research_reports/RR2662.html

sophisticated levels of roadmanship alter routes and mission plans[159] to avoid risky situations beyond just driving defensively.

Roadmanship is, however, only part of the set of skills necessary for safe driving. Even a human driver who is essentially flawless at handling difficult road situations can have issues if there is an equipment failure. Additionally there can be problems when encountering a situation that has not been included in training or is beyond the capabilities of the equipment to handle.

A good driving skills course will, for example, teach how to recover from a spin. But expert drivers might also have learned how to stop a vehicle safely despite total main service brake failure (to the degree it is physically possible), loss of a wheel, complete loss of visibility (sheet of mud suddenly covering the windscreen), loss of steering power assistance, or other equipment failures. An AV also needs to be able to assure a reasonable level of safety if the ADS computer itself suffers a failure.

The normal notion of roadmanship is about being able to handle the vehicle despite environmental challenges. To achieve practical safety an AV design must also be able to ensure safety despite internal failures in equipment, gaps in training, or outright software defects.

4.2.3. Provably safe driving behavior

Potential claim: Our vehicles have provably safe behavior.
- Same questions as for roadmanship
- How reasonable are the assumptions made by the proofs?
- What happens when the AV is forced into a provably unsafe situation?

Some AV design approaches are based on a claim that the AV has been proven safe with mathematical rigor. A highly visible example is the work on Responsibility Sensitive Safety (RSS).[160] Other researchers make narrower claims of safety properties for various aspects of machine learning research.

Formal proofs of safe behavior and other properties of AVs and their components can provide valuable insight. In the case of RSS, an analysis via classical Newtonian physics of vehicle acceleration and distances can lead to insight into what safe following distances are under a given set of assumptions, and how to ensure that the desired amount of buffer time and space is left between vehicles in other situations.

Those insights can significantly help assess the safety of AV behaviors. For example, all things being equal, RSS can help ensure an AV remains a

---

[159] UPS famously minimizes left turns during delivery route planning. This brings benefits for travel speed and fuel economy, but also can reduce crash rates. See: https://www.thestar.com/business/2014/04/07/why_ups_said_no_to_left_turns.html Additionally, left turns are said to cause a quarter of pedestrian crashes. See: https://www.npr.org/2015/05/25/409531218/left-turns-cause-a-quarter-of-all-pedestrian-crashes-in-u-s

[160] See: https://www.mobileye.com/responsibility-sensitive-safety/

safe following distance behind a lead vehicle that gives it time to stop even if the lead vehicle does a panic stop.

The issue with any formal proof is what assumptions it is based upon, and how realistic those assumptions are for the real world. In the case of RSS (and any other mathematical analysis for something such as safe following distance) assumptions have to be made about the ability of the lead vehicle's maximum braking ability, whether the coefficient of friction of the road surface is different under the two vehicles, whether the road slope is about to change dramatically, and so on. Stopping distance on a slippery downhill following a sports car that has high-performance tires and brakes can be a lot more harrowing than following an average car on a flat dry road. Those factors can be accounted for to a degree, but worst-case assumptions can easily lead to AV behavior that is too conservative to be practical. So some amount of sensing and estimation of road conditions and capabilities of other vehicle behaviors is required to use these techniques in practice.

In reality, what you end up with is a situation in which safety is proven under a set of assumptions, but the assumptions have some uncertainty to them. Seen another way, all the uncertainty has been swept out of the proofs and into the assumptions. Such an approach can still have significant value. But any statement that the AV has been proven safe does not mean that safety is absolutely guaranteed.

Another issue with proofs of safety is what happens when an AV is forced into a situation in which the proof fails to hold. If an AV is in dense traffic it might not be able to maintain a safe following distance. If it constantly jams on the brakes to open up mathematically required headway, that can do more harm than good. An important question to ask is how the system deals with situations in which the proof assumptions are invalid, or in which the proof shows that it is impossible to be provably safe. If the proofs show that safety cannot be guaranteed, you want the AV to perform in a best-effort way to maximize safety rather than simply give up and decide it is OK to crash.

4.2.4. Does better at avoiding crashes

A specific type of argument that an AV can behave safely on the road is that it is designed to avoid the types of crashes that human drivers make.[161]

The idea is that a list of human driver crashes is ranked, and the most common crash scenarios are identified. A default starting point is the NHTSA pre-crash scenario typology which lists several dozen crash types with break-downs of other factors such as speed, driver condition, weather, driver mitigation attempts, and crash outcomes.[162] An AV simulator recreates

---

[161] A conspicuous example of this is a claim made by Waymo in 2021. See Rodrigo: https://thehill.com/policy/technology/542222-waymo-says-their-autonomous-car-ai-would-avoid-fatal-human-crashes/
[162] See NHTSA DOT HS 810 767, April 2007: https://www.nhtsa.gov/sites/nhtsa.gov/files/pre-crash_scenario_typology-final_pdf_version_5-2-07.pdf

the different types of crash scenarios and determines that the AV would successfully avoid those types of crashes.[163]

Certainly being able to mitigate the risk of typical crash scenarios is a good thing. However, care must be taken not to over-claim. An AV that avoids human crash scenarios might very well have different crash scenarios that are still a problem. It will be no surprise if AVs still make driving mistakes, but they are simply different driving mistakes than human drivers will make.

Saying that an AV avoids common human driver crashes is good. Implying that this means AVs will never crash is, however, an unsupported result.

4.3. Road testing

Summary: Road testing is required to demonstrate safety, but it is impractical to prove safety via brute force road testing alone.

If there has not been enough experience to have statistically significant road data about safety outcomes, many AV companies will emphasize how many road testing miles they have. Even having millions of test miles does not necessarily mean an AV will be safe when deployed. A few million miles does not begin to be enough for statistical significance. Not all miles are created equal, and testing only on "easy" miles does not necessarily prove much. If the software gets changed daily or weekly, in the end the final version itself has only been slightly tested and all the other millions of miles of testing software that is different than what is in the final vehicle provide uncertain support for any claim of safety.

4.3.1. Millions of miles

Potential claim: Our vehicles are safe because we have done millions of miles of testing on public roads.

- Do you really have enough miles?
- Are the miles driven representative?
- Are all the miles on the system you plan to deploy?

The reality is no company can afford to do enough real-world test miles to ensure safe deployment. (Simulated miles might be affordable, but have other issues covered in the next section.)

4.3.1.1. Millions of miles of road testing

While having driven millions or tens of millions of miles of road testing is an impressive accomplishment, that number of miles pales in comparison

---

[163] For example, see: https://blog.waymo.com/2021/03/replaying-real-life.html

with the number of miles required for statistical confidence in whether AVs will be at least as safe as human-driven vehicles.[164]

The starting fact for an analysis is that the US fatality rate is ballpark one fatal crash per 100 million (100M) miles.[165]

Now consider a brute force testing approach in which the only means of validating testing is road miles. Making a number of questionable, but favorable, assumptions, the statistical confidence increases as an AV team accumulates testing miles. Say we want to use such an approach for fatal car crashes to establish that our AV has a mean time to fatal crash of more than 100 million miles. We would have to test for the following number of miles depending on how many fatal crashes were observed during testing:

Confidence	No crashes	One crash
99%	461M miles	664M
95%	300M	474M
90%	230M	389M
80%	161M	299M
70%	120M	244M
60%	92M	202M
50%	69M	168M

Table 4.1 Number of test miles required to achieve stated confidence of no worse than 100 million (100M) miles between fatal crashes.[166]

Two things jump out when looking at the numbers in Table 4.1. The first is that the numbers are huge. Brute force testing is not viable in the best of situations, and with issues such as resetting the test odometer for each bug fix it just gets even worse. The second is that the amount of testing required gets much worse if there actually is a crash.

Even worse, a crash is quite likely to happen during such testing even if the system is acceptably safe. That is because the test length requirement for no-crash confidence is longer than the average crash rate above a confidence

---

[164] For a general discussion of miles required to prove safety, see Kalra et al. 2016: https://www.rand.org/pubs/research_reports/RR1478.html

[165] We use 1 fatal crash per 100M VMT as an illustrative round number representative of pre-COVID-19 era traffic patterns. The fatal crash rate varies slightly from the fatality rate because some crashes result in multiple fatalities. In 2020 the fatality rate was 1.34 per 100M VMT, with about 1.23 fatal crashes per 100M VMT. This is substantially higher than previous years, with fatalities per 100M VMT increasing 21% from 2019. Remarkably, at the same time overall injuries were down 17%. The takeaway here is that "better than human driver" is a moving target. See: https://crashstats.nhtsa.dot.gov/Api/Public/ViewPublication/813266

[166] Computations performed with the tool at: https://reliabilityanalyticstoolkit.appspot.com/mtbf_test_calculator

level in the high 60s.[167] So a brute force test campaign has to get quite lucky to see no crashes.

The general rule of thumb is you need to drive at least as far as your safety target with no crash for medium confidence that your safety target has been reached. That increases to three times your target with no crashes for high confidence. If you have crashes, you will need perhaps ten times your safety target to have confidence that the average is at least as good as you need it to be.[168] If you set a higher target of perhaps 200M miles per fatality to subtract out the effects of the most egregiously impaired human drivers weighing down conventional vehicle data, you can easily need a billion or more miles of testing to validate safety. That is simply not going to happen.

Anything less, such as 10M miles, tells you almost nothing about safety in terms of confidence. However, if you do have a significant crash in 10M miles, you know that very likely you are not acceptably safe. The reality is that a road testing campaign is a reasonable sanity check on engineering rigor. It is also an effective way to find out if an AV is dramatically unsafe (because there will be an early crash). But it has very limited power in supporting a safety case based on brute force testing alone.

A related approach of showing an hour-long video of a drive with no mistakes made by the AV is a helpful confidence builder. But an hour-long video serves mainly to show that the AV basically works. If the hour-long video took multiple takes, then it should be obvious there is an issue. Regardless, any such video falls far short of providing enough data to predict crash rates.

4.3.1.2. Representative miles

Which miles an AV drives in road testing matters. Driving a million times around the same block mid-day in sunny weather proves almost nothing – unless perhaps you are planning to build a low-speed shuttle that goes around

---

[167] It is important to note that the 300M mile testing target (for 95% confidence) is with zero crashes – which is pretty unlikely to happen if the AV just barely meets its crash rate goal. For a 100M mile between crash AV, you'd expect about 3 crashes to happen in 300M miles of testing. But with the first crash you'd need 474M miles, which probably results in 4 or 5 crashes, and so on. Pretty soon it ends up that the AV needs a billion miles or so of testing for the random crash arrivals to even out into statistical significance.

[168] The range of testing or experience of 3 to 10 times the target value appears several times in this book. It comes from an approximate rule of thumb that with no events and about 3 times the expected arrival time there 95% confidence that the system is at least as good as expected. However, by then it is pretty likely an event will have happened. Depending on how luck runs, it might take up to 10 times longer than the expected arrival time for statistical fluctuations to even out. If the system is dramatically worse than expected, it will take fewer miles to see too many crashes.

that same exact block for its entire operational life and shuts down whenever it is not dry, sunny weather.[169]

Similarly, most miles are boring in that nothing much challenging happens. Perhaps you can operate a shuttle for 364 days in the downtown business district with no problem. But if that 365th day you are sharing the route with the Thanksgiving Day parade you had better be able to deal with it. Yes, you can take the shuttle offline that day. But someone has to know to do that before a crash has a chance to happen.

Safety does not live in the boring miles; it lives in the interesting miles. More precisely, once a system mostly works, safety issues tend to hide in the rare situations that are seldom seen in testing.

To address safety, testing coverage needs to account for risk. A high-risk event that occurs only once every 10M miles might not be seen at all in a road test campaign, and yet might present unacceptable risk many times per the 100M miles (or more) used as the basis for a fatality risk budget. Low probability events with high consequence need to be addressed thoroughly to achieve an acceptable safety outcome.

All this means that a careful design of experiments approach must be taken to make sure that various factors are addressed. All relevant aspects of the ODD need to see some testing. Additionally, low probability but high consequence events need to be tested to the extent practicable to ensure they have been handled.[170]

4.3.1.3. Which version of the system?

Typically omitted from any claim of millions of miles of testing is how often the software was updated during the test campaign. If the software is updated daily or weekly during testing, then the "testing" campaign was really a "debugging" campaign, which is a lot different.

In typical software development there is a phase during which the software is written, tested, debugged, software defects are fixed, and then tested some more.[171] Only after the software is thought to be ready to deploy does a phase called acceptance testing start. The debugging tests do not count

---

[169] A few such cases might exist, such as parking lot shuttles at airports and theme parks. However, those applications hardly justify investing tens of billions of dollars of venture capital with a five-year exit expectation.

[170] Some events are too risky to test thoroughly on public roads, such as vehicle behavior in near hit situations, or seeing if children are recognized crossing in front of an AV. Those need to be validated via a combination of closed-course testing, simulation, and ensuring that the validation is predictive of real world performance.

[171] By the time software is in "beta test" it is (at least in the critical software world) supposed to be essentially finished, with perhaps only some unexpected customer usage patterns revealing requirements gaps. Silicon-valley style companies have since corrupted that traditional use of the term beta testing to instead mean they are still debugging while customers providing free testing workloads. There is probably no rolling the abuse of the terminology back, but such an approach causes deep dysfunction with life-critical system development processes.

much for software reliability, because any change to the software – no matter how small – can in principle (and often does) introduce new defects.

If a claim is being made that an AV is safe because there are millions of miles of testing, that testing odometer must necessarily be reset to zero every time there is a software update. That includes both bug fixes directly programmed into the vehicle as well as over-the-air software updates made after deployment.

There is a technique called impact analysis[172] that might be used to argue that a specific software bug correction is so minor that it does not affect safety. However, in AVs a typical bug fix is supposed to fix a driving behavior error and is therefore difficult to claim as a "minor" fix. Moreover, there is no accepted notion of impact analysis for retraining a machine learning-based component. The default expectation has to be that every software update to an AV driving system makes changes so widespread that no credit can be taken for previous testing unless a compelling impact analysis shows otherwise. Any change resets testing to start over again.

With all these limitations, one might wonder why it is worth doing road testing at all. First and foremost, at least some amount of road testing is needed to make sure there was no mistake in other methods being used to ensure safety. That means a regime of closed-course testing and road testing needs to be done to some degree after virtually every software update not to prove safety per se, but rather to demonstrate that there has been no process defect in the other techniques used to ensure safety. In other words, road testing is a last line of defense sanity check on the engineering process, not the primary method of ensuring safety.

Summarizing, a claim of millions of miles of road testing shows that the AV design team has put significant resources into testing. If it has happened without a crash this is better news than if a crash did occur. But road testing is not enough on its own to support a credible claim that an AV will be safe enough.

4.3.2. Miles between disengagements

Potential claim: Our vehicles are safe because we can go 10,000 miles between disengagements on public road testing.

- Disengagements are a better measure of un-safety than safety.

The idea of a testing disengagement is that the autonomy function has been turned off during testing for some reason. Disengagement numbers are widely reported in the press in large part because they have historically been one of the few scraps of data publicly reported by companies doing AV

---

[172] Impact analysis is a process within the larger scope of engineering change management. See: https://en.wikipedia.org/wiki/Change_management_(engineering)

testing.[173] At that, the reporting has only been done because the California government requires it.[174]

One source of disengagement is that the autonomy system has disabled itself during testing. Another source is that a safety driver has turned off the autonomy function or over-ridden it for some reason. In any event, the expectation is that a human safety driver takes over vehicle control when needed for safety.[175]

Different companies report disengagements differently. It seems reasonable to not report disengagements that occur because the test session has ended and the safety driver is taking over to return the vehicle to the garage. Other disengagements might be due to a safety driver being more cautious than strictly necessary. Some companies are more aggressive, only reporting disengagements they believe would have resulted in a crash if a safety driver had not intervened.

Given that California makes disengagement reporting metrics public along with testing miles driven, there is a market incentive to show the highest number of testing miles possible with the fewest disengagements.

While intuition might say that a longer time between disengagements means technology is more mature, there are a number of problems with that interpretation. Different companies might be testing in different parts of their ODD. Companies might have ODDs as different as a city robotaxi vs. a highway trucking route. Different companies and different safety drivers within each company might have different standards for how aggressively they take over if they are not sure if the test platform is behaving properly.

If all disengagements are reported and used to keep score on progress, that creates incentives to only test easy miles. It also potentially incentivizes safety drivers to let the AV they are testing take more chances on the road by delaying takeover until there is no doubt that a crash is about to happen. Minimizing the number of disengagements can make numbers look more favorable, but can also increase the risk of a close call turning into a real crash.

From an AV developer point of view, data that determines how well the simulation campaign predicted behavior in the real world is the most valuable information. For those developers, each disengagement indicates a place where their simulation failed to predict the real world, although prediction failures can be found even without disengagements.

Some developers have under-invested in simulation, and so seek out disengagements as a way to determine what parts of their design need more work. A high disengagement rate might mean the system has low maturity, but might also mean that the company's testers are simply good at finding

---

[173] More recently NHTSA has started requiring reporting of crash reports beyond the California requirements. See: https://www.nhtsa.gov/laws-regulations/standing-general-order-crash-reporting

[174] See: https://www.dmv.ca.gov/portal/vehicle-industry-services/autonomous-vehicles/disengagement-reports/

[175] The topic of road testing safety is revisited in section 9.5.

areas that need more work. From a cost point of view, any boring miles with no disengagements are wasted money if the road testing is really a debugging or requirements discovery exercise instead of a validation process.

From a regulatory point of view, disengagements do not give much useful information, even if they are something that can be measured and reported. Regulatory agencies measuring testing safety would be better served monitoring metrics such as frequency of safety driver attention lapses and how often the safety driver fails to disengage in a high-risk situation. These types of metrics should be more predictive of the risk presented to the public by the road testing campaign itself.[176]

In terms of a prediction of deployment safety, disengagement numbers suffer from the same problem as bulk accumulation of testing miles. Any disengagement that requires human safety driver intervention during any feasible amount of testing tends to show that the system is not safe enough to deploy. Disengagements caused by the equipment itself that are followed by a safe Failover maneuver with no safety driver intervention are not a problem for safety, because that is what an uncrewed vehicle would also be designed to do.

Lack of disengagements simply shows that no dangerous situation has been seen in a comparatively short testing campaign. Zero disengagements initiated by a human safety driver does not on its own prove safety at the level of 100M miles or more between potentially fatal crashes. However, as with any road testing, due to the small mileage amounts involved even a single disengagement that avoids a crash provides compelling evidence that the AV is not ready to deploy without a safety driver.

Measuring disengagements at most can prove an AV developmental system is unsafe if safe disengagements are disregarded. However, zero disengagements for even a million miles does not prove safety all on its own.

4.4. Simulation

Summary: Simulation is an attractive supplement to road testing due to its lower cost and the absence of risk imposed on other road users. However, ensuring accurate coverage of all relevant scenarios and sufficient fidelity with regard to real-world safety outcomes is a significant challenge.

Given the expense and general impracticality of racking up billions of miles of pre-deployment testing for an AV, companies tend to turn to using simulations. Simulated vehicles are much cheaper per mile to run than real ones. More importantly, simulations can be scaled up by using large data centers much more easily than building out thousands of custom test vehicles.

---

[176] Regulators should be in the business of ensuring public safety, not keeping score in the race to autonomy.

A well-funded AV developer can realistically plan to test for billions of miles in simulation. Road testing could then be done at a much smaller scale, both to do a final high-level check on AV performance and, just as importantly, to validate that the simulator outputs are accurate enough to predict real-world AV performance and safety.

4.4.1. Billions of simulation miles

Potential claim: Our vehicles are safe because we have done billions of miles of simulation.

* Does your simulation include perception?
* Does the simulator match real-world safety outcomes?[177]
* Do your simulator models include billions of miles of real-world long-tail events?

4.4.1.1. Simulation scope

Perception is one of the most challenging functions performed by an AV. As complex as it is to deal with all the different traffic scenarios that can occur, reliably identifying specific types of objects and events using machine learning-based approaches is even more difficult.

Perhaps it will come as a surprise that when some developers say they have thorough simulation results, they are only simulating the traffic scenarios, and are assuming that perception is perfect. Yes, really. If a simulator tells the AV software what objects it is sharing the road with, then perception is not really being tested in simulation.

Simulation might omit the perception aspect because the AV company is buying a perception solution from some vendor, and then declares perception accuracy to be that vendor's problem. But if that vendor has not done the billions of miles of testing (simulated or otherwise), then how does the AV company know that the perception is reliable enough? From a vehicle safety point of view, if perception produces inaccurate information about the outside world, the AV is going to struggle to be acceptably safe. Adding another wrinkle, if a perception company trains and tests its system on simulated images, how does that align with real-world perception performance?

It is important to ask the question: what is the scope of the simulation? If an AV maker says they have billions of miles of simulation, does that include billions of miles of simulating the perception system? Or just vehicle maneuvering? If it is just vehicle maneuvering, what is the plan for trusting the parts of the ADS not tested via simulation? Unquestioning trust in a

---

[177] There is a common saying that "simulation is doomed to succeed." The general meaning of that saying is that because simulations are comparatively inexpensive to run and have clearly defined pass/fail criteria, engineers will iterate until the simulation passes. What that leaves out is all the factors involved in mismatches between the simulation's predictions and real-world failure outcomes.

supplier who similarly does not have an acceptable combination of simulation and road testing miles is an insufficient plan for safety.

4.4.1.2. Simulation ability to predict real-world safety

Simulation proponents often say that if they have enough fidelity they can accurately predict safety. That is not the whole story.

Simulator fidelity is the level of realism represented in the simulated world the AV design is being tested in. Fidelity can be thought of as how fine-grained objects and images are, how realistic vehicle motions are, and how nuanced models are at accounting for subtle interactions among objects in the simulated world. While one simulation might model roads as a perfectly smooth surface with constant friction, another simulation might include patches of ice and model the momentum transfer effects of gravel being sprayed into the air by spinning wheels. To a point, more fidelity is better.

Increased fidelity comes at a cost both in creating more detailed models and running more complex simulations. At some point, increased fidelity is a waste of computing resources if it does not affect the accuracy of safety predictions. Some things require more fidelity than others. Light absorption properties of dark clothing on pedestrians and pedestrian body posture are likely to matter more than variations in the shape of individual tree leaves. However, modeling trees with leaves vs. trees without leaves might be relevant to a lidar system that uses the position of trees as part of its localization scheme.[178]

Rather than chasing high fidelity at any cost, the objective should be to make sure everything within the simulation has at least enough fidelity to predict real-world AV performance and safety. This will likely include not only simulator capability to do modeling of light bouncing off various types of surfaces, but also models of the various objects in the environment. Those objects include not only the AV itself, but also other vehicles, pedestrians, animals, objects at the side of the road, buildings, billboards, street surfaces, and so on.

Fidelity is sufficient when the results of a simulation accurately predict what happens in the real world. Because economics dictates running many more simulated miles than real-world testing miles, there needs a way to build confidence in the simulations for scenarios that will not be reproduced in the real world. To ensure simulated miles are useful in predicting safety outcomes, you need a careful design of experiments approach that includes not only covering the full ODD for testing, but also covering the range of models and interactions in the simulator to ensure that the simulator is accurate enough across the ODD to make valid predictions.

From this point of view, the main purpose of a road testing campaign is not to prove that the vehicle is safe on its own. Rather, the simulations are supposed to predict that the vehicle is safe, leaving open the question as to

---

[178] One AV had a problem in Spring when trees grew leaves. See Faulkner 2019: https://ecori.org/2019-8-2-little-roady-shuttle-reaches-milestone-hits-speedbumps/

whether the simulator's predictions are accurate. The road testing campaign is not primarily done to prove safety, but rather to build confidence that simulator results predicting safety are accurate.[179]

4.4.1.3. Long-tail simulation events

A significant potential hole in a simulation-based safety approach is accounting for so-called long-tail rare events. These are events that are so rare that they are unlikely to be seen in a road testing campaign, but nonetheless will happen often enough to a large deployed AV fleet that they must be dealt with to assure acceptable safety.[180]

Some of these rare events might be no surprise to humans in retrospect, such as the possibility of animals with jumping movement in Australia.[181] Others might only be obvious to someone who has previously encountered it (for example, pedestrians in costumes other than on Halloween[182]). And some might be subtle things that could confuse an AV perception system that a human would not think unusual at all (for example, bare legs in summer mistaken for tree trunks due to a system being trained only on winter data in which vertical things that are shades of tan and brown are tree trunks). Infrequent environmental events might also qualify, such as road flooding, wildfires, mudslides, and earthquakes.

This is not to say that an AV has to operate with perfect availability in all conditions, but rather that the types of things that will happen to the fleet over time need to be handled in a graceful way to yield acceptable safety. Slowing down for safety if something unusual is happening is usually fine. Hitting a pedestrian mistaken for a shadow is not. Achieving safety despite rare events occurring requires that a wide variety of rare events be modeled in the simulation, especially if they lead to high-risk scenarios.

From a simulation point of view, billions of miles of simulation will not make a kangaroo appear out of thin air if one hasn't been modeled as a possible animal within the simulated world. Nor will a simulator create mudslides that cover the road if that condition has not been made part of the environmental model.

---

[179] Will you still want road testing as a sanity check on each software release? Sure. But the bulk of road testing should be for simulation validation, not brute force road testing just for the sake of accumulating miles.

[180] Any event that is rare can be said to be long tail (infrequent). A heavy-tail distribution means that there are so many different long tail events that, in aggregate, they contribute so much to risk that they must be dealt with rather than dismissed as inconsequential fluke events.

[181] Kangaroos famously confused a particular AV test vehicle when it started operations in Australia. See Evans 2017: https://www.abc.net.au/news/2017-06-24/driverless-cars-in-australia-face-challenge-of-roo-problem/8574816

[182] For example, an annual anthropomorphic convention held in Pittsburgh. See: https://www.anthrocon.org/

There are two ways to address this problem. One is to use a starting list of foreseeable long-tail events. The ANSI/UL 4600 standard has a list of what can be loosely called #DidYouThinkOfThat road obstacles and situations.

An additional approach that should also be used is analysis of road data from non-AV vehicles. For example, commercial fleets of delivery vehicles, postal vehicles, and long-haul trucks can accumulate billions of miles of data and, if instrumented suitable, provide a source of long-tail data for the many aspects of the environments they operate in without the need to do billions of miles of testing specific to that purpose. There will be data that is more difficult to gather that way, such as human driver reactions to any quirks of AV-operated vehicle behavior. That having been said, gathering fleet data should be an excellent start.

Addressing long-tail events in a simulation requires gathering enough data to know what they are. You might not need a billion miles of road testing if the rare events can be accounted for in simulation and closed-course testing. track. Nonetheless, you are likely to need a billion miles of looking for long-tail events in the environment so that they can be put into simulations.

4.4.2. Shadow mode testing

Potential claim: Our vehicles are safe because we have done many miles of shadow driving.

- Does your shadow driving cover the full ODD sufficiently well?

A somewhat different approach that for practical purposes is a type of simulation is so-called shadow mode operation. In shadow mode an automated driving system mounted on a real vehicle watches sensor inputs and computes its intended driving responses, but does not control the vehicle. It is in effect a simulation, but using live road data instead of a playback of recorded road data[183] or synthesized simulated road data.

4.4.2.1. Shadow mode challenges

A computer's driving actions are unlikely to match the normal variation of behaviors of a human driver of the shadow mode vehicle exactly. Handling the difference between a live vehicle driver's control actions and the corresponding shadow mode ADS intended actions presents challenges. An exact match is unlikely to occur, but is not necessarily required for safety. Motions of the vehicle indirectly affect motions of other road users who respond to changing road situations, so small differences in own vehicle behavior can lead to potentially divergent road scenarios compared to what the shadow mode ADS was expecting to happen.

Anyone dealing with shadow mode testing will have to come to terms with issues such as divergent behaviors between what would have happened with the shadow mode system in command and the real-world vehicle driver's

---

[183] Playback of recorded data as part of a simulation is called "resimulation" and can be considered a middle ground between simulation and shadow mode operation.

control actions. The complexities of getting shadow mode to really work are beyond what we are concerned about here. For safety validation purposes, we will assume that designers have figured out a viable approach to obtaining useful shadow mode testing results.

4.4.2.2. Shadow mode ODD coverage

The potential virtue of shadow mode operation is that an ADS under test can be deployed on a production vehicle fleet without introducing testing risk (assuming that the ADS or person driving vehicles in the fleet is already acceptably safe). If the fleet is large enough, that can provide exposure to many more miles than a small test fleet. As an example, a 1 million car test fleet can reasonably cover about a billion miles of driving within a month with ordinary commuting and local trip vehicle use.

This approach addresses some of the issues with road testing as a claim to safety validation because it permits a much larger number of miles. However, there is still the question of whether the miles cover the full scope of the ODD.

One could argue that a million vehicles are likely to see a full scope of road conditions and traffic conditions that are representative of usage. That is mostly true, although biases such as regional concentration of early adopters and other similar factors need to be taken into account. Attention must be paid when deploying a vehicle validated by shadow mode testing to a region that has not accumulated shadow mode testing miles.

A larger concern is that testing for only a month will not expose the fleet of vehicles running in shadow mode to yearly seasonal cycles. A billion miles gathered in summer will not validate behavior in winter driving conditions. On the other hand, miles gathered in winter are likely to have less exposure to road construction in colder climates.

An additional concern is that some rare events are synchronized in the real world rather than being random independent events. A month-long shadow mode validation period might not happen to experience holiday weekend traffic, a severe storm, unusual pedestrian behavior, or other events that only occur occasionally. Halloween costumes, marathons, parades, and even burning couches in the street[184] cannot be ignored, but can easily be missed in only a month of testing.

The underlying issue is that shadow mode exposure by its very nature is not done according to a test plan that methodically covers all the nooks and crannies of an ODD, but rather relies upon opportunistic exposure to events.

One possible way to get ODD coverage might be to analyze shadow mode results and perform supplemental road testing and simulation to additionally cover areas that have been missed. Regardless of the method used, more than shadow mode will be required to validate safety due to likely gaps in ODD coverage.

---

[184] Also a thing. See 2015: https://ftw.usatoday.com/2015/04/morgantown-bans-outdoor-furniture-west-virginia-fans-fires

4.5. Safety standards

Summary: Industry-created safety standards that cover a large bulk of AV safety requirements already exist. They should be used to ensure AV testing and deployment safety.

A significantly different approach to claiming safety is not to talk about how much testing or validation has been done, but rather claim to have followed some set of safety standards that impart a presumption of safety.

Several relevant safety standards apply to AVs, with more standards under development. The basic standards for AV safety at the time of this writing are:

- ISO 26262, which addresses Functional Safety (sometimes abbreviated FuSa) for road vehicles.[185] At a high level, functional safety means that if there is a fault inside the vehicle equipment, that fault is handled in a way that is safe, usually involving shutting down the operation of a malfunctioning feature. This standard was primarily created for human-driven vehicles. Nonetheless, it is applicable to many aspects of functional safety within an AV. This standard is more than a decade old, with a second edition issued in 2018.

- ISO 21448, which addresses Safety Of The Intended Function (SOTIF).[186] At a high level, SOTIF helps make sure that the various scenarios an AV will encounter have been considered in the design process. The goal is to have the fraction of novel scenarios that have been missed during design be low enough that the system will have acceptable safety. This standard was initially written to cover driver assistance features, then revised to encompass fully automated vehicles. Whereas functional safety is about faults inside the vehicle, SOTIF emphasizes avoiding requirements gaps caused by unknown operational conditions and dealing with the reality that sensors return imperfect measurements of the external world.

- ANSI/UL 4600, which addresses system safety. [187] This standard provides an umbrella framework for creating a safety case to address a broad range of issues relevant to AVs, including: driving, passenger safety, equipment maintenance, and operational infrastructure. It is designed to provide a general framework for using ISO 26262 and ISO 21448, as well as any specific techniques that might be used by an AV design team beyond those standards. One especially important feature is extensive lists of potential hazards that need to be considered in ensuring acceptable safety. It also requires the use of Safety Performance Indicators as discussed in chapters 7 and 8.

---

[185] See: https://en.wikipedia.org/wiki/ISO_26262
[186] See: https://www.iso.org/standard/77490.html
[187] See: https://users.ece.cmu.edu/~koopman/ul4600/index.html

- SAE J3018, which addresses road testing safety. [188] The approach assumes that testing safety is the responsibility of human safety drivers. Aspects covered include safety driver selection, training, monitoring, and operational procedures.

- Security standards. A suitable security standard is required in practice for ANSI/UL 4600 conformance. The ISO/SAE 21434 road vehicle cybersecurity engineering standard [189] is a relevant starting point, although security is beyond the scope we will cover here.

- Other relevant safety standards. At the time of this writing, an effort is being made to develop ISO 5083 as a comprehensive AV safety standard. [190] It is too early to say anything substantive about how that effort will turn out. Another standard, IEEE 2846:2022 lists some scenarios and assumptions that should be considered in AV safety. [191] Many other standards and guidelines have been issued or are being created. This list is just a core starting point rather than an attempt at a complete list.

- Safety Management System (SMS). A safety management system tracks operational metrics and uses them to ensure the continued safety of the system in practical use, whether it be for road testing or production vehicle operation. An essential part of an SMS is a continuous improvement approach to detecting and correcting potential safety issues. At the moment there is no automotive-specific SMS standard, but there is a relevant non-consensus recommended practice. [192]

The above standards were created by industry stakeholders using a consensus process [193] through an accredited standards development organization. In other words, they are publicly available standards created by the industry for the industry. In the case of SAE J3018, ISO 21448, ANSI/UL 4600, IEEE 2846, and the ISO 5803 development effort the standards are specifically intended to cover AVs.

It is important to note that the SAE J3016 standard is intentionally missing from the above list. That is because SAE J3016 is definitely not a safety standard in any form. Nor does J3016 itself purport to be. Nor would the lead authors of that standard describe it as such. [194] Nonetheless, the claim that conformance to SAE J3016 will bestow some manner of safety standard

---

[188] See: https://www.sae.org/standards/content/j3018_202012/
[189] See: https://de.wikipedia.org/wiki/ISO/SAE_21434
[190] See: https://www.iso.org/standard/81920.html
[191] See: https://standards.ieee.org/ieee/2846/10831/
[192] AVSC Information Report for Adapting a Safety Management System (SMS) for Automated Driving System (ADS) SAE Level 4 and 5 Testing and Evaluation AVSC00007202107, July 16, 2021.
See: https://www.sae.org/standards/content/avsc00007202107/
[193] Except for the SMS document, as noted.
[194] Personal communications with the SAE J3016 leads in 2022.

benefit has been publicly stated as part of a law-making process.[195] So we note here that any statement claiming that SAE J3016 provides a safety conformance benefit is flatly incorrect.[196]

Other life-critical application areas such as aviation, petrochemical processing, rail, and medical devices all follow industry-appropriate safety standards. Safety standard compliance is seen as a normal and required part of engineering for every safety-critical industry – except automotive.[197]

Cars in general, and AVs in particular, are not required by automotive equipment safety regulators to follow any of the above relevant industry-written safety standards.[198] That makes it important to ask an AV company claiming that they are "safe" which industry safety standards they actually follow, if any.

4.5.1. We use concepts from safety standards

Potential claim: We use concepts from relevant safety standards.

- What does that even mean? Either you conform to a safety standard or you do not.

It is common to find phrasing in documents such as Voluntary Safety Self-Assessment (VSSA) reports[199] that amounts to a roll call of safety standards but with no hard commitment to following any specific safety standard.

Wording such as having considered concepts, using a standard as a framework, using selected portions of relevant safety practices, or other similar less-than-complete efforts do not really mean anything concrete. Either an AV company follows a safety standard or they do not.[200] The official term for following a safety standard is that one "conforms" to it (or an AV would "comply" if the standard were required by regulations). If an AV company does not unambiguously state that it is conformant to or

---

[195] See this press conference in which an AV primary bill sponsor references SAE J3016 (the only SAE standard referenced in that bill) as something that "will ensure the safe design of" AVs. See January 5, 2022 video at time 14:53:
https://www.senatorlangerholc.com/2022/01/05/langerholc-introduces-legislation-to-create-a-roadmap-for-highly-automated-vehicles/
with mirror at https://youtu.be/ewULUNDBZO4

[196] Section 2.2 goes into the safety issues with J3016 in detail.

[197] Individual engineers and some companies might see safety standards as important, but as a whole the automotive industry has fought hard against any regulatory requirement to follow their own safety standards.

[198] There are scarce exceptions regarding safety driver standards such as New York City requiring conformance to SAE J3018 for road testing. But there is no requirement in any US jurisdiction to conform to AV design safety standards such as ISO 26262, ISO 21448, and ANSI/UL 4600.

[199] See NHTSA: https://www.nhtsa.gov/automated-driving-systems/voluntary-safety-self-assessment

[200] See section 4.10.7 "the spirit of the standard" for a discussion of how this can go wrong.

compliant with a specific standard, then really it is just so much waving of hands with regards to safety.

It is important to note that mainstream AV safety standards (SAE J3018, ISO 26262, ISO 21448, and ANSI/UL 4600) leave plenty of room for tailoring or customizing application of the standard in a way that is appropriate to a specific AV's technology choices and operational context. There is no prescriptive requirement to include any particular technology. It is entirely possible to conform to all these safety standards without locking the AV design into untenable or outdated technology choices.

It is possible that an acceptable alternative standard might be used as a replacement (for example IEC 61508[201] or MIL-STD 882[202]). However, any standards used should be clearly stated in terms of conformance and should cover all relevant areas of safety.

4.5.2. We use proprietary safety approaches

Potential claim: We use a proprietary safety approach that is better than somehow inferior industry safety standards.

- How exactly are the industry safety standards inferior?[203]
- Why do you not add your secret sauce safety approach on top of conforming to a standard?
- Many companies helped write the existing safety standards. Why did they vote to approve one that is inadequate? Why will not they follow a standard they helped create?

It is common to see proprietary safety practices being followed rather than a standards conformance approach under some claim that the existing practices are "as good as" the standards, the practices are "better than" the standards, or even that, somehow, following standards would overall reduce safety by forcing AV designers to be less safe.[204]

An opaque claim that there is a better way than following standards at best suffers from a lack of transparency. At worst it is simply an evasion of the practice of following industry safety standards (see section 4.10.5).

In some cases it is worth digging deeper into what "better" actually means. From personal experience, we have seen that proprietary practices being considered "better" tends to have more to do with being quicker and cheaper – usually at the cost of increased risk – rather than resulting in comparable or improved safety. Better for profits and time to market at the expense of failing to achieve acceptable safety is a problem for at least some stakeholders.

---

[201] See: https://en.wikipedia.org/wiki/IEC_61508

[202] See: https://webstore.ansi.org/Standards/DOD/MILSTD882E   It is common to find free, but non-authoritative, sources for this document on a web search.

[203] The usual answer to this question is simply the sound of crickets chirping.

[204] It is astonishing that AV company representatives can say this with a straight face. But they do.

In some cases, companies are avoiding conformance with safety standards that in fact they themselves helped write. For all public consensus standards, stakeholders have been provided an opportunity to provide comments and point out potential problems. If a company has a smarter, better way to approach safety, they will have had ample opportunity to submit that idea to the standards processes.

Additionally, some companies propose their own practices via best practice publications or as a starting point for industry standards. There are processes in place to make such proposals public quickly. We have yet to see a reasonable basis for a claim that any company's safety engineering practices are so incredibly superior that they need to keep them secret. Rather, companies often publish their safety approaches in conferences and workshops to take credit for their safety efforts and, at times, raise the safety bar for their competitors. Any claim that any company has secret sauce safety practices that are so effective that they obviate a need to follow industry standards, but are so secret they cannot be revealed, should be regarded with skepticism.

Importantly, none of the safety standards prohibits companies from going beyond what is in the standard. ANSI/UL 4600 in particular strongly encourages going beyond the required elements of the standard.

It is not so much to ask the automotive industry to conform to their own industry-developed, consensus-based standards. At the very least, each AV company should clearly state which standards they conform to. Eschewing industry-created safety standards in favor of opaque proprietary standards should be treated as being unwilling to commit to achieving acceptable safety.

On the other hand, a statement that an AV company conforms to specific, relevant safety standards and uses additional proprietary safety approaches should be fine.

4.5.3. We use a safety case

Potential claim: We are building a safety case.

- Does it include a relevant claim of safety supported by argument and evidence?

A reasonable definition of a safety case is: "A structured argument, supported by a body of evidence, that provides a compelling, comprehensible and valid case that a system is safe for a given application in a given environment."[205]

One expects the claims to be relevant to actual operational safety, such as "This AV will be at least as safe as a human driver[206] in comparable driving

---

[205] Defence Standard 00-56 Issue 7 (part 1): Safety Management Requirements for Defence Systems, UK MoD, p. 26. Available via registration at: https://www.dstan.mod.uk/StanMIS/indexes/DefenceStandards
[206] We'll get to what "as safe as a human driver" might mean in chapter 5.

situations." Claims should be backed up by a credible argument to provide reasoning for why the claims are supported, and evidence that the argument relies upon. A safety case breaks one high-level claim down into a number of sub-claims, arguing down toward evidence in a structured manner.[207]

Other types of structures are sometimes called "safety cases," so it is important to understand what an AV maker means by that term. For example, a brief text document with no evidence might informally discuss safety, but it is not a safety case.[208]

Alternately there might be a "safety case framework" that has claims and arguments, but no tie to evidence. This can be a good start, but is not a finished safety case due to the lack of incorporated evidence.

ISO 26262 requires a safety case. However, that safety case is by default limited to functional safety, and does not cover system-level safety unless it goes well beyond the requirements of the standard. In practice such safety cases are often a pile-o-documents approach without any argument that ties them together. As with a safety case framework, this can provide useful raw material, but is insufficient to establish overall AV safety on its own.

Ideally, the safety case conforms to ANSI/UL 4600, which is a standard specifically written to ensure that an AV safety case supports a claim of acceptable safety.

4.5.4. We conform to safety standards

Potential claim: We conform to {ISO 26262, ISO 21448, ANSI/UL 4600, IEEE 2846, …}.

- Sounds promising, but is it for the whole vehicle, or just a part of it?
- Is the standard referenced sufficient to cover everything that matters?

Following industry-created consensus-based safety standards is the cornerstone of life-critical system design in other industries. The AV industry should do this as well.

It is important to be transparent about what aspects of the system and what part of the standards are being followed if the situation is either less than the entire system or less than the entirety of the standard is being followed.

Some examples of reasonable, transparent conformance statements might be:

- "Our vehicle conforms to ISO 26262 for all functional safety aspects of the design."
- "We conform to the normative sections of ISO 21448."[209]

---

[207] We use "claim" in a generic sense. Saying goals instead of claims for fans of Goal Structuring Notation (GSN) is fine.

[208] In particular, we have not seen a VSSA that would qualify as a safety case.

[209] A significant portion of ISO 21448 is informative rather than normative. That means only a fraction of the standard actually needs to be addressed to legitimately claim conformance. So this is a narrower statement than might be apparent without reading the standard in some detail. Nonetheless, it is an encouraging statement. A

- "Our vehicle conforms to ANSI/UL 4600, with independent assessment performed by an independent internal group of accredited safety assessors."

An example of a potentially misleading statement is a somewhat common approach of: "Our hardware conforms to ISO 26262." ISO 26262 covers both hardware and software, so what this statement really means is that software does not conform to the requirements of ISO 26262. That is potentially a huge deal for life-critical software in an AV, but is a claim that has been made by some companies when trying to convince stakeholders that they have safety covered. We consider such statements to be "ISO-washing" in that they invoke a veneer of conformance to safety standards without actually conforming in full.

Another potentially misleading statement would be "we conform to the scenarios and other requirements for the AV safety standard IEEE 2846." There is nothing wrong with that statement so long as it is part of a much more comprehensive safety standard. That standard has a small fraction of the scenarios that would be needed to build a safe AV, and is expressly intended as a starting point, not a comprehensive list of requirements for AV safety. The problem is not with conformance to that standard, but rather over-claiming what that conformance means in terms of system-level safety. In fact, any statement that one single standard is all that is needed to achieve AV safety is highly suspect. Rather, it should be expected that a combination of standards will be required.

Anything less than a direct statement of conformance and the scope of such conformance might mean that pieces of the standard have not been conformed to. Especially problematic are claims of near conformance or "in the spirit of" types of statements. Either an AV conforms to the standard or it does not. Any other statement that dances around whether conformance has been achieved, or at least will be achieved before deployment, should be treated as marketing puffery.

It is important to realize that conformance to a standard all on its own does not guarantee acceptable safety. Any standard can be gamed. But that is no excuse to avoid standards. Rather, safety standards serve the purpose of providing guidance and a grading rubric for teams trying to do the right thing.

In practice it is unlikely that AV design teams will achieve acceptable safety without addressing the topics found in standards, especially ANSI/UL 4600. The question is simply whether they follow the standards or try to get there some other way. If they follow their own path, it is difficult to know what they might have missed and, in practice, they are likely to miss important aspects of safety. Conformance to safety standards is an essential part of getting to safety in every domain, including AVs.

---

better statement would also address what was done about the multiple informative sections.

4.5.5. We conform to FMVSS

Potential claim: We meet all required Federal safety standards.

- Conforming to FMVSS covers vehicle basics unless subject to an exemption, but not AV functions.

The set of US Federal Motor Vehicle Safety Standards (FMVSS)[210] forms a regulatory mechanism to assure a minimal set of safety capabilities in road vehicles. This is a baseline safety standard for conventional vehicles, defining a minimum set of functionality that supports, but does not ensure, that the vehicle is safe to operate for a human driver.

FMVSS covers things such as whether headlights are bright enough, whether the brakes can stop the vehicle fast enough in at least some test conditions, whether a low tire pressure warning can be activated in specific test conditions, airbags, rearview cameras, and so on.

The FMVSS suite does not attempt to measure software quality or software safety, let alone the effectiveness of automation capabilities. Nor is it intended to. It defines a set of vehicle tests that can be run to ensure a baseline level of capability for some safety-related vehicle functions.

As regulations evolve it might be that FMVSS includes some basic AV functionality testing. However, no such tests will exist any time soon. Moreover, any such "driver's license road test" approach can at best confirm minimum driving competence, but cannot be robust enough to ensure acceptable safety all on its own.

FMVSS tests can sometimes present a burden for an AV because they are defined assuming a human driver is able to sit in a driver's seat at a steering wheel, looking at a dashboard display. This can be problematic, especially for delivery vehicles that do not have a driver's seat, or do not have a physical dashboard to display mandated warning symbols. Such vehicles might be exempted from FMVSS conformance so long as there is an equivalent way to achieve the same functionality. But none of that serves to ensure safety for the vehicle automation functions themselves.

A recent move to modify FMVSS for AVs did not set standards for AV safety, but rather adjusted FMVSS crash safety standards to accommodate the somewhat different needs of AV crash safety, such as not having a steering wheel-based airbag for vehicles with no steering wheel.[211]

In short, FMVSS conformance is good for ensuring that the brakes and lights work. That should only be modified or waived if equivalent functionality is available to accomplish the intended safety purpose behind

---

[210] See: https://www.nhtsa.gov/laws-regulations/fmvss

[211] An example of misinterpretation in the popular press is an article headline of: "Buckle up, autonomous vehicles finally get federal safety standards" with article text that more accurately states: "update the safety requirements for occupants in vehicles that don't have traditional manual controls associated with a human driver. https://techcrunch.com/2022/03/10/nhtsa-first-autonomous-vehicle-occupant-safety-standards/

the test. Regardless, FMVSS conformance has almost nothing to do with whether an ADS knows how to drive safely.

4.5.6. We got five stars on crash tests

Potential claim: We are safe because we have five-star safety performance.

- Doing well on crash tests is reassuring in case something goes wrong. But AV safety should be primarily about avoiding crashes in the first place.

A system beyond FMVSS is the so-called star system for crashworthiness. This is the New Car Assessment Program (NCAP) in the US, with a parallel but more stringent cousin in Europe (Euro NCAP). These are programs that produce ratings on a scale from one star to five stars. [212] There is no regulatory requirement to receive a certain score, but the system has been successful in putting pressure on carmakers to improve at least some aspects of crash safety. [213]

Classical NCAP-style testing involves crash testing, and has brought fame to the notion of an instrumented crash test dummy. Crash tests have evolved over time to address related factors such as collision avoidance technology and pedestrian harm reduction, although the specifics vary depending on the testing regime and region of the world. [214] There are also some criticisms that it is possible (and potentially common) to game NCAP tests so that actual crash performance degrades significantly for even small differences in collision geometry between NCAP test results and real-world crashes. Nonetheless, NCAP-style tests have helped improve crash safety, even if safety proponents would like to see more stringent tests.

It is common for car companies to trumpet a variation of being "the safest car on the road" with some potential market segment qualifiers based solely on NCAP testing results. However, this is a very narrow view of safety. It only addresses safety when the car gets into a crash. Most car occupants and especially vulnerable road users have a more expansive notion of safety that emphasizes not getting into crashes in the first place.

High scores on crash safety ratings are a good start, but only deal with a small fraction of the entire safety problem. NCAP ratings are only a part of predicting AV safety outcomes.

---

[212] A NHTSA summary of NCAP can be found here: https://www.nhtsa.gov/ratings
[213] The Global NCAP project attempts to improve car safety worldwide.
See: https://en.wikipedia.org/wiki/Global_NCAP
[214] An interesting overview of various types of NCAP type testing for different regions can be found here from 2017:
https://www.marklines.com/en/report_all/rep1657_201712

4.6. Risk management and insurance coverage

Summary: Risk management approaches including insurance have a role to play, but are not on their own able to ensure acceptable safety, nor do they provide compelling incentives to be acceptably safe.

Sometimes a company will say their AV is safe because they do risk management or because they can afford insurance. The two concepts of risk management and safety are related – but not identical. The differences can be subtle in the abstract, but are extremely important to stakeholders who live in deployment areas and from a more general ethical point of view. The differences can become especially relevant when dealing with companies that concentrate more on valuation than steady state profitability.

4.6.1. We do risk management

Potential claim: We are safe because we do risk management.
- Risk management tends to reduce risks to a point, but is not necessarily incentivized to reach acceptable safety.
- Is the business plan optimizing for a short-term exit vs. long-term sustainable safety?

Risk management involves minimizing the expected cost of adverse events via a combination of selectively investing in risk mitigation, smoothing out the cost of losses over time via insurance, and simply accepting some risks.[215] This includes identifying risks, estimating the likely cost of each risk, and reducing risk where it is economically beneficial to do so. In other words, finding ways to spend a little money to reduce risks can result in avoiding potential large payouts from those risks turning into loss events. Spending a bit more money than expected losses is justified if you receive a benefit from having reduced uncertainty. An example of paying a bit more than expected losses is purchasing an insurance policy that charges a premium compared to estimated losses, but in return provides economic protection against a potential catastrophically high-cost loss event.

This classical portrayal of risk management assumes you have a steady state business situation with a goal of improving profitability by getting a better handle on risks. You have already decided to conduct some business activity that has some risk associated with it, and are already conforming with suitable safety regulations. You are trying to optimize costs from risk overall while blunting the possible consequences of high severity events. That usually involves some combination of reducing some risks, insuring most others, and just accepting the need to pay out compensation in some cases.[216]

---

[215] For an overview, see: https://en.wikipedia.org/wiki/Risk_management
[216] A crucial part of this framing is that there is some sort of regulatory mechanism that is already making the situation safe enough to meet societal expectations. Risk

To some degree risk management can be aligned with improving safety. That alignment happens when high costs of potential losses drive risk mitigation to reduce the risk of those high-cost losses.

However, this view of risk management is relative in terms of reducing risk, and is not absolute. Even reducing the risk of something dangerous can still result in a system that is unsafe according to societal norms. You can do risk management to reduce the number of deaths associated with extreme sports such as jumping off buildings with a parachute or jumping off cliffs with a wing suit. But no amount of risk management is likely to make those activities as safe as riding a conventional elevator. While there is risk tolerance for extreme sport casualties, making an elevator as risky as an extreme sport would not be societally acceptable.

The "reduce cost of losses" view of risk management diverges from safety in large part because it implicitly excludes the most important part of the cost equation for AVs: potential profit from taking increased risks as part of a deliberate business strategy. The true risk management equation that matters is not whether risk mitigation costs save money compared to the expected cost of adverse events. What matters for a company is total profits taking into account the cost of risk. As long as high risk is associated with high profit, the risk is economically viable, regardless of where adverse events might fall on an absolute scale of safety and personal harm.[217]

For startup companies, risk management is even more decoupled from safety. For them, the question is what risk-taking behavior will result in the highest possible company valuation while still having an acceptable risk of company failure due to adverse news events. If the CEO and Board are willing to gamble, they can further decide that as long as they perceive the probability of catastrophic events to be low, their risk management plan can simply be to roll the dice on catastrophic events and plan to get lucky[218] (especially if they have a good crisis management team to clean up any messes created as they go). They do not have to build AVs at scale for 10 years and account for the average cost of lawsuit settlements. They just have to get cool enough demos to cash out their stock. That financial exit could occur before the deployed fleet has scaled up, and possibly before there is a chance for too many lawsuits to pile up even if crashes happen. To be sure,

---

management is about optimizing risk/reward within the constraint of already being responsibly safe.

[217] For example, if you can capture a market segment by selling "beta" quality AV capabilities that might be less safe on the road than conventional human-driven vehicles, the value increase of the company due to having such a product could far exceed the costs of settling litigation related to crashes. Hypothetically.

[218] Keep in mind that a significant majority of venture-backed company fail. Rolling the dice on a risky deployment might be seen as well within risk tolerance limits in such a situation. Generally, consider Eisenmann 2021: https://hbr.org/2021/05/why-start-ups-fail

not all founders think this way, but there is palpable economic pressure to take this path. We will revisit these topics later in the ethics chapter.[219]

In sharp contrast, with safety the goal is to reduce harm (injuries and fatalities) to some societally acceptable level, even if doing so requires a slower pace for time to market and increased product cost. Furthermore, there are basic safety practices that should be implemented even if a purely monetary risk analysis shows that doing so is a bit more expensive versus paying cost-of-lives-lost settlements. In other words, safety is about reasonable measures to prevent harm to people rather than pure optimization of profits and/or total business value. Risk management, on the other hand, is more compatible with optimizing for maximum returns from an Initial Public Offering, acquisition, or other liquidity event that allows initial investors to cash out and collect profits.[220]

4.6.2. The cost of risk forces us to be safe

Potential claim: The financial incentives to reduce risk will force us to devote resources to become acceptably safe.

- As with risk management in general, the financial incentive to reduce risk is too weak to ensure safety is acceptable.
- Is the assessed cost of life used in figuring risk in line with US DOT figures of about $12M per life?

The usual definition of risk is probability times cost. In other words, you look at how likely a loss event is to occur, figure out the average cost of each loss event, and sum up the cost of the number of expected losses to determine the total cost you expect to see in paying out for repairs, injury compensation, and fatality compensation. This sounds a lot like safety in that you are trying to minimize net risk. But it is different to the degree that equipment damage cost is traded off against human harm, the book-keeping cost of human harm is discounted from societal norms, or low hanging safety fruit is neglected because it is small compared to overall net risk.[221]

For systems that cannot hurt or kill people, maximizing overall profit via risk management is an economically rational approach. That involves

---

[219] See section 10.5 for more on this topic.

[220] Does this mean that early investors and founders are 100% focused on the money? It depends on the people involved. But leadership has significant pressure to act that way due to their obligations to stockholders. In some cases they might need to justify that safety increases company value within the few-year planning horizon of venture capital better than a narrower risk management approach.

[221] It is common to see recall decision criteria include whether a known safety defect will affect many vehicles or only a few. Under an assumption of fixed resources to process recalls, those that only affect a few vehicles might be foregone entirely, or downgraded to repairs that are only made in response to customer complaints. That can happen even though it is foreseeable that people might be harmed as a result of that decision.

spending money to mitigate risk only to the degree there is a positive return on investment. If total cost of mitigation plus remaining risk is lower with the mitigation, then spend money on the mitigation. If the mitigation is more expensive than the savings, do not bother.

However, when injuries and fatalities are at stake, economic optimization can be at odds with safety.

Like it or not, eventually there is a monetary cost put on the value of a human life by society. One manifestation of this is the US Department of Transportation's value for a "statistical" average human life at USD $11.8 million for 2021 based on a survey of various sources.[222] In practice, the actual cost of paying out for a car occupant fatality can be substantially lower.[223]

A classic conflict between risk management and safety occurs when safety features are slightly more expensive to implement than the expected overall risk value. There is a long history in the automotive industry of claiming that safety features proposed by regulators would cost too much. The implicit argument is that the risk reduction will cost more than consumers are willing to spend, and thus reduce sales of newer cars that have newer mandated safety features, reducing overall safety. This is complicated by the inherent nature of buying safety equipment that might never be used. If the cost of safety features is made transparent to customers, they might feel like it is buying a lottery ticket in which you only "win" (the money you spent saves your life) if you are in a severe enough crash. Money spent on safety equipment that you feel will never be used (because it is natural to believe that major crashes only happen to other people) can feel like it is wasted.

There is an additional issue that high production volume drives down costs in the automotive market. But starting the journey to scale up is difficult because costs are high for the initial units that are built before getting to scale. In the face of this dynamic it is common for car companies to put safety innovations only on high-end, high-margin vehicles and safety-focused brands. Features then percolate down into low-end vehicles over time. Features that do not seem to motivate car purchases take longer, perhaps requiring a push from regulators.

Adoption issues notwithstanding, over time safety features have been incorporated into cars, from seat belts to airbags to crumple zones to automatic emergency braking features. Vehicle safety features paid for by

---

[222] See: https://www.transportation.gov/office-policy/transportation-policy/revised-departmental-guidance-on-valuation-of-a-statistical-life-in-economic-analysis

[223] In the only jury trial held for the infamous Toyota Unintended Acceleration cases the jury awarded $1.5M for the death of Ms. Barbara Schwarz in a manufacturers' products liability claim. The amount of punitive damages is unknown due to a last-minute settlement, but would have been capped at an additional $1.5M: https://www.beasleyallen.com/wp-content/uploads/toyota-sua-jury-verdict-form-schwarz.pdf That is far less than the DOT amount of $9.2M for a 2013 fatality. Cases in other states might result in a higher payment, but negotiated pre-trial settlements would be expected to be lower than corresponding average trial awards.

customers regularly prevent fatalities, and over time new safety features such as seat belts and airbags have become required equipment.

A scenario that brings the difference between risk management and safety to a head occurs when a car maker decides not to mitigate a risk based on a purely economic analysis. Such analysis determines that a risk mitigation (such as a repair to a discovered design defect) would cost more than settling claims via payments to victims,[224] and is not required by regulators.

The poster child of risk mitigation gone wrong is the famous Ford Pinto fire problem, in which vehicles were discovered to be susceptible to fuel tank fires in moderate-speed rear-end collisions. At trial, a memo[225] was exposed with a cost of mitigation for the problem of $11 per vehicle and total of $137 million yearly for to fix the problem on all vehicles produced. On the other hand, expected costs for paying out to settle claims was predicted to be significantly lower, at only $50 million. The memo estimated the costs as: $200,000 per death, $67,000 per injury, and $700 per vehicle while predicting 180 burn deaths. There are subtleties involved with the case and interpreting the memo, but for our purposes it suffices that the outcome of the court case decision punished Ford for making a decision to save money by not mitigating a risk, even though mitigating the risk was more expensive than simply payout out settlements.

Based on the Ford Pinto story, it could be said that at least in some cases the wrong tradeoff is being considered. The tradeoff typically portrayed is between cost to mitigate vs. cost to pay out. In practice, however, a higher stakes tradeoff is also being made at the same time: the cost to mitigate vs. the possibility of getting caught and punished for not mitigating. The cost of punishment for failing to report a defect can be high[226] and there can be significant brand tarnish in addition to compensation costs.[227]

The tension between safety and risk management can get worse when there is a high cost associated with delaying deployment of a system to improve safety. If a large AV maker is burning through millions of dollars

---

[224] Recall that even these payments tend to be discounted from a more neutral evaluation of the cost of a human life.

[225] See:
https://www.autosafety.org/wp-content/uploads/import/phpq3mJ7F_FordMemo.pdf

[226] Toyota paid a $1.2 billion fine and admitted that it "misled US consumers by concealing and making deceptive statements about two safety-related issues affecting its vehicles, each of which caused a type of unintended acceleration" relating to non-software issues it claimed were a cause of some unintended acceleration events.
https://abcnews.go.com/Blotter/toyota-pay-12b-hiding-deadly-unintended-acceleration/story?id=22972214
Anyone involved in decisions about how to handle a safety-related automotive defect should read the Toyota signed statement in its entirety. See:
https://www.justice.gov/sites/default/files/opa/legacy/2014/03/19/toyota-def-pros-agr.pdf

[227] See the General Motors ignition switch recalls:
https://en.wikipedia.org/wiki/General_Motors_ignition_switch_recalls

per day in funding until it can deploy, the cost to pay out for a few injuries or fatalities can be perceived as economically attractive compared to the cost of extending development time by months or years. In other words, paying out for a fatality during testing is just a few days of operational costs, and might (ethics aside) simply be seen as the cost of doing business.

A purely risk-driven approach also runs into problems with achieving safety when the cost of compensating victims for harm can be manipulated to be cheaper per person than societal norms. One manipulation strategy might be concentrating testing in areas populated by road users who have limited access to legal counsel to pursue claims for injuries or fatalities. Another strategy might be testing or operating in jurisdictions with limits on awards to any road user who has been harmed to limit the cost of any potential crash. A third strategy might be ensuring that state laws are written in such a way that expensive and time consuming litigation would be required to resolve intentionally inserted ambiguities and conflicts, increasing pressure for victims to settle for lower compensation.[228] A significant flaw in typical risk management decisions is assigning a risk of zero to brand tarnish if loss events blow up into a public spectacle.

From another point of view, if pure economic pressure from risk management were enough to ensure acceptably safe outcomes, there would be no need for safety regulatory agencies such as NHTSA, FMCSA, FAA, FDA, FRA, and OSHA at the Federal level, plus state and municipal regulators. Much of the responsibility of those agencies is to force companies to make safety improvements despite company complaints that doing so will increase their overall economic costs or deter customers from making purchases due to cost.

Sadly, in practice it is often seen as profitable, or at least expedient considering short-term incentives, to build systems that are not as safe as they should be given an objective societal value of human life. This can be especially true in situations that present significant competitive pressure with an accompanying temptation to roll the safety dice for a quicker win, hoping to get lucky.

To be clear, we are not proposing spending billions of dollars beyond accepted safety practices to avoid a single statistical potential death across a huge fleet of vehicles. Ultimately there is a range of cost per human life

---

[228] It seems difficult to prove that this mechanism is in action in any specific situation. However, it is hard to believe that the prevalence of problematic proposed state bill wording is entirely due to a lack of skill of drafters. This is especially true given the close involvement of highly compensated AV industry representatives in the drafting process. For an example see:
https://safeautonomy.blogspot.com/2022/01/comments-on-pa-sb-965-regulating.html
While speculative, it is somewhat easier to believe that at least some problematic bill wording can be attributed to a strategy of trying to increase transaction costs for victims facing a process in which the meaning of laws can only be determined via lengthy and expensive litigation. Considerations related to this topic are discussed in sections 10.6.2 and 10.6.5.

saved that is sustainable. However, in practice it is too easy for businesses to use a practical value of human life during risk analysis that is net lower than is societally appropriate. It is also all too easy for risk managers to low-ball the expectation of harm if there is business pressure to come up with an optimistic answer. This means that some form of risk management is indeed an important component in achieving safety, but only if the true value of harm (rather than expected out of pocket cost to the company) is properly accounted for and combined with responsible safety engineering practices.

Risk management can surely pressure a grossly unsafe system to become less unsafe. However, things become more complicated when considering the lack of strong incentives to improve a somewhat-safe system to become an acceptably safe system. Incentive structures that have outsized rewards and reduced penalties for risk-taking behavior that degrades or fails to provide safety become highly problematic. Anyone who says that risk management, insurance premiums, or other similar forces will ensure acceptable safety is simply not accounting for the dynamics involved.

4.6.3. The insurance company gave us a policy

Potential claim: The insurance company gave us a policy, so that must mean we are safe.

- Insurance policies are not issued on the basis of safety, but rather whether the insurance company can characterize risk and sell policies for a profit.

4.6.3.1. Insurance policies do not make you safe

Getting an insurance policy does not mean you are objectively "safe." You can insure plenty of things that might be considered risky by everyday standards: skydiving injury insurance, commercial rocket launch payload insurance, marine piracy insurance, [229] and life insurance for front-line military personnel are all routinely issued.

An insurance company issuing a policy does not mean any particular activity in general or AV in particular is objectively safe. Rather, it means that the insurance company thinks it understands the risks well enough to set a policy rate that is, on average, economically attractive (profitable to the insurance company) across the members of the risk pool.

Taking a lot of risk? Expect a higher premium. But you will still get an insurance policy for high-risk activities so long as the insurance company feels comfortable it can estimate likely future losses and charge accordingly.

To be sure, the insurance industry does support improving safety. Historically, the insurance industry has spawned activities to create safety standards and help their customers manage risks. [230] Organizations such as the

---

[229] Yes, this is a thing even for ships without sails and cannons.
See: https://en.wikipedia.org/wiki/Captain_Phillips_(film)
[230] Underwriters Laboratories was founded in the 1890s to help improve fire safety in partnership with the insurance industry. See: https://www.ul.com/about/history

Insurance Institute for Highway Safety (IIHS)[231] are both active and vocal in support of vehicle automation safety. Insurance companies typically have a loss prevention activity to support their clients as well. So these remarks should not be interpreted as indicating industry disregard for safety.

Nonetheless, the economic reality of the situation is that you can get insurance for activities that are objectively dangerous so long as you are willing to pay the required premium. With a multi-billion dollar war chest for AV development and aggressive timelines to deploy, reducing insurance costs is nowhere near the top budget item of concern until well after deployment. Higher insurance premiums are unlikely to drive safety improvements very hard until the industry is operating at significant scale. And even then, other issues discussed regarding risk mitigation incentives will still apply.

4.6.3.2. Low premiums do not necessarily mean low harm

A crucial aspect of insurance for vehicle crashes is that total cost of insurance bundles together harm as well as property damage. For personal policies the contributing costs are broken out into several categories. But if you are tracking business profitability what matters is the total insurance cost, which includes both harm to people and property damage. If the property damage risk far outweighs the risk of harm, there is reduced economic pressure to mitigate harm.

An everyday example of divergence between insurance premiums and fatality rates can be seen in motorcycles.

Overall, motorcyclists account for 14% of all traffic fatalities, with those fatalities occurring nearly 27 times more frequently than for passenger cars on a per-mile basis. [232] Even though motorcycles are 27 times more dangerous in terms of risk of death per mile, motorcycle insurance costs about half that of car insurance. This difference is attributed to motorcycle crashes causing much lower equipment damage bills (both to the motorcycle and any other vehicle hit) that more than offset the cost of increased fatalities.[233]

Based on motorcycle insurance alone, it is clear that insurance cost can be a poor prediction of occupant harm because of the influence of property damage on insurance rates. Cheaper insurance does not necessarily mean a vehicle is safer. By the same token, more expensive insurance on an expensive-to-repair vehicle chock-full of crash safety technology does not mean such a high-end vehicle is less safe.

In short, insurance rates are not necessarily predictive of safety.

---

[231] See: https://www.iihs.org/about-us

[232] Source: https://crashstats.nhtsa.dot.gov/Api/Public/ViewPublication/812979

[233] Source: https://policyscout.com/auto-insurance/learn/motorcycle-insurance-vs-car-insurance A possible confounder is number of miles per year driven by motorcycles being less than for cars. But that is unlikely to explain the entire difference here.

4.6.3.3. Insurance premiums will not force acceptable safety

You can perform risk management exclusively by purchasing insurance and doing no risk mitigation whatsoever, so long as you can afford the premiums. People and businesses do precisely that on a regular basis.[234] However, there is economic pressure for sophisticated companies to perform risk mitigation to lower insurance premiums – to a point.

In principle, risk mitigation will lower your insurance premiums, but that might or might not be worth your while. If hypothetically you are spending $1 per mile to run a vehicle and insurance costs $0.05 per mile, the theoretical limit to the benefit of risk mitigation is only 5% of your costs. You might be better off from a purely economic point of view spending management attention on optimizing the other $0.95 per mile of cost. Note that safety does not enter into such an insurance-driven risk management calculation – it is purely about optimizing profits.

Yes, if insurance is 95% of your cost, you have strong incentive to reduce risk. But as insurance cost becomes small compared to other factors, there is less and less pressure to do risk mitigation to further reduce costs. This is especially true if you are in a fast-moving business where things like time to market and ability to scale the fleet quickly are an existential threat to your business vs. a few cents per mile of insurance cost.

In other words, the ability to buy insurance does not mean that an AV is safe, but rather that the insurance company has decided they are willing to get paid a certain amount to cover any potential losses, and the AV maker has decided they can afford to pay that amount while achieving their goals. If you have a company spending more than a million dollars a day on engineering costs, a few dollars extra of insurance cost for test fleets is inconsequential. Perhaps insurance costs will be optimized after deployment, but even then it is economically pressing to do so only when all the much greater business costs have been optimized on a large deployed fleet.

It is unreasonable to expect an AV developer to delay market introduction to improve safety simply to shave a few pennies per mile off their insurance costs. Rather, they will be incentivized to deploy as soon as they can to capture market share – even if they lose money on every mile driven to do so – and worry about incrementally reducing insurance costs later.

Still another consideration is that insurance companies might low-ball quotes to obtain market share. The theory is that if AVs become a big insurance market, it is advantageous for insurance companies to use early policies as loss leaders to in effect "buy" part of the market by establishing early relationships with AV developers. That might mean, for example, that a company could write a policy for an AV tester that is the same rate as for an ordinary vehicle even if the risk might be higher or even largely unknown. Given a fixed payout limit set by a policy cap, the worst-case downside for a

---

[234] If you doubt this, the next time you are at a rental car counter during a quiet shift, take a few minutes to ask the attendant for their worst horror story of damage carelessly or perhaps even intentionally done to a vehicle for which someone purchased the expensive zero deduction insurance waivers.

crash is limited to that policy cap. The upside is preferential access to a potentially huge future insurance market.

Insurance premiums are further reduced by artificially low insurance policy cap requirements compared to the risk that is likely being taken during testing and early deployment. State laws require insurance maximums to be much lower than reasonably expected jury compensation awards, sometimes no larger than the state insurance minimum requirement for human drivers.[235]

Insurance provides a comparatively weak economic incentive to be "safer." But as with risk management, that economic incentive runs out of steam when the expected insurance cost becomes small compared to other financial considerations and management imperatives.

4.7. Safety culture

Summary: A robust safety culture is required to achieve acceptable safety for any real-world product. Achieving that requires more than smart people and good intentions.

Another category for arguing that AVs will be safe holds that really smart, well-intentioned people are working hard to make the world a better place, with safety their #1 priority. So of course what they produce will be safe.

These assertions are often made by organizations and people that by all appearances are sincere, but are also subject to immense economic pressure to show progress. When tens of billions of dollars of investment are on the line to show results on an overly aggressive timeline, it seems prudent to ask for evidence of safety beyond statements of good intent. It is also reasonable to ask if the people making those statements have the necessary grasp of safety engineering as the basis for making such statements.

A robust safety culture is essential to achieving safety in the real world. However, good intentions and rhetoric are not enough.

4.7.1. Trust us, we are smart and work hard

Potential claim: We're experts in AV technology. We're smart, and we work hard. Trust us. It will be safe.

• Do you also have strong safety engineering capability?

The skill set held by core ADS designers (robotics and machine learning) has little overlap with a safety engineering specialty skill set. Those are

---

[235] State insurance requirements for AVs range from state minimums of $25K to $50K up to a high of $5M. Even if a court verdict is higher, the insurance company is only on the hook for the maximum, with the rest of any potential liability falling back on responsible parties – if the plaintiff can manage to collect. For a list of state insurance requirements see:
https://www.iihs.org/topics/advanced-driver-assistance/autonomous-vehicle-laws

different specialization areas that historically have been done by different people with different educational backgrounds. There is no reason to expect that a typical smart, capable, ADS designer will have safety skills.[236]

Achieving AV safety will require a team that integrates several different skill sets including: (1) robotics and machine learning to build autonomous capability, (2) automotive expertise to build a vehicle and lifecycle support system that can be deployed at scale in real-world conditions, and (3) safety expertise that goes beyond the traditional automotive paradigm of relying upon a human driver to handle issues not mitigated via usual functional safety approaches.

As AV companies get closer to deployment, many of them have been building up both their automotive engineering capability and their safety teams. But approaches vary widely. It is important to understand the team composition to ensure that sufficient capability in each area is available. It is also crucial that the safety team be integrated into the overall project rather than told to keep out of the way of other teams making the fastest possible progress to autonomy deployment.

We are likely to see increased emphasis on safety staffing and effort as companies get close to at-scale deployment. It seems likely there will be a broad spectrum of how much safety is incorporated into the mainstream engineering process. Most of the industry is still closer to the beginning of this journey than they are to the end.

4.7.2. Safety is our #1 priority

Potential claim: Safety is our #1 priority.
- How do we know this is more than a corporate slogan?

Saying that Safety is #1 is a nice sentiment and a worthy organizational priority. But does the organization take action on this? Does that priority permeate the organization? Or is it just a slogan?

If safety is really important to an organization, you should expect to see a robust safety culture backed by evidence of accomplishments and data transparency. Slogans aren't enough, especially if they are not representative of what is really going on inside the company.[237]

4.7.3. We have a robust safety culture

Potential claim: Our safety culture ensures we will create a safe AV.

---

[236] Nor will most safety engineers have ADS developer skills.

[237] One AV company, Otto, was said to have an internal slogan of "safety third." The reader is left to ponder any potentially indirect relationship between this and the fact that the fatal testing crash the following year involved Uber, which had purchased Otto. See Balakrishnan 2017: https://www.cnbc.com/2017/03/16/anthony-levandowski-ubers-self-driving-car-engineer-safety-lawsuit.html

- Do you follow best practices for building and maintaining a robust safety culture?
- Do you have a comprehensive Safety Management System (SMS)?

A safety culture reflects the values and practices of how an organization does business with regard to safety.[238]

An informal way of describing a robust safety culture is that: your boss and organization want to hear about safety concerns, and you can count on them to act upon what you tell them without punishing you. In recent years this general idea has crystalized into the notion of "Just Culture."[239]

Beyond the strictly cultural aspects, a robust safety culture needs to be accompanied by processes and activities to ensure that safety is indeed prioritized within the organization. Typically there is a Safety Management System (SMS) that emphasizes operational safety. Example SMS activities for AVs would include ensuring all safety drivers are trained, having viable processes to ground the operational fleet if a significant safety issue is discovered, and keeping metrics on the effectiveness of operational safety practices.

Beyond an SMS, there also needs to be a robust safety engineering activity for the AV design and deployment process. While only a rough guideline, one would expect to see perhaps 10% of the engineering workforce engaged in system and safety engineering, with perhaps one quarter of that (2.5% of the workforce) specifically dedicated to specialized safety activities such as hazard analysis.[240] These benchmark numbers come from non-autonomous vehicle development, so higher numbers might easily be required for especially complex AV efforts.

A robust safety culture is essential for producing a safe AV.[241] If a robust safety culture is indeed in place, it should be easy to provide ample evidence of its existence, including conformance to industry best practices and published guidelines.

---

[238] There are various definitions and frameworks for safety culture that end up in similar places. For a reasonable overview starting point, see:
https://en.wikipedia.org/wiki/Safety_culture
[239] "Just" is used in the sense of "justice." For example, see:
https://airlines.iata.org/analysis/just-culture-can-improve-safety
[240] See: https://youtu.be/5ythLOzQav0
[241] ISO 26262-2:2018 Sub-clause 5.4.2 requires a good safety culture. Annex B of that document has a two-page table with some example characteristics of good and poor safety cultures. Examples of a poor safety culture include lack of specific accountability and a reward system that favors cost and schedule over safety and quality. Clause 5.6 of ANSI/UL 4600 includes a number of attributes relevant to a good safety culture.

4.7.4. We have excellent system engineering

Potential claim: Our system engineers are very good, so safety will naturally be addressed as we execute our design process.

- Do your system engineers perform hazard identification and risk mitigation as an explicit part of their workflow?

Sometimes companies do not feel a need to specifically address safety as an internal activity because they believe they have a strong system engineering organization. However, doing system engineering alone is insufficient to reach acceptable safety.

While system and safety engineering are cousins, safety engineering involves a specific set of activities and skills that are distinct from more general system engineering. Safety activities might be included under a system engineering umbrella, but system engineering does not automatically achieve safety engineering without specific attention to safety.

System engineering tends to deal with design, integration, and management of complex systems, such as a car. It tends to emphasize a methodical design process, addressing life cycle considerations, managing the supply chain, and so on. Good system engineering is essential for safety, but does not cover everything.

Safety engineering starts with the concepts of system engineering and adds a set of activities and work products specifically intended to deal with safety.

Some key elements in safety engineering include:

- Identify risks, especially considering the severity of potential loss events
- Identify safety goals and architectural approaches to mitigate risks
- Create safety requirements in the context of the system architecture and safety goals
- Ensure that risks are adequately mitigated in the design
- Foster and ensure the health of a safety culture for both design and operations
- Independently evaluate the effectiveness of risk mitigation approaches
- Independently evaluate the effectiveness of safety processes

It is common for system engineering and safety engineering roles to iterate between those two perspectives with different architectural approaches. System engineers might propose an approach that provides redundancy to help mitigate equipment faults, but safety engineers might in turn identify issues such as single points of failure. That in turn prompts a revision from system engineers, with the iteration continuing until both sides can be sure the result is acceptable.

At a more philosophical level, it is common for system engineers to focus on the question "will these pieces work together?" Safety engineers spend more focus on "what will happen when pieces break?" There is certainly overlap between the two fields, but a distinct safety engineering effort is required to achieve acceptable safety. If someone says that safety engineering is not needed because they have system engineering, then expect that team to have safety issues.

4.8. Human drivers are bad

Summary: Saying that human drivers are bad does not necessarily mean an AV will be safe. Computer-based systems have their own failures and weaknesses too.

A common argument for AV adoption revolves around statements of the form: humans are poor drivers, so of course a computer-based system will be better. However, this type of argument tends to assume that computers will function perfectly. Anyone who has experienced a computer "glitch," or had to turn the power off and then back on to fix a problem with any piece of electronics should know better.[242]

4.8.1. Human drivers are terrible, so AVs will be safe

Potential claim: Everyone knows human drivers are terrible, so anything involving technology doing the driving is sure to be safer.

Alternate claims: Human drivers cause huge numbers of deaths on the road each year, so computer drivers will be safer.

- Human drivers are not as incredibly bad as the talking points imply.
- This assumes that AVs will not have their own failures.

Any argument of the form "human drivers are bad, so computer drivers will be better" misses the obvious point that computers will make mistakes too – just different ones. While an obviously invalid argument for AV safety, this type of messaging is nonetheless a frequently encountered support for the proposition that AVs will be safe.[243]

Before we get to the problems about computers not being able to drive perfectly, we should first examine the presumption that humans are bad drivers. The claim that humans are bad drivers is not as clear-cut as AV proponents make it out to be.

We will get into the complexities of human driver mishap rates in a later chapter, but for now consider that in the US there is one fatal crash about every 100M miles of driving – including all the crashes from drunk and distracted drivers. For an average vehicle use of about 30 miles per day, that is more than 9000 years of daily driving between fatal crashes for a single driver. Yes, we would like it to be a lot better. But when you consider how often consumer electronics suffer hardware and software failures, that is far

---

[242] Yes, this includes rebooting entire vehicles. For an example, see Roper 2019: https://insideevs.com/features/380532/how-to-rebot-tesla-model-3/
[243] See also the "94% human error" myth discussed in section 4.10.1.

fewer failures than we demand of any other computer-based system used in daily life.

A related statement is that human drivers kill something like 40,000 people a year in the US, so computers will do better. There is no doubt that this is a tragic number that can and should be reduced. But people in the US also drive an incredibly large number of miles. That 40,000 fatalities is simply another way of saying about one fatal crash per 100M miles.

Humans are amazingly good drivers considering the complexity of the task and the comparatively low amount of training and operational oversight involved with the driving public. Doing even better is a worthy goal to be sure. But saying that human drivers are terrible is a disingenuous narrative when comparing them to typical computer-based technology. Getting AVs safe will take a tremendous amount of work, and simply cannot be taken for granted as an inevitable outcome.

A related point is that human drivers are quite good at compensating for failures in the underlying vehicle equipment. If you read a typical high-profile story for an automotive recall, you will often see that there are thousands of complaints on file about the problem, compared to perhaps a few dozen fatalities. As an example, a recall for General Motors antilock braking issues was associated with 10,861 complaints to NHTSA, 2111 crashes, 293 injuries, and no fatalities.[244] That means that human drivers were able to avoid crashes almost 80% of the time there was a malfunction severe enough to take the time to complain about (and likely many more incidents that did not even generate a complaint). Even if a crash happened, 86% of the time there was no injury, and there were no fatalities at all, at least in part because the driver was able to partially mitigate the severity of the crash.

To be as safe as human drivers, AVs will need to not only be able to drive nearly mistake-free, but also be able to compensate for problems that happen in the vehicle and compensate for unsafe environmental situations. An anti-lock braking system failure can happen just as easily on an AV as it can on a conventional vehicle. Designing in failure compensation skills will require significantly more effort than teaching an AV how to drive in well-behaved environments with a defect-free vehicle.

It is unclear how long it will take AV technology to mature to the point that it can operate as safely as a human driver in open-world environments such as public roads. Given that tens of billions of dollars are being spent to get there, one can argue it is just a matter of time and money. But we are not there yet, and nobody really knows when we will get there at enough scale to make a significant difference in road safety. Statements that AVs will inevitably be safer than human drivers are purely aspirational.

The most that can be said now is that AV technology holds the *promise* of *potentially* improved safety.

---

[244] See: https://www.nytimes.com/1999/07/22/us/gm-admits-brake-flaws-after-inquiry.html

In highly constrained, structured environments it is likely that AVs will eventually become safer than even expert human drivers. Consider that airport inter-terminal shuttle light rail systems have been safely operating with no human minder for decades. However, the structured environment for those trains typically includes automated access doors and other measures to keep people and other obstacles off the tracks so there is nothing for the trains to hit. Deploying a similarly constrained AV system safely should be achievable. But expanding beyond a very heavily controlled, constrained environment is still a work in progress.

4.8.2. AVs won't drive drunk

Potential claim: AVs won't drive drunk, so they will be better than human drivers.

Alternate claims: AVs won't text and drive...; AVs won't drive impaired...; AVs won't experience road rage...; AVs can avoid the most common crashes for human drivers...

- These claims ignore that AVs will make different mistakes than human drivers. It is unclear whether the net result will be safer or not.

Computers will not literally drive drunk, but they do lack common sense. In particular, machine learning-based systems are notoriously brittle to slight changes to situations compared to data they have been trained on. They can also be confused by novel situations which they incorrectly determine match their training data.[245] They can also game incentives in unexpected ways that do not align with what a human would perceive to be the intended goal. The stories of failures of systems using this technology are legion.[246] Overall, machine learning has a number of limitations that need to be considered when incorporating that technology into a safety-critical system.[247]

Given the significant reliance of most AVs on machine learning-based technology, is likely that computer-driven vehicles will make different mistakes than humans. Those mistakes are likely to involve limitations to AV designs rather than decision making impaired by alcohol, drugs, fatigue, or distracted driving.

While computers not making the same mistakes as humans is a start, safety outcomes cannot be predicted without accounting for mistakes that AVs will inevitably make.

---

[245] As an example, there was the incident in which an automated camera system repeatedly confused a linesman's bald head for a soccer ball. See Vincent 2020: https://www.theverge.com/tldr/2020/11/3/21547392/ai-camera-operator-football-bald-head-soccer-mistakes

[246] For a sampling of failures in consumer goods, see Leadem 2017: https://www.entrepreneur.com/slideshow/289621

[247] An overview identifying seven areas of limitation with examples is provided by Choi 2021: https://spectrum.ieee.org/ai-failures

4.9. An AV safety hierarchy of needs

Summary: Safety does not mean just one thing. There is a set of things that all must be considered, ranging from the ability of the AV to drive down the road without hitting things to functional safety to a Just Culture organizational approach.

It is clear that when people talk about safety, they mean significantly different things. For some, safety means competent driving. For others, safety encompasses rare (but relevant) equipment failures that could make an otherwise competent automated driver crash. Many of the claims of safety we have just covered are relevant, and the issue is how to combine them rather than choosing one point of view as somehow the best.

Figure 4.1 An AV safety hierarchy of needs.

To make sense of the different points of view, we propose a maturity model for an organization's consideration of safety. An inspiration for this idea is Maslow's famous hierarchy of needs.[248] All levels in the hierarchy shown in Figure 4.1 are required to drive with acceptable safety. However, organizations developing autonomous vehicles have to take care of the lower levels before they are likely to have the luxury of addressing higher levels.

To draw the parallel to Maslow's needs hierarchy, if a company is starving for cash to run its operations, they are going to care more about getting the

---

[248] Summary here: https://en.wikipedia.org/wiki/Maslow%27s_hierarchy_of_needs

next demo or funding milestone compared to lifecycle system safety and socio-technical considerations. That might put such a company down at the bottom-most level of basic driving functionality. Once the organizational survival needs for safety (do not hit stuff on the road during the demo) are taken care of, more sophisticated aspects of safety can then be addressed. Progressing up the hierarchy happens when basic driving is taken care of, and funders include higher levels of safety maturity in progress milestones.[249] The layers are as follows.

Basic driving functionality: The vehicle works in a defined environment without hitting any objects or other road users, perhaps for a funding milestone demo.

Defensive driving: The vehicle has expert driving skills, actively avoiding driving situations that present increased risk. This is analogous to the outcome of sending a human driver to defensive driving school. At some point the automated driver becomes as good as an expert human driver for the driving task itself. Assuming no malfunctions in the equipment, the AV can drive as well as an experienced human driver who is free of impairment, proactively handles potentially risky situations, and does not make reasonably avoidable driving errors.

Systematic hazard analysis: Engineering effort has been spent analyzing and mitigating risks not just from driving functions, but also potential technical malfunctions, forced exits from the intended operational design domain, and so on. An example approach would be to complete a Hazard And Risk Analysis (HARA) from ISO 26262, although this might not be sufficient for an AV.

Functional safety: Redundancy and engineering rigor have been used according to a principled approach (e.g., based on ASILs per ISO 26262). All risks stemming from technical faults inside the system have been mitigated to an acceptable level.

Safety of the Intended Function (SOTIF): "Unknowns" have been addressed, as well as potential functional insufficiencies due to imperfect operation of sensors and actuators in dealing with the real world (e.g., not all radar pulses sent out will successfully result in a signal returned to the radar's sensor). Any requirements gaps have been closed, and the use of machine learning has been accounted for in validation. All of this might be done in conformance with ISO 21448.

System-level safety: Safety analysis and risk mitigation have accounted for things beyond just the driving task, including lifecycle considerations. Hazard analysis and mitigation have been extended to both engineering and support process aspects, and a safety case has been used to ensure acceptable safety. All this might be done in conformance with ANSI/UL 4600.

Socio-technical considerations: Aspects of interaction among the AV, other road users, regulators, and other stakeholders have been considered

---

[249] To be clear, higher levels of safety should be addressed on a safety roadmap from the beginning. This hierarchy is an attempt to explain what happens in many projects and why it happens rather than how things would be in an ideal world.

with regard to safety. One example is resolving how and when an AV might acceptably violate traffic laws.

Just Safety Culture: The culture of the organization building, operating, and maintaining the AV continuously improves safety according to Just Culture principles in a blame-free manner.

As with the Maslow hierarchy, the levels are not exclusive. Rather, all levels need to operate concurrently, with the highest concurrently active level indicating progress toward safety maturity. An additional consideration that must be addressed is cybersecurity. Rather than being a level in safety, this might be thought of as having its own maturity levels and its own journey that runs in parallel with safety.

4.10. Misleading AV industry talking points regarding safety

Summary as a riddle: How can you tell a government relations specialist from the AV industry is spouting misinformation when they promote AV safety and champion an AV industry self-governance policy?

In this section we consider a set of talking points used by the AV industry to spread what seems best described as disinformation.[250] Some of the points sound similar to the safety definitions already discussed, such as the "94% human error" myth. However, the emphasis here is on outright myths rather than points of view that might be reasonable if the contextual limitations are made clear. Thus, none of the talking points in this section are legitimate statements to make about safety. Rather, when we see them employed they tend to be aimed at deflecting, defusing, or otherwise evading legitimate concerns about safety in a way that lets the industry shrug off its obligation to ensure the safety of both its customers and other road users.

The talking points here are presented as "myths" in contrast to claims, with each "myth" being a statement that is false but presented as true. The various myths have been collected from both written sources and verbal discussions at conferences and other venues which are not readily citable. However, anyone who has watched a panel session[251] or heard a pitch by industry promoters of lax AV regulation will find most if not all of these myths familiar. No attributions are made. The point here is to discuss the industry as a whole rather than indict a particular industry representative who happened to be the one we saw spouting the usual talking points trotted out by most all of them.

---

[250] This section is an expanded version of: Koopman, "Autonomous Vehicle Myths: The Dirty Dozen," EE Times, Oct. 22, 2021. https://www.eetimes.com/autonomous-vehicle-myths-the-dirty-dozen/

[251] These events are difficult to access and cite, but a representative summary of one is (paywall, but free trial available) Yoshida 2021: https://ojoyoshidareport.com/u-s-lawyers-perpetuate-regulation-myths-at-the-autonomous-2/

It is our hope that other stakeholders, policymakers, and regulators can use this myth list to recognize the disinformation for what it is and steer conversations back to productive directions that support safety. We need more transparency and honest discussion — not a continuation of this empty rhetoric.[252]

It is important to be clear that, from everything we have seen, the rank-and-file engineers, and especially the safety professionals (if the company has any) are trying to do the right thing within the constraints they must live with. It is more the influencers, government relations staff, and policy people, not the engineers, who are providing the facile talking points. And it is the high-level managers — the ones who set budgets, priorities, and milestones — who determine whether safety teams have sufficient resources and authority to build an AV that will be acceptably safe.

4.10.1. 94% human error

Myth #1: 94% of vehicle fatalities are due to human error.

Alternate myths: 94% of fatal crashes are due to bad human choices; drivers cause the vast majority of crashes; …

• This incorrectly characterizes the underlying study data.

US Department of Transportation, among many others, spent years promoting the notion that "the major factor in 94 percent of all fatal crashes is human error"[253] typically shortened in verbal presentations to 94% of fatal crashes are due to human error, or sometimes 94% of crashes are due to bad choices made by human drivers. This is typically followed by a mention of how much of a problem impaired and distracted drivers are. An implied claim is that AVs will be almost 20 times safer (only suffer from that remaining 6% of crashes) if we get rid of those oh-so-unreliable human drivers. Claims from other sources of "90% of crashes are due to bad human drivers" and the like seem to stem from the same source material.

To be sure, impaired human driving is a problem. But the statistic being quoted does not support the claim being made.[254] Rather, the statistic reflects that 94% of crashes are said to have human error as a contributing factor. The DOT publication quote in full that is the source of this statistic says:

> *"The critical reason was assigned to drivers in an*
> *estimated 2,046,000 crashes that comprise 94 percent of*

---

[252] We have numbered the myths for easier reference. Making yourself a bingo card and bringing it to the next regulatory/policy panel session you attend to see if you can score a win is optional.

[253] NHTSA, Automated Driving Systems 2.0: a vision for safety, 2017, page i: https://www.nhtsa.gov/sites/nhtsa.gov/files/documents/13069a-ads2.0_090617_v9a_tag.pdf

[254] For a more detailed analysis, see: https://safeautonomy.blogspot.com/2018/06/a-reality-check-on-94-percent-human.html

the NMVCCS crashes at the national level. However, in
none of these cases was the assignment intended to blame
the driver for causing the crash."[255]

A "critical reason" in the reported data is "the immediate reason for the critical event and is often the last failure in the causal chain." Critical reasons attributed to a driver include "panic"[256] – which sometimes means that the vehicle equipment or roadway infrastructure failed catastrophically, and the driver succumbed to panic rather than avoiding a crash. The source also says "Normally, one critical reason is assigned per crash and as such can be subjective in nature." Importantly, the critical reason "may not be the cause of the crash nor does it imply the assignment of fault to a vehicle, driver, or the environment in particular."

In English: sometimes the driver causes the crash. But at other times something goes wrong, and a driver who fails to avoid a crash caused by that something else gets left holding the bag. If the driver fails to avoid a theoretically avoidable crash, then the driver's imperfection is the critical reason.

Yes, drivers should try their best to avoid crashes regardless of circumstance. And as we discussed in section 4.8.1 overall human drivers are quite good at that. But they are not perfect – nor is it reasonable to expect them to be.

Sometimes a critical reason assigned to a driver does indeed mean that the driver made a mistake that caused a crash. But even then, an AV might make the same mistake. Mistakes such as "recognition error" assigned to human driver crashes are likely to be made by AVs as well. Machine learning-based perception systems are notoriously brittle to unusual shapes and objects, and can misclassify things just as people can. So even if you believe it is really the human driver's fault, an automated driver might well make exactly the same error.

Other human "errors" are failures of a human driver to compensate for some problem in the environment or vehicle failure that happened through no fault of their own. Say a wheel falls off the car or a tree falls into the road, but an analyst judges that a human driver should have been able to stop safely anyway. For whatever reason the human driver fails to stop safely, perhaps because of "panic." It is hardly fair to say that "human error" or "bad judgment" was the primary cause of the crash. Rather, the human failed to perfectly prevent a crash when presented with a high-risk situation. An AV might – or might not – do better.

---

[255] Traffic Safety Facts: Crash Stats, Critical Reasons for Crashes Investigated in the National Motor Vehicle Crash Causation Survey, February 2015, DOT HS 812 115, https://crashstats.nhtsa.dot.gov/Api/Public/ViewPublication/812115
[256] The Feb 2015 brief report summarizes and puts a bit of quotable spin on the underlying data report, which is National Motor Vehicle Crash Causation Survey, July 2008, DOT HS 811 059. See:
https://crashstats.nhtsa.dot.gov/Api/Public/ViewPublication/811059

Some human drivers do make bad choices and drive incompetently. But the cited data makes it clear that the result is nowhere near 94% of crashes that could be avoided by replacing human drivers with AVs – even assuming AVs are as good as a person who does not make "bad choices." In 2019, alcohol was a factor in 28% of fatalities, and distracted driving was a factor in 8.7% of fatalities.[257] There is a big gap between that and 94%.

After a sustained campaign to debunk the 94% narrative, including highly visible statements by the Chair of the National Transportation Safety Board, NHTSA finally backed away from the disinformation and the AV industry has modified its approach.[258] The AV industry talking point is now a somewhat narrower "human error is a factor in 94% of fatal crashes" or the like. While technically accurate, it has the same rhetorical effect as the myth and does not further the safety conversation in a productive manner.

The question that matters is when AVs will be at least as good as human drivers, given that there will no longer be a human driver to blame for whatever might go wrong on the road. Anyone invoking the 94% statistic as a compelling safety reason to adopt AVs is pumping the technology rather than encouraging an informed discussion about safety.

4.10.2. Regulation vs. Innovation

Myth #2: You can have either innovation or regulation, not both.
- You can easily have both innovation and regulation so long as the regulation is not based on a fixed functionality test or a "building code"-style implementation constraint.

Current automotive safety regulatory approaches are largely based on performance tests that demonstrate a particular safety feature functions in a particular way. In the name of repeatability and objectivity, they go so far as to specify distances from particular pieces of vehicle equipment, shape of warning symbols, brightness of lights, and so on.

For example, Federal Motor Vehicle Safety Standard (FMVSS) 138[259] specifies the symbol that needs to be displayed when tire pressure is lower than a specific amount under specific test conditions of temperature, road speed, driving times, and so on. This makes for an unambiguous testing specification that might indeed stifle some types of innovation that would nonetheless accomplish the intended goal of making sure failure of a low pressure tire does not cause a crash during driving. Nonetheless, this specificity and inflexibility is seen as providing a level playing field for all

---

[257] To be sure, 37% of fatalities involving alcohol and distraction leaves serious room for improvement. But is nowhere close to 94%, and other factors such as roadway construction can also be factors in such crashes. Data source: DOT HS 813 060: https://crashstats.nhtsa.dot.gov/Api/Public/Publication/813060

[258] See Wilson 2022: https://usa.streetsblog.org/2022/01/31/it-aint-94-percent-ntsb-chair-jennifer-homendy-on-the-role-of-human-error-in-car-crashes/

[259] See: https://www.law.cornell.edu/cfr/text/49/571.138

carmakers and, more importantly to the industry, is said to provide regulatory certainty.[260]

Because of their nature, some FMVSS rules require there to be a steering wheel or a driver visible dashboard. This might make no sense in an AV that does not need a steering wheel or a dashboard, perhaps because there is not even a driver compartment. Such rules can indeed impede the deployment of autonomous cargo vehicles.

But the point of FMVSS rules is not the measurements, the dashboard icons, the steering wheel, the rearview camera display, and so on. The point is to ensure that vehicles implement countermeasures to safety defects that have caused crashes in the past such as: driving with deflated tires, ineffective crash protection for passengers, headlights that are too dim for proper visibility, poor rearward visibility causing run-overs of children when backing, and so on.

Evolving beyond the current FMVSS approach requires moving away from an overly prescriptive testing regime to something more goal oriented. For example, the requirement can be that the manufacturer must demonstrate that a tire with out-of-specification pressure will be detected and corrected within so many miles of driving by an alternate method if the FMVSS test is unsuitable. This approach would not be a trivial effort, but it can be done without abandoning the concept of having safety regulations.[261]

A more general approach to less constraining regulations is to get the government out of the business of creating safety standards. Instead, the government could use a regulatory approach based on requiring compliance to standards the industry itself has written.

To consider a simple example, the government could, to a large degree, regulate road testing safety by requiring compliance to the SAE J3018 on-road testing safety standard with related reporting of safety metrics.[262] That standard is all about making sure that the human safety driver is properly qualified and trained. It also helps ensure that testing operations are conducted in a responsible manner consistent with good engineering

---

[260] A frequent AV regulatory talking point is that companies want "regulatory certainty." It is advantageous to be able to create a design knowing exactly what test regulators will run, and having no concern other than passing that very specific (and limited) test. On the other hand, tests of that sort are wholly unsuited to validating software safety. Other life-critical industries use other compliance models largely based on industry standards, especially when computer-based system safety is a core concern.

[261] One point of view is that the car companies have nobody but themselves to blame for insisting over the years that NHTSA create a regulatory approach that is so dependent on precise, inflexible FMVSS tests. For a proposed alternative see Koopman, 2018: https://thehill.com/opinion/technology/394945-how-to-keep-self-driving-cars-safe-when-no-one-is-watching-for-dashboard/

[262] See: https://www.sae.org/standards/content/j3018_202012/

validation and road safety practices. It places no constraints on the autonomy technology being tested.[263]

The primary industry standards for deployed AVs in the US are ISO 26262 (functional safety), ISO 21448 (safety of the intended function, or SOTIF), and ANSI/UL 4600 (system-level safety). Indeed, there has already been a US DOT/NHTSA regulatory proposal to require the AV industry to conform to precisely those standards. [264] None of the standards stifle innovation. Rather, they promote a level playing field so companies cannot skimp on safety to gain a competitive time to market advantage while putting other road users at undue risk. Most importantly, these standards have been written by many of the very companies that complain about overly burdensome regulations.

If a company states that safety is its #1 priority, how can that possibly be incompatible with regulatory requirements to follow industry consensus safety standards written and approved by the industry itself?

4.10.3. We already have regulations

Myth #3: States and the federal government already have regulations in place for AV operations that cover safety, so no additional regulations are needed.

- The federal government has no regulations in place specific to autonomous vehicle safety, nor of automotive software safety in general.[265]
- Paradoxically, even as they say regulations are sufficient, the AV industry has been waging a state-by-state barnstorming campaign to create a "regulatory path" to deployment by pushing for new state AV safety regulations. Those regulations dramatically favor the AV industry at the expense of protections for public safety.

For all practical purposes, there are no US Government rules requiring AV companies to ensure that their autonomous driving functions are safe when they are deployed. Existing Federal vehicle regulations (FMVSS) do not cover autonomous vehicle safety other than to modify existing FMVSS rules to permit driverless interior configurations (e.g., eliminate a requirement for a steering wheel airbag if there is no steering wheel to mount one on).

---

[263] That standard presumes the driver is inside the vehicle being tested. Adapting that standard for cargo delivery AVs with no passenger compartment and remote operators could certainly be done.

[264] See NHTSA 2020:
https://www.nhtsa.gov/sites/nhtsa.gov/files/documents/ads_safety_principles_anprm_website_version.pdf

[265] NHTSA has started required crash reports for vehicle automation technology as a standing general order, but has no requirement for regulatory approval so long as the vehicle is self-certified to FMVSS.
See: https://www.nhtsa.gov/laws-regulations/standing-general-order-crash-reporting

States have a variety of regulatory approaches. But with few exceptions those approaches leave all requirements for autonomy safety engineering and testing safety in the hands of the AV companies with minimal oversight. If the AV company can manage to test a few vehicles for a moderate number of miles without causing embarrassing crashes or otherwise irritating enforcement officials, it can do whatever it wants so long as it takes out a required minimum insurance policy. That can continue until there is a crash too scary to ignore.[266]

Recently the AV industry has campaigned state-by-state for extraordinarily lax regulatory terms in the name of promoting jobs and economic growth. States are pitted against each other with a narrative that if one state does not pass favorable rules the industry will just spend its money in another state. If that does not work, states (and the Federal government) are threatened with the prospect of China beating the US with autonomous vehicle technology. There is every indication this regulatory campaign will continue indefinitely.[267]

There are a few exceptions to this trend. New York City DOT adopted a rule that requires conformance to the SAE J3018 road testing safety standard.[268] Massachusetts requires that testers "review and understand" SAE J3018, although it does not require them to comply with that standard.[269]

No jurisdiction in the US requires conformance to industry safety standards for deploying AVs.

4.10.4. Recalls and lawsuits mitigate risk

Myth #4: We do not need proactive regulation because fear of litigation and NHTSA recalls will force AV companies to do the right thing.

- Recalls and lawsuits do not happen until after the harm has been done, and have an uneven record of effectiveness.

There are no federal regulations restricting deployment of AVs so long as they are self-certified to (or exempted from) FMVSS requirements. As a practical matter, under current regulations NHTSA gives AV companies a

---

[266] Regulations are changing all the time, but the current trend as this is written is for more permissive regulations. A significant amount of testing, especially of heavy trucks, occurs in Texas. Their regulations incorporate typical features of such approaches. For example, there is no requirement for a driving test or other assessment of ADS driving competence before granting the ADS a license to drive, even for heavy trucks on public roads. Here is the Texas 4-page regulatory regime: https://capitol.texas.gov/tlodocs/85R/billtext/pdf/SB02205F.pdf

[267] Case study material for several states including bills and hearing videos can be found at: https://safeautonomy.blogspot.com/2022/02/kansas-av-regulation-bill-hearings.html

[268] See: https://rules.cityofnewyork.us/rule/autonomous-self-driving-vehicles/

[269] See: https://www.mass.gov/doc/memorandum-of-agreement-to-test-automated-driving-systems-on-public-ways-in-massachusetts/download

free pass on ADS safety until it can be proven vehicles already on the road have significant safety defects.[270] The main regulatory mechanism is the possibility for NHTSA to address unreasonably dangerous design features after the fact via recalls.

Contrary to some popular belief, a recall is not the act of taking a vehicle to a dealer to get something repaired. The potential repair itself is one way to accomplish what is termed a remedy. A recall is an administrative process by which the vehicle maker notifies NHTSA of a need to remedy a safety defect. Whether that remedy is an over-the-air software update,[271] mailing owners a sticker to put in their owner's manual, or a dealer visit to reprogram or replace parts, it is still a recall.

NHTSA and the AV maker work together to conduct a recall when there is a problem discovered on cars already on the road. Carmakers are required to inform NHTSA of problems in a timely manner and fix the problem according to the recall process. They also must notify NHTSA about progress made (or lack thereof) on deploying the remedy to affected vehicles. That process can easily take months while the car company and potentially NHTSA investigate. There is no routine NHTSA penalty invoked by a company deploying a dangerous vehicle, so long as the company follows the recall process. While it is important and good that such a process is in place, this process routinely leaves dangerous vehicles on the road for months at a time or longer while the process plays out.[272]

Sometimes signs of potential defects are found by NHTSA via analysis of customer complaints or analysis of crash trends. Interventions based on such findings cannot take place until enough incidents have occurred that customers are prompted to complain, or statistical crash data becomes obviously problematic. As an example, an investigation was launched into

---

[270] There are informal mechanisms to discourage release of problematic features and put pressure on car companies to improve safety. But as we have seen especially with Tesla those less formal mechanisms can be ineffective in deterring the release and subsequent need to recall vehicle features with safety defects. As an example, see Muraf 2022:
https://www.cnn.com/2022/02/13/business/tesla-recall-boombox/index.html

[271] The recall process is showing signs of strain under the realities of continual over-the-air software updates, but that issue goes beyond the scope of our discussion. Until regulations change, over-the-air software updates relevant to safety must still follow the recall process. Among other things, this enables NHTSA to track the fraction of the vehicle population that has received applicable remedies.

[272] It is sometimes said that over-the-air recalls permit essentially instant fixes to safety defects. This narrative is then used to justify a relaxed need for validation because fixes are so quick and cheap. The reality is that in practice it can take months to trace road incidents, injuries, and sometimes even deaths back to a particular defect, especially if driver error is initially blamed for what turns out to be a vehicle defect. Once the defect is understood maybe it can be fixed in perhaps a week. But while that fix might take a week, the vehicles were in fact dangerous and potentially causing harm for many months overall.

Tesla driver assistance Autopilot systems crashing into emergency responders, typically at night when emergency flares and responder vehicle lights were active. By the time that investigation was launched there had already been 11 such crashes resulting in 17 injuries and one death, with the crashes spanning 3.5 years. [273] Crashes continued to occur during the investigation, which is ongoing at the time of this writing.

There can be enormous financial pressure for car companies to bargain with NHTSA regarding the scope of a recall, or attempt a remedy that is only partially effective if it costs much less. For example, it is common to see software workarounds for hardware defects, which might not necessarily be fully effective at mitigating the underlying safety issue. NHTSA is incentivized to bargain if for no other reason than significant resource limitations. When the recall system suffers significant delays or fails to react strongly enough to a problem, deaths and injuries can continue for years.[274]

The threat of litigation by victims or their surviving families does put some pressure on car companies toward safety. However, this pressure suffers from the same limitations as insurance motivations to improve safety. An AV can easily be many times more dangerous than a human driver while still being affordable from a liability point of view. Paying a few million dollars per fatality for a road testing campaign or initial deployment is a drop in the bucket compared to the operating costs of an AV development effort. If victims and their families that do not want to settle, it is a simple matter to drag out legal processes for years to give the AV company time to find an investor exit. And even then, awards are still likely to be small compared to the money to be made by cutting corners on safety to speed up the race to market.

While both recalls and threat of litigation have a small moderating effect on AV company risk taking, neither are anywhere near sufficient to ensure that AVs will be deployed with societally acceptable safety.

4.10.5. Standards???

Myth #5: Existing safety standards aren't appropriate because (pick one or more of):
- they are not a *perfect* fit;
- no *single* standard does everything required for safety;
- they were not written *specifically* for AVs;
- they would reduce safety because they prevent the developer from being safer than the standard permits;
- they would force the AV to be less safe;
- standards are "unproven" or not in common industry use.

---

[273] See: https://static.nhtsa.gov/odi/inv/2021/INOA-PE21020-1893.PDF

[274] The Takata airbag fiasco lasted more than a decade, and has been said to involve both industry and NHTSA being slow to react and slow to issue recalls. See Tabuchi 2014: https://www.nytimes.com/2014/09/12/business/air-bag-flaw-long-known-led-to-recalls.html

- Standards? We ain't got no standards. We don't need no standards! *I don't have to show you any stinkin' standards!*[275]

- Such statements are a combination of rhetorical tricks and misrepresentations.

The variations of these talking points amount to excuses as to why the AV industry does not conform to standards. They are a combination of rhetorical tricks and outright misrepresentations of how relevant safety standards work. ISO 26262, ISO 21448, and ANSI/UL 4600 all permit significant flexibility to be used in a way that makes sense. All three work together to fit any safe AV. We will address the talking points in turn.

"Not a perfect fit" amounts to saying that the company only wants a bespoke safety standard instead of getting its safety standards "off the rack" so to speak. But the use of the word "perfect" here is typically disingenuous. A standard that is a 99.999% fit is not a 100% fit, and therefore not "perfect." The question should be whether safety standards are usable in practice. Moreover, all three safety standards permit significant flexibility and permit the majority of written standard's content to be adjusted to suit if a reason is documented why that makes sense.

No "single" standard does everything required for safety because the standards are purposefully written to cover different parts and work together as a team. The industry teams who write these standards have liaisons to avoid overlap as well as shared voting committee members across ISO 26262, ISO 21448, ANSI/UL 4600, and other relevant standards. One single standard for everything in an AV would simply be too big a chunk to bite off at once. Given the existence of pre-AV automotive safety standards, creating a one-stop-shopping AV standard would violate standards organization operating procedures due to the impermissible overlap between standards that would result.

The statement that safety standards were not written "specifically" for AVs is plainly incorrect and beside the point. What matters is which standards get the job done, not whether they also might help make non-autonomous vehicles safe. The scope of ISO 26262 is for all vehicles, including relevant aspects of AVs. The initial version of ISO 21448 was just for driver assistance systems, but the currently issued version explicitly covers autonomous vehicles. Without question, ANSI/UL 4600 has been specific to autonomous vehicles from the start.

The notion that safety standards prevent developers from being safer than they would otherwise be is utter nonsense. The safety standards being discussed set minimum requirements on safety, not maximum permitted safety practices. This talking point is simply made up from whole cloth.

The notion that safety standards will incentivize AV developers to be less safe than not using standards comes from a presumption that AV developers

---

[275] Really, all the variants boil down to this one. Shameless parody of: https://en.wikipedia.org/wiki/The_Treasure_of_the_Sierra_Madre_(film)#John_Huston's_screenplay

will actively game the standard. This talking point often says that standards force AV developers into a "checkbox" mentality of doing the minimum necessary. The reality is that any automotive company already has its own internal engineering processes that it follows – or it has no business building safety-critical systems. The point of the standards is to make sure that the internal engineering processes are robust enough and are being followed. If an AV company plays a "check the boxes" game with conformance theater for safety standards, there is nothing to stop them from doing it with their own internal standards. Adopting an industry standard is not the factor forcing any degradation of safety culture.

Finally, industry standards are said to be "unproven" or not in widespread industry use. All three of ISO 26262, ISO 21448, and ANSI/UL 4600 are in their second version. ISO 26262 in particular has been in existence for more than a decade. Having an industry refuse to adopt standards – that they themselves wrote – because they are "unproven" means they will never get proven and therefore never be in widespread use. This is just another variant of finding an excuse not to use the standards.

The reality with these talking points is that the automotive industry has had the luxury of regulators who do not force them to conform to their own industry-written safety standards. Industry regulatory advocates will say whatever it takes to keep it that way, even if what they are saying is laughable. (It is.)

4.10.6. A patchwork quilt of regulations

Myth #6: Local and state regulations need to be stopped to avoid a problematic patchwork approach that inhibits innovation

- Any patchwork effect is largely of the AV industry's own making

US states and municipalities control driver qualification, set traffic laws, and perform traffic law enforcement. In contrast, the federal government via NHTSA deals with equipment safety standards. The relatively clean separation between these two roles becomes murky when the equipment is doing the driving rather than a human driver.

For crewed AV testing, it is clear that the predominant factor in safety is the human safety driver. Thus, it makes sense for states to take the lead in regulating and enforcing rules related to safety drivers. States also set insurance requirements for all vehicles, issue driver's licenses, and so on. It seems reasonable for each state to set requirements and enforce those requirements for AV driving behavior on its roads.

Harmonization of laws across states in general has been accomplished over time not with federal laws, but rather with a collaborative state process through the Uniform Law Commission. Indeed, there is a model Automated Operation of Vehicles Act, but that model has not been adopted by any states[276] and such a uniform approach to state regulations does not seem to be supported by the AV industry.[277]

Municipalities are further empowered to set additional traffic rules to ensure safety in the face of local conditions. They can limit what types of vehicles are permitted on some roads, set speed limits, and enforce state traffic rules within their municipality. Municipalities in particular have an interest in ensuring the safety of their constituents during AV testing. They also should have a reasonable right to demand operational data from testers to ensure that their constituents are not being placed at undue risk.

The AV industry has lobbied aggressively for regulations in states they wish to operate in, with their proposals heavily favoring the industry. Regulation was discussed in section 4.10.3, but three characteristics are relevant to this section. The first is that every state bill turns out a little differently due to negotiations needed to get a bill passed. The objective of the AV industry seems to be getting the most favorable bill they can on a state-by-state basis rather than coordinating precisely the same bill language across all states. In these regards, any patchwork is of the AV industry's own making, especially since they decided not to support the uniform state regulation mechanism that was previously tried.

Another problematic characteristic of a typical state bill supported by the AV industry is a municipal preemption clause that prevents municipalities from overriding state AV regulations. This takes away the ability of a city to curb irresponsible AV developer behavior or adapt AV operational constraints to local conditions without petitioning the state to do it for them. If state regulations do not prohibit testing heavy trucks on any particular roads, a city is not able to stop big rigs from doing testing next to schools and playgrounds. Similarly, a city under the burden of a preemption clause cannot curtail failed testing attempts disrupting traffic in a downtown business district if test vehicles become immobilized. Municipal preemption can especially become a problem when AV lobbyists successfully convince a state legislature to force municipalities to accept undesired testing activity via a process we call autonomandering.[278] The AV industry derides any attempt of a municipality to impose safety restrictions on AVs as impeding progress via creating a patchwork of regulations.

---

[276] See: https://www.uniformlaws.org/committees/community-home?communitykey=4e70cf8e-a3f4-4c55-9d27-fb3e2ab241d6

[277] Auto Alliance response to draft Highly Automated Vehicles Act of June 15, 2018: https://www.uniformlaws.org/HigherLogic/System/DownloadDocumentFile.ashx?DocumentFileKey=feaf72ec-473e-5a78-0621-a5119a10eec4

[278] Autonomandering occurs when state representatives from one part of a state who control a key part of the state legislative process are lobbied to use municipal preemption to force the population from a different part of a state to be exposed to risks from AV testing and deployment that they would not voluntarily consent to. See section IV of: https://uclajolt.com/autonomous-vehicle-regulation-trust-the-impact-of-failures-to-comply-with-standards/

A third problematic issue is that the AV industry has successfully removed any licensing requirements from being imposed on operation without human safety drivers. Companies themselves are, in effect, authorized to issue a license for their own vehicle with little or no state oversight. In such states, any AV is presumed to be a competent driver with no examination and no road test. While this is presumably based on a narrative that companies have an interest in not being involved in crashes, it calls into question how issues such as license revocation based on an accumulation of moving violations ("points" systems) might work, or what the state can do to revoke a driver's license of an AV that proves unreasonably dangerous on public roads.

This area is still in flux. Nonetheless, in practice any time the word "patchwork" is invoked in an AV regulatory conversation, the real objective of the speaker is typically to be as close to unregulated as possible on a state-by-state basis.

4.10.7. The spirit of the standard

Myth #7: We conform to the spirit of ISO 26262, etc.

- Anything less than an unambiguous statement of conformance is just handwaving.

Often an AV company will mention one or more safety standards to give the impression they are following them, but not fully committed. In written documents phrases such as "use key principles from" or "follow practices drawn from" or "follow internal standards based on" refer to industry-written standards, but do not commit to following them. In verbal conversations one might hear that a company "follows the spirit of" a particular safety standard.

AV developers typically justify their "in the spirit of" statements by advancing the theory that there might be a need for deviation from the standard (beyond any deviations that the standards already permit). The statements never specify what the possibly required deviations might be, and we have never heard a concrete example of why such a deviation should be required. In practice there probably is no legitimate need for deviation driven by safety considerations.

As discussed in section 4.5.1, any "in the spirit of" statement is meaningless. Industry safety standards are all flexible enough to permit conformance, and permit safety activities above and beyond what is required by the standard. In reality, this type of statement is more likely to be an attempt to say that they do not follow the standard, but they want people to think they do, at least mostly.

A possible motivation for making such statements is that lawyers might want to avoid committing to something if nobody is forcing them to do so. That is understandable from their point of view in terms of giving up the least amount of ground possible in a perceived battle with regulatory authorities, but it impairs transparency. The dark side of the strategy is that it provides cover for companies that are not the best actors to hide any corner-cutting on safety. If companies are worried that they will be called out for not following a standard after a crash, they should spend the resources to actually follow the standard. Or they should not spend so much effort making public claims about safety being their top priority. Companies that are truly doing their best on safety should be transparent about conforming to industry consensus standards to raise the bar for others.

Consider whether you would ride in an airplane whose manufacturer said, "We conform to the spirit of the aviation safety standards, but we are very smart and our airplane is very special so we skipped some steps. It will be fine. This aircraft type hasn't killed anyone yet, so trust us."

Now ask yourself if you'd want to share the road with a test AV whose developer has said it wants the flexibility of not conforming to the road testing industry standards that the developer itself helped write.

4.10.8. Government regulator skills

Myth #8: Government regulators are not qualified to regulate the technology.

- Regulators can pick industry standards instead of writing their own from scratch.

This myth tends to operate in multiple parts. First it assumes that only test-based standards are appropriate, despite every other industry using process-based safety engineering standards. Then it criticizes government regulators for being too slow to write test-based standards (which, in fairness, are very difficult to write in a way to address industry criticisms – but the real problem is that test-based standards are the wrong way to go here). The final criticism is that regulators do not understand the technology well enough to write test-based standards for AVs, and so should not be allowed to regulate them. Instead, the argument continues, the industry should just be allowed to do what it wants to avoid "impeding innovation."[279]

NHTSA has already proposed invoking industry standards instead of writing new standards as previously discussed.

If we could trust industry – any industry – to self-police safety in the face of short-term profit incentive and organizational dysfunction, we would not need regulators. But that is not how the real world works. Trusting the automotive industry to self-regulate the development of immature, novel technology is unlikely to end well. It is possible, and important, for the industry to achieve a healthy balance between taking responsibility for safety and accepting regulatory oversight.

Telling regulators to sit on the sidelines until after the crash victims start piling up is not the right balance. The good news is now that AV-relevant safety standards exist, government regulators can simply require their use instead of having to create their own standards.

---

[279] It is almost as if the industry is painting the regulators into a corner to make sure it is as difficult as possible to regulate. Hmm.

4.10.9. Revealing the secret autonomy sauce

Myth #9: Disclosing AV testing data will give away the secret sauce intellectual property for autonomy.

- Testing safety is not about the autonomy's construction, but rather effectiveness of human test driver safety supervision.
- The relevant standards for AV safety do not require public disclosure of intellectual property.

Road testing safety is all about whether a human safety driver can effectively keep a test vehicle from creating elevated risk for other road users. That has nothing to do with the secret sauce autonomy intellectual property. It is about the effectiveness of the safety driver. Additionally, companies often say it would be too difficult or expensive to get or provide data to regulators. This does not make any sense.

AV companies loudly proclaim that safety is #1 and that their vehicles are or will be safer than human vehicles. They justify public road testing because they say they need to collect and analyze data from that testing. They can only know this by creating metrics for road safety and collecting data to prove that their claims are true. If they do not have any safety data from their testing, then they are just making up their safety claims. If they are just making up their safety claims, they should not be operating on public roads. On the other hand, if they do have data to back up their safety claims, they should be able to share it with regulators.

From a public policy point of view, states and municipalities are providing AV testers and for-profit AV operators with free access to a shared public resource in the form of public roads and human test subject road users. Given that AV technology is still immature, AV companies are planning to profit massively from access to this public resource, while putting other road users at potentially elevated risk. In exchange for the privilege of accessing that shared public resource, they should have an obligation to provide data demonstrating they are not subjecting the general public to undue risk.

If companies do not have data to prove that they are testing safely, they shouldn't be testing. If they think that providing testing safety data is too expensive, they cannot afford the price of admission for using public roads as a testbed.[280]

There is a potential issue with the data being requested. Some data is more about the maturity of technology, such as California disengagement reports.[281] To the degree those reports provide a horse race scorecard in the race to autonomy, that information is not relevant to public safety. Rather, regulators should collect data that indicates what level of risk is being presented to which portion of the population.

---

[280] Compared to the cost of renting out a dedicated test track and setting up various physical scenarios for testing, the cost of providing safety data to public stakeholders is a bargain.
[281] See: https://www.dmv.ca.gov/portal/vehicle-industry-services/autonomous-vehicles/disengagement-reports/

Test miles (risk exposure), zip codes of operation (who is exposed to the risk), and traffic violations [282] (measures of potentially reckless driving) should all be reported. AV testers should also report metrics of safety driver performance such as how often they suffer alertness lapses, how often they fail to take over when they should (for example, automation prevents a crash after the safety driver should have intervened), and whether tester qualification procedures are being followed.

The important thing is that metrics should be relevant to public safety rather than technology maturity. If an AV test platform regularly suffers near hits or its testers regularly fall asleep, that might be embarrassing to the company. But such road testing safety metrics certainly do not reveal the inner workings of its secret autonomous vehicle technology. Besides which, we all know that unprotected left turns are going to be tough. It's not a secret.

Currently, AV testers and even operators of advanced driver assistance systems are already required to provide data on all significant mishaps to NHTSA. [283] States and municipalities whose constituents are put at potential risk by AVs should be entitled to receive that same data. Moreover, that data collection should be expanded to include near hits, traffic rule violations (for example running red lights), and other safety-relevant data. If the companies do not know when there is a safety problem on the road, they cannot be said to be testing in a responsible manner. All data relevant to public safety should be reported to regulators in return for the privilege of testing on public roads.

4.10.10. Delaying AVs is murder

Myth #10: Delaying deployment of AVs is tantamount to killing people.

Alternate myth: AVs are sure to improve road safety, so any harm done short term by hasty deployment will be overwhelmed by long-term good. Therefore, there is a moral imperative to conduct hasty, potentially unsafe early operation.

- While we hope it will eventually be true, there is not yet any proof that AVs based on current technology will ever be safer than human drivers. Any harm now is weighed against only the hope of future benefit, not the certainty of future benefit.

---

[282] These are not traffic violations that were attempted by the automation features under test, but rather actual, real-world traffic violations that were not prevented by the safety driver. If a test platform blows through a stop sign that is a danger to the public, and no amount of "but muh secret sauce" protestations should permit a tester to hide that such an event happened. A disengagement that prevents a traffic violation, on the other hand, arguably need not be disclosed because that was the safety driver performing as expected to ensure safety.

[283] See NHTSA Standing Order from 2021: https://www.nhtsa.gov/laws-regulations/standing-general-order-crash-reporting-levels-driving-automation-2-5

The safety benefits of AVs are aspirational and targeted for some time in the future. Every year, that time seems to get further away. Given the track record of promises and delays, nobody really knows how far in the future. Moreover, there is no real proof to show that AVs will ever be safer than human-driven vehicles, especially with human-driven vehicles becoming ever safer themselves over time due to the addition of passive and active safety technology.

With tens of billions of dollars being spent on AV technology, plenty of investors are making big bets that the technology will succeed. And it seems reasonable to expect AVs will reach a point where they can be acceptably safe in appropriately restricted operational design domains (ODDs). But the "when" still remains a question mark, as does whether the net safety benefit will be compelling. Or there will be a net safety benefit at all.[284]

Ignoring industry best practices to put vulnerable road users at risk today should not be permitted in a bid to maybe, perhaps, someday, eventually save potential later victims if the technology proves viable.

A RAND study[285] urging early deployment is sometimes inaccurately invoked by proponents of the urgency to save lives narrative. That study indicates that if AVs are even slightly better than human drivers there can be long-term net reduction in harm. As the RAND study puts it, it can be beneficial to deploy while good rather than waiting for nearly perfect. However, the matter of uncertainty as to how safe (or dangerous) AVs will be at deployment was not addressed in that study. Most importantly, that study does not advocate deploying AVs when they are known to be more dangerous than human drivers in hopes that later savings of lives will compensate for initial harm.[286] Rather, it simply points out that even a little better than human drivers might be enough, rather than waiting for perfection.

If saving lives on the road today is indeed the No. 1 priority, then a small fraction of the tens of billions of dollars being spent on AVs could be spent on reducing the drunk driving rate (shockingly high in the US compared with some other countries[287]), improving roadway infrastructure, improving speed limit strategies, installing safer pedestrian crossings and bikeways, and so on – not on increasing near-term risk via premature deployment or irresponsible testing of AVs.

An additional consideration is that if saving lives is truly an AV company's #1 mission, bad press from a high-profile mishap can easily set the whole industry back, and potentially derail that mission for years.[288]

---

[284] It might be that society will eventually accept AVs that are modestly more risky than human drivers. But if that is where we end up, any argument that it is OK to kill more people now for a safety benefit later will have been based on a false promise.

[285] Kalra & Groves 2017: https://www.rand.org/pubs/research_reports/RR2150.html

[286] We revisit this report in section 5.3.2.

[287] See McCarthy 2016: https://www.forbes.com/sites/niallmccarthy/2016/08/11/the-worst-countries-in-the-world-for-drunk-driving-infographic/

[288] Just ask Uber ATG. Oh, wait, you can't, because they don't exist anymore.

4.10.11. No deaths ... yet

Myth #11: We haven't killed anyone yet, so that means we are safe.
* Getting lucky does not bestow safety.

In the context of a test program or small-scale deployment, having suffered no major crashes is statistically insignificant. Such arguments are really saying: "we have gotten lucky so far, and our plan is to continue to get lucky." If there is no evidence of robust, systematic safety engineering and operational safety practices, this amounts to a gambler on a winning streak claiming they will keep winning forever. Such a strategy works right up until the time when it stops working. Usually that happens sooner rather than later.

The implications of accepting this myth are disturbing. If every AV tester gets to make an unsupported claim of safety from the day they start road operations (which they have), they can operate however they like until there is a severe crash. In other words, every AV company gets one "free kill" before they are held to account for safety. Even if they believe they are 100 times more dangerous than a human driver (i.e., 1 million miles per fatality), they have a strong financial incentive to roll the dice for a few thousand miles of testing in hopes of being acquired by a big player before their luck runs out. While any single company might in reality get lucky, across an entire industry that will result in an unnecessarily elevated rate of public harm.[289]

We should not be giving developers a free pass on public safety, looking into the matter only after they have killed someone.

4.10.12. Fear of missing out

Myth #12: Other states/cities/countries let us test without any restrictions, so you should too.
* If all your friends jumped off a cliff, would you do that too?

Whether regulators are willing to put their constituents at increased risk in exchange for some economic benefit is a decision they are permitted to make. But the hard reality is that any tester who is not at least doing as well as SAE J3018 for road testing safety is not following accepted practices and is likely putting the local population at *unnecessary* risk.

In the board hearing for the 2018 Tempe AZ testing fatality, the NTSB Chair pointed out that other companies did not need to have a similar crash to learn the lessons of having a strong safety culture and a robust Safety Management System.[290] Many of the lessons from that tragedy were incorporated into a revision of SAE J3018 for road testing safety. If testers

---

[289] We revisit this topic in more detail in section 8.4.1 on bootstrap safety arguments.

[290] Anyone involved in AV safety and in particular AV testing safety should listen to the NTSB hearing on the Uber ATG fatality in Tempe AZ, and especially the first five minutes or so. A direct link to the part where safety culture is stressed within that hearing is: https://youtu.be/mSC4Fr3wf0k?t=178

refuse to follow that consensus industry standard, they have not taken that lesson to heart.

The responsibility of safety regulators is to promote safety, not pander to investors and economic development interests. Vulnerable road users should not act as unwitting test subjects for AV road testers who cannot even be bothered to commit to following accepted industry safety practices. Regulators should not feel inhibited from merely asking developers to follow the industry safety standards that, in many cases, the developers themselves helped write.

4.10.13. Testing deaths are a regrettable necessity

Myth #13: Testing deaths are a regrettable, but necessary price to pay for improved safety.

- The statistical budget for any company doing responsible public road testing is approximately zero fatalities.
- The correct metric is deaths per vehicle mile. Citing deaths per day or death counts compared to human-driven vehicles without normalizing for the huge disparity of exposure is a misrepresentation of the issue.

Usually, this argument is accompanied by an observation that approximately 100 people die per day on US roads from human-driven vehicles, so why get excited about one death from an AV? However, the proper risk comparison is not the number of deaths, but rather fatality rate per mile, or possibly per vehicle. Any comparison of AV or even automated driver assistance features needs to be in proportion to the use of the automated feature, not compared to the number of events happening in a much larger human-operated vehicle fleet.

In the US, fatal car crashes happen approximately once every 100 million miles. The entire industry has not yet accumulated 100 million miles of AV road testing, but we have already seen a testing fatality (Uber ATG in 2018). It is unlikely that AV test fleets will rack up more than 100 million miles of AV feature testing anytime soon,[291] so the industry has already over-spent its fatality "budget" for AV testing deaths over the foreseeable future. There is no justifiable reason to road test in a way that is likely to result in further testing-related fatalities. Following industry standards for safe testing is the very least that testers should be doing.

4.10.14. Self-certification

Myth #14: Self-certification has served the industry well, so it should not be changed.

- The industry will fight as hard as it can to avoid giving up their self-certification perk. However, no other major safety-critical industry is permitted to operate this way.

---

[291] A possible exception is Tesla FSD beta considered as an AV testing platform.

The US automotive industry has long enjoyed a perk not available to other regulated safety-critical industries: self-certification. With self-certification, a car company can deploy vehicles on the road without regulatory approval in advance. The company "self-certifies" that it meets any required safety standards. Application for self-certification approval is not required. The company just ships the cars when it thinks it is OK to ship. (In Europe they have type approval[292] that involves independent checks for conformance to relevant standards before shipment is authorized, but not in the US.)

Victims and their families involved with numerous wide-scale safety and environmental issues might think that self-certification has not served them well, even if the industry is happy with the situation. Exercise: Pick your favorite automotive industry safety or emissions scandal. Be sure to include class actions and death and injury suits, as well as criminal proceedings, verdicts, and settlements.[293] Ask how well self-certification has served the public.

It is important to remember that industry "self-certification" is only to FMVSS, and not to any functional or software safety standard. Companies are not even required to self-certify anything related to software and computer-based system safety. From a practical point of view, self-certification for computer-based system safety is currently meaningless.

Other industries follow their own safety standards (aviation, rail, chemical, power, mining, factory robotics, and building climate controls are examples). As far as we can tell, many automotive original equipment manufacturers (OEMs) – the companies that sell cars, rather than those companies' suppliers – do not. Suppliers often follow safety standards if OEMs pay accordingly. But the ball gets dropped at the OEM level for many if not most companies as far as we can tell.[294]

Automotive is the only life-critical equipment industry that is not required to follow its own industry safety standards.

Let that sink in.

With regard to self-certification, a core concept of safety standards and safety is independence. Without independence, it is in practice impossible to get sustainable safety. That is because there is always significant business pressure to take shortcuts or skip process steps to meet sales quotas or profitability goals. The Boeing 737 MAX scandal is largely attributable to a

---

[292] See: https://en.wikipedia.org/wiki/Type_approval#Automotive_industry
[293] Here is a list to pick from that includes automotive scandals:
https://safeautonomy.blogspot.com/p/safe-autonomy.html
[294] Companies do not disclose standards compliance so it is difficult to be sure, but this is the sense we get based on many interactions with industry.

compromise of such independence, in that case due to undermining of the independence of FAA oversight.[295]

Yet carmakers continually push back on any external oversight as well as even standards that require internal, but independent, checks and balances.

4.11. Summary

A reasonable description of safety is likely to combine a number of the different perspectives on safety we have discussed, while hopefully avoiding the myths and various pitfalls.

A statement that an AV is safe might mean a combination of statements that the AV:

- is expected to have fewer crashes, injuries, and/or fatalities than a human driver, perhaps with some additional safety margin
- has been tested for millions of miles with a low failure rate
- has been simulated for billions of miles with a low failure rate
- uses one or more design approaches to safety, which should include conformance to industry safety standards
- has had its overall risk reduced to an acceptable level (e.g., affordable insurance)
- does not present unreasonable risk to particular demographic segments of road users beyond just having overall acceptable risk
- addresses all the levels of the AV safety hierarchy of needs described, all the way up to and including having a robust, just safety culture
- does not indulge in statements perpetuating AV industry myths.

Each of the different definitions of safety has some applicability to achieving a level of safety that is likely to be considered societally acceptable. However, each concept of safety presented has limitations, ranging from pure marketing puffery to technically substantive portions of a credible overall safety plan.

Ultimately what matters is an AV design team explaining what exactly they mean by "safe" in a way that stakeholders not privy to the design details can reasonably understand. Once the meaning of a claim of safety is understood, there needs to be a reasonable expectation that the AV will actually be as safe as claimed.

---

[295] See: US House Committee on Transportation & Infrastructure report, 2020: https://transportation.house.gov/imo/media/doc/TI%20Preliminary%20Investigative %20Findings%20Boeing%20737%20MAX%20March%202020.pdf

5.   Setting an acceptable safety goal

We have looked at risk acceptance frameworks and the various types of things that people tend to be thinking of when they talk about safety. Now we can get down to the central topic of setting a baseline goal for "how safe is safe enough." We refer to the idea of "safe enough" throughout this book as *acceptable safety*.

ANSI/UL 4600 defines "acceptable" as: "sufficient to achieve the overall item risk as determined by the safety case." This means that safety is "acceptable" not because someone subjectively thinks it is, but rather because there is a claim that the AV is reasonably expected to present a quantified overall risk that is acceptable to all stakeholders as backed up by argument and evidence. Acceptability is an engineering statement, not a subjective thought.

The question of acceptable safety involves setting a quantified risk threshold for acceptability and determining what dimensions of risk should be included in that risk threshold. Those dimensions of risk should include not only expected rates of harm, but also address uncertainty inherent in predicting expected rates of harm.

5.1. Positive Risk Balance

Summary: Positive Risk Balance has become a default safety expectation. It means that an AV is at least as safe as a human driver.

The center of gravity of the safety discussion seems to be converging on "safe enough" being at least as safe as a human driver. That has come to be known by the term Positive Risk Balance (PRB), meaning that risk is lower ("positive balance") for AVs compared to conventional vehicles with human drivers. PRB is commonly messaged by European car companies and seems likely to become the overall automotive industry position on what acceptable safety might be.

You might think PRB would be an obvious starting point. However, some initial risk discussions envisioned that early adoption of a technology more dangerous than human drivers might be desirable if it resulted in safer technology more quickly. The argument was based on a premise that sacrificing fewer lives in the near term was acceptable if it meant saving more lives in the somewhat longer term. Such arguments typically take for granted that AVs would be dramatically safer than human drivers, and do not consider that it is also possible that near-term fatalities could be sacrificed for no long-term gain if the best AVs can do is merely as good as a human driver.

A European Commission report on automated vehicle ethics centered the discussion on PRB instead. That report said that acceptable safety requires that AVs "decrease, or at least do not increase, the amount of physical harm [compared to] conventional driving."[296]

Considering a goal of PRB in light of the variety of definitions of "safe" in chapter 4 sheds light on some of the rhetorical tricks being played in public messaging. For example, stating that human drivers are bad drivers (which is not really true to the degree usually stated) only addresses half of the risk balance, leaving the other half of the risk balance regarding whether AVs will be less risky unaddressed.

Saying that AVs will be safer than humans is a GAMAB-style approach of comparison against a human driver baseline.[297] There are important implications of a PRB approach based on a GAMAB risk acceptance framework:

- A specific baseline must be defined for human driver safety both in terms of which drivers and what operational conditions apply.
- In contrast to a MEM approach, PRB AVs would likely be more dangerous than most other everyday hazards, just as human-driven vehicles are. Presumably an initial PRB deployment strategy is accompanied by a hope that safety will improve over time, but initially PRB is satisfied if the safety situation is made no worse than it is for human-driven vehicles.
- In contrast to an ALARP approach, there is no obligation to improve safety beyond PRB, even if doing so would be comparatively cheap and easy. PRB does not, however, prohibit doing better.
- Risk shifting would be permitted in a simplistic PRB approach, using decreased risk in some situations to subsidize increased risk in other situations. However, the European Commission report includes a section on fairness to address this topic. PRB should be considered to also import other considerations from that report, and so does not permit substantive risk shifting.

These implications do not necessarily mean that a PRB approach is undesirable. They are simply the types of outcomes implied by a PRB approach unless additional constraints are added. It can be argued that the PRB approach is the minimum socially acceptable deployment criterion, along the lines of a "do no harm" ethical framework. In this book we argue that more than a simplistic PRB approach is almost certainly required for practical deployment.[298]

---

[296] See European Commission, 2020, Page 25: https://doi.org/10.2777/035239 Anyone studying this book in depth should also read the EC report in its entirety.

[297] See Section 3.1 for a discussion of the risk acceptance frameworks including GAMAB, MEM, and ALARP.

[298] To be clear, the European Commission report addresses many of the topics beyond PRB, so this is not intended as a criticism of that report. Rather, it is

5.2. Baseline human-driven vehicle safety

Summary: To determine PRB you need a baseline human driver for the comparison. Easier said than done. Human drivers and the conditions they drive in vary significantly. You need to decide which human driver to pick as a basis for PRB comparison.

A PRB approach starts with characterizing human-driven vehicle safety. We mostly use 2019 data in this book to avoid the worse (but anomalous, one hopes!) US safety data from the COVID-19 pandemic years starting in 2020.

Because most transportation is about getting from Point A to Point B rather than driving for its own sake, we use safety statistics based on Vehicle Miles Traveled (VMT) rather than hours of exposure. This normalizes the fatality and injury rates against total miles driven, giving a measure of risk that accounts for the length of a trip being taken by an individual passenger.[299]

Unless otherwise noted, the sources for US statistics and the graphics in this section are US DOT publication HS 813 060 Traffic Safety Facts: Overview of Motor Vehicle Crashes in 2019.[300]

5.2.1. Baseline US road fatality and injury rates

US total public road fatalities decreased from 44,525 in 1975 to 36,096 in 2019, attributed to improvements in a combination of vehicle safety, road safety, and driver behavior improvement (figure 5.1). The fatality rate per 100 million vehicle miles traveled (100M VMT) dropped much more dramatically, from 3.35 fatalities per 100M VMT in 1975 to just 1.10 in 2019. The disparity between this drop and the total fatality change is due to significantly more miles being driven by the population, which totaled 3.267 trillion miles in 2019.

---

important not to lose the other relevant factors for ethical AV deployment that go beyond the PRB punchline of "better than a human driver."

[299] A case can be made at a societal level for using fatalities per population size to measure the harm done by personal vehicles. However, the question we consider is whether AVs will be safer than conventional human-driven vehicles, all things being equal. We revisit when things might not be equal in chapter 10.

[300] US DOT/NHTSA publication DOT HS 813 060, 2020: https://crashstats.nhtsa.dot.gov/Api/Public/Publication/813060

Fatalities and Fatality Rate per 100 Million VMT, 1975-2019

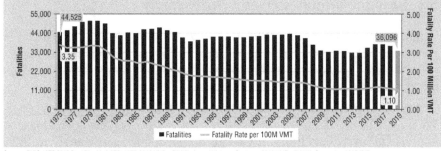

Sources: FARS 1975-2018 Final File, 2019 ARF; 1975-2018 VMT – FHWA's Annual Highway Statistics; 2019 VMT – FHWA's September 2020 TVT

Figure 5.1: Fatalities and fatality rate per 100M VMT. Source: NHTSA

People Injured and Injury Rate per 100 Million VMT, 1988-2019

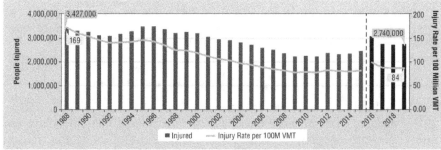

Sources: FARS 1988-2018 Final File, 2019 ARF; NASS GES 1988-2015; CRSS 2016-2019; 1988-2018 VMT – FHWA's Annual Highway Statistics; 2019 VMT – FHWA's September 2020 TVT
Note: CRSS estimates and NASS GES estimates are not comparable due to different sample designs. Refer to end of document for more information about CRSS.

Figure 5.2: Injuries and injury rate per 100M VMT. Source: NHTSA

Injury rates have similarly dropped over time, from 169 per 100M VMT in 1988 to 84 in 2019 (figure 5.2). During that same time, NHTSA shows that police reported:

- Fatal crashes = 33,244   (1.02 per 100M VMT)
- Injury crashes = 1,916,000   (58.6 per 100M VMT)
- Property Damage Only crashes = 4,806,000 (147 per 100M VMT)

Minor injury and especially property damage crashes are not always reported to police, so these should be considered underestimates of the true crash rate. Even with the under-reporting of less severe crashes, there is a clear trend that fatal crashes are rare compared to injury and property damage only (PDO) crashes.

When considering crash rates compared to death and injury rates, the number of passengers per vehicle becomes relevant, with the number of crashes generally lower than the number of fatalities and injuries. This is due to some crashes involving multi-occupant vehicles or at times multiple occupied vehicles, in addition to pedestrians and other vulnerable road users (multiple victims from a single crash).

An alternate view of road deaths and injuries is compiled by the National Safety Council (NSC). Their numbers tend to be a bit higher than NHTSA numbers due to their inclusion of fatalities that occur on non-public roads. That data might be relevant as an alternate baseline value for ODDs that include non-public roads. For example, in 2019 NSC reports 39,107 fatalities, [301] which is significantly higher than the 36,096 reported by NHTSA, which is in turn higher than the 33,244 included in police reports. A data source that accounts for the full number of comparable loss statistics will have to be made as a first step in computing PRB, with substantial differences in numbers between sources.

Taking just the NHTSA data for public roads, an (overly) simplistic starting point for PRB might be fewer than 1.10 fatalities and fewer than 84 injuries per 100M VMT. This could be converted to approximate vehicle collision rates based on the police-reported collision damage to create a likely conservative estimate of permissible injury and PDO crash rates. More precise methodologies to estimate unreported crashes especially for PDO events should be used, so this is just a starting point to such an approach.

However, some complications require thought before setting a PRB value for any particular vehicle deployment.

5.2.2. Risk variation due to operational conditions

All road miles are not created equal in terms of risk. Driving conditions have a significant influence on risk. A simple example from 2019 is that NHTSA reports 0.86 urban fatalities per 100M VMT, but almost twice the fatality rate for rural driving at 1.65 fatalities per 100M VMT.[302] Both urban and rural fatality rates differ significantly from the overall average of 1.02 fatalities per 100M VMT.[303]

The significant difference in fatality rates shows that using a national average PRB baseline can set an inappropriate safety target for a more limited ODD. An AV that experienced 1.00 fatalities per 100M VMT could be said to have PRB at slightly better than an average vehicle. However, if it spent all its time in urban settings, it would be considerably less safe than human urban drivers who experience only 0.86 per 100M VMT fatalities. 1.00 fatalities per 100M VMT might even be worse than comparable highway fatality rates if the AV only operates in sunny dry weather on interstate highways compared to the figure for all rural driving that includes night, rain, ice, and winding two-lane roads.

---

[301] See: https://injuryfacts.nsc.org/motor-vehicle/overview/preliminary-estimates/

[302] A higher fatality rate is not the same as a higher crash rate. A vehicle that claims to have fewer crashes overall might still have higher fatality rates if it has crashes that are less survivable due either less effective passive safety features or higher exposure to more severe crashes that can result from high travel speeds.

[303] IIHS breaks down urban vs. rural crash fatalities here: https://www.iihs.org/topics/fatality-statistics/detail/urban-rural-comparison

Looking a bit deeper, risk variation is much higher when accounting for differences in ODD. While a detailed analysis is beyond our scope, some other examples of significant risk variability can be seen in state-by-state data. Some highlights of this data are:[304]

- A 3.4 times spread for fatality rates from US state to state:
  - Massachusetts: 0.51 fatalities / 100M VMT
  - US average: 1.11 fatalities / 100M VMT
  - South Carolina: 1.73 fatalities / 100M VMT
- A 7.7 times spread for traffic fatalities based on population for US states:
  - District of Columbia: 3.3 deaths per 100K people
  - Wyoming: 25.4 deaths per 100K people
- A significant spread for rural non-Interstate freeways and expressways
  - Eight states: 0 / 100M VMT
  - US average: 0.99 fatalities / 100M VMT
  - Louisiana: 4.04 fatalities / 100M VMT
- A significant variation for local roads
  - Three states: 0 fatalities / 100M VMT
  - US average: 0.69 fatalities / 100M VMT
  - Rhode Island: 4.42 fatalities / 100M VMT

There are many different data breakdowns available from the sources cited, as well as others. This description is simply meant to illustrate that the variations can be dramatic from one geographic region to another. This means that saying an AV is better than the national average at the types of roads it tends to operate on might not give an accurate accounting of PRB compared to local drivers in the AV's operational area.

Additionally, one would expect risk to vary significantly depending upon environmental conditions (day/night, wet/dry/icy) and the quality of prevalent roadway infrastructure in a deployment area (crash absorbing barriers vs. obsolete guardrail types vs. no guardrails at all). Questions about whether trading off risks for different operational conditions will need to be asked. Is it OK to be twice as dangerous as human drivers in the rain if you can, on average, more than make up for that by being twice as safe as human drivers in sunny weather? Perhaps, but perhaps not.

If 100% of the vehicle fleet were AVs then these variations would not really be a problem, and a fleet average might be a reasonable measurement of safety. However, phased deployment of an AV fleet is likely to favor

---

[304] Data drawn from the Insurance Institute for Highway Safety:
https://www.iihs.org/topics/fatality-statistics/detail/state-by-state#fatal-crash-totals
and the US Federal Highway Administration
https://www.fhwa.dot.gov/policyinformation/statistics/2019/fi30.cfm
Note that the US averages given differ slightly, perhaps due to revisions of the total US VMT in updated reports. They are reported as given in the underlying documents. Also, the number and type of roadways vary by state.

easier driving conditions first, within the limits of business objectives. That is a reasonable approach while the technology is maturing. However, for a fair comparison it is important for the PRB baseline to be picked based on the characteristics of actual deployment. If deployed first in easy conditions, that means that the PRB baseline needs to be more stringent than a simple national average. Otherwise, vehicles might well be more dangerous than human drivers operating in the same local conditions, while at the same time claiming to be "safe" based on a comparison to a national average.

5.2.3. Risk variation for different types of road users

Different road users are exposed to different levels of risk. Pedestrians are more vulnerable in a crash than a seat belted, airbagged, and crumple zone protected vehicle occupant. Additional variables are the number of vulnerable road users in a particular operational area (more in dense urban centers; fewer on remote interstate highways) as well as the fraction of crashes that involve different types of road users.

IIHS has published data based on road user type and state in terms of percent of fatalities by road user type that shows that the outcomes are highly variable.[305] Lows and highs for each type are shown:

- Percent of fatalities that were car occupants:
  - Hawaii: 19%
  - US overall: 34%
  - Vermont: 45%
- Pickup and SUV occupants:
  - New Jersey: 12%
  - US overall: 27%
  - Idaho: 42%
- Large truck occupants:
  - District of Columbia, Rhode Island, Hawaii, New Hampshire (tie): 0%
  - US overall: 2%
  - Wyoming: 6%
- Motorcyclists:
  - Mississippi: 6%
  - US overall: 14%
  - New Hampshire: 30%
- Pedestrians:
  - Kansas: 4%
  - US overall: 17%

---

[305] IIHS 2019 data archived at:
https://web.archive.org/web/20210707072124/https://www.iihs.org/topics/fatality-statistics/detail/state-by-state

- o   District of Columbia: 39%
- Bicyclists:
    - o   Vermont, Wyoming, Nebraska, New Hampshire, Rhode Island (tie): 0%
    - o   US overall: 2%
    - o   Florida, Delaware, New York (tie): 5%

It would be expected that some variations in numbers above are due to the prevalence of different types of road users and the mix of vehicle types in use. Nonetheless, the spread of data shows that a one-size-fits-all approach to PRB baseline selection according to a national average is likely to be a mismatch to local conditions for a geographically limited AV deployment.

Beyond the numbers reported, there is the issue of the risk presented to smaller classes of road users that do not appear in these summaries. For example, if an AV were particularly prone to hitting people dressed in high visibility clothing such as construction workers (a weakness we saw in a widely used research computer vision system), that is unlikely to be acceptable even if the overall pedestrian fatality rate is otherwise acceptably low. The same problems could occur if a system had difficulties handling children, people using mobility aids, people with darker skin color, people wearing uncommon headdress styles, and so on.

In general, anyone who does not look or behave like a "typical" pedestrian might be under-represented in AV training data sets, simulations, and road testing campaigns. That could create problematic structured weaknesses in AV performance that might nonetheless seem to meet PRB target values in aggregate.

Dealing with all the possible variations between and within operating locations will require a relatively fine-grain approach to risk evaluation of both human drivers and AVs in varying operational situations. The time to find out if your safe-enough-on-average AV is (hypothetically) struggling to avoid hitting wheelchair riders during sun glare conditions is before there has been a collision, not after.

5.2.4. Risk variation due to driver experience

Just as not all VMTs are created equal, not all driver performance is equal. Figure 5.3 provides some potentially counter-intuitive data showing driving safety improves with age up to a point a lot older than many would have thought.

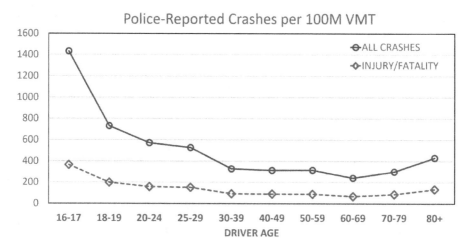

Figure 5.3 Police-reported crashes per 100M VMT by age range.
Data source: AAA Foundation.[306]

The minimum risk age interval is at 60-69 years old for crashes, injury crashes, and fatal crashes. The data report states that "drivers ages 60-69 were the safest drivers by most measures examined." Even drivers over 80 have a lower crash rate than drivers under 30 years old.[307]

There is a divergence between crash rates and fatality rates with increasing age, in that fatality rates increase more quickly than crash rates. That likely has more to do with an 80-year-old's reduced ability to survive a severe crash than it has to do with driving skill. The same age-related survivability effect would be expected to occur for older passengers in AV crashes.

Two implications stem from this data. The first is that a PRB goal should specify the experience of the baseline driver. As a minimum risk target, the PRB baseline should be set at an unimpaired 50- or 60-something- year-old driver, not a driver under 30.

The second implication is that the fatality rate for an AV will in part depend on the age and health fragility of the passengers. Deploying AVs to provide increased mobility for elderly passengers could, perhaps paradoxically, make the AVs seem more dangerous because fragile passengers are more likely to be killed in any given crash. Compensating

---

[306]See data tables at: https://aaafoundation.org/rates-motor-vehicle-crashes-injuries-deaths-relation-driver-age-united-states-2014-2015/

[307] Anecdotal stories about old people being bad drivers are ubiquitous. Indeed, it is possible older drivers are involved in more minor crashes not reported to police. However, they also tend to self-limit their risk, especially by not driving at night or in bad weather. They also commonly stop driving at some point. Be that as it may, the point here is that AVs need to be better than the many 20-something year old software developers helping build these systems who might incorrectly think they are the safest drivers.

target fatality rates for the age range of passengers could be reasonable in such a situation.

5.3. How positive should Positive Risk Balance be?

Summary: Human nature and uncertainty require an ample engineering margin to be added to a PRB. Perhaps up to a factor of between 10 and 100.

A narrow reading of PRB is that it suffices for the net risk related to harm to be just slightly better (or at least no worse). As we have seen from the preceding sections, nailing down the baseline for what human drivers and driving conditions might be used for the human driver baseline is complicated. Nonetheless, for this section we assume you have an answer to the baseline question and have a multi-dimensional metric that defines precisely where the PRB limit of exactly equal to human safety is drawn with regard to the span of operational environments.

But you are not done yet. The next question is, how positive does the PRB need to be? Is parity with human driver risk enough? Is 10% safer enough? Is it 10 times safer? Or is more required?

5.3.1. Consumer attitudes and trust

One of the biggest challenges facing the AV industry [308] is public perception of safety and trust in the companies.

While attitudes change over time, a representative snapshot of public attitudes[309] showed that 23% of US adults said they would ride in an AV, 34% said no, and 37% were on the fence.[310] While those numbers could be worse, they reflect a significant need to earn trust.

5.3.1.1. Consumers want far better than minimal PRB

One way to earn trust is to promise (and deliver) AVs that are seen to be noticeably safer than human drivers. It gets more complicated because consumer attitudes can be inaccurate, overestimating how safe human-driven cars really are. This combination of human tendencies likely pushes AVs to be significantly better than an engineering analysis of PRB would otherwise indicate to achieve a perception of being safer by the general public.

A related effect is that most human drivers believe themselves to be better than average. (Just ask them – they'll tell you!) They also tend to prefer

---

[308] Apart from getting AV technology to work dependably in the real world!

[309] Morning Star 2021: https://morningconsult.com/2021/09/02/autonomous-vehicles-safety-consumer-interest-polling/

[310] The trust for our first ride in an AV test platform was primarily based on having the head of safety also in the back seat. Listen to: https://player.fm/series/no-parking-podcast/building-trust-and-reliability-in-autonomous-vehicles-with-dr-phillip-koopman

situations in which they feel in control. It is likely that they do not want their AV to be better than average if they are to give up the control of driving. Rather, they will want their AV to be significantly better than they perceive themselves to be as an individual, even if that perception is inflated compared to reality.[311]

This suggests that a PRB threshold must be based on an exaggerated perception of human driver safety rather than an objective measurement of on-road human driver safety. That will require adding a significant improvement beyond net-zero PRB.

Requirements for risk reduction might be even higher because of a phenomenon known as algorithm aversion,[312] in which people distrust machines compared to people, even if the machines are provably safer.[313]

One analysis based on three studies[314] concluded that due to psychological factors including the better-than-average effect and algorithm aversion, consumers will demand that an autonomous vehicle be as good as an 80th percentile human driver – approaching an expert level of proficiency in driving. The authors believe that the biases involved will be very hard to overcome. In fact, those authors propose that the industry should not be selling AVs on safety at all because of these effects, but rather sell AVs based on some other attractive characteristics.

While perhaps selling AVs to the public primarily on safety might have been a strategic mistake, the industry has already invested heavily on that path, and arguably it is too late to change that narrative. Moreover, even if the AV industry were not selling on safety, the issue of acceptable safety would still have to be answered, because it would quickly arise as a topic of public concern once crashes started happening in at-scale operations, if not before.

5.3.1.2. The dread risk effect

A commonly cited issue with consumer acceptance of AV risk is the so-called dread risk effect, in which losses that receive dramatic media attention are weighed more heavily in the public consciousness than an equal amount of harm experienced in smaller, less publicized doses.[315] As an example, an

---

[311] See Nees 2019:
https://www.sciencedirect.com/science/article/pii/S0022437518304511

[312] Summary at: https://en.wikipedia.org/wiki/Algorithm_aversion

[313] This means there are two comparative issues at work here. People tend to trust others to be in control less than themselves. But they might trust computers even less than they trust other people, at least until they have built confidence in the computers. As we will discuss in the next subsection there is an additional effect in which people are too quick to trust computers, then too slow to re-trust computers after the computers have made a mistake. All this needs to be taken into account when trying to apply PRB in practice.

[314] Shariff et al. 2021:
https://www.sciencedirect.com/science/article/abs/pii/S0968090X21000942

[315] See: https://en.wikipedia.org/wiki/Risk#Dread_risk

airplane crash that kills 50 people and makes headlines all over the world induces more concern for safety than might a US routine daily total of over 100 fatalities in assorted car crashes.

Dread risk for AVs cuts both ways. If AVs suffer crashes that result in small amounts of harm for each crash, there might long-term be little public backlash even if the total harm done exceeds that from human drivers. Once the novelty of it being an AV crash wears off, it might just be seen as another tragic loss on already dangerous roads. Whether the industry can survive the scrutiny that will attend the first such crashes is unclear, but people have a way of adapting to a new normal even it is worse than their old normal. Perhaps this is what will happen over time if AV safety proves too challenging, and the industry deploys without even achieving PRB.

On the other hand, computer technology is prone to large coordinated incidents across large numbers of systems. The AV industry will perpetually be one bad software update from a large number of near-simultaneous vehicle crashes due to a software defect common cause failure. Such an event would be likely to invoke the dread risk effect and result in a significant backlash against at least a specific company, but perhaps against all AVs.

5.3.1.3. Over-trust and loss of trust

A counter-intuitive effect that has been widely reported is that when someone gets into an AV for an actual ride, within minutes they stop paying attention and feel that the ride is safe so long as the vehicle seems to be well behaved. This is part of a more general pattern of automation complacency in which people over-trust automation based on personal experience far too quickly in practice, compared to the trust they should have based on the amount of data they have available.

This quick over-trust effect can be used by the industry to build public confidence in the technology by offering widespread familiarization rides, either solely for publicity purposes or as part of a pilot deployment program. Social media campaigns of early adopters showing great on-road performance can also help build public confidence, which is likely to invoke this over-trust effect. This is not to say that pilot programs and demonstrations are inherently bad. Rather, it should be expected that a brief demo ride will build a level of public trust that could set safety expectations higher than they really should be given the current state of the technology.

The other side of the over-trust coin is that people are even quicker to lose trust if a seemingly dangerous behavior or an actual crash occurs. Trust, once lost, is difficult to regain. Loss of trust that feels like a betrayal to those who became true believers might well be even worse.

A significant loss of trust in AVs and the AV industry resulted from the Uber ATG testing fatality in Tempe Arizona in 2018.[316] An ironic aspect of that tragic mishap is that the Uber ATG testing fatality involved a vehicle that was not operating as an AV, but rather was an AV test platform

---

[316] NTSB Accident Report HAR-19/03:
https://data.ntsb.gov/Docket?ProjectID=96894

supervised by a human safety driver. The fatality was due to unsafe testing practices, and had essentially nothing to do with the likely safety of any finished and deployed AV. Nonetheless, headlines stated that a self-driving car had killed a pedestrian, harming public perception of AV safety overall.

Crashes involving Tesla Autopilot have continued to erode trust in AV technology. An extended marketing campaign[317] has confused the public narrative regarding the capabilities of the Autopilot system, even though drivers are told that it is a driver assistance system rather than an autonomous driving feature. Nonetheless, it is common in public discussions to hear Tesla crashes being considered as an indication of issues with AV safety, eroding trust in the whole industry. Again, headlines often state that a "self-driving car" has been involved in a crash when Autopilot is implicated, even if the text of the accompanying article clarifies that it is a driver assistance feature.

Many common behaviors by the AV industry tend to additionally erode trust. These include aggressively pushing back against regulatory attempts to ensure testing and deployment safety; lobbying for federal legislation to preempt what state safety regulatory oversight there might be; widespread lack of commitment to follow relevant industry-created safety standards; and lack of transparency regarding the safety criteria being used by companies to initiate deployment.[318] Additionally, the myths discussed in section 4.10 further erode trust once stakeholders realize that they have been fed industry propaganda.

No matter how safe an AV is on an objective basis, pure bad luck (wrong place at wrong time in wrong circumstance) can cause a fatality to happen a lot sooner than the average arrival rate. Even if it is much longer to the next loss event, that first event is likely to get extensive media attention and will erode public trust. Once that trust erosion has occurred, safety requirements might well be increased before there has been enough operational experience to determine if the first loss event was really a fluke.

The probability math works against the industry here. If PRB is perhaps one fatality per 200M VMT[319] to be approximately on par with a good unimpaired human driver, public opinion would likely be averse to a fatality happening before 200M VMT had been traveled. Yet, according to

---

[317] We consider all forms of marketing relevant here, whether directly paid for by Tesla, indirectly incentivized, press coverage, or just created by eager fans.

[318] For a more lengthy discussion on how the AV industry acts in ways that erode trust in the industry and its products, see Widen & Koopman, 2022: https://uclajolt.com/autonomous-vehicle-regulation-trust-the-impact-of-failures-to-comply-with-standards/

[319] It is surprisingly difficult to pin down the exact fatality rate per VMT due to statistics including multiple potential contributing causes for each fatality as well as fatalities in which the driver of a different vehicle is impaired or distracted rather than the own-vehicle driver. This is an approximation for unimpaired drivers. One fatality per 200M VMT should not be used nor cited as an authoritative number.

straightforward reliability probability math, there is a 63% chance the first crash will happen before 200M VMT.[320]

There are two ways to address this issue. The first way to have a better chance of weathering an adverse event is to have credible trust from the public so that they will believe an "early" crash is a random statistical fluctuation that caused an unlucky break for an otherwise safe system.

The other is to have an AV so much safer than a baseline human driver that the probability is quite low that such an unlucky break will occur during initial deployments. For example, if an AV is ten times safer for fatalities than the baseline target driver, the chance of having a fatality before the baseline target number of miles has been reached drops to less than 10% instead of 63%.[321] That is still a risk, but a much reduced one.

The lower the trust, the more important it is to have a large PRB risk surplus to reduce the chances of an unlucky crash severely damaging the reputation of the company making the AV, or potentially the entire industry.

5.3.2. The RAND report and 10% safer

A RAND report delved into the topic of how safe was safe enough, and included a tradeoff study as to what might happen in various deployment scenarios, concentrating on fatalities.[322] The heart of the study was whether society should wait until AVs have 90% of the fatality rate, 25% of the fatality rate, or only 10% of the fatality rate of human drivers. This is meant to span the range of a little better (ten percent better), quite a bit better (four times better), or dramatically better (ten times better).

The study also included factors such as the time it will take to convert a substantial portion of traveled miles from human-driven vehicles to AVs, safety improvements in both human-driven vehicles and AVs over time, and how much safer AVs will ultimately be than humans in the 30-50 year timeframe.

At a high level, the RAND study's conclusion was that deploying AVs as soon as they are 10% safer than human drivers can potentially save more lives than waiting until they are four times or ten times safer than human drivers. In essence, the argument is there is no point in waiting longer than it takes for AVs to be a little better than human drivers. The saving of lives starts the moment AVs are even a tiny bit better than human drivers. There is also the possibility that early deployment with only slight safety improvement will enable the technology to mature more rapidly.

---

[320] Reliability when mission time is equal to the failure rate is about 37%, meaning a 63% chance a failure will occur before the rated time to failure. This is worse than the more intuitive (but incorrect) 50% one might suppose. See slide 10 at: https://users.ece.cmu.edu/~koopman/lectures/ece649/19_dependability.pdf

[321] The relevant math is to treat this as reliability for a mission time of one-tenth the failure rate. $R(t) = e^{-\lambda t} = e^{-0.10} = 90.49\%$ chance of running with no failure for failure rate of 10 times the mean time to failure.

[322] Kalra & Groves, 2017: https://www.rand.org/pubs/research_reports/RR2150.html

There is a significant limitation to the RAND study in that it does an extensive sensitivity analysis for many variables, but assumes certainty for the most important variable of all – how much safer AVs will be. The issue with a 10% safer deployment strategy is, how sure are you that the AVs will be 10% safer?

What if you think you are deploying with AVs that are 10% safer with a margin of error of +/- 60 percentage points? The AVs might be 70% safer than human drivers. Or they might kill people much more often than human drivers because they are really -50% instead of +10% safer. On the other hand, if you are 10% safer with a +/- 5 percentage point margin, you know they will be at least a little safer regardless of uncertainty with a range of 5% to 15% safer, and it is fine to deploy.

One could decide to live with large uncertainty because you believe that AVs will ultimately be much safer than human drivers in the long term. However, that position is ethically fraught, because it involves a probability of excess near-term fatalities against the hope of future long-term gains. If you could prove definite long-term overall gains, that is still a potentially problematic ethical situation. However, there is no proof that AVs will save lives in the long term, so society would be gambling by incurring near-term deaths against a hope (not a certainty) of long-term wins in overall reduced fatalities.

An important question to ask based on the RAND report is not really how much better AVs need to be worth deploying in terms of saving lives. Any amount better is in principle justifiable, subject to considerations such as risk transfer issues. The more important question is what to do about the likely situation that you will be uncertain as to how many lives will be saved. If you cut it close (such as only 10% better) your safety estimate might be off by so much that you reduce rather than improve safety at initial deployment. This argues for a bigger margin than 10% to account for uncertainty.

5.3.3. The case for 10 to 100 times safer than human drivers

There is a case to be made that at-scale AV deployments should be at least ten times safer than human drivers, and perhaps even safer than that. The rationale for this large margin is leaving room for the effects of uncertainty via incorporating a safety factor of some sort.[323]

---

[323] Safety factors and derating are ubiquitous in non-software engineering. It is common to see safety factors of 2 for well understood areas of engineering, but values can vary. A long-term challenge for software safety is understanding how to make software twice as "strong" for some useful meaning of the word "strong." Over-simplifying, with mechanical structures, doubling the amount of steel should make it support twice the load. But with software, adding twice the number of lines of code just doubles the number of defects, potentially making the system less reliable instead of more reliable unless special techniques are applied very carefully. And even then, predicted improvement can be controversial.
See: https://en.wikipedia.org/wiki/Factor_of_safety

Consider all the variables and uncertainty discussed in this chapter. We have seen significant variability in fatality and injury rates for baseline human drivers depending on geographic area, road type, vehicle type, road user types, driver experience, and even passenger age. All those statistics can change year by year as well.

Additionally, even if one were to create a precise model for acceptable risk for a particular AV's operational profile within its ODD, there are additional factors that might require an increase:

- Human biases to both want an AV safer than their own driving and to over-estimate their own driving ability as discussed in a previous section. In short, drivers want an AV driving their vehicle to better than they think they are rather than better than they actually are.

- Risk of brand tarnish from AV crashes which are treated as more newsworthy than human-driven vehicle crashes of comparable severity. Like it or not, AV crashes are going to be covered by news outlets as a consequence of the same media exposure that created interest in and funding for AV developers. Even if AVs are exactly as safe as human drivers in every respect, each highly publicized crash will call AV safety into question and degrade public trust in the technology.

- Risk of liability exposure to the degree that AV crashes are treated as being caused by product defects rather than human driver error. For better or worse (mostly for worse), "driver error" is attributed to a great many traffic fatalities rather than equipment failure or unsafe infrastructure design. Insurance tends to cover the costs. Even if a judicial system is invoked for drunk driving or the like, the consequences tend to be limited to the participants of a single mishap, and the limits of personal insurance coverage limit the practical size of monetary awards in many cases. However, the stakes might be much higher for an AV if it is determined that the AV is systematically prone to crashes in certain conditions or is overall less safe than a human driver. A product defect legal action could affect an entire fleet of AVs and expose a deep-pockets operator or manufacturer to having to pay a large sum. Being seen to be dramatically safer than human drivers could help both mitigate this risk and provide a better argument for responsible AV developer behavior.

- The risk of not knowing how safe the vehicle is. The reality is that it will be challenging to predict how safe an AV is when it is deployed. What if the safety expectation is too optimistic? Human-driven vehicle fatalities in particular are so rare that it is not practicable to get enough road experience to validate fatality rates before deployment. Simulation and other measures can be used to estimate safety but will not provide certainty. The next chapter talks about this in more detail.

---

https://en.wikipedia.org/wiki/Derating
and https://en.wikipedia.org/wiki/N-version_programming

Taken together, there is an argument to be made that AVs should be safer than human drivers by about a factor of 10 (being a nice round order of magnitude number) to leave engineering margin for the above considerations. A similar argument could be made for this margin to be an even higher factor of 100, especially due to the likelihood of a high degree of uncertainty regarding safety prediction accuracy while the technology is still maturing.

The factor of 100 is not to say that the AV must be guaranteed to be 100 times safer. Rather, it means that the AV design team should do their best to build an AV that is expected to be 100 times safer plus or minus some significant uncertainty. The cumulative effect of uncertainties in safety prediction, inevitable fluctuations in operational exposure to risky driving conditions, and so on might easily cost a factor of 10 in safety.[324] That will in turn reduce achieved safety to "only" a factor of 10 better than a baseline human driver. That second factor of 10^{325} is intended to help deal with the human aspect of expectations being not just a little better than the safety of human drivers, but a lot better, the risk of getting unlucky with an early first crash, and so on.

Waiting to deploy until vehicles are thought to be 100 times safer than humans is not a message investors and design teams are likely to want to hear. But it is, however, a conservative way to think about safety that leaves room for the messiness of real-world engineering to deploy AVs. Any AV deployed will have a safety factor over (or under) PRB.

The question is whether the design team will manage their PRB safety factor proactively. Or not.

5.4. Summary: an acceptable PRB baseline

Typical discussions about an AV safety goal do a cursory look at human driver fatality rates and assume that doing better than those average numbers will be fine. In this chapter we found out there is a lot more to it than that. Using a gross national average is overly optimistic for easy miles, and might unnecessarily penalize an AV that is being designed to operate in particularly challenging environments that humans do poorly in.

Setting a fair PRB goal should encompass at least three areas: selecting a baseline, accounting for operational conditions, and adding sufficient engineering margin.

In selecting a baseline, consider the type of human driver you should be comparing against. A top-level national average is far too simplistic. Using a

---

[324] For better or worse – but given the optimism ingrained in most engineers, probably not for better.

[325] Some good news here – by the time you have a safety factor of 10 or more, nuances such as driver age and geofence zip codes start being small compared to the safety factor. If someone says they have a safety factor of 10, it is OK not to sweat the small stuff.

teenager driving late at night in an ice storm as a risk baseline is not reasonable. Using something like a 60-year-old, 80th or even 95th percentile ability, unimpaired, undistracted driver is likely to be a more socially acceptable baseline, and be a start at building in a safety factor.

Any AV operational constraints such as geo-fencing and environmental limitations should also be considered. If an AV only operates in fair weather, it should be compared to fair weather human driver operation. Risk should further be adjusted based on the specific locations being driven, which varies significantly by road type and geographic location. For all but the most simplified operational concepts, this will require a fine-grain evaluation of risk to ensure there are no systematic patterns to high risks related to environmental conditions, other road users, vulnerable road users, own vehicle maneuvers, etc.

Finally, it is advisable to add some engineering margin to the PRB goal. Some margin should account for uncertainty in the predictability of deployed safety (discussed at length in the next chapter). Additional margin should be added to provide a clear improvement of AVs compared to human drivers. A factor of 10 seems prudent at a minimum, and a factor of 100 is even better – even if that is an unpopular message. Using a smaller engineering factor is done at everyone's risk.

6.   Measuring safety

A few years after AVs deploy at scale, we will know how safety is turning out overall. But by then any harm to road users will have been done. It might be an improvement compared to harm that would have been done by human drivers, or it might be much worse. The trick is being able to predict with reasonable accuracy how safe AVs will be up-front, at the earliest stages of deployment. We should only put AVs on the road when there is a reasonable, good faith belief that they are acceptably safe for whatever ODD and operational concept is being used.

Setting a safety acceptability threshold and collecting outcome data is in many ways the easy part. A more challenging part is setting up a measurement approach to make the safety prediction before deployment.[326]

The array of possible safety metrics is dizzying. Potential metrics vary in difficulty of data collection, likely safety relevance, and likely ability to predict deployed AV safety. The entire AV safety metric topic is very much a work in progress. In this section we will walk through a variety of different types of metrics and metric strategies that are being used, that have been proposed in guidance documents, that do not really help, and that seem like a good idea.[327]

6.1. Leading vs. lagging metrics

Summary: Leading metrics help predict safety before deployment, while lagging metrics see how road safety turned out. A good metrics strategy uses both.

Lagging metrics tell you how things turn after deployment. However, waiting until after deployment to see how safety turns out is unlikely to sit well with many stakeholders, and is likely to enable deployment of an AV that turns out to have unacceptable safety. You will also need leading metrics

---

[326] We are mindful of "Goodhart's Law" regarding the tendency of metrics to lose utility when there is an incentive to optimize them. But that is not a valid excuse to avoid measurement. At some point, metrics are necessary to ensure safety. The SPI approach described in chapters 7 and 8 is intended to make metric optimization more likely to have good outcomes by aligning metrics with claims in the safety case. See: https://en.wikipedia.org/wiki/Goodhart%27s_law

[327] This chapter is based on a podcast series on metrics. See: https://users.ece.cmu.edu/~koopman/lectures/index.html#podcasts

that include not only testing results, but also process quality metrics and product maturity metrics.[328]

- *Lagging metrics* are things you can only measure when you see how safety turns out. In other words, lagging metrics tend to measure outcomes. They are called lagging because the information provided lags after operation has already taken place. Examples of lagging metrics include: fatalities per 100M VMT, injuries per 100M VMT, and Property Damage Only (PDO) crashes per 100M VMT.

- *Leading metrics*, on the other hand, measure things earlier in the design and deployment process, ideally before any loss event has occurred. Examples of leading metrics might include: software defect rates, percentage of pedestrians detected, how frequently an AV must transition to a degraded operational mode due to an internal fault, and how often an unexpected scenario outside the Operational Design Domain is encountered during operation. These metrics can be collected during simulation, during road testing, and after deployment. The importance of these metrics is that at least some of them can be used to predict safety outcomes without waiting for loss events recorded by lagging metrics to happen.

In a strict sense, leading vs. lagging has to do with whether a safety metric is collected before or after there is a loss event. Because safety is determined to a large degree by the rigor of the engineering design process, many leading metrics go beyond operational data and reach their tendrils into measurements of the design process itself. That includes metrics regarding engineering rigor, component performance, and test results.

In practice, leading metrics will be required to predict the safety of new AVs and software updates before they are put on public roads to ensure that undue risk is not involved with deployment. Building confidence that leading metrics are predictive of safety outcomes will be crucial.

It can be helpful to think about leading vs. lagging as less of an either/or classification and more of a spectrum according to where in the development and deployment a measurement can be made. For example, a metric of how often an AV passes closer to a pedestrian than it should might be seen as lagging in that it measures actual road events during operation. However, such a near-hit metric is leading in terms of its ability to potentially predict the risk of a pedestrian collision before any collision occurs. Presumably there will on average be more near-hits than actual hits, so detecting near-hits gives more favorable odds of detecting and correcting problems that could result in a pedestrian fatality compared to waiting for actual collisions to

---

[328] The distinction of leading vs. lagging metrics with regard to AV safety was popularized by Fraade-Blanar et al., 2018: https://www.rand.org/pubs/research_reports/RR2662.html

detect a problematic trend. [329] This type of leading metric can build confidence during testing if it shows extremely low rates of near-hit situations. It can also continue to monitor safety after deployment.

Not all things that might feel like leading metrics will turn out to be predictive of safety. In some cases there might be higher-level system behaviors that seem related to safety, but might not be predictive in practice. For example, high braking force could be a sign of a vehicle that is having trouble detecting objects on the road – or merely a sign of a vehicle that needs to be tuned to have a less aggressive braking deceleration profile for improved passenger ride comfort.

6.2. Vehicle-level metrics

We will somewhat arbitrarily bin metrics into two categories: vehicle-level metrics and engineering metrics. Vehicle-level metrics are based on safety-relevant measurements of the entire vehicle, while engineering metrics concentrate more on component performance and engineering process metrics. Those classifications are independent of the leading vs. lagging characteristics of any particular metric.

6.2.1. Crashes and other loss events

Summary: The most obvious vehicle-level metrics are lagging metrics that align with the baseline human driver metrics selected for the PRB approach such as crash rates. Be careful not to be distracted by blame issues.

Every AV project should collect lagging metrics that align with the metrics used to establish the PRB baseline. That will include not only recording crashes that cause harm, but other road events that are clearly undesirable.

Setting up metrics to track crashes should go without saying. [330] Other lagging metrics that are likely to be relevant to any safety case include unreasonable bending of rules of the road, [331] violation of traffic laws, and proximate involvement in loss events even though a collision has not occurred. As an example, if an AV has a close encounter with a cyclist who

---

[329] There is no guarantee that the first event won't hit a pedestrian, but it is common to have many warnings before a bad outcome, and even more warnings before loss event trends would become evident – if one is paying attention to looking for them.

[330] Implementing such metrics might be more challenging than is readily apparent. For example, where is the border between a tire lightly tapping a curb and a curb strike so hard that the wheels will need realignment? If an unoccupied vehicle does not see a small pedestrian at all, will it be able to sense the impact of the ensuing crash? And so on. Nonetheless, these types of information are likely to be needed to measure safety.

[331] See section 10.4.3 for a discussion on bending the rules.

departs the roadway to avoid being hit, that is an issue that should be considered in lagging metrics regardless of whether the AV made physical contact with the cyclist.

A critically important factor in these metrics is that blame is a secondary concern. If a loss event occurs and the AV is not to blame, it must still be asked whether the AV could have done something differently to have reduced the probability or likely severity of the outcome. The rate and severity of loss events over statistically significant operational intervals is the ultimate lagging metric for safety. Assigning blame is irrelevant to those numbers.[332]

6.2.2. Measuring road miles

Summary: Miles for the sake of having lots of miles is an inefficient use of resources. Which miles under which conditions matters much more.

While road miles have the advantage of being real-world testing, there can be lots of "boring" miles that do not challenge the AV at all, mixed in with a few important safety-critical events. Additionally, using public road testing to accumulate road miles is expensive and potentially hazardous to other road users. It is infeasible to collect the hundreds of millions of road miles required to establish acceptable fatality rates. It is better to have a limited number of high-value road miles combined with other metrics compared to a huge number of essentially meaningless road test miles that do not cover the ODD well.

At least for the first few years of the so-called race to autonomy, it was common to hear someone say that whoever had the most testing miles was winning that race. But there has always been more to it than that.

Some companies have millions of miles of road testing experience. There is no doubt that this an impressive accomplishment. If they have that many miles, certainly they have an incentive to boast about it by saying, "Look how many miles we have." At least in the early days, the press went along, equating the number of miles with progress. But mileage accumulation does not show who is safer or even necessarily ahead. Rather, mileage mostly reflects how much money is available to be burned via deploying a test fleet.

If you have lots of money, you can buy a lot of cars, hire lots of people, and put them out there to rack up the miles. Sure, having lots of resources can make progress easier, and initial road testing is an expedient way to understand the strengths and weaknesses of your AV strategy. Any company too poor to have a test fleet will eventually run into problems trying to validate its design for deployment. But miles alone do not make an AV safer.

More recently, some companies have taken pride in reducing their testing road miles and instead put resources into simulation and other sorts of

---

[332] See section 10.4.8 for a discussion on the safety problems with playing the blame game. Short version: having twice the crashes but being able to blame the other guy for every single crash still means the AV had twice the crashes as a human driver.

engineering activities other than road testing. That is a generally positive sign in progressing toward a more principled engineering approach to AV design.

Even if you have a lot of miles, not all miles are created equal. Okay, so we have a billion miles – are they in simulation around the same block? Are they all in sunny weather – or do they include rain and hail and ice and all those other types of weather conditions you care about? Are they in a place with wide roads and no pedestrians or are they in a chaotic urban center? Was that urban center at 4:00 AM with empty streets, or was it at rush-hour with a maximum volume of pedestrian and vehicular traffic?

If somebody wants to talk about miles, they should also talk about how those miles show they have covered the entirety of their operational design domain. Did you include construction zones, Halloween costumes, and all sorts of things that do not happen that often, but that still need to be handled? Did you try driving across all 446 bridges in Pittsburgh during a blizzard?[333]

There is also a potential problem with using miles as a measure of progress because they can motivate the wrong behavior. If progress is judged solely on how many miles have been driven, then there is an incentive to drive more easy miles.

Worse, every mile on public roads is a chance to make a mistake. Even if you have the best possible safety drivers, every test mile adds some risk. So every mile costs not only money, but also presents additional risk of adverse news or some unfortunate event.

AV companies should think carefully about driving a lot of miles for the sake of miles. Rather, it is better to ensure that miles earn their keep by intentionally and methodically testing things that ought to work to make sure they really do. Another reason to accumulate miles is to gather long tail examples of objects and events, although much of that work might be done using human-driven data collection vehicles rather than AV test platforms.

Having no miles on public roads probably means you are not ready to deploy because you have not checked to make sure the AV works. But having a huge number of miles does not mean an AV is better than something with fewer miles. More likely it just means the development effort is well funded.

If you want to know how an AV development effort is doing, it is not just the number of miles. Rather, which miles is what matters, as well as how those miles go together with all the other engineering activities. Meaningless miles are no substitute for a solid engineering approach to designing a safe AV.

---

[333] Yes, 446 bridges. https://en.wikipedia.org/wiki/List_of_bridges_of_Pittsburgh Each bridge presents a potential challenge to an AV due to metal structure reflections affecting radar performance and general lack of buildings alongside the road for many of them to help with localization. Additionally, bridges might be more prone to icing in cold weather.

6.2.3. Disengagement metrics

Summary: We should be worried about road testing safety metrics, not disengagements.

A disengagement happens when an AV detects an internal problem and deactivates vehicle automation functions, or a human test driver takes over control of an AV test platform because of safety concerns. These metrics have become famous because AV developers must report disengagements to California.[334]

The apparent rationale for requiring disengagement reports is that all things being equal, disengagements per mile might decrease over time as technology matures. Eventually, when disengagements reached zero, you might think it is time to deploy the vehicle without a human test driver.[335]

The problem is this model is much too simplistic and – more importantly – not all things are equal. As we've already discussed, not all miles are equal. But beyond that, not all safety drivers are equal. Some safety drivers will be more prone to be cautious and others less cautious. Hopefully there is rigorous driver screening so that safety drivers are the right amount of cautious, but in fact, this is still an area the industry is working on. So even with the best intentions, all disengagements might not be equal.

After this disengagement data is collected, the metrics get published and that leads the media to trend those published metrics into the Great Disengagement Metric Horse Race. Pundits opine about which company is in the lead. Companies who are ahead brag about their miles. Companies who are behind say it is not about the miles. Occasionally companies flip-flop as they gain and lose leadership position in miles. It is difficult to blame people for doing this because the developers operate in such great secrecy there are no other metrics available, and reading audiences do love a horse race.[336]

A major issue is that disengagements do not mean that much for public safety. In fact, publishing a combination of testing miles and disengagement rates as California is doing can incentivize harmful behavior.

A disengagement metric penalizes companies who tell their safety drivers to be extra safe by being extra quick to disengage. That means there is an incentive to tell drivers to give their vehicles a little more slack, which might or might not be as safe as it should be. One hopes this does not lead to reckless driving. However, in a very competitive environment there will be

---

[334]   See: https://www.dmv.ca.gov/portal/vehicle-industry-services/autonomous-vehicles/disengagement-reports/

[335] In reality when disengagements reach zero you have just solved all the common problems. No practical amount of road testing can prove acceptable safety on its own. See section 4.3.1.

[336] This dynamic is exemplified by an article which explains why everyone is said to hate the disengagement metric, acknowledges the problematic nature of the data, and then presents the numbers because everyone wants to know how they turned out. Hawkins 2020: https://www.theverge.com/2020/2/26/21142685/california-dmv-self-driving-car-disengagement-report-data

natural pressure to let borderline situations slide. That might make disengagement numbers look better, but it is likely to increase risk as well if safety drivers have an "I can get away with this" attitude or, worse, "I'll get fired if I have too many disengagements and make the company look bad" instead of an abundance of caution.

Another problem is the metric penalizes companies who are working on difficult operational design domains and instead incentivizes them to chase easy miles that do not help mature the technology. There are good reasons why a company making excellent progress would see its disengagements increase rather than decrease. Perhaps a company has expanded its operational design domain to handle more challenging situations and is concentrating road testing in those new situations. The week that an AV development team starts operating in the rain they might see the disengagement rate go up, but that does not mean their vehicles necessarily got worse in the previously validated sunny weather conditions.

Because companies are being judged on disengagements, there is an incentive to game them. For example, the AV company might find excuses to not count a disengagement motivated more by metric pressure than reality, potentially burying a legitimate safety problem. There might be systematic under-reporting of disengagements that makes the system look good, but also suppresses data about problems that should be addressed before later deployment.

For example, consider a company that only reports disengagement if an after-the-fact simulation confirms that the AV would have hit something. That can be part of a reasonable approach to mitigating metric pressure against better-safe-than-sorry disengagements. During road testing an AV comes too close to a pedestrian for comfort, so the safety driver disengages. If the AV would have missed the pedestrian by 10 to 20 feet, perhaps omitting the disengagement from a report would be OK. But what if the AV would have only missed the pedestrian by one inch? A miss is a miss, so that incident might be counted as a false alarm disengagement and not reported. But a near hit that could easily have turned into a real hit should still count as a safety failure for system testing.

Here is another hypothetical example. An AV test vehicle is going to run a red light unless the driver disengages. But it is late at night and there is no traffic anywhere to be seen. Perhaps the driver, knowing that some colleagues were fired for being too eager to disengage, just lets the vehicle run the red light to make disengagement numbers for that shift look better. Maybe a pedestrian the safety driver did not notice gets hit. More likely not. But either way the driver in that situation would be reacting to an incentive to value disengagement metrics over safety.

Disengagements might be useful input to some parts of an engineering process, but in a hypercompetitive market, they provide all the wrong incentives for road test safety. Reporting disengagements at best says essentially nothing about testing safety, and at worst incentivize testers to behave in an unsafe way to make the metrics look better.

Is it appropriate to have Departments of Transportation measuring the development progress of companies? Their job ought to be keeping people safe on the road, not keeping score in the race to autonomy. The emphasis should instead be on road testing safety metrics.

6.2.4. Road testing safety metrics

Summary: To build trust, self-driving car companies should be transparent about operational safety metrics for road testing, such as how often the safety driver fails to react as required to a dangerous situation.

AV road testing involves a human acting as a safety driver to ensure that any potential design or other defects will not result in a crash. The important thing to keep in mind is that if you ask the question, "How safe is testing," you are not asking about the safety of the AV technology. What is relevant is whether or not the human safety driver is able to properly supervise the safety of the AV test platform overall and do the right thing when something inevitably goes wrong. Safety of public on-road testing is mainly about the human safety driver's performance. To understand that let us consider the types of things that a safety driver must do.[337]

The safety driver has to build and maintain situational awareness to anticipate what is likely to happen next in a continually evolving road situation. The safety driver has to notice something is going wrong with the AV test platform and intervene at exactly the right time. While this is happening, the safety driver is under some pressure to balance getting operational data with maintaining safety. After all, sitting in the garage with the car turned off is safer, but does not gather public road testing data.

During testing the safety driver has to figure out how to react when other drivers do things that are weird, illegal, dangerous, or just plain crazy. On the other hand, sometimes it is the AV test platform itself that misbehaves due to a software defect or other technology issue. When something bad happens, the safety driver must take over control of the vehicle while taking care not to make a dangerous situation worse.

Most of the time being a safety driver for a reasonably mature AV test platform is an exceptionally boring job.[338] The car just keeps doing the thing it is supposed to be doing and the driver sits there watching and waiting. The driver must continuously keep a strong situational awareness, determine when the vehicle behavior deviates from expected behavior, and be able to instantly do the right thing to avoid a collision when something goes wrong.

Considering that the role of the driver is to intervene when something goes wrong, measuring disengagements is precisely the wrong metric for public safety. Safety is not about how many times the safety driver intervenes to

---

[337] See section 9.5 for additional considerations regarding road testing safety

[338] A testing organization might give the safety driver other work to do, but in general that is a bad idea. The safety driver should be focused on the monitoring task and not other obligations.

prevent a bad thing from happening. Rather, safety is about how often the safety driver fails to intervene in a timely and correct way. Not all those failed interventions will result in a reportable crash, but every missed or late intervention represents an elevated risk to other road users. It is not the disengagements that matter, but rather the times when disengagement did not happen but should have.

It might seem that measuring something that almost happens (a near hit that the safety driver fails to prevent) might be tricky. But if AV companies do not spend the time to figure that out, they have no credible basis for claiming that their testing is acceptably safe, much less their end product.

Examples of metrics that can help with missed disengagement detection might include after-mission analysis to find situations in which the vehicle passed dangerously close to something without the safety driver intervening, whether the safety driver intervened later than appropriate for a particular situation, warnings issued by a driver monitoring system, and inappropriate startle-type reactions from safety drivers when they do intervene that indicate lack of situational awareness. These metrics generally require analysis of testing data after the fact, but the whole point of testing is to generate data to be analyzed, so this should not present an excessive burden on the AV development team.

There should also be metrics tied to the safety of the testing plan overall. For example, driver alertness is expected to degrade over time, so alertness metrics should be used to ensure drivers are taking necessary rest breaks at frequent enough intervals.

Monitoring data should not be used to punish drivers, but rather to feed a continuous improvement process for testing safety. Drivers having trouble remaining alert and engaged could point to a training problem, testing plans that allow insufficient breaks during testing, or drivers with insufficient rest between shifts. Drivers reacting late or missing required interventions could be due to attention issues, but could also be due to over-trust in the system or inaccurate mental models of how the system should handle situations for which the need for intervention is in doubt.

Some driver performance problems could be due to drivers simply not having the ability to perform that job function safely (not everyone can). If data of that type emerges during operations, the training program should be revisited to understand why it did not find the incompatibility before the driver graduated from training to road testing operations. While telling a driver that they cannot continue acting as a tester is a difficult conversation, having that conversation is much better before rather than after a crash.

False alarm interventions should be tracked, but not used to punish drivers for being too careful. Rather a high false-alarm rate suggests that drivers are having trouble predicting what should happen next, or the vehicle is cutting things too close for drivers to be able to intervene in time if something does go wrong, with driver disengagements expressing their discomfort.

At the level of the overall vehicle, safety violations during testing indicate a problem with the ability of the safety driver to oversee operation.[339] Traffic violations should be monitored during testing. Examples include: running stop signs, running red traffic lights, operating in off-limits lanes (bike lanes, tramways, bus-only lanes), and other dangerous behavior even if no harm was done due to the absence of other road users who would otherwise have been put at risk.

Probably the most important thing to measure is near misses (or the more accurate term of near hits[340]) where the margin for error was just too small even if you got lucky and nothing bad actually happened. For example, maybe you leave too little buffer room for a bicyclist, or a pedestrian has to jump back up onto the curb to avoid being hit as you take a turn too tightly. If your safety driver intervenes, then that is good. If the safety driver does not intervene, something needs to change to improve the ability of safety drivers to intervene when and as necessary. Either way, vehicle behavior that almost causes a collision needs to be rectified before the testing program gets unlucky and hits another road user. However, the testing safety question is not the technical defect, but rather whether the safety driver intervened properly and whether testers are avoiding exercising dangerous behavior until the defect it has been fixed.

No safety metric is going to show that safety is perfect. It is unreasonable to expect AV testing to be absolutely perfect with not even a fender bender. Surely mishaps will happen, especially when interacting with human drivers on public roads. But there has to be some sort of way to monitor the risk being experienced during road testing before crashes occur, and ensure that the risk being presented by testing is not unreasonable.

To build trust, companies should be exposing at least the high-level rollup of testing safety metrics to public safety stakeholders. They have nothing to do with the secret sauce behind the AV, but they have everything to do with the safety of the general public as this technology is being tested on public roads. From a trust point of view, if AV companies withhold transparent testing safety statistics, it should be assumed that they are doing so because the numbers show they are unsafe.[341]

---

[339] A video of an AV truck testing incident shows a safety driver who reacted promptly still being unable to prevent a collision with a barrier. Regardless of the circumstances that lead to the incident, this was unsafe testing behavior on a public road. Note the near hit with the white pickup truck to left of the AV. See: https://www.theverge.com/2022/8/4/23288794/tusimple-self-driving-truck-crash-investigation

[340] Preferred by comedian George Carlin: https://www.goodreads.com/quotes/98951-here-s-a-phrase-that-apparently-the-airlines-simply-made-up

[341] If they have no data as to whether their testing is safe, that should be just as concerning to safety regulators.

6.2.5. Driving test metrics

Summary: The part of the driving test that is problematic for AVs is deciding that the system has maturity of judgment. How do you check that it is, in effect, grown up enough to drive?

At some point, companies are done testing and they need to make a decision about whether it is time to operate their vehicles without safety drivers. The important change here is that there is no longer a human responsible for continuously ensuring operational safety. That changes the complexion of safety, because now there is no human driver to rely upon to take care of anything weird that might go wrong.[342] Metrics for safety when deploying (are AV behaviors safe) are different compared to those used during road testing (is the safety driver able to keep vehicle behaviors safe despite potentially misbehaving AV features).

One way people talk about determining when it is time to deploy is to give the car a road test, just as is done for human drivers. There is significant appeal to something quick, cheap, and direct to decide whether a self-driving car is ready to go, and a driving test superficially sounds like it will do the job. Indeed, if a car cannot pass a driving test, then truly that is a problem.

But is passing a driving test enough to show an AV is acceptably safe? There are multiple parts to a driving test, and the question is whether they are enough to assure AV safety.

There is a written test. Well, surely an AV needs to know the rules of the road, just like a person. For an AV it is a little more complicated, because the required knowledge is not just the rules of the road, but also what to do about conflicting rules or incomplete rules, and how to handle justifiable rule-breaking. [343] If the designers have enumerated all driving scenarios and simulated them, they should be able to show that they have been checking for rule-breaking behavior as part of the simulation results.

Another thing needed is a vision test. Surely AVs need to be able to see things on the road. For a person, the vision test amounts to a simple eye chart to ensure they have adequate prescription lenses if needed for driving. But for an AV it is more complicated, because there must be a demonstration of not only detecting objects on the road, but also contextualizing what is being seen. The part that matters is building an internal world model accurate enough to use for driving based on sensor inputs. The vision test for AVs needs to be about a lot more than the ability to make out letters on road signs at a distance. It needs to be whether the AV's sensors can build an accurate model of a sometimes chaotic world.

For most human drivers, the biggest hurdle is the road skills test. Surely an AV needs to be able to maneuver the vehicle in traffic and account for all the things that happen. But again, for AVs it will be more complicated than a typical human driver road test. There is a presumption that with comparatively little practice a human driver will be able to learn vehicle

---

[342] Or blame for not having mitigated safety issues.
[343] Section 10.4.3 covers rule-breaking behavior.

control tasks in a wide variety of conditions. A road skills test might take place on a few selected roads on a sunny day, but the human driver passing such a test is licensed to drive in essentially all locations in all environmental conditions. We already know that an AV that can drive in fair weather can have serious problems handling snow, heavy rain, or novel road situations. Anyone designing an AV road test needs to determine how far to go with requiring the road test span the entire AV ODD.

Even if an AV driving test addresses rule knowledge, a vision test, and a road skills test, there is still one critically important test to go. A person getting a driver's license must prove they are old enough to qualify for a license and, implicitly, that they are a human being with all the cognitive abilities and experience that comes with that.

The age requirement is used as a proxy for maturity of judgment. Just as importantly, it is used as a proxy for having seen enough of how the world works that the driver can do a reasonable job of handling unexpected situations and displaying at least some level of common sense. There are of course limits to both maturity and common sense in licensed drivers, but as a society we have decided a particular place to draw those boundaries. Sometimes we also put restrictions on licenses for younger and inexperienced drivers to reduce risk.

How do we measure maturity and common sense ability to handle the unexpected for an AV? Calendar year age does not make sense, both because nobody wants to wait 16 years for a piece of software to mature, but also because we know that machine learning struggles with common sense no matter how many years it has taken to develop it. While we can hope to cover all possible driving situations with a comprehensive set of scenarios used in simulation and testing, a lack of common sense will make missing even one real-world scenario from the set potentially catastrophic.

The limitations of applying a driving test approach should not be a surprise. We have known for decades that testing alone cannot prove a system is safe, because there are always more ways things can go wrong than there is budget to test.[344] Testing gives confidence that engineering design rigor is sufficient for safety, but does not prove safety on its own.

An AV driving test can and should be administered as a sanity check to make sure that the vehicle really will drive safely. Relevant metrics will include the fraction of driving scenarios completed without making a driving skills or road rule knowledge mistake, perhaps based on a combination of simulation and public road testing. However, the argument that an AV's behavior is sufficiently mature and able to handle unusual events will need to be supported by evidence of engineering rigor that goes well beyond a typical driving test.

---

[344] See: https://betterembsw.blogspot.com/2014/09/go-beyond-system-functional-testing-to.html

6.2.6. Coverage metrics

Summary: Coverage metrics help track that all known aspects of system operation are exercised during testing, simulation, and other validation.

Because brute force testing over many miles is not enough to demonstrate safety, some combination of simulation, testing, and engineering rigor will be required. Economic reality dictates that road testing in particular will need to emphasize quality over quantity. Given a finite validation budget, it is important to be sure that all cases that matter for AV safety are accounted for.

As a thought experiment, consider what would be happening if an AV testing program involved driving billions of miles on public roads with the same mix of operating conditions that would happen in deployment. There are two things happening that are intertwined. One is that the failure rate is being measured to ensure that harm happens sufficiently seldom (for example, if an average of 5 fatal crashes per billion miles with sufficiently rare serious injuries might meet Positive Risk Balance criteria with sufficient confidence).

But a second thing is also happening with a huge road testing campaign. That is exposing the AV to a mix of representative operating situations. That mix includes things that might happen only once in hundreds of millions of miles, but that still matter for acceptable safety.

If the AV validation activities switch to brute force simulation, that requires both billions of miles of simulations and a way to know that a billion miles worth of rare events are occurring during the simulation campaign as well. In other words, you need to make sure that the combination of road testing and simulation is getting robust coverage of events that can happen within the ODD, including very rare ones. This in particular includes long-tail events discussed in section 4.4.1.3.

Coverage is central to any testing, simulation, or validation approach. It is important to ensure that every single function in the system works properly. Coverage at this level is the fraction of intended functionality that is exercised by the validation campaign via a combination of simulation, road testing, and other methods such as closed track testing. For safety-critical systems, you need as close to 100% validation coverage as is practicable.

If an AV testing campaign is based upon a set of thousands of scenarios, then it is important for a combination of simulation and testing to exercise every scenario that has been defined. Each scenario should be checked for safe operation with a variety of parameters according to the scenario definition. The coverage for this type of approach is first that every scenario has been exercised, and second that each scenario has been exercised across the ranges of its parameter values.[345]

---

[345] Scenario approaches tend to use parameterized generic scenarios that for example have a range of vehicle speeds, distances, and other conditions. A generic scenario of unprotected left turn might have oncoming traffic at a variety of distances and speeds in its variable parameters. Specific values for each parameter are chosen for a test

Other types of coverage are important as well to the degree they are not explicit parameters of a scenario. These include testing across all different types and presentations of objects, all equipment configurations possible for degraded operational modes, all factors that are relevant to the ODD (weather, lighting, road surfaces, etc.), and so on.

A different type of coverage is measuring how well the ODD corresponds to the Operational Domain (OD – the real world) the AV will be operating in. The ODD will inevitably be an incomplete model of the OD.[346] Therefore, it is important to understand how well the ODD covers conditions in the OD relevant to safety.

Coverage metrics are essential for any AV validation campaign regardless of the underlying approaches being used. Relevant metrics will include fraction of scenarios tested, fraction of high criticality areas of each scenario tested, and fraction of ODD characteristics successfully mapped to test runs in the real-world OD. It is important to ensure that validation covers all functions and situations that are relevant for safety. It is also important that validation ensures that the coverage model itself (e.g., covering all scenarios) sufficiently covers the real world so that validation results will predict real-world safety.

6.2.7. Physics-based risk metrics

Summary: Approaches to safety metrics for motion ultimately boil down to ensuring adequate separation between road users according to Newton's laws of motion. Implementation in the real world also requires the ability to understand, predict, and measure both the actions of others and environmental conditions with particular emphasis on frictional forces between vehicle tires and the road surface.

6.2.7.1. Criticality metrics

The general idea of a metric for physics-based motion safety is to determine how well an AV is doing at avoiding hitting things in the

---

(oncoming vehicle X meters away traveling Y kph), with multiple tests required to span the range within each generic scenario (many different distances at many different speeds). That means you need both coverage within each scenario (did you sweep across all parameter values for each generic scenario) as well as coverage of the entire set of scenarios (did you validate every single generic scenario in the scenario catalog).

[346] The ODD only needs to model the aspects of the OD that are relevant for safety, so some types of incompleteness are OK. For example, the color of leaves on a tree need only be modeled if they are relevant to safe operation of the AV. If leaves are always green and that does not affect safety, then the model is still useful. On the other hand, if red leaves behind a sign render stop signs undetectable, then color of the leaves needs to be modeled. See "All models are wrong, but some are useful": https://en.wikipedia.org/wiki/All_models_are_wrong

roadway.[347] A classical metric of this type is Time To Collision (TTC). In its simplest form, TTC is how long it will take for a vehicle to collide with something if there are no changes in trajectory. For example, if one car is following another and the trailing car is going faster than the leading car, eventually, if nothing changes, they will hit. How long it will take for the collision to happen depends on the relative closing speed and gives the TTC.

The general idea is that the smaller the TTC, the higher the risk, because there is less time for a driver to react and intervene. TTC can also be measured to a fixed obstacle. TTC has a limitation, however, in that two cars can be in a high-risk situation in which they will not quite collide, but a very small change in course will cause a near hit to turn into a collision, such as cars passing head-to-head on a narrow two-lane road while safely in their own lanes. Cars not on a collision course might have an infinite TTC, and yet be only one steering wheel twitch away from a nearly instant crash.

TTC helps understand how much reaction time is available to a driver to act to avoid a collision, which encompasses not only how safe a particular plan might be, but also how much slack is available if motion is perturbed by unexpected forces such as a strong gust of wind or a patch of ice.

Numerous criticality metrics exist beyond TTC, each with its particular use.[348] They are considered to be surrogates for criticality to be used as makes sense for a particular application and roadway geometry. Ultimately these are leading metrics that can be used to determine which of a set of alternative actions might be deemed to be less risky when planning vehicle maneuvers.

6.2.7.2. Newtonian physics

Several proposals attempt to give a comprehensive view of risk by considering all possible traffic participant geometries and potential near-term future actions that might be taken by each road user. Some examples are Mobileye Responsibility-Sensitive Safety (RSS),[349] NVIDIA Force Fields,[350] and the NHTSA Instantaneous Safety Metric.[351] These ideas came into play in creating the IEEE 2846 Standard.[352] But rather than go into the details of each of these individual approaches, we will just sketch out some of the high-level characteristics, ideas, and issues.

---

[347] The section for any particular metric discussion is somewhat arbitrary. Not hitting things also includes aspects planning, perception, and prediction. We discuss it here as a matter of convenience for the flow of the chapter.

[348] Westhofen et al. 2021 review a wide variety of criticality metrics: https://arxiv.org/abs/2108.02403

[349] Mobileye, https://www.mobileye.com/technology/responsibility-sensitive-safety/

[350] Nvidia, https://www.nvidia.com/en-us/self-driving-cars/safety-force-field/

[351] Weng et al., 2020, https://arxiv.org/abs/2005.09999

[352] The issued standard concentrates on the types of assumptions that might be made for safety-related models for AVs: https://standards.ieee.org/ieee/2846/10831/

The first big idea is that this is just physics. No matter how you package it, Newton's laws of motion[353] come into play. The rest of it is just about how to encode those laws, reason about them, determine values to put into equations relevant to operational conditions, and apply them to everyday traffic. Some of these approaches attempt to provide mathematically proven guarantees of no at-fault collisions. And that can work, provided the assumptions behind the guarantees are correct.

A big consideration with a comprehensive framework is that a static notion of risk based on current road user status is not sufficient. You also need to consider likely near-term changes in behaviors. For example, tailgating a leading vehicle at identical speeds is dangerous not because you will hit the other vehicle right now, but rather because you might not have time to react if the lead vehicle performs an aggressive braking maneuver. Predicting likely future actions is essential to evaluating the risk inherent in vehicle placement and planned maneuvers.

While all this might seem pretty straightforward for someone who survived a college physics course, when you try and apply it to real cars in the real world, things get a bit more complicated.[354] Various geometries and situations are just the start, encompassing leader/follower, head-on in separate lanes, merging, crossing, and so on. You then determine equations for safe separations and behaviors given distances, directions, speeds, and possible maneuvers by each vehicle involved.

You also have to consider the worst-case actions of other objects. For example, some cars can brake very quickly while some brake comparatively slowly. Characteristics tend to be different for different classes of objects such as trucks, cars, bicycles, and pedestrians. One way or another, you have to consider all the possibilities of one of these objects exercising its maximum turning authority, maximum braking authority, maximum acceleration authority, or some combination, in all types of different physical positions so you can avoid a collision.

Some situations are notoriously difficult to handle, such as a cut-out maneuver, discussed in section 2.4.9 on reaction challenges. Nonetheless, a robust physics-based framework can set the stage for evaluating which reactions to sudden changes in driving situations are least risky in light of other road user potential future actions.

6.2.7.3. Assumptions and measurement uncertainty

Environmental factors matter as well. The coefficient of friction of road surfaces, steepness of the road grade (both hills and banked turns), tire grip, braking capability, and other factors that influence the results of Newtonian motion equations must be known or estimated to compute safe separation distances while driving.

---

[353] Summary: https://en.wikipedia.org/wiki/Newton's_laws_of_motion
[354] For a description of the types of issues that arise, see Koopman, Osyk & Weast 2019: https://arxiv.org/abs/1911.01207

There are also special cases to consider that violate the usual assumptions made in mathematical safety formulations. For example, it might seem reasonable to assume that a truck in front of you that is in forward gear will move forward when applying engine power. However, if you are traveling up a steep hill on ice, the heavy truck in front of you might not go forward, but instead slide backward into your vehicle.[355] So you can hit a vehicle in front of you even if you are at a complete stop and the lead vehicle is in forward gear – on an icy hill. While that might sound like a trick question in a physics test, it is the type of thing that needs to be considered when applying motion analysis to the real world.[356]

An AV will also need the ability to predict other system capabilities and decide what assumptions it is going to make. For example, it might be reasonable to assume that a world champion sprinter is not going to suddenly cross a four-lane road in the middle of the block at a fast run. But it might well be that a pedestrian dashes across a road at a fast trot to catch a bus on the other side of the street about to leave a bus stop. A related assumption is that a leading vehicle is not able to brake at more than 1g because if it can, the AV's brake and tire combination may not be good enough to stop in time.[357]

Any proof of safety is only as good as the estimates of environmental conditions: the AV's ability to brake, the other vehicle's ability to maneuver quickly, road conditions, and absence of special situations such as sliding backward down a hill. That does not mean the situation is hopeless, but rather that there are limits to the real-world applicability of a mathematical proof of safety. Those proofs only hold when you can accurately estimate necessary environmental conditions and the assumptions made in the math are valid. At least some of this can be addressed by making defensible assumptions about the future behavior of other road users.

Mathematical proof techniques that guarantee proven safety do not mean there will be no crashes. That is because at least some assumptions can be violated, even if no road user is doing anything improper according to the rules of the road. Nonetheless, using physics-based safety metrics can provide helpful guidance for avoiding crashes in cases where assumptions hold and the environment is reasonably well understood. Physics-based approaches are helpful, but not bulletproof.

From a metrics point of view, time spent in situations that the physics-based risk approaches say are risky is worth tracking and reducing where

---

[355] Been there. Done that. Fortunately, got out of the way in time to avoid being hit.

[356] It is all well and good to assume that trucks will not move backward in a travel lane. But that assumption will not pay your body shop repair bill.

[357] Sports cars can brake more aggressively than 1g (the amount of acceleration imparted by Earth's gravity) using high-grip sticky tires and high-performance brakes. Tailgating sports cars is an especially bad idea. But knowing that a leading vehicle is likely to be a sports car with performance brakes requires much finer grain object classification than "that is a car."

possible. This is especially true if less risky driving behavior was practical under those same operating conditions.

6.2.7.4. Best effort when safety cannot be proven

Typical physics-based approaches attempt to prove that an AV will be safe by ensuring it has enough room to stop or can otherwise maneuver to avoid collisions at all times. But what happens when you ask the physics equations if there is any way to make the AV provably safe, and the answer is "no" – provable safety is impossible in a particular situation?[358]

Perhaps the AV is in traffic so heavy that it is impossible to leave enough following room due to continuous cut-ins. Or the AV is driving in an urban setting so densely packed with vehicles that avoiding collisions requires other drivers to restrain themselves from making worst-case maneuvers to avoid a crash. Even in everyday driving at moderate speeds, it can be impossible for an AV to avoid a collision if a vehicle in opposing traffic suddenly swerves over the centerline right in front of the AV.

Dangerous situations should be avoided to the degree it is reasonable to do so. There is no need to tailgate a leading vehicle on an otherwise empty road. However, when it is impractical to operate in a way that is proven safe, an AV should do better than simply declare safety defeat and drive recklessly. To do better we need a notion of best-effort safety and maneuvering in a way that reduces risk, even if a collision cannot be prevented.

The question is, how do you behave when you have been placed in a situation that is provably unsafe in the worst case? To address that you not only need rules for ensuring you are perfectly safe given assumptions, but also rules for reasonable behavior to restore safety or minimize the risk if you are put in an unsafe situation and you have to operate there for a while. This is where risk metrics such as TTC come into play. They do not purport to prove perfect safety, but rather seek to estimate risk exposure given a situation that has some amount of danger so that risk can be reduced. While there has been progress in this area, more work remains to be done.

---

[358] Physics math can give answers to questions under assumptions. Understanding the precise question that is useful to ask and what the answer truly means is the tricky bit. There is a spectrum of assertions to check with math possible such as:
- provably safe under given assumptions
- comparatively low risk (e.g., any impact can be proven to be less than 5 mph under given assumptions)
- safe under more constrained assumptions (e.g., assuming the lead vehicle brakes moderately but not a panic braking event)
- no collision with current situation, but collision likely if another road user maneuvers for a reason not readily apparent
- collision will occur unless own vehicle maneuvers
- collision is inevitable regardless of own vehicle maneuver, but collision energy can be reduced by {braking, turning, …}

6.2.7.5. Permissiveness vs. safety

Part of managing the risk of collision is the fundamental consideration of the tradeoff between permissiveness and safety.[359] Permissiveness is how much freedom of movement the AV has. The more freedom of movement, the more permissive the safety policy. An AV that never leaves the garage is a lot safer than one that drives on high-risk stretches of road, but due to lack of permissiveness is not particularly useful as a vehicle. One of the potential pitfalls of AV safety is creating an AV that might be provably safe, but has driving behavior so conservative that nobody will want to ride in it.

Permissiveness vs. safety is a fundamental tradeoff that cannot be escaped. There will always be risk involved in driving. However, permissiveness can be managed. Within the context of this book, we assume that the strategy will be to maximize permissiveness while still remaining acceptably safe. This means that the definition of acceptable safety will be entwined with how performant an AV is in any particular ODD.

Safety assurance frameworks more comprehensive than the special case of provably safe will be needed to provide permissiveness that stakeholders find reasonable in most open road situations. A first level approach will be to set a limit on risk (e.g., Positive Risk Balance with an appropriate safety margin) and then increase permissiveness as much as possible within that risk limit. A more nuanced approach might be to reduce risk further so long as the permissiveness cost is low, even if the original behavior was still within the PRB limit.[360]

How to play the permissiveness vs. safety tradeoff is a decision that AV design teams will need to make, informed by regulatory requirements and public policy considerations. Ultimately, they must do so within the context of their overall acceptable safety strategy.

However, it is important to remember that physics will not be denied.

$$F = MA$$

It's not just a good idea. It's Newton's <u>LAW</u>!

---

[359] The notion of permissiveness in this context was identified by Machin et al., 2014: https://hal.archives-ouvertes.fr/hal-01207152/document

[360] As an example, some groups advocate a "20 Is Plenty" strategy to reduce city speed limits from 25 mph to 20 mph. This is based upon data showing pedestrian fatalities are substantially reduced at 20 mph. Sometimes even a comparatively small change in speed or ODD permissiveness can have significant safety benefits.

6.3. Engineering metrics

Some metrics have more to do with components, engineering processes, and generally leading metrics that are not directly related to vehicle level performance. Here we somewhat arbitrarily call them engineering metrics.

6.3.1. Planning metrics

Summary: Planning metrics should cover whether paths avoid collisions and are otherwise safe, taking into account the full range of the ODD.

Planning metrics deal with how effectively a vehicle can plan a path through the environment, obstacles, and other road users. Often, planning metrics are tied to the concept of having various scenarios and actors that a vehicle might encounter, along with associated behaviors, maneuvers, and other events that need to be dealt with. Leaving perception and prediction issues to other sections, we assume for the purposes of planning that the AV knows where everything is on the roadway along with associated predicted trajectories and expected behaviors. The objective of a planner is to find a route and speed profile that makes progress without causing incidents.

6.3.1.1. Avoiding collisions and near hits with buffers

Some path planning metrics are tied closely to distance from other objects. An AV planner that commands the vehicle to hit a pedestrian that is otherwise avoidable clearly has an issue. But even near hits are also an issue.

Consider an AV that creates a path that purposefully misses collision with a pedestrian by one foot. That intended one-foot separation at closest point of approach could evaporate by the time the AV gets there due to inaccuracies in sensor readings that lead to slightly incorrect predictions of future position of the pedestrian and the AV. Beyond that, even small changes in pedestrian movement such as slowing down, speeding up, or turning slightly can put the pedestrian in an unexpected location. Also, even if the body of a pedestrian is in the expected location, an outstretched arm might be hit, or a loose article of clothing might be snagged by the AV, resulting in the pedestrian being tugged off-balance or even pulled down the road. Even if no physical contact is made, a too-close pass from an AV moving at speed is likely to distress or startle the pedestrian.

Avoiding near hits requires adding some sort of time and/or space buffer around objects and other road users. The amount of appropriate buffer will depend on factors such as accuracy of object state measurement (position, speed, direction of travel), vulnerability of the object (pedestrian vs. bush vs. trash barrel), relative speed during close approach (1 mph is much different than 50 mph), and uncertainty as to ability to ensure that the AV itself accurately follows the planned path. Also, the amount of time remaining until closest approach matters, although that factor cuts both ways. A longer time to close approach means more time for the AV to replan in case of a prediction error, but also more time for the object being approached to vary from its expected position as well.

The highest risk situations are likely to be highly vulnerable road users who have an ability to dramatically change their behavior in short periods of time but are nonetheless going to be approached closely. For example, pedestrians on the edge of sidewalks at city street corners.

In most cases it is likely that buffers used for planning are larger for situations involving higher vehicle speeds and objects with greater behavioral uncertainty. Buffer size in particular should be based on expected uncertainty when predicting future object motion, and should collapse to a minimum keep-away distance as the AV reaches the closest point of approach to each object.

Given the concept of a buffer, the most important safety metrics for object avoidance are not how close the AV comes to another road user on an absolute basis, but rather whether the AV path planner violates an appropriate safety buffer. A related metric has to do with the acceptability of buffer choices themselves. A metric for that is how often a path planner obeying buffer selection rules nonetheless has an incident such as passing closer than a safe keep-away distance. If an incident occurs due to an insufficient buffer, the buffer size or prediction capability will need to be improved.[361]

6.3.1.2. Scenario and ODD coverage

Consider a scenario-based design approach in which all the various situations and maneuvers that the AV can experience are broken down into a catalog of scenarios.[362] Examples of individual scenarios might include the AV changing to a faster lane to overtake a slow vehicle, the AV making an unprotected left turn that needs to cross oncoming traffic, and the AV turning right at a signalized intersection. In each case there is a specific sequence of actions covering a relatively short span of time that involves different road situations, obstacles, and other road users. There are many more considerations of scenario-based approaches, and this is just a high-level notion of the idea.[363]

Metrics related to scenario-based design largely have to do with coverage. By coverage we mean, for example, that the set of all scenarios taken together does not miss any relevant situations. Any scenarios that might

---

[361] Another way to look at this is a buffer is always the minimum keep-away distance as a function of space and/or time, and some other accounting mechanism is used to handle future uncertainty. The details of any particular approach are not as important as ensuring safe outcomes.

[362] The Pegasus project has done a significant amount of work on scenario-based approaches for AV design: https://www.pegasusprojekt.de/en/pegasus-method That material points out that a MEM approach might be divided by 20 to account for other technical systems also accounting to the MEM.

[363] The ASM OpenSCENARIO project defines a format for representing scenarios for use in simulations: https://www.asam.net/standards/detail/openscenario/

happen in the real world but are not in the scenario database are a coverage gap. Types of coverage metrics that might be useful include: whether the set of all defined scenarios in aggregate covers the entire ODD, whether all scenarios have been tested in simulation, whether parameters in generic scenarios have been exercised in simulation, and whether enough specific parameter setting combinations have been validated in road testing.

From a safety point of view, it is also important to ask whether all possible exits from the ODD are covered by scenarios. While the ODD specifies situations in which the AV is intended to operate, the AV could be forced out of its ODD due to situations beyond its control, such as a sudden rain squall or an unanticipated road infrastructure failure. While the AV need not complete its current driving mission when it is pushed outside its ODD, it still needs to ensure acceptable safety. That means that scenarios should not only cover the full ODD, but also cover ODD exit situations to ensure acceptable safety.[364]

6.3.2. Perception metrics

Summary: For a mature AV design there will likely be two limits to perception performance. The first will be encounters with novel presentations of objects the AV has not been trained on, and the second will be common cause failures across sensor modalities.

The main role of perception is to take information from an array of sensors and convert it into a model of the outside world. That model is used by the AV as the basis for planning and predicting the future locations of other road users. It is also used to characterize the driving environment and determine the location of the AV on the roadway.

Major concerns for perception metrics are classification accuracy and vulnerability to common cause failures.

6.3.2.1. Classification accuracy

Classification accuracy[365] as a general concept deals with the ability of the AV to take incoming sensor data and accurately determine which type of objects have been detected. Classification and related operations take sensor data as input and propose likely real-world objects that correspond to that

---

[364] An alternative is to expand the ODD to include Fallback situations as a type of degraded operating mode. But either way, safety must be assured in response to the AV being pushed out of its normal operating environment.

[365] We use (some might say abuse) both the terms classification and accuracy in an intentionally generic and simplistic way here because our focus is on general approaches to metrics and not on the nuances of designing systems that do object classification using machine learning-based techniques. Much more goes on that is described here in terms of mechanisms as well as measurement. To dig further on metrics, a good starting point is ROC curves:
https://en.wikipedia.org/wiki/Receiver_operating_characteristic

data. For cameras this would be a cluster of pixels that correspond to an object. For lidar this would be a cluster of 3-D voxels measured by laser pulse returns that correspond to an object. The output of a classification process is a categorization of the object that has been sensed, such as pedestrian, vehicle, pothole, road surface, and so on.

It is helpful in such discussions to define the terms of a confusion matrix.[366] We do this with the example of a pedestrian, although it is a much more general concept that applies to any detected object or environmental feature:

- True Positive (TP): a pedestrian is really there, and the AV senses the pedestrian.
- True Negative (TN): there is no pedestrian, and the AV senses no pedestrian.
- False Positive (FP): there is no pedestrian, but the AV senses a pedestrian that does not really exist in the real world.
- False Negative (FN): a pedestrian is there, but the AV does not sense them.

What is desired is that an AV has a very high fraction of results that are either TP or TN, corresponding to accurate sensing of the real world. However, in any practical system it is impossible to completely avoid FP and FN results, both of which cause problems.

We will discuss the FP and FN issues at two levels: sensing some object, and correctly classifying the type of object.

For an AV, an FN for an object of concern is the worst-case sensing outcome. There is something there that might be hit, but the AV does not know it is there. Unless the path planner gets lucky and avoids it by chance, there will be a collision.

An FP for an object might be seen as merely an inconvenience for an AV, because when it decides there is an object in what is really an empty roadway (sometimes called a phantom object), the AV will need to do a safety stop or swerve to avoid a potential collision. However, if that object shows up suddenly at close range, the AV might be forced to panic brake to avoid collision, known as phantom braking. That phantom braking increases the risk of being hit from behind by a trailing vehicle

It gets worse, because there is an inherent tradeoff between FNs and FPs. At some point there needs to be a threshold below which the perception algorithm decides a weak detection is a negative, and above which a strong detection is a positive. Setting that threshold lower avoids false negatives because even weak detections will be classified as real objects. However, some of those weak detections are phantoms, so reducing FNs tends to increase FPs. This is an essential tradeoff for all classification systems – you

---

[366] Graphically this is often drawn as a 2x2 matrix grid, but we'll just do the text version here. See: https://en.wikipedia.org/wiki/Confusion_matrix

can have good FN performance, or good FP performance, but you cannot have both.[367]

This tradeoff means that a fundamental set of metrics for perception is the fraction of false negative (FN) and false positive (FP) detections for various types of objects compared to a budget tied to risks. The risks include both collisions with objects not sensed and crashes caused by panic braking or swerving to avoid hitting sensed phantom objects that aren't really there.

Given that an object has been accurately sensed, there is still the notion of classifying the object as to what it might be. Partly this helps feed prediction (discussed in a later section), because different object types have different motion expectations. Cars, bicycles, horse riders, and pedestrians all have different expected speeds and agility as well as behavioral rules in traffic situations. So an accurate classification is important for predicting future changes in motion.

A more difficult issue is handling classification errors that convert objects from obstacles to non-obstacles. Real-world examples include a drawing of a person on a road that looks like a real person to a camera, but is in fact a drawing. Or a person wearing a disposable rain poncho that is characterized as a plastic bag blowing in the wind and therefore not an object of concern to an AV. To the degree that the AV decides it is OK to drive through some types of objects, a misclassification amounts to an FN or FP in terms of object avoidance consequences.

Classification type errors are important metrics for measuring both detection of objects and ability to correctly classify objects.

6.3.2.2. Sensor fusion and common cause failures

Sensor fusion involves taking inputs from multiple sensors and combining them to create a single model of objects and other aspects of the external environment.

The main benefit of sensor fusion is that weaknesses in some types of sensors can be compensated for with other types of sensors. For example, it is much easier for lidar to measure distance to an object that is moderately far away than for a camera to do so. On the other hand, if that object is a sign, the lidar will not be able to read the sign lettering, whereas that is a camera's strong suit.

Additionally, sensor types can work together to disambiguate situations that are potentially difficult for one sensor mode. A camera might see a person, but a lidar with fine grain depth perception might do better and determining if it is a real three-dimensional person standing on a road, a

---

[367] A better perception system has a more forgiving tradeoff between FNs and FPs, which is where the ROC curves previously mentioned come in. But there is no free lunch to be had here. For any given system there is at least some level of tradeoff between FNs and FPs.

photo of a person,[368] or a convincing optical illusion picture of a person painted onto a road.[369]

A beneficial metric associated with sensor fusion is that the false negative and false positive rates might be improved by cross-checking sensor types against each other. Sensors of the same type can also be cross-checked if they have overlapping fields of view. Additionally, fusion across multiple sensor types that accounts for environmental conditions can help enlarge the safe ODD by placing more importance on sensors that are not compromised by current operating conditions.

A naive approach to metrics simply measures the FN and FP improvements from sensor fusion and takes credit for improved safety. In an ideal world, a hypothetical 99% accurate camera combined with a 99% accurate lidar would be 99.99% accurate so long as their failures are completely independent. However, there is a catch associated with that independence assumption.

Some types of objects and some types of situations can be prone to causing multiple different sensors to fail together, creating a common cause failure scenario. If, for example, each sensor type has 1% inaccuracy, and that inaccuracy happens to be for the same objects for each sensor, then there is no benefit from sensor fusion because the failures are not independent. Fused sensors will fail 1% of the time if two 99% accurate sensors always fail at the same time.

As a physical object that might create a common cause failure, consider a detached truck tire tread on fresh asphalt. A tire tread is relatively flat, and might be missed by radar. The black rubber might be good at absorbing lidar pulses rather than reflecting them, and cameras will struggle with a black object on a black background. But hitting that debris might cause significant problems to a car nonetheless, and human drivers responding to that debris might swerve suddenly for no reason predictable to an AV that has had trouble detecting it.[370]

If environmental conditions degrade operation of some sensor types, full credit can no longer be taken for sensor diversity. Lidar, cameras, and radar might provide three independent views of other vehicles on the roadway in fair weather. However, in heavy snow both the lidar and camera sensors

---

[368] An advertisement on the side of a bus with a photo of a person was mistaken for that person jaywalking in real life by an automated enforcement system. See Liao 2018: https://www.theverge.com/2018/11/22/18107885/china-facial-recognition-mistaken-jaywalker

[369] Even if it is an optical illusion, that illusion might be intentionally deployed as a traffic calming measure. In case the reader is skeptical that anyone would take the time to do such a thing, a collection of optical illusion paintings on roads found in the wild is Flynn 2018: https://www.hotcars.com/20-weirdest-things-people-painted-on-roads-to-slow-down-speeding-cars/

[370] So-called road gators (detached truck tire treads) are one of the many types of road debris that contribute to thousands of crashes and injuries each year. See: https://www.dispatch.com/story/news/2018/09/04/road-gator-can-bite/10845128007/

might be compromised, leaving the AV vulnerable to collisions that aren't handled well enough by the radar alone.

An especially important category of metrics is determining how often common cause failures occur across sensor types. Those failures can be affected by object type, operational conditions, or both at the same time.

6.3.2.3. Edge cases

The bane of any machine learning-based system is the topic of edge cases, in which some rare objects or situations occur in the real world that are not adequately represented in the training and validation data. The challenge of edge cases was covered earlier in section 2.4.12, but has special relevance for perception.

A classification system that has no defined type for a novel object has an issue to resolve. Ideally it has a bin for "unknown" objects. However, it might instead guess wrong and classify an object by assigning it a classification bin that it thinks is close to the object, but that in reality is quite different in terms of motion planning and prediction characteristics. For example, the visual difference between a person riding a bicycle and a person walking next to a bicycle is small, but the likely speed of motion and road rules that apply are dramatically different.[371]

A critical metric for predicting AV safety is the anticipated arrival rate of perception edge cases and their effect on system safety. If unusual presentations of high-criticality object types cause false negatives at any appreciable rate, that can present an especially risky FN issue. As an example of an unusual presentation, if a system has never been trained on people wearing bright green clothing, then a person wearing dayglo green might not be detected due to that unusual coloration.

While it is inevitable that edge cases will cause issues, the relevant metrics to consider have to do with how often that happens, and how severe the safety consequences are when it does happen.

6.3.3. Prediction metrics

Summary: You need to drive not where the free space is, but where the free space is going to be when you get there. Predicting what happens must encompass not only current motions, but also potential changes in motion.

Prediction metrics deal with how well an AV is able to take the results of perception data and predict what happens next so that it can create a safe plan. A major part of prediction involves "free space" which corresponds to

---

[371] It is not just the expected speed and maneuverability that differ. A bicycle with rider is typically considered a vehicle that must obey vehicular rules of the road. However, a dismounted person pushing a bike is typically considered a pedestrian, with significantly different privileges and right of way priorities compared to vehicles.

areas on the drivable road that are free of obstacles and other road users. By definition, if an AV only drives on the free space it will never hit anything.

The catch is that free space changes over time as other road users move. Thus, an AV cannot simply plan to drive where the free space is. It needs to drive where the free space is going to be when it gets there. Prediction is largely about figuring out where the free space is going to be as the AV progresses along its path.

There are different levels of prediction sophistication required depending on operational conditions and desired AV capability.

6.3.3.1. Keep-out zone

The first, simplest prediction capability is, in effect, no runtime prediction at all. Just measure the current space along the vehicle path and make sure that the vehicle can stop before it can possibly hit anything. For stationary objects that means never get closer than the required AV stopping distance. For moving objects that have the same stopping distance as the AV, stay twice as far away as the AV stopping distance so that the AV can be fully stopped and, assuming the other object does the same, avoid collision.

Consider a low-speed vehicle in an operational design domain in which everything is guaranteed to also be moving at low speeds. Think of a closed business office campus with a slow-speed shuttle on a dedicated path that is only shared with pedestrians at designated crossings. The requirement boils down to other objects normally being far enough away and moving slowly enough that the worst case permits the AV to come to a complete stop before there is any possibility of a collision – even if some object pivots and immediately attempts to collide with the AV at its top speed. Such a system can be designed to stop anytime something gets too close with no need to predict future motion. In effect, a fixed design time prediction is used: any object will behave in a worst-case way within a set of assumptions. The AV comes to a stop if any object gets close enough for that worst case to be a problem, whether the other object actually behaves that way or not.

This approach is a riff on factory robot safety in which there is a keep-out zone. If anything enters the keep-out zone, the robots stop motion immediately. The difference here is that the keep-out zone travels as a sensed area surrounding the AV instead of being a stationary painted or fenced area on a factory floor.

A useful metric for such a proximity-stop system is the maximum speed seen in other objects in the environment. If other objects move faster than assumed or have trouble stopping within the distance assumed, lack of collisions is no longer assured.

6.3.3.2. Motion extrapolation

AVs that operate faster than a low-speed shuttle will need some sort of prediction based on likely object movement. For example, at an intersection an AV might need to pass fairly close to pedestrians and cross-traffic due to the geometry of the intersection itself. If the cross traffic is stopped and the pedestrians are all moving in a crosswalk parallel to the direction of straight

AV motion, there cannot be a collision – assuming their motion behavior does not change and the AV travels straight through the intersection.

With motion extrapolation, the AV assumes that every object will stay on its current trajectory (motion and speed) indefinitely. The path planner then creates a set of extrapolated paths for each object in the environment. The AV path then takes these into account and makes sure that the AV will not end up at the same place and time as another object. If the AV and anything else in the environment are expected to occupy the same space at the same time, that is a collision and needs to be avoided. (From an alternate point of view, if the AV plans to occupy space that will not be free when it gets there, that is a collision.)

The issue with simple motion extrapolation is that other objects in the environment can and will change their behavior. Vehicles start, stop, and turn. Pedestrians step off a curb to cross the street, stop in the middle of walking, and change directions for any number of reasons. Any change in motion throws off the entire prediction, changing what might have been a collision-free plan into a plan that suddenly will involve a collision.

In some situations, motion extrapolation can be sufficient so long as the AV can rapidly re-plan and the changes in motion are limited. Periodically, usually multiple times per second, a plan is computed that ensures a collision-free path for the AV. If anything changes its direction or speed a new path is planned that ensures a new collision-free path. Sometimes changes are benign, and the AV continues on its current path. But sometimes changes would result in a collision, causing the AV to maneuver to a new path or speed to avoid collision. As a simple example, if a leading vehicle slows down, the AV must also slow down to avoid a rear-end collision.

As long as the motion of other road users changes a small amount compared to overall motion, this reactive replanning approach can provide safety. However, if other road users can quickly perform significant changes to their behavior, it might not be possible to avoid collisions in the absence of prediction of such changes, which would not be done with this approach.

Pure motion extrapolation might work well in relatively low-speed, benign ODDs. That is especially true if other road users have high physical inertia and simply cannot make radical speed and direction changes in a very short period of time. It will struggle in chaotic situations in which many other road users might make dramatic sudden maneuvers, such as a pedestrian-rich shopping district or parking lot.

Motion extrapolation safety metrics should be used to determine how often and how dramatically other objects in the environment change their motion, and whether those changes are significant enough to impair the safety of this approach.

6.3.3.3. Prediction motion changes

Some believe that motion extrapolation plus rapid replanning is sufficient for acceptable safety. However, we believe that predicting motion changes will be required to some degree in all but the most benign and well-controlled ODDs. The question for acceptable safety is how accurate such predictions will need to be.

An AV operating in any but the most benign real-world conditions will experience situations in which operating in a way that is provably free of collisions is either excessively constraining or impossible. For example, every time an AV encounters an opposing vehicle on a two-lane road, both the AV and the other vehicle are counting on the fact that the two drivers will do their best not to swerve across the lane into a head-on collision. To assume otherwise would mean slowing to a crawl for every opposing vehicle encountered, making for an excruciatingly slow road travel experience.

One reason humans do well as drivers is that they are continually making predictions of the behaviors of other road users not only based on current actions, but also by taking into account possible future actions that involve changes in speeds and direction.

The basis for predictions varies widely. We expect a vehicle moving on an entrance ramp to a highway to attempt a merge operation. A car slowing down at a stop sign should stop at the sign. A pedestrian standing with toes hanging off the edge of a curb at a crosswalk is supposed to wait for the light to change to green in their direction. And a pedestrian waving wildly at a bus driver not to leave a stop across the street is likely to make a dash for it, even if doing so violates the traffic signal.

To the degree that we can make valid assumptions about the worst-case behaviors, we can use a physics-based approach to predict where free space will be (see section 6.2.7 on physics-based risk metrics). However, there is a permissiveness tradeoff between how much change in behavior is permitted by the assumptions behind the math used in those approaches and how aggressively the AV itself can operate.

More difficult are significant behavioral changes that we might assume will not happen most of the time, but occasionally do happen. Pedestrians do not jump off the pavement into the road mid-block – except when they do. Turn signals indicate that a vehicle is about to turn, except when it goes straight (or perhaps turns in the other direction). Lack of turn signals means that a vehicle is going straight, except when the driver does not use a turn signal. And so on.

If you see another driver not slowing down for a stop sign on a cross street, it is wise to assume they will miss it and try not to be in a position to be hit.[372] If you see a pedestrian with a red traffic light walking towards a crosswalk while completely engrossed in a smart phone interaction, it is a good idea to drive a bit more conservatively when approaching in case that pedestrian keeps walking into the street against the light. And so on.

The issue in building a sophisticated autonomous driver is that most predictions are not a single prediction, but rather a set of alternative predictions with associated probabilities. To make things even more complex, those probabilities often change in reaction to the behaviors of the AV itself.

---

[372] As they say, the right of way is not a right worth dying for.

The prediction probability cloud around each road user [373] is usually heavily weighted toward current motion. But the possibility of significant motion changes is there for even the least agile vehicles, if for no other reason than another vehicle experiencing a collision can make it decelerate far faster than mere braking. As a simplified example, the probability set for another vehicle on the road might be (hypothetical numbers) 80% goes straight, 7% left turn, 10% right turn, 2.5% normal stop, just under .5% panic stop, and 0.0001% hits another vehicle and stops instantly in a crash. The probability set for a pedestrian waiting at a red signal at a corner might be (again, hypothetical) 95% stands still, 4% backs away from the corner, .999% enters intersection against the light, and 0.001% trips and falls into the intersection.

Human drivers are remarkably good and predicting the potential behaviors of other road users, often using very subtle behavioral clues combined with expectations based on societal norms to adjust expected probabilities. "That driver is clearly from out of town, so let's give them extra room," "that traffic light cycle is too long, so locals are likely to run into the intersection just as it turns red to cross and avoid a long wait," and "that pedestrian is buried in their phone, so I expect they'll cross against the light because they did not notice it just changed to red" are the kind of judgment calls that human drivers make all the time to prevent crashes. To at least some degree, AVs will need to do this as well.

From a metric point of view the variety of potential behavioral cues and behavior predictions are immense. Starting down this path should involve at least two types of metrics. The first is building context-dependent probability clouds for different road actors. Different road users will have significantly different behavioral prediction profiles. Time of day and weather is likely to play a role too. [374]

Given a set of behavioral predictions, the most relevant safety performance metric is likely to be how well predictions work. While it might be difficult to judge how good a prediction is at the time it is made, it can be easy to score predictions in retrospect. For each prediction made, see how the real world turns out. If the probabilities of the predictions do not match the distribution of real-world outcomes, the prediction models need to be improved.

---

[373] The probability cloud idea is discussed in section 2.4.1 under the "predict" bullet.

[374] Are you more likely to be aggressive crossing a street as a pedestrian if caught without an umbrella in the rain? Are other drivers more likely to be aggressive at traffic signals and other driving near a large facility if their start of shift happens in only a few minutes?

6.3.3.4. Object permanence

A different aspect of prediction has to do with object permanence, in which the AV builds a world model that tracks the presence of objects even though they might not be sensed.[375]

A sequence of sensor readings might identify and categorize an object correctly for several consecutive sensor sweeps, then fail to detect that object. The detection failure does not mean that the object has suddenly evaporated, but rather object permanence and inertia dictate that it is likely to be more or less where it was predicted to be based on the last sensor sweep.

A detection failure could be due to a transient performance failure in sensors. Sensor data is never perfect, and it is to be expected that detection failures happen once in a while. Likely a prediction system will assume the object has continued on its previous trajectory from its previously detected position for a short while. If the object is not detected for some longer length of time, the system will assume it is no longer relevant and eventually abandon attempts to predict future positions as the probability of changes in motion accumulates over time.

While some objects disappear due to limits on sensor abilities, other objects disappear due to occlusions, in which some nearer object blocks the ability of a sensor to detect an object further away. A large truck might pass in front of other road users, temporarily occluding those further-away road users. A large parcel carried by one pedestrian stepping onto a sidewalk might occlude another pedestrian about to enter the roadway. A bus preceding the AV might occlude traffic signals at an oncoming intersection. And so on.

Tracking objects through occlusions is an important prediction capability. Such tracking can improve the ability to predict and avoid collision with objects that were previously detected and tracked, but temporarily occluded. This avoids starting from scratch figuring out object classification and likely trajectory plans when the object reappears.

A relevant metric for object permanence is how accurately the system is able to track objects through occlusions, and well it does at matching objects that disappear with their reappearance.

While tracking objects through occlusions sounds like a "nice to have" rather than an essential feature, that capability is often used to improve classification capabilities in ways that can be much more safety-critical. Consider a stream of classification results for a sequence of sensor readings of a single object of: person, person, tree, person, person. One would expect the system to recognize that the intermediate "tree" classification is a mistake, perhaps due to a person wearing a green shirt and brown pants, and not the result of momentary transmorgrification.[376] Any plan that assumed the object suddenly acquired the motion probability cloud of a tree – even if

---

[375] We use the term object permanence in a similar manner to childhood development terminology: https://en.wikipedia.org/wiki/Object_permanence
Freshman Psych. class strikes again!

[376] See: https://calvinandhobbes.fandom.com/wiki/Transmogrifier

for a short while – has a problem, because object permanence dictates the "tree" is really a person despite an obvious classification error.

While object permanence can help smooth out classification errors, it is important that any assumptions regarding classification error frequency and duration be monitored with metrics such as burst length of how many misclassifications occur in a row. While some bursts might be due to temporary occlusions such as street light poles or random variation in sensor performance, other bursts of incorrect classification might be due to more worrisome types of correlated classification failures. As an example, a classifier might lose track of pedestrians who are standing near scaffolding, presumably due to the strong vertical edges in the camera image, even though the pedestrian is in plain view and is completely unobstructed.

Related to object permanence is predicting whether a previously unseen object is hiding behind an occlusion that might suddenly appear inside the safe reaction range of the AV. Classic scenarios include the children running out between parked cars, and debarking bus riders crossing traffic after appearing from in front of the stopped bus. While it is impossible to predict every object that might appear from every occlusion, AVs should be at least as conservative as human drivers in this regard. Children tend to appear randomly near play areas, and every ball rolling into a roadway should form a basis for predicting a child following it. Extra caution should be used when passing stopped public buses even if there is no crosswalk.

Speculatively predicting the potential presence of a vulnerable road user causes a tradeoff between permissiveness in driving vs. reducing the probability of a collision with a newly revealed road user. Just as human drivers should slow down when approaching intersections with poor cross-street visibility, playgrounds, and stopped transit vehicles, AVs should operate more cautiously when there is an elevated risk of obscured road users.

From a metrics point of view, AVs should track the probability of an occluded road user appearing based on the situation, and should be operated more conservatively when that probability is elevated. Whatever risk calculation is used by the AV should be continually checked against real-world outcomes.

6.3.4. ODD metrics

Summary: Operational Design Domain metrics (ODD metrics) deal with how thoroughly the ODD has been validated, the completeness of the ODD description, and how often the vehicle is forcibly ejected from its ODD.

An ODD is the designer's model of the types of things that the AV is intended to deal with. The actual world will have things that are outside the ODD. As a simple example, the ODD might include fair weather and rain, but snow and ice might be outside the ODD because the vehicle is intended to be deployed in a place where freezing weather is rare. It might well be that freezing happens yearly in the real world at some location, and its omission from the ODD simply means the AV is not put into operate on those very cold days.

Several types of ODD safety metrics can be helpful. One is how well validation covers the ODD. That measures whether the testing, analysis, simulation, and other validation cover everything in the ODD, or have gaps in coverage.

When considering ODD coverage, it is important to realize that ODDs have many dimensions, going well beyond geofence boundaries. Some obvious variables are day versus night, wet versus dry, and freeze versus thaw. But different driving locations and times can also have differences in traffic rules, condition of road markings, the types of vehicles present, the types of pedestrians present, whether there are leaves on the trees that affect lidar localization, and so on. All these things and more can affect perception, planning, prediction, and motion. And all of them must be considered in measuring how well validation has covered the ODD.

Another type of metric is how well the system detects ODD violations. At some point, a vehicle will be forcibly ejected from its ODD even though it did not do anything wrong, simply due to external events. A freak snowstorm in the desert, a tornado, or the appearance of a new type of completely unexpected vehicle can force an AV out of its ODD with essentially no warning. The system must recognize when it has exited its ODD and be safe, even if being safe means an orderly shutdown procedure to leave the vehicle in a safe off-road location. Metrics related to this are how often ODD violations are happening during testing and on the road after deployment, and what fraction of those ODD violations were recognized by the AV itself rather than identified some other way.

Coverage of the ODD is important, but an equally important question is how good is the ODD description itself? If an ODD description is missing many things that happen every day in the actual operational domain (the real world), then that AV is going to have problems operating. If we hypothetically assume that an AV is perfectly safe within its ODD, then that simply pushes safety issues into the disparities between the ODD and the real world.

A higher-level measurement strategy is ODD description quality, which can take many forms. The frequency of ODD violations during road testing can inform how well the ODD covers the real world as a supplement to pre-deployment analysis.

How often the vehicle fails to follow the commanded trajectory can predict missing environmental characteristics in the ODD model. For example, cobblestone pavers will have significantly different driving dynamics than a smooth concrete surface, leading to motion control problems that are due to the omission of that type of road surface from design validation.

Metrics showing frequent perception failures could be due to poor training of machine learning capabilities, but could also indicate an odd object breaking the ODD object taxonomy for which there is no training data. For example, a new aggressive clothing style or new types of vehicles appearing on roads could create a mismatch between the ODD and the real world if they cause perception failures.[377] Similarly, planning failures could be due to planning software defects, but could also be due to the ODD missing descriptions of informal local traffic behavioral conventions.[378]

A metric tallying prediction failures might find prediction algorithm issues, but could also find missing actor types with atypical behavior compared to other road users. For example, large groups of runners in formation near a military base might present a challenge if formation runners are missing from training data. It might be fine to have an incomplete ODD so long as the AV can always tell when something is happening that forced it out of the ODD. But it is important to consider that metric issues in various areas might be due to an unintentionally incomplete ODD model compared to the real world.

Summing up, ODD metrics should address how well validation covers the whole ODD and how well the system detects ODD violations. It is also useful to consider that a cause of poor metric results in other areas might be that the ODD description is missing something important compared to what happens in the real world.

6.3.5. Surprise metrics

Summary: You can estimate how many unknown unknowns are left to deal with via a metric that measures the surprise arrival rate. All things being equal, a low surprise arrival rate for a significant time spent testing or operating suggests a similarly low surprise arrival rate for upcoming miles.

A significant threat to the safety of machine learning-based systems is encountering surprises in the form of input data representing unknown unknown objects or situations. That means there will need to be a way to measure and predict how often surprises will be encountered as part of predicting on-road safety.

---

[377] It might seem a bit odd that a new vehicle type or hairstyle could break the ODD. The idea is that the ODD necessarily contains a taxonomy (implicit or explicit) of all the objects relevant to safe operation that need to be recognized and reacted to. If a new vehicle shape or color scheme causes a perception failure, whatever is unique about that vehicle needs to be accounted for in the taxonomy so that perception training and validation make sure the vehicle is recognized as a vehicle. In other words, that new vehicle characteristic introduced a critical difference between the ODD (model of the real world) and the operational domain (the real world), requiring an ODD update to close the gap.

[378] For example, the infamous Pittsburgh Left. See Blackley 2020: https://www.wesa.fm/development-transportation/2020-07-28/how-the-pittsburgh-left-became-embedded-in-city-driving

6.3.5.1. Software reliability growth modeling

Your first reaction to thinking about measuring unknown unknowns may be: how in the world can you do that? How can you measure something you don't know about?

It turns out that the software engineering community has been working on just the approach we are looking for over many decades: software reliability growth modeling.[379] That area has a rich history and solves a very similar conceptual problem of estimating the arrival rate of surprises. In particular, one aspect of that approach is estimating how many more unknown things might be discovered with a certain amount of additional effort.

Software reliability growth modeling deals with estimating how many software defect bugs are left in a system based on how many software defect "bugs" have been found during testing. (Our surprises are, in terms of this approach, analogous to the bugs.) If you spend a week testing and find 100 bugs, it is a really good bet that the number of remaining bugs is greater than zero. But the question, is how many more bugs are left to find?

You can glean more information about how many bugs are left to find by looking at trends. As an example, consider a situation in which you find 100 bugs the first week, 20 on week 2, and 10 on week 3. All things being equal you'd expect to find only a few bugs if any on week 4, and by week 5 or 6 you might stop finding bugs.[380] Or you might get to a steady state situation of finding several bugs a week for many weeks in a row, depending on your testing strategy and the quality of the software.

The idea is that if week after week the bug count goes down, you can start forming expectations about an upper bound on how many bugs you expect to find during the next time interval, all things being equal. The software reliability growth modeling research area proposes a variety of mathematical functions and approaches to estimate the shape of the defects-found-over-time curve. But even a simple hand sketch of a curve fit can have some value here in setting expectations of how many software defects are likely to be found with additional testing effort. If the number of bugs found is nicely following a trend line over time, it is reasonable to expect that trend line to continue if there are no major changes to the software or the testing strategy.

One of the many important limitations to such an approach is that when you get to zero bugs found with a certain amount of effort it does not mean there are no bugs left in the software. Rather, it means there are no bugs left that can be found via whatever testing technique you are using. If the

---

[379] A dizzying array of work on this topic exists, most of which is too specialized to be a good first read on the topic. The general idea relevant to surprise metrics is using historical arrival rates of discovered defects to predict the future discovery of defects. Wood's paper from 1996 seems a reasonable starting point, describing the concept as used by a high dependability computing company applied to production software: https://www.hpl.hp.com/techreports/tandem/TR-96.1.pdf

[380] There are any number of reasons that expectation might not be fulfilled, especially including making major changes to the software during debugging. This is a simplistic view to illustrate the concept.

software is used in a way your testing method did not anticipate, expect more bugs to show up in the field. That is why it is so important to do testing that reflects the types of situations that can cause problems during real-world usage.

While you would like to get to zero bugs in testing, it is common to not ever get there. In non-life-critical systems, testing is often terminated when the number of bugs being found in testing is deemed to be "small" and/or the testing time and monetary budget has been spent. Even then, tracking the trends of bugs being found gives some expectation of how rough the ride will be for users when the software is released.

A related approach is to arrange a stress test of a system, especially for complex multi-user systems. If the original system fails after a few minutes of stress testing, system robustness might be improved over time until the failures become sufficiently infrequent to be tolerable. Perhaps if the system can run for ten days without failing under high stress it is deemed time to ship it, while scheduling a maintenance reboot every weekend during operation for good measure.

A much more troubling situation occurs when the number of bugs found in each week of testing is too high for comfort, but does not decrease over time. Stories abound of projects that are perpetually a couple of months away from shipping, either dying from budget exhaustion or being shipped with poor quality. Software like that typically has modules that are poorly designed in a way that makes them a so-called "bug farm." Continued testing and defect removal will not resolve the situation without stepping back to do a major redesign of the bug farms within the software.

The metric that matters most for software reliability growth modeling is the projected number of defects that could be found with additional testing. When that number gets low enough to present acceptable risk, it is time to ship. That approach might be used to track surprise metrics and get a handle on unknown unknowns.

6.3.5.2. Surprise arrival rate modeling

We might be able to use the main idea of software reliability growth modeling to manage the arrival of unknowns for AV deployment. In software reliability growth modeling, each defect that remains undiscovered is an unknown, and the point is to find those unknowns during testing instead of operation as much as possible. We assume effort has already been made to fix for traditional software defects in an AV, so this discussion is about handling unknowns for machine learning training data and system requirements. This corresponds to the SOTIF idea of discovering and then resolving unknown unsafe triggering conditions.

For grappling with unknown unknowns, we need to estimate not the defects in implementation, but rather the gaps and defects in requirements and training data. Nonetheless, an approach similar to software reliability growth modeling could work. For both software reliability and surprise arrivals, what we care about is estimating the population of things that would be found if we did more testing and/or operation.

The main metric we propose for managing unknown unknowns is tracking the arrival rate of surprises. How often are surprises arriving? The longer it is between surprises, the more mature the AV design can be considered to be.

A surprise can be anything that causes the AV to fail, or the AV to experience something it was not intended to handle, such as some edge case in the environment. It need not be a crash, but rather any violation of expectations (a surprise) exposes a gap or defect in the system requirements that should be addressed.

Ideally, AV designers start measuring surprises during the design process. If a simulator is generating randomized driving scenarios, measuring surprises (failures to handle a particular combination of driving conditions) can provide a measure of how well the design is progressing. Later, the surprise arrival rate during road testing gives an idea of how well the simulations are doing at predicting real-world driving conditions.

Surprises should still be tracked during deployment. It is likely that surprises will arrive in real-world operation no matter how hard the design team has tried to find them all before deployment. However, as long as surprises are relatively infrequent and vast majority of surprises are benign, this might still be fine. The arrival of a surprise while driving amounts to the AV being ejected from its ODD. So long as it can detect the surprise, it can respond with a graceful Fallback maneuver.

Fixing surprises that arrive even after deployment can help with continuously improving safety. Moreover, noticing a cluster of surprises can signal that the operational environment has changed in some important way, prompting an ODD update to match the new environment. We will revisit this idea in section 8.4.2 and use it as the basis for a bootstrap safety argument.

6.3.6. Conformance and engineering rigor metrics

Summary: Metrics that evaluate progress in conforming to an appropriate safety standard can help track safety during development.

Conformance metrics have to do with how extensively a system conforms to a safety standard. They are not measuring direct safety outcomes, but rather how complete engineering efforts have been in designing and validating safety.

A typical software or systems safety standard has a large number of requirements that must be met. A typical functional safety standard has extensive tables of engineering techniques or technical mitigation measures that need to be done based on the risk presented by each hazard. While mitigating a low-risk hazard might just need normal software quality practices, a life-critical hazard might call for dozens of very specific safety and software quality techniques to make sure the software is not going to fail in use. The higher the risk, the more process rigor table entries need to be performed in design validation and deployment.[381]

The simplest metric related to a safety standard is as a simple yes/no question: Do you conform to a relevant safety standard? However, there are nuances that matter. Conforming to a standard might mean a lot less than you might think for any number of reasons.

Given a statement that some AV conforms to a standard, the first question is what is the scope of the conformance? For example, is conformance just hardware components, or is it both hardware and software? It is somewhat common to see a claim of conformance to ISO 26262, and then find out it is only for hardware or for design processes – but not the software. For AVs, conformance needs to include software, or it is a rather hollow standards claim.

If conformance does cover the software, what scope? Is it just self-test software that detects hardware failures (again, a common conformance claim that omits important aspects of the product)? Does it include the real-time operating system? Does it include all the application software that is relevant to safety?

If a conformance claim is made that includes software, is that claim just for a part of the system, or is it for the entire vehicle? Does it cover both the vehicle and its cloud infrastructure and the communications to the cloud? Does it cover the system used to collect training data that is assumed to be accurate to create a safety-critical machine learning-based system? And so on. If you see a claim of conformance, be sure to ask what exactly the claim applies to, because it might not be everything that matters for safety.

Conformance can have different levels of credibility.[382] The weakest claim might be that an AV has been designed "in the spirit of the standard," which in real life is an essentially meaningless claim. A close cousin is "we use an internal standard that we think is equivalent to this international standard" which in practice is almost certain to be weaker than the actual standard. Or it might be that the standard is conformed to in theory, but the independent assessment is performed by a team with too much pressure to approve even if the conformance is not really complete.

For life-critical systems it is essential that any claim of conformance be checked in its entirety by an independent team of technically competent assessors. Independence must first include an independent boss (for example, someone who does periodic performance assessments and raise determinations for the assessors) who is not incentivized to approve deployment. If the person who can reward or punish the assessors for their independent evaluation of conformance gets a big cash bonus for shipping on time, that is not independent enough. Independence also needs to consider individual incentives to assessors. If an assessor has a huge pile of stock options that gain value when a conformance milestone is met, that is also a problem for independence. While there can be exceptions for very large,

---

[381] Here we are referring to SIL approaches as discussed in section 3.1.6.2.

[382] This section expands on the theme in section 4.10.7.

diversified corporations that have a highly independent assessment business unit, in getting sufficient independence for final conformance sign-off often means using external assessors.

Another dimension of conformance metrics is: how much of the standard is being conformed to? Is it only some chapters or all of the chapters? In some standards most of the text is not required to claim conformance.[383] Did only the required text get addressed or were the optional parts addressed as well?

Has the standard been aggressively tailored so that it weakens the value of the claim conformance? Some standards permit skipping some clauses or interpreting the standard in a very weak way under funding and deadline pressures. It is important to understand how tailored the standard was. Was the full standard conformed to? Were pieces left out that should have been left in? Were practices required by the standard interpreted in an unreasonably weak way?

Aggressive tailoring or conformance to only part of a standard is problematic for life-critical systems. It is common to see misunderstandings based on one or more of these issues. Somebody claims conformance to a standard, but does not disclose the limitations. Then somebody else gets confused and says, oh, well, the safety box has been checked by standards conformance, so nothing to worry about. However, excessive tailoring or partial conformance might leave the resultant system with substantive safety issues unaddressed.[384]

During development (before the design is complete), partial conformance and measuring progress against partial conformance can be an important part of a safety roadmap. Ideally, there is a safety case that documents the conformance plan and has a list of how you plan to conform to all the aspects of the standard that are relevant by the time a product is put into service. A metric then measures progress against the completeness of the safety case. The progress is probably not linear, and not every requirement from the standard takes the same amount of effort. But just looking at what fraction of the standard that has been addressed can be helpful for managing the engineering process. However, by the end of the engineering effort the entire standard must be covered.

---

[383] In standards terminology, only text that is "normative" is required. Text that is "informative" is a suggestion or explanation only, and is not a direct factor in determining conformance. A mix of both normative and informative text is common. As an example, ISO 21448 (FDIS version) has 190 pages including guidance annexes, but only page numbers 1-56 are normative content.

[384] In practice a Safety Manual or other similar document is supposed to be delivered with any component or subsystem that has been assessed for conformance to a safety standard. That safety manual documents the boundaries and limitations to any conformance claim. If the higher level system does not respect those boundaries or takes credit for safety beyond those boundaries, the result will be unsafe even though the component was assessed for conformance.

Summing up, conforming to relevant safety standards is an essential part of ensuring safety, especially in life-critical products. Metrics, measures, and ways to assess how well that conformance is going will help ensure progress toward acceptable safety. If for some reason a product or component is released with only partial standards conformance, metrics indicating the situation will be important to document what has and has not been done.

It is important to make sure an AV conforms to the right standards, with the right scope, and with only absolutely justified tailoring. Otherwise, a conformance claim can end up being a paper tiger that does not assure safety in the real world.

6.3.7. Causal rather than correlative metrics

Summary: Metrics that are correlative rather than causal can give false indications of potential AV safety. Hard braking might be a symptom of unsafe operation – or it might just be the way the AV is built.

An important piece of the metric puzzle is making sure that any metric is predictive of safety outcomes. Not all things that can be measured relate to safety, and not all things that might intuitively seem to be related to safety will turn out to be predictive of safety, especially if there are design or operational incentives to game the metrics.

Take for example the classical human driver safety metric of hard braking. Insurance companies who do real-time driver monitoring typically say that hard braking events are associated with risky driving. They have determined that hard braking is a useful risk metric for setting insurance rates. But that does not necessarily mean that lack hard braking is causally predictive of safe AV driving skills. Considerations include:

- Some hard braking events are legitimately necessary for safety, such as if another vehicle runs a stop sign and the AV is forced to brake hard to avoid a crash. From a risk point of view hard braking might still be reasonably predictive of crashes, because a vehicle being driven in an area in which other vehicles frequently run stop signs is still at higher risk of a crash, regardless of who might be at fault. While in this case hard braking is necessary to avoid a crash, each hard braking event "blames" the AV for unsafe driving. From a safety metric point of view, that punishes drivers who avoid a crash in such situations, and rewards drivers who do not even notice the other vehicle running a stop sign but get lucky and do not happen to get hit. The presumption here is that drivers mostly will brake to try to avoid getting hit due to a self-preservation instinct – something that an ADS does not really have. Hard braking might reflect that something dangerous has happened, but not that the AV was doing anything dangerous itself.[385]

- The risk of rear-end collision from hard braking depends to a large degree on whether there is a trailing vehicle that might cause the hit from

---

[385] Other than perhaps driving in a neighborhood full of crazy other drivers.

behind, which is not included in the metric. If an AV is sophisticated enough to alter its braking force based on the size and position of trailing vehicles, it can significantly mitigate rear-end collision risk. An AV strategy that brakes hard only if there is no closely following vehicle might be quite safe, but would be punished by a simplistic hard braking metric.

- Hard braking might be a useful proxy for behaviors such as aggressive speed control and inattention causing last-second panic stops in human drivers. If we assume hard braking due to inattention and poor driving skills overwhelms hard braking to avoid crashes, maybe hard braking is a reasonable metric for human drivers. However, the envisioned benefits of AVs include that they will have good driving skills, will be able to maintain excellent 360-degree situational awareness, will not get distracted, and will not drive aggressively due to emotional state. If all the distracted driving and road rage hard braking events are avoided, it would be no surprise if the remaining hard braking events correlate poorly with AV driving skills.

- An engineer designing an AV (or a sophisticated human driver) who is being measured on hard braking is incentivized to avoid hard braking, even if it slightly increases the risk of converting a near-hit situation into an actual collision by reducing braking force.[386] In particular, if a specific threshold value is used for hard braking, an AV designer is incentivized to build a maximum braking force slightly below the threshold and blame any collision on being due to a situation in which it was (given the artificial limit on braking ability) impossible to brake in time to avoid a collision.

For the example of hard braking, a metric that is correlated with risk for human drivers is not necessarily a good safety metric choice. Partly that is because lower risk is not the same as safety. But also that is because an AV designer judged on this metric will have significant incentive and ability to evade and game the metric in a way that might actually compromise safety.

The real issue is that lack of hard braking is not inherently tied to safety, but rather seems to be correlated to it for a typical human driver. The relationship is not "I'm a safe driver because I never brake hard" but rather "in the absence of a strong incentive to game the metric, lack of hard braking suggests that I am at lower risk of a crash." While an AV that slams on its brakes with maximum force at every stop does not sound desirable, an AV that has weak brakes installed to ensure it cannot possibly brake hard when it needs to does not seem likely to be safe.

---

[386] This situation was said to occur when Tesla drivers were incentivized to improve their so-called "safety score" to qualify for Full Self Driving beta privileges. Drivers responded by moderating their braking force even in situations where they admitted it increased collision risk. See Ruffo 2021:
https://www.autoevolution.com/news/tesla-safety-score-beta-shows-its-impact-and-raises-doubts-a-few-hours-after-release-170309.html

When picking metrics, it is important to be able to relate the metric values to safety outcomes, preferably via a tie to an engineering-based reason why the vehicle is safe. Correlation is not causation,[387] and confusing the two can lead to problematic outcomes.

6.4. Metric proposals

Summary: There are several metric proposals out there, but we like Safety Performance Indicators (SPIs). SPIs help ensure that assumptions in the safety case are valid, that risks are being mitigated as effectively as you thought they would be, and that fault and failure responses are working the way you thought they would.

In addition to the various types of metrics discussed in preceding sections, there are two overall proposed approaches to safety metrics: Safety Performance Indicators (SPIs) and a set of behavioral metrics proposed by various industry sources.

6.4.1. Safety Performance Indicators (SPIs)

Safety Performance Indicators, or SPIs, are safety metrics defined in the ANSI/UL 4600 standard.[388] The 4600 SPI approach covers many different ways to approach safety metrics for an AV, divided into several categories. A distinctive characteristic of an SPI is that it is linked to a specific claim in a safety case, and is used to detect when that claim might be rendered false by observed data. Any of the types of metrics previously discussed might be an SPI so long as each SPI is linked to a claim in a safety case.[389]

One type of 4600 SPI safety metric is a system-level safety metric. Some of these are lagging metrics such as the number of collisions, injuries, and fatalities. But other SPI metrics associated with driving have leading metric characteristics because they are intended to predict loss events. Leading metrics gathered during operation include SPIs for which no loss occurs, but for which the AV's behavior is clearly dangerous. Examples include near hits and traffic rule violations. The idea is that continual near hits and traffic rule violations will eventually lead to a loss event, so measuring such problematic behaviors can help predict overall safety.

---

[387] Obxkcd: https://xkcd.com/552/

[388] Safety Performance Indicators from ANSI/UL 4600 intentionally have the same name as a similar concept in aviation. In aviation they tend to be used for operational safety: see ICAO Annex 19 – Safety Management at:

https://www.icao.int/nacc/documents/meetings/2014/sspsmsant/annex19.pdf

Consistent with ANSI/UL 4600, we consider SPIs in a much more expansive manner to cover design and other lifecycle considerations including operations.

[389] The relationship between SPIs and safety cases is discussed in more detail in chapter 7.

Another type of 4600 metric is intended to deal with ineffective risk mitigation. An important type of SPI relates to ensuring hazards and faults are not occurring more frequently than expected in the field.

As a narrow but concrete example, consider an AV design that takes into account that a vehicle control data network might lose one network message out of a million due to electrical noise. The AV can withstand such occasional data loss and still be safe. But say that one day the AV starts losing one out of a thousand network messages. With such a high data loss rate the AV might still be acting more or less safely, but something is clearly wrong. Something should be done to address network reliability before a clump of lost network messages can happen at the wrong time and cause a crash. In this example the SPI is monitoring whether the message loss rate used in engineering analysis (one per million on average) is holding true during operation.

A broader example is that a rare hazard might be deemed acceptable without mitigation because it is thought that it will never happen in practice. But just because a member of a design team has never seen it happen does not mean it never happens in the real world, especially if millions of AVs are deployed. A one-in-a-million type event can easily happen every day somewhere in a large fleet of a million vehicles. A false sense of security for events that are expected to "never" happen can be mitigated by creating an SPI to measure if such an event does in fact happen.[390] If not, then that is great. But far too often "never" turns out to be wishful thinking with a large fleet of safety-critical systems.[391]

Another type of SPI for field data is measuring how often components fail or behave badly. For example, an AV might have two redundant computers so that if one crashes, the other one will keep working. What if one of those computers is failing every 10 minutes? The AV might drive around for an entire day and not crash because the second computer did not fail at all that day. But if the reliability calculations assume each computer might fail once a year and instead there is an internal failure every 10 minutes, both will fail at the same time much sooner than expected. It is important for SPIs to confirm that component failure rates are as expected, even if failures have been masked by redundancy so far.

---

[390] For example, some engineers might say that lightning strikes on a moving car are an unrealistic concern and will never happen in practice. However, a quick web search reveals many examples, including videos of such strikes. It is worth considering how an AV will respond to loss of all of its electronics due to a direct lightning strike while driving, and how that fits in a claim of acceptable safety. See Parrish, 2014: https://edmonton.ctvnews.ca/it-sounded-like-a-sonic-boom-couple-describes-lightning-strike-while-on-highway-1.1855556

[391] One million hours is about 114 years. An event that happens once per million hours can easily never happen to any particular human over an entire lifetime, but will be expected to happen daily somewhere in a fleet of a million vehicles operating just one hour per day. Engineers saying something cannot happen because they have never seen it is a common fallacy in safety engineering.

A related type of SPI has to do with classification algorithm performance for AVs. When doing safety analysis, there will be set criteria for permissible false positive and false negative rates for the perception system. While those rates can be validated in testing, there is every reason to expect that real-world performance might be different. SPIs are important to ensure that perception performance is as accurate in operations as required.

Another type of SPI is related to recoveries from faults and failures. It is common to argue that safety-critical systems are safe because they use fail-safes and fallback operational modes. If something bad happens, the argument is that the fail-safes will ensure the system remains safe. However, fail-safes themselves are imperfect, so there is also a reasonable limit on how often it is acceptable to exercise the fail-safes before the system gets unlucky and is too likely to encounter a fail-safe malfunction. SPIs should measure how often fail-safes are exercised, and how often they work as intended even if there is no actual loss event.

Chapters 7 and 8 have more detailed discussions of how SPIs related to safety cases and how they might be applied in practice.

6.4.2. AVSC metrics

The Automated Vehicle Safety Consortium (AVSC) is a closed-membership group of automotive industry companies that publishes recommended practice documents[392] for some aspects of AV safety through SAE. One of those documents is: *AVSC Best Practice for Metrics and Methods for Assessing Safety Performance of Automated Driving Systems (ADS)*, AVSC00006202103.[393]

The AVSC metrics document proposes a variety of safety performance metrics in the categories of crash statistics, traffic regulation compliance, maintaining safety envelopes, contextually safe vehicle motion control, and object/event reaction time.

The crash statistics and traffic regulation requirement metrics measure the observable behavior of a vehicle operating on roadways. The other metrics involve leaving sufficient room around the vehicle (safety envelopes). Vehicle motion and reaction time are treated as leading metrics along the lines of roadmanship.

Appendix C of the AVSC metrics document lists other proposed metrics based on a survey of various papers and standards, and is worth a look for any team brainstorming potential metric candidates. Examples of metrics

---

[392] It is important to note that AVSC documents do not have the status of regular SAE standards documents because they are not subject to a public consensus process. This is true even for versions of AVSC documents that are published by SAE via their partnership arrangement. AVSC publications can evolve into SAE standards documents via an additional more open consensus process, typically undergoing extensive revision in the process before being assigned an SAE standards "J" document number.

[393] See: https://www.sae.org/standards/content/avsc00006202103/

identified in the appendix include scenario completeness, near misses, system error rates, and instantaneous risk.

While the AVSC document surveys a broad variety of potential metrics, it does not attempt to create a specific link between leading metrics and safety outcomes.

6.5. Metric thresholds

Summary: At some point every metric needs to have an acceptance threshold. "Up is good" for a metrics chart sounds nice, but how far up is "up" enough for acceptable safety for a particular metric? There needs to be a threshold. Moreover, for safety it is often the case that even a very small number of problematic metric values can make the system unsafe overall,[394] so average metric values might not be useful.

6.5.1. Safety is statistical

A significant challenge with any safety metric is reconciling the desire to know if a vehicle's behavior is safe at any particular moment compared to the reality that the safety of an AV should ultimately boil down to the frequency of rare mishaps. There are two sides to this coin. One side is that if an AV goes a million miles without a fatality it could still be 10 to 100 times less safe than a human driver and the fatalities just haven't happened yet. Lack of a crash so far does not necessarily mean the vehicle is acceptably safe. The other side of that same coin is that a big crash in the first million miles does not necessarily mean the AV will crash every million miles – it could simply be that the AV was unlucky and the next crash will not happen for hundreds of millions of miles, although that is unlikely.[395] Safety ends up being not a moment-to-moment state, but rather a statistical property averaged over huge fleet sizes and numbers of miles traveled.

In a similar vein, counting up only the number of crashes does not necessarily give much information about safety. When an AV prototype has a crash, advocates for AV technology often say something along the lines that one death is no big deal since traditional vehicles killed perhaps 100 people that same day. What they overlook is that a test fleet of perhaps a few dozen operational vehicles killing one person (1 death over a few dozen

---

[394] Very often safety is not about how many things go right, but rather about how many things go wrong. One bad pipe out of 10,000 in plumbing still means a flood.

[395] Smart money would not bet that an AV that crashes in the first million miles is acceptably safe. The point here is that we need to be more sophisticated about probabilistic characterizations of safety beyond simple "without crash means safe" and "any crash means technology will never work" type news headlines.

vehicles) is a much different proposition than 100 deaths caused by just under 300 million conventional vehicles.[396]

Any particular vehicle having a crash – or not – is not a particularly useful indication of safety unless taken in the context of the exposure of vehicles of that type compared to stakeholder expectations for safety. Setting acceptable thresholds for metrics needs to take this into account. With small fleet sizes such as seen in AV test fleets, pretty much any adverse event is a problem, because the exposure is low compared to conventional vehicles. But as fleet sizes grow, catastrophically bad events are to be expected even for acceptably safe AVs.

A significant practical challenge for setting thresholds for metrics is that the acceptable failure rates for high consequence crashes are so low we need to aggregate metrics across many vehicles rather than just a single vehicle to understand overall safety.

6.5.2. Extreme values matter more than average metrics

An AV safety metric needs to do better than being an instantaneous measure. A metric that says "nothing bad has happened in the last hour" does not mean the AV is safe. Rather, some sort of metric processing is needed to understand safety of an AV fleet over large numbers of vehicles and long time intervals.[397]

To assess overall AV safety, we need average metrics that account for behavior over time. This might seem straightforward, but in practice looking at safety as an average of risk overall for behaviors is not the best way to frame the problem. The part that matters is not the average. Rather, safety is limited by infrequent instances of dangerous behaviors and situations.

Consider an AV traveling down a road with concrete barriers on each side of the lane. The AV could keep in the center of the lane to within an inch for an entire hour-long trip – except for a few seconds during which it managed to hit both the left and right barriers. The trip average might be exactly centered. And indeed, for almost the entire trip it was nicely centered in the lane. But it is the crashes into the side barriers we care about for safety, not the other miles where nothing happened.[398]

---

[396] Yes, on other days AV technology did not cause deaths. But that simply emphasizes the point here. Vehicle safety needs to account for both the numerator of mishaps and denominators of exposure and scale. Anything else is merely marketing talking points rather than objective statements about safety.

[397] There is a place for instantaneous risk prediction metrics in deciding if a vehicle has gotten itself into an overly risky situation and should take mitigating action. But such metrics are more about behavioral control of the AV rather than assessing overall safety outcomes.

[398] Advocates for vehicle automation often become incensed during discussions about dangerous AV testing incidents, complaining that nobody is talking about the amazing things that are shown in crash-free driving videos. But the crashes are the part where people get harmed.

Consider a similar trip in which a car wanders back and forth in the lane by a foot or two instead of staying exactly centered, and on average is six inches skewed to the left of the center of the lane. But in this case no side barrier is hit. The wandering might be a sign that the vehicle's control system is less stable and possibly not as safe overall. Or it might be a sign that the vehicle is avoiding potholes, optimizing trajectory on curves, or driving in high winds that are pushing the car around. The safety outcome is that nothing was hit, making this vehicle safer than the other one that hit barriers for only a few seconds of an otherwise perfect trip.

Measuring the average offset from center of lane is a common performance indicator for system automation. But might have little, if anything, to do with safety so long as the average offset is much smaller than the width of the lane.

Some systems are obviously dangerous, and that is easy to spot.[399] But the difference between a system that is not obviously dangerous and a system that is safe can only be measured by looking at reactions to rare but dangerous situations in which the system struggles to stay safe. What we need is not a measure of how good the average looks, but rather a measure of how often the system is misbehaving or doing something riskier than it should.

6.5.3. Metric thresholds

For the single-lane example with side barriers just discussed, from a safety point of view how well the vehicle centers is irrelevant, within broad limits. The metric that matters is how often the vehicle crashes into walls, and likely how often it has near hit encounters with walls. For that we do not care about distance from center of lane – we care about distance from walls. And not even average distance from walls, but rather time spent dangerously close to walls. In other words, we want to track how much time and/or how often the AV violates some sort of metric threshold that indicates dangerous operation.

While picking a metric that is related to dangerous behaviors rather than normal behaviors is an important start, just defining such a metric does not get the job done. It is also important to address the question of how dangerous is really a problem.

For the car driving down a road with side barriers example, the way to address safety is to base metrics on how often or how much time is spent dangerously close to a side barrier. For this example, let us assume that the vehicle's safety concept is that it is designed to never get closer than one foot to a side barrier. This means design engineers have taken into account the types of things that can disturb a car's path, and have determined that as long

---

[399] Brute force road testing is really about testing for un-safety. If an AV is overtly dangerous, it won't take too many miles to see a crash or need a safety driver to intervene to prevent a crash. If you can go a lot of miles without a crash that shows it is not obviously dangerous. But further determining the AV is safe requires going beyond road testing.

as the car is at least one foot away from a barrier there is a sufficiently low probability of a crash to meet the overall AV's risk goal. This suggests the following metric thresholds:

- Time spent closer than one foot to a side barrier as a fraction of driving time.
- Number of times per hour the vehicle approaches within one foot of a side barrier.
- Impacts with side barriers per mile.

The two metrics regarding violating the one-foot buffer zone of a barrier give a way of knowing when the vehicle has violated its safety goal of staying at least a foot away. Even if no crash occurs, that one-foot buffer zone should never be violated, so every such buffer violation situation is unsafe by this definition *even if a crash never occurs*. Whenever the AV is too close it is simply a matter of luck whether a strong cross-wind or pothole in the road slams the vehicle into the wall. If the AV spends enough time too close to the wall, eventually there will be a crash. You do not have to wait for a crash to know that operating only two inches from the wall is a safety issue.

Another metric of actual crashes shows how often the loss event of hitting the barrier occurs. One would expect that there would be many more encroachments within a foot than there are crashes. That would permit using the encroachment metrics as a predictor of loss metrics. Frequent encroachments suggest a crash is more likely to happen, while fewer encroachments suggest better safety outcomes.

It is important to avoid bargaining about the threshold. The threshold needs to be set to a particular value rather than jiggled around if field data shows the threshold is not being met. An argument that leads to unsafe outcomes might go something like this. If 12 inches is the safety distance, then an AV that spends an entire trip at 12.01 inches is safe, but one that spends an entire trip at 11.99 inches is unsafe. Someone might say that makes little sense, since the measurement accuracy is probably worse than that 0.02 inch difference. So 11.99 inches is safe. A while later the number is reduced to 11.9. And then 11.8. And so on, with the threshold being lowered until a catastrophic mishap occurs revealing the core fallacy: getting away with violating a threshold a few times does not make you safe; it just makes you lucky. Until your luck runs out.[400]

The reality is there must be some buffer distance away from walls in the lane barrier example. Above a stated distance is considered safe, and below that distance is considered unsafe. Considerations such as measurement error should be built into the threshold. In other words, there is a threshold beyond which the system is determined to be acting unsafely; no bargaining allowed

---

[400] Re-setting safety rules based on having gotten away with a rule violation is called normalization of deviance. Doing this with successively colder launch temperatures that reduced flexibility of a rocket booster joint seal was a primary factor in the traffic space shuttle Challenger disaster. See:
https://en.wikipedia.org/wiki/Normalization_of_deviance

past that point. How often that threshold might be violated while still achieving acceptable safety depends on other factors, and in particular how a safety case argues that buffer distance contributes with other factors to achieve an overall acceptable safety outcome. We will continue that discussion in chapter 7 on safety cases.

For those who think that a fixed distance buffer does not make sense, that is fine. There can be a mapping from a more complex evaluative function to a binary safe/unsafe output value that takes into account vehicle speed in addition to distance to a barrier. When determining how much time spent near the barrier is unsafe you might create a points system with a certain number of points assigned for every second the AV spends within 0-3 inches away from the barrier, fewer points from 3-9 inches, and minimal points from 9-15 inches. A threshold approach would determine the threshold had been violated if more than a certain number of points were accumulated within five or ten seconds of operation. As long as the grading scheme makes sense in the context of the AV's operational concept that is fine. But ultimately there must be operational behavior limits that show the vehicle is not acting as safely as it should be, and a threshold should exist that can be triggered without requiring a loss event.

6.6. Summary

A wide variety of metrics can be used to measure and predict safety. Lagging vehicle metrics that directly measure the contributing factors to a safety goal (e.g., actual crashes) are straightforward to justify assuming that a concrete safety goal has been articulated.

Leading metrics at the vehicle level can make intuitive sense, but can be difficult to calibrate. Intuitively, a higher rate of incidents (near collisions or other vehicle misbehaviors) seems to correlate with higher risk. But the multiplier between incidents and crashes might be difficult to know in the abstract until there is some field experience. Leading metrics can serve as Key Performance Indicators suggestive of likely risk, but do not necessarily predict safety because they might rely on factors that can change over time or that are not under control of the design team.

Metrics that are predictive for human drivers need to be considered carefully because they make assumptions based on human behavior that are not necessarily applicable to AVs. As an example, the classic "hard braking" metric used by some insurance companies to rate human driver risk might not be as useful for optimizing AV safety.

Leading metrics based on subsystem performance such as vision system false negative rates for pedestrian detection can seem obvious candidates for measurement. However, setting a threshold value can be difficult without knowing a lot about the context. For example, one would expect camera performance would need to be better on an AV that has only cameras and no other sensors compared to an AV that also has lidar and radar to supplement camera performance. It seems unlikely that a single one-size-fits-all threshold for any sensor type will be useful for predicting safety across all AVs.

One metric pitfall is measuring things that sound nice but are not actually predictive of risk. Sure, a smooth ride inspires confidence in passengers and might be critical to market acceptance. But a smooth ride might have little predictive power for safety outcomes.

Another metric pitfall is setting up metrics that present perverse incentives. The most obvious such metric is disengagement rates, which incentivize taking more chances during testing by avoiding disengagements, or saying that a particular incident does not count because the vehicle would have gotten lucky without a safety driver intervention. It is important that metrics not only predict safety, but also that improving performance on metrics necessarily incentivizes better safety outcomes.

In chapters 7 and 8 we discuss the idea of using a specifically formulated Safety Performance Indicator approach that addresses metric challenges by tying each metric to a specific claim made by a safety case.

7.   Safety cases

The key to picking meaningful leading metrics is to find a compelling, causal explanation for why each metric selected is connected to safety outcomes. While you can always use some metrics picked based on subjective opinion, that leads to two problems. The first is whose opinion you want to use. Selections based on human driver safety metrics might not only be inaccurate, but also provide perverse incentives for more dangerous overall behavior given the differences between AV and human driver strengths and weaknesses.

The second problem is that even if you do identify a good predictive metric, you need to know what the acceptance threshold is for that number. Suppose you decide to use pedestrian detection false negatives as a leading metric for camera-based sensing. Surely it makes sense that not seeing a pedestrian is a problem. And a smaller number (fewer missed pedestrians) is likely better. But how small is small enough to be acceptably safe? And what is the point below which smaller does not improve things enough to matter? Or perhaps the issue is not how often a particular sensor fails to detect pedestrians, but rather that the undetected pedestrians have some common property that also makes them difficult to detect with other sensor types. The answer depends on what other sensors are on the AV and how they are used.

The challenge is that you do not know how good is good enough for any leading metric unless you know the role of that leading metric in the overall reasoning as to why the system is acceptably safe. For that, you need a safety case.

7.1. Safety cases and SPIs

Summary: In this section we explain what safety cases are and how they relate to SPIs.

A *safety case* is a structured argument, supported by a body of evidence that provides a compelling, comprehensible, and valid case that a system is safe for a given application in a given environment.[401] For our purposes, the system is the AV combined with all off-vehicle support required for safety, and the "given environment" is the environment the AV operates in.

Every ethically deployed AV has some manner of safety case. The level of formality, as well as the amount of detail and rigor contained in the safety case tends to vary, as do validity and soundness.

---

[401]UK MoD Def Stan 00-56 Part 1 Issue 7, 2017. Access to this standard via free registration at: https://www.dstan.mod.uk/StanMIS/

7.1.1. Safety case structure and notation

Safety cases can be generically described in terms of claims, argument, and evidence.[402] Figure 7.1 illustrates key elements of a safety case.[403]

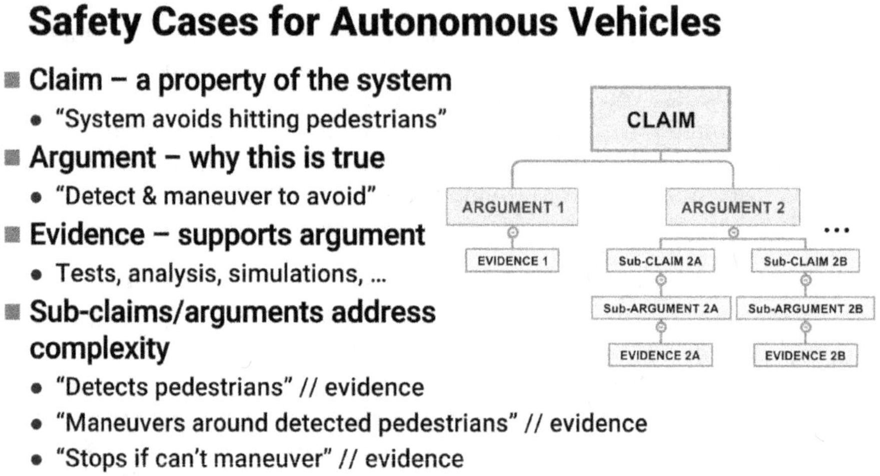

Safety Cases for Autonomous Vehicles

- **Claim – a property of the system**
  - "System avoids hitting pedestrians"
- **Argument – why this is true**
  - "Detect & maneuver to avoid"
- **Evidence – supports argument**
  - Tests, analysis, simulations, ...
- **Sub-claims/arguments address complexity**
  - "Detects pedestrians" // evidence
  - "Maneuvers around detected pedestrians" // evidence
  - "Stops if can't maneuver" // evidence

Figure 7.1. An illustration of safety case structure and elements.

A claim is a falsifiable statement of a desirable property, such as "The AV has acceptable safety" or "the false negative rate for pedestrian detection is less than 0.1% per frame from the camera system for non-occluded pedestrians closer than 25 meters" or "the real-time operating system conforms to ISO 26262 ASIL D." There is typically some context connected to each claim. An important contextual element is the concept of operations for the AV, such as robotaxi or low-speed shuttle. Another important contextual element is the intended operational environment. For an AV the given environment in terms of the definition of safety is the operational domain (OD).[404]

---

[402] Terminology varies, and there are typically more building blocks used in a safety case. A popular approach is Goal Structuring Notation (GSN) which uses the term "goal" instead of "claim." The discussion in this book should be considered neutral in terms of which nomenclature and terminology might be useful for any particular situation. For information on GSN including access to the latest community standard, see: https://scsc.uk/gsn

[403] For a narrated video explanation see: https://youtu.be/iDLSNsIzDHo

[404] The Operational Design Domain (ODD) is the design model of the real environment, which is the Operational Domain (OD). Part of the role of the safety case is arguing that the design model (ODD) is an acceptable representation of the real world (OD). We discourage use of the term ODD to refer to the real-world environment because it obscures a key issue that a lot of safety problems live in the gap between the ODD and the OD.

Evidence is some sort of factual support, often in the form of engineering analysis or testing data, that is used as the ultimate basis of support for the claim being made. In some cases, evidence might be more subjective, and could consist of an expert opinion or even just an assumption being made by the designers.[405]

The structured argument is some sort of reasoning that connects the evidence to the claim. Some more classical approaches to safety cases treat this as an exercise in deductive logic, in which claims inexorably arise from the evidence if the right argument connective structure can be found in the manner of a mathematical proof. As we shall discuss, safety cases for AVs will have to be handled in a more open-ended way[406] because of the inevitability of uncertainty in many dimensions.

There are two crucial evaluation criteria for safety cases: validity and soundness. A safety case is *valid* if the claims are necessarily true given that the evidence provides the purported support. A safety case is *sound* if the safety case is not only valid, but the evidence provides the support required for the claim to be true. For example, a safety case that has an assumption that is untrue might be valid but would be unsound.

So-called *safety case frameworks* are the argument without the evidence. A safety case framework can be useful in describing a strategy to assure safety and provide a working framework during AV development. When it comes to deployment, such frameworks are potentially valid, but should be considered unsound by default until evidence is provided.

An important observation about the scope of a safety case is that it might be silent about what happens in instances of misuse or operation outside the specified environment. For a human-directed system that is the human's problem, because a human supervisor is supposed to ensure a system is only used according to its limitations in an appropriate environment.

The whole point of having an autonomous system is to dispense with the human supervisor. From a definitional point of view this can be addressed by including misuse in the scope of the safety case. While it is all well and good to have intended uses and a model of the "should be used like this" world for engineering analysis, the actual product needs to be safe in use in the real world, with all its attendant issues and messiness.

We have seen safety cases that range from vigorous hand-waving nonsense,[407] to a powerpoint slide deck,[408] to slick marketing brochures

---

[405] Whether the assumption is true is a different matter. Functionally, assumptions might be treated as evidence by the argument. In logic these assumptions are called the premises.

[406] Engineers tend to believe the difference between theory and practice is smaller in theory than it is in practice. (For the origins of this saying, see: https://quoteinvestigator.com/2018/04/14/theory/)

[407] See the Chewbacca defense: https://en.wikipedia.org/wiki/Chewbacca_defense

[408] The first safety case powerpoint deck we were to review had been lost when the employee who created it left the company. We were told that the missing the safety case was truly superb. The review of the system itself did not go as well.

replete with rhetorical devices and eye candy, to engineering white papers, to extensive engineering analysis reports, to rigorous safety cases with graphical notation for key parts of the safety argument.

For more rigorously expressed safety cases there are defined notational standards. Goal Structuring Notation is a widely known example.[409] At a higher level of abstraction is the Structured Assurance Case Metamodel (SACM).[410] There is no inherent reason that a safety case must be graphical in nature, although using a graphical approach for viewing at least regions of a safety case has some appeal. In practice it would be no surprise if practical safety cases have a database or tabular internal structure that can optionally be viewed at least in part in a graphical manner.

Different types of safety cases are suitable for communicating to different audiences. A 10,000 page safety case with obscure formal notation is not likely to communicate well to a non-technical decision maker.[411] On the other hand, a slick marketing brochure is not going to have enough substance for technically sophisticated stakeholders to build comfort that a safety case is credible.

In our view, an ideal situation is one in which there is a substantive, technically detailed safety case that accounts for all relevant aspects of AV safety, such as one that is conformant to ANSI/UL 4600. Other lighter-weight safety case representations can be created to communicate to audiences other than technical specialists, but each alternate representation should be directly traceable to the detailed version. In other words, you need a technically detailed safety case as a foundation, but various summarizations can be prepared to be relevant to different audiences.

In some application domains safety cases do not necessarily go all the way down to fine grain specifics. This might be justifiable if there are accepted practices that can be relied upon to do the heavy lifting. For example, if there is a credible domain-specific system safety standard, a safety case might largely be a justification that a particular safety standard is applicable and is being followed in an appropriate way, without attempting to argue in detail that the safety standard is credible.[412]

7.1.2. Safety cases and leading indicators

From a metrics point of view, a significant reason a safety case is so important is that it can inform both the selection of relevant metrics and their corresponding acceptable threshold values. A measurement derived from the safety case has two advantages: it traces directly to the reasons the AV is

---

[409] See GSN Community Standard 2021: https://scsc.uk/scsc-141C

[410] See: https://www.omg.org/spec/SACM/

[411] Unless the objective is to impress with a huge stack of paper via thud factor. Yes, that is most definitely a thing.

[412] To be sure, the credibility of the safety standard is crucial. But if a widely adopted standard with an established track record is used to provide some aspect of safety, there might be little point in rehashing that topic in a safety case.

expected to be safe, and it comes with a ready-made context to determine how good the metric value needs to be to support a claim of acceptable safety.

Looking at a safety case, there are many layers between a top-level vehicle safety claim and the underlying evidence. Each claim in the middle collects a set of underlying evidence and intermediate argument to provide a piece of the overall safety puzzle, with bigger and bigger pieces being assembled going up the safety case structure and eventually reaching the overall top-most safety claim.

Using a safety case point of view, we can think of leading indicators in the context of claims in the middle of the safety case that are violated.

As a simplified, hypothetical example, a path down the safety case levels might include the following, with claims progressing at successively lower levels of the safety case with each bullet point below:

- Topmost Claim: AV is acceptably safe (with context for what "acceptably safe" means)
- ... various increasingly narrow claims ...
  - Sketch of general argument: if the camera pool has a false negative rate for pedestrians of no higher than 0.0001% over $1/5^{th}$ of a second, the rest of the claims involving tracking objects over time and other sensing modes ensure that the AV is acceptably safe
- Claim: The pool of cameras has a false negative rate for close pedestrians no worse than 0.0001% over any $1/5^{th}$ of a second time interval
  - Context: "close" pedestrians are less than 10 meters away.
  - Argument: Any pedestrian of interest will be seen by at least two cameras. Each camera will have no worse than a 0.001% false negative rate over a $1/5^{th}$ of a second time interval (6 image frames in a row at 30 frames per second). Correlated detection failures between cameras will be low enough to provide a factor of 10 improvement to 0.0001%. Correlated failures will be sufficiently random to avoid detection failures biased against identifiable sub-populations of pedestrians.
  - (Supporting claim regarding correlated failures to support ten times improvement and lack of bias omitted from this example.)
  - (Supporting argument that pool of cameras provides sufficiently overlapped fields of view omitted from this example. This should take into account occlusions and fraction of pedestrian in-frame for each camera at each pedestrian position.)
- Claim: Each camera has less than 0.001% false negative rate for any pedestrian closer than 10 meters across 6 image frames in a row
  - Evidence: there is no 6 frame image sequence in a sufficiently large and representative data set that misses a pedestrian detection, supporting a statistical conclusion of 0.001% false negative rate at a 95% confidence level.

In this example, one generic type of leading metric might be the false negative rate for pedestrians for the pool of cameras. Another would be the false negative rate for pedestrians for a single camera. A third would the fraction of correlated failure rate across pairs of cameras.

However – and this is critical – the generic leading metric does not necessarily predict safety for any particular AV without more information. Moreover, that information is likely to be very specific to that particular AV.

Consider the single camera metric. Sure, knowing how often a single camera misses seeing a pedestrian has to be related in some way to safety. And one would expect that all things being equal, a lower false negative rate of undetected pedestrians is better. But how low is low enough, given that getting all the way to zero is unrealistic? In the example, the 0.001% per camera came with some contextual statements: 1/5th of a second was a long enough time interval to support safely spreading detection across multiple frames, only a ten times improvement in detection was required despite likely common cause failures, and 10 meters (which corresponds to a certain number of pixels in size) is the right distance for a "close" passenger given that particular AV's context of operational speeds in the relevant environment. In another AV any of these contextual statements might well be different.

The only way to know whether a leading metric looks good enough is to understand how it fits within a safety case.

The point here is that it is not hard to pick a leading metric that sounds like it should be useful: "let's measure false negatives on pedestrians." However, unless you understand the precise measurement thresholds and the budget for failures given by the surrounding safety case context, you are just guessing. Without a safety case to support it, your leading metric might predict safety, or it might just be a comforting number that means almost nothing.

Because of this, setting generic safety requirements for individual components or sensors is likely to be unproductive. For example, saying something like "an AV lidar must have a 50% probability detection range of 100 meters" could have little to do with safety. That range might be much longer than needed for long-range urban applications and yet much shorter than needed for highway applications. Whether such a lidar is sufficient will also dependent on the type of camera, radar, HD map, or other information that is available from other sensors, as well as how much operational environment conditions within the ODD are likely to degrade lidar operation in practice.

7.1.3. SPIs used in safety cases

A Safety Performance Indicator (SPI) is, in general terms, a metric that is associated with the safety of the design or operation of a system.[413]

---

[413] ANSI/UL 4600 gives a very generic definition of SPI as a "metric used to quantify safety performance."

SPIs have been used in the aviation industry for operational safety as part of a Safety Management System (SMS). Aviation SPIs can include metrics such as in-flight engine shutdowns and number of non-compliance findings in a safety audit. [414] Aviation SMS activities in general assume that the underlying equipment has been designed to be acceptably safe, and are primarily intended to make sure that lifecycle activities are performed well enough to ensure safe operation.

ANSI/UL 4600 takes a broader view of SPIs for AV design, using that term for any metric used to quantify safety performance. 4600 SPIs, which are what we are interested in here, include metrics related to the AV design itself, the design process, and SMS-related metrics. Many types of SPIs are described in 4600, with significant emphasis on detecting and reporting various types of equipment failures, incidents, violations of assumptions, and other events that are likely to be predictive of downstream system-level failures. In particular, at least some SPIs are intended to detect ineffective risk mitigation, violations of statistical assumptions baked into the safety case, and other types of problems with the safety case. Moreover, 4600 requires using SPI data as a feedback mechanism to find and fix problems in the system and its safety case.

7.1.4. Safety Performance Indicators revisited

A more precise definition of a Safety Performance Indicator (SPI) for our purposes is that it is a way of combining the concepts of a measurable value, an acceptance threshold, and a relationship to a safety argument:[415]

An SPI is a metric supported by evidence that uses a threshold comparison to condition a claim in a safety case.

We can break this definition down term by term:

SPI (Safety Performance Indicator): A {metric, threshold} pair that measures some aspect of safety relevant to an autonomous vehicle according to the stated definition.

Metric: A value, typically related to one or more of product performance, design quality, process quality, or adherence to operational procedures. Often metrics are related to time (e.g., incidents per million km, maintenance mistakes per thousand repairs) but can also be related to particular release

---

[414] For a definition and concrete examples of aviation SPIs see:
https://www4.icao.int/demo/SMI/9.5.4%20SM%20ICG%20Measuring%20Safety%20Performance%20Guidance%20for%20Service%20Providers.pdf
[415] This definition was first published in:
https://safeautonomy.blogspot.com/2021/06/a-more-precise-definition-of-ansiul.html
It is included as a Highly Recommended approach in the voting draft of ANSI/UL 4600 version 3 at the time of this writing.

versions (e.g., significant defects per thousand lines of code; unit test coverage; peer review effectiveness).

Evidence: The metric values are derived from measurements rather than non-measurement sources.

Threshold: A metric on its own is not an SPI because context within the safety case matters. For example, false negative detections on a sensor as a number is not an SPI because it misses the part about how good the metric has to be to provide acceptable safety when fused with other sensor data in a particular vehicle's operational context. ("We have 1% false negatives on camera #1. Is that good enough? Well, it depends...") There is no inherent limit to the complexity of the threshold determination if such complexity is justified. But in the end the answer is some sort of comparison between the metric and the threshold that results in true or false.[416] We call the state of an SPI threshold comparison being false an *SPI Violation*.

Condition a claim: Each SPI is associated with a claim in a safety case. If the SPI threshold comparison is true, the claim is supported by the SPI. If the SPI threshold comparison is false, then the associated claim has been falsified. SPIs based on time series data could be true for a long time before encountering a situation that makes them go false, so this is a time- and state-dependent outcome in many cases.

Safety case: Per ANSI/UL 4600 a safety case is "a structured argument, supported by a body of evidence, that provides a compelling, comprehensible and valid case that a system is safe for a given application in a given environment." In the context of that standard, anything that is related to safety is in the safety case. If it is not in the safety case, it is by definition not related to safety. Figure 7.2 illustrates the concept.[417]

---

[416] Multi-valued operations and outputs are OK if you are using multi-valued logic in your safety case. Some notion of a threshold would still have to be used to assign a specific logic value or fuzzy logic value tuple nonetheless.

[417] For a narrated video explanation see: https://youtu.be/1hWYd2vizSQ

SPIs Instrument a Safety Case

■ SPIs monitor the validity of safety case claims

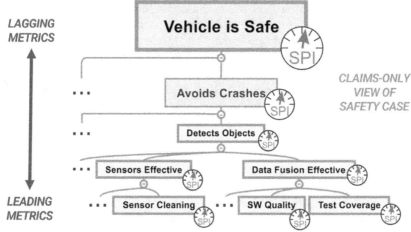

Figure 7.2. A conceptual illustration of SPIs in a safety case.

A direct implication of the SPI definition is that if a metric does not have a threshold, or it does not condition a claim in a safety case, then it cannot be an SPI.

Less formally, the point of an SPI is that you have built up a safety case, but there is always the chance you missed something in the safety case argument (omitted a relevant reason why a claim might not be true). Or you might have made an assumption that is not as true as you thought it was in the real world. Or there is otherwise some sort of a problem with your safety case that makes in invalid or unsound. An SPI violation amounts to: "Well, you thought you had everything covered and this claim was always true. And yet, here we are with the claim being false when we encountered a particular unforeseen situation in validation or real-world operation. Better update your safety argument!"

In other words, an SPI is a measurement you take to make sure that if your safety case is invalidated you will detect it and notice that your safety case has a problem so that you can fix it.

An important point of all this is that not every metric is an SPI. SPIs are a very specific term. Any metric that does not qualify as an SPI could still be called a Key Performance Indicator (KPI).[418] KPIs can be very useful, for example in measuring progress toward a functional system. But they are not SPIs unless they meet the definition given above.

There are some notes associated with this definition:

---

[418] We take the view that SPIs should be a subset of KPIs that meet our additional definitional constraints. See: https://en.wikipedia.org/wiki/Performance_indicator

- Aviation uses SPI for metrics related to the operational phase and SMS activities. The definition given here is one relevant to ANSI/UL 4600 and is a superset of the aviation use, including technical metrics and design cycle metrics as well as operational metrics.
- In this formulation, an SPI is not quite the same as a safety monitor. It might well be that some SPI violations happen to use the same {metric, threshold} comparison as logic that might trigger a vehicle safety shutdown. But for many SPI violations there might not be anything actionable at the individual vehicle level.[419] Indeed, some SPI violations might only be detectable at the fleet level in retrospect. For example, if you have a budget of 1 incident per 100 million km, an individual vehicle having such an incident does not necessarily mean the safety case has been invalidated. Rather, you need to look across the fleet data history to see if such an incident just happens to be that budgeted one in 100 million based on operational exposure, or is part of a trend of too many such incidents.
- We pronounce "SPI" as "S-P-I" rather than "spy" after a very confusing conversation during which we realized we needed to clarify to a government official that we were not proposing that the CIA send field agents to validate autonomous vehicle safety.[420]

The implications of an SPI approach to metrics are subtle but important. Most importantly:

> SPIs measure the validity and soundness of the safety case, not just safety outcomes.

This is in line with the purpose of the safety case being a proactive argument about why the AV is expected to be safe going forward. Metrics that trace to the safety case might include some lagging metrics ("we've been acceptably safe to this point"), but those lagging metrics do not prove the AV will be safe in the future. Rather, they provide a basis for building additional confidence in the safety case.

Every time an SPI is violated, that means that at least a portion of the safety case has been rendered unsound, and the system is *potentially* unsafe. It is possible the system is still safe if there is some engineering margin in the safety argument. But once any claim in the safety argument has been shown to be false, all bets are off as to the soundness and potentially the validity of the entire safety case. Once a safety case claim has been falsified, the system should be presumed to be unsafe until shown otherwise. An important special case is that if a top-level safety claim regarding lagging metrics is false, then the system is definitely unsafe (e.g., an SPI violated regarding the overall

---

[419] Section 8.3.4 discusses how to respond to an SPI violation in more detail.
[420] True story. Some older lecture videos do not have that correction, and you are welcome to laugh at that misstep if you like.

crash fatality rate is no longer a potential problem, but a proven actual problem).

7.1.4.1. Importance of SPI threshold values

A metric without a target value is not that useful as a leading indicator. Consider some hypothetical SPI metric that has a value of 90 events per million miles. You then improve the metric to 80 events per million miles. That must be better, right? Well … maybe.

If the target for your hypothetical SPI is 70, then 90 to 80 is half the way to the goal value. But what if the target is 100? Or 10? Or 1? Or 0.0001? A metric improvement might be made to a number that is already good enough for safety, or might make little practical difference to a metric that is wildly bad.

Without a target value you can collect SPI metric data and tell if you are improving, but you have no idea how much relative progress you are making, or when you have reached a reasonable leading metric goal.

For this reason, an SPI is not just a metric, but rather is a {metric, threshold} pair, with the threshold being the acceptable goal value. In practice the threshold is often not a single numeric value for comparison, but rather some evaluative function that gives a result of acceptable or not acceptable. For example, the SPI threshold might be a line drawn on an X-Y graph plane, with below the line being acceptable. Or the threshold might be a complex 3-D surface in an X-Y-Z graph space with acceptable being above that surface in the Z direction. And so on into many dimensions. The point is that each SPI metric is some combination of data values derived from evidence, and there is a defined way to know if any particular SPI value is acceptable.[421] Section 8.3 has a more detailed discussion about sources of data and possible approaches to acceptable threshold functions.

7.1.4.2. SPIs as statistical monitors

While comparing a metric value to a threshold sounds like a mechanism that triggers when any data sample crosses the threshold, typical SPIs are more likely to be statistical in nature. So for things that are not loss events themselves, it is not a single data sample, but rather a pattern of data samples that is often problematic.

Consider a hypothetical SPI of 1.5 PDO crashes per 1M VMT (Property Damage Only crashes per 1 Million Vehicle Miles Traveled). If you have 100 million miles of data, you expect to see no more than 150 PDO crashes plus or minus statistical fluctuation. But what does that mean at a finer granularity?

---

[421] A more general description is that the threshold is violated if the data from the metrics stream fails a suitable "acceptance test" in the sense that term is used in the fault tolerant computing discipline. In that framework the "recovery block" is not a runtime mitigation, but rather a data reporting function regarding the SPI violation. See Randell 1975: https://dl.acm.org/doi/10.1145/390016.808467

Consider that same hypothetical SPI in the context of a single vehicle. Say that vehicle drives 200K (200,000) miles with no crash. The SPI looks good so far. Then the AV has a crash at 250K miles. That is worse than the SPI value of 667K miles per crash. But that one vehicle has insufficient miles to build statistical significance, so is it really an SPI violation? Perhaps is, but perhaps that was the one vehicle that got unlucky out of 1000 vehicles, and the other 999 vehicles had no crashes. There is no way to resolve this if we only have data from a single vehicle.

Knowing that an SPI violation has occurred requires statistical confidence in the metric data. For many SPIs this is going to require not just single-vehicle data, but rather will require collecting data across many vehicles. For one or two PDO crashes per 1M VMT you will need to several million miles of data to know if the SPI threshold has been violated with high confidence depending on statistical fluctuation of PDO crash arrivals.

On the other hand, knowing an SPI violation has occurred can happen much sooner. For example if you see 10 crashes in 100K miles, it is a pretty sure bet that the system is worse than the target of one crash in 667K miles. Even then, it takes multiple such crashes to be sure that the first crash is due to missing the SPI target rather than simply getting unlucky.

A typical operational SPI is statistical in this way. In the common case it will take data aggregation from multiple AVs to know whether an SPI threshold has been violated. We pick up this topic again in section 8.3.3 in the context of monitoring SPI violations.

7.1.4.3. SPI vs. runtime safety monitoring

The use of SPIs can be a bit non-intuitive because they sound similar to runtime safety monitors – but they are not. Each SPI uses a problem detection mechanism that is similar to a runtime safety monitor. However, the problems being detected are often different, and the results of that monitoring play a very different system role.

A runtime safety monitor collects data during operation and *invokes a safety mechanism* if a metric violates a threshold. For example, a physics-based distance monitor might force an AV to slow down if it is following a leading vehicle too closely to leave adequate braking room. The idea is that violation of a runtime safety monitor triggers an AV response to reduce risk in real time, affecting the specific AV that has experienced the problem.

In contrast, an SPI collects data during operation or other phases of the design process and *raises a process alarm* if a metric violates a threshold. The SPI does not tell the AV to jam on the brakes. Rather, data is fed to an aggregator that does statistical analysis to see if the SPI threshold has been violated for spending too much time at impermissible following distances. If that threshold is violated, an engineering response is initiated to find the root cause and correct it via a software update, a change in ODD limitations, a design quality process intervention, or some other means.

In other words, an SPI violation triggers an engineering process response, not an AV vehicle action. Also, the SPI violation is more likely based on a statistical average across many AVs rather than a single situation affecting a single AV.

For the car-following distance example, a runtime safety monitor will slow the vehicle when the following distance is too small. But an SPI is more likely to count up how often following distance is too small, and compare it against a defined risk budget, triggering a violation only if it happens too often. The SPI might well set a somewhat more stringent threshold than the safety monitor, triggering an SPI violation even if the runtime monitor has not been triggered. A strategy might be to track how often the runtime safety monitor was *almost* invoked to solve any problems before there is a physical danger of collision in the real world. A variation on the theme would be an SPI that counts up the number of safety monitor activations and declares an SPI violation if safety monitors are activated more often than designers expected.

Again, the point of the SPI is to feed metrics regarding unexpectedly high risk back into the engineering process rather than to directly signal the AV to slam on the brakes. An acceptably safe AV is likely to have SPIs that track each runtime safety monitor, as well as SPIs that measure other things.

7.1.4.4. What does an SPI violation actually mean?

When an SPI is violated, it does not quite mean that the AV is unsafe.[422] Rather, it means that the safety case has been proven to be incorrect in some sense. Put another way, an SPI violation means you thought a certain thing could not happen, yet nonetheless it just did happen in the real world.

This might be counterintuitive. If a car has just had a fatal crash, it is easy to think that this must mean that the car is unsafe in an everyday sense. But the fact that a fatal crash has occurred, while tragic, does not on its own demonstrate a lack of safety for the AV deployed fleet as a whole. If there is a fatal crash "budget" of 5 fatal crashes per 1000M VMT (a hypothetical threshold about twice as good as current US rates including impaired drivers), then in terms of a fatalities/1000M VMT SPI the fleet is acceptably safe despite a few such crashes. Safety is not about that one crash, but rather about how often such crashes are occurring.

To be sure, after each fatality it is important to dig deep and see what could have been to prevent that fatality so as to continuously improve safety. But the point here is that SPI violations are about the overall trend, and not about any particular incident or loss event.

For a lagging metric such as crashes per VMT, an SPI violation would directly show that the AV is unsafe, and that decisive action is needed to correct the situation. But what about leading metric SPI violations in the absence of associated lagging metric SPI violations?

The violation of a leading SPI does not necessarily mean that the AV is unsafe, but rather that safety is no longer assured. The AV might be unsafe, but it might also be that there is enough engineering margin in the overall

---

[422] As mentioned earlier, the exception is that if an SPI monitoring a top-level safety claim is violated, such as overall fatality rate, that also means the AV is unsafe.

risk mitigation approach that the AV will be acceptably safe in practice. With a leading SPI violation we simply do not know which is the case. The prudent approach is that if safety is in doubt, the AV should be considered provisionally unsafe pending an investigation.

A more technically detailed interpretation is that a leading SPI violation means that one or more claims in the safety case have been falsified (shown to be false) by newly collected data. That falsification could be due to an invalid safety case (e.g., a defective argument), an invalid assumption, or newly discovered data that revealed some other sort of previously unknown issue. Some newly arriving operational data caused us to discover the problem, or some change in the world broke a previously sound safety case. Regardless of the root cause, an SPI violation means that you can no longer count on your AV being safe.

Once an SPI violation has shown that a safety case no longer supports a claim of acceptable safety, consideration should be given to additional risk mitigation for operating AVs, up to and including making a decision to ground the entire fleet pending investigation. The actual decision in any particular situation will need to consider which SPI was violated, by how much, and what the likely operational risk presented by the SPI violation might be. In some cases, restricting the ODD might be a reasonable response, especially if the SPI violation is in response to a particular environmental circumstance, or the claim associated with the SPI is associated with a particular operational mode that can be temporarily avoided pending investigation.

Addressing an SPI violation might be done in a variety of ways, depending on the nature of the SPI violation and the safety case. Examples include the following:

- **Reallocate risk budget.** It might be that an SPI has a somewhat arbitrary threshold set as part of a risk budget. For example, the design team arbitrarily sliced up a total false negative budget and allocated expected contributions to cameras, lidars, and radars. If one sensor is doing better than expected based on field data, then its threshold can be lowered and that change in risk budget allocated to another sensor. If lidars are doing better than expected and cameras doing worse, then take some of the false negative risk budget away from lidars and give it to cameras. If that new threshold is not violated by collected data, the problem might be solved simply by changing the safety case. There is a moral hazard here of jiggling threshold numbers to make problems go away based on random variations in data rather than fundamental engineering analysis. But if solid data is available to support risk budget reallocation, then this can work.

- **Manage a reserve risk pool.** If a portion of the overall risk budget is set aside at design time, it can be used to absorb unexpected risk that arises due to SPI violations. This is also a risk budget reallocation exercise, but is done from a spare reserve pool of risk rather than stealing risk budget from another part of the safety case. At some point the reserve risk pool needs to be paid back, either by mitigating the risk identified by the SPI violation or by finding unused risk budget in other portions of the design. This approach can help avoid restricting fleet operations if minor SPI violations are quickly assessed as resulting in small increases of risk that can be absorbed by the reserve risk pool. This lets the fleet keep operating while any problems are addressed to repay the risk reserve pool. This approach is a more explicit way of handling the traditional engineering practice of building design margin into a system, making it safer than strictly necessary to provide slack for unanticipated issues.

- **Mitigate the discovered risk.** If the SPI indicates that risk is significantly higher than expected or a critical safety principle has been violated, the AV fleet might need to be grounded pending a fix for the problem. The root cause of the SPI violation will need to be discovered, which might involve a gap in the argument, a logic error in the argument, the discovery that evidence was biased, a change in the operational environment that requires a modification to the safety case, or some combination of problems. The safety case will need to be modified, and depending on the new argument there may need to be technical risk mitigations added to the AV. Mitigation of discovered risk might involve a combination of hardware, software, electrical, and even mechanical changes depending on the nature of the problem. After resolution, the safety case would be updated to match the new system design.

It is important to note that simply raising the SPI threshold alone to get rid of the violation is not an acceptable way to resolve a problem. Any change to the SPI threshold must be accompanied by some analysis justifying that change. Typically there will need to be a reallocation of risk budget from another part of the safety case, addition of a technical risk reduction mechanism, or more detailed analysis to support a more tightly defined SPI threshold for the claim under investigation.

7.2. Real-world safety cases are not deductive

Summary: Safety cases cannot guarantee complete coverage of AV safety due to the messy nature of the real world. Rather, a well-constructed safety case provides confidence that relevant factors have been considered, and provides a framework to continually check to see if something has been missed.

A significant issue with a typical safety case approach is that it is primarily based on deductive reasoning. In a purely deductive safety case, the evidence and assumptions march relentlessly up through layers of argument and claims, driving inexorably to the overall highest level safety claim being made with complete certainty. This works well for arguments that are essentially mathematical proofs. And it can work well in closed systems which are extremely well understood. But it falls short of representing many complex, messy real-world systems, with AVs being one of the messiest engineered systems due to their interactions with an unstructured, unconstrained external environment full of heterogeneous actors.

Safety cases that deal with AVs are not fully deductive because they have inherent gaps in knowledge and understanding due to unknowns. Each claim is supported by some combination of lower-level claims and evidence. But there is always the possibility that a claim thought to be true will be discovered at some later date to be false due to some unknown gap in the argument, or some as-yet-unseen evidence that falsifies the claim.

The classic example of a falsifiable claim is the black swan story. At one time all swans were said to be white, and all swans observed by Western naturalists had indeed been white – until they visited Australia and saw black swans. The claim of all swans being white was falsifiable by a single sighting of a black swan, which eventually happened. But, up until that black swan sighting, a claim that all swans were white was both plausible and useful in practice.[423]

The same type of issue can arise with AV technology, especially when machine learning (ML) techniques are used. ML techniques are inherently inductive in that they make generalizations based on a finite set of examples. Specifically, ML approaches "learn" statistical properties based on training data. If you train an ML system on a million white swans, it is likely to indeed learn that all swans are white, and conclude that any black bird is not a swan – even if it is in fact a black swan.

While the theory of logical arguments might seem a bit like an academic exercise, this issue is at the center of ensuring safety in AVs. Just because the ML part of an AV has been trained on examples does not mean it really "understands" anything about the real world. It is simply determining the closest statistical match to something new compared to what it has been trained on. If it sees something novel it might not know what to do, or might match it to something completely ridiculous (to a human observer) based on how the statistical properties turn out.

Some examples of incorrectly learned statistical characteristics one might see in an ML-based system include: all stop signs are red (except for blue stop signs on private property in Hawaii); all pedestrians wear clothing covering their legs (for data collected in cold weather, but not so much during the summer); all creatures have at least one foot on the ground plane being used for distance estimation (except for galloping horses, kangaroos, and running people); all traffic lights show a yellow light before a red light (except any remaining old traffic lights that do not have yellow bulbs at all, or ones with a burned out yellow bulb); all people seen in an intersection are pedestrians (except for pictures of people on bus-mounted advertisements); all mapped bridges provide passage across some sort of ditch or gap in the roadway (except bridges that have just been washed out or collapsed) and so on.

---

[423] In other words, we view claims in a safety case not as mathematically proven statements, but rather as falsifiable scientific statements. For a discussion on falsifiability and the black swan story see: https://en.wikipedia.org/wiki/Falsifiability

The problem is the unknowns, and in particular the unknown unknowns: things that were not included in the training data that even the designers do not know are missing from the training data. In the real world there are, for practical purposes, an infinite number of potential unknowns for any ML-based system. When something previously unknown is encountered in the wild, it might falsify some claims in the safety case.

7.2.1. Defeasible reasoning and defeaters

The unknowns make it impractical to use a purely deductive safety case approach.[424] We are trying to argue safety for an AV that uses inductive techniques to create its behavioral functions. As a practical matter there is no descriptive function of the AV's behavior that can be subjected to deductive reasoning about safety. Additionally, the real world is unbounded, making it impracticable to fully enumerate all possible cases that must be handled safely by an AV. We do not fully understand how the AV behaves, and we do not fully understand the environment the AV interacts with. A proof of safety that handles all possible situations is simply not feasible given that lack of knowledge.

However, that does not mean we give up on safety cases. Rather, it means we need to consider an approach that is not a purely deductive safety case. One approach that is sometimes proposed is abductive reasoning, in which a possible conclusion is stated that seems strongly supported by evidence.[425] We prefer a different kind of non-demonstrative approach known as defeasible reasoning,[426] because it provides a more robust framework for understanding the interaction of SPIs and the safety case.[427]

Defeasible reasoning involves an argument that is rationally compelling but is falsifiable due to the possibility of missing information involved in drawing the conclusion.[428] The safety case is logically compelling, valid, and sound *as far as we know*. Yet that safety case might have flaws due to exceptions or counter-examples that we simply have not thought of and have not encountered in testing. A claim can be thought to be true, but then later be shown to be false if new evidence that disproves the claim arises. This is not a defect in the safety case approach – it is a fundamental consequence of trying to understand the complexity of the world around us.

Defeasible reasoning is a pragmatic approach enable use of a safety case approach despite the unknowns. However, it fundamentally changes what a

---

[424] One can try transforming a non-deductive AV safety case into a deductive format by sweeping the unknowns into a special argument pattern, which ends up in more or less the same place we are going with this discussion.

[425] See: https://en.wikipedia.org/wiki/Abductive_reasoning

[426] See: https://en.wikipedia.org/wiki/Defeasible_reasoning

[427] See Goodenough, Weinstock & Klein 2015: https://www.researchgate.net/publication/272678149_Eliminative_Argumentation_A_Basis_for_Arguing_Confidence_in_System_Properties

[428] See https://plato.stanford.edu/entries/reasoning-defeasible/

safety case really is. It is no longer a mathematical statement that is "proven" true in some sense. Rather, it is our best effort at showing via a combination of analysis and scientific observation that a claim is true as far as we know.

To avoid the pitfall of confirmation bias[429] and to improve belief in the truth of safety claim cases, it is a best practice to consider *defeaters* in constructing the safety case. A defeater is evidence (or more generally an argument supported by evidence) that would be relevant to disproving a claim. With defeasible reasoning, the idea is to not only argue why the claim is true, but also argue why the claim is not false. Defeaters are reasons that the claim might be false that seem worth considering.

Using an example of stop signs, a claim that all stop signs are red (have red sign background color with white lettering) is supported by observation ("here are photos of all the stop signs we've ever seen, and they are all red"), and an argument that a defeater has been addressed ("what if we missed non-red stop signs in our analysis?" – "we've spent as much budget as we can afford looking for non-red stop signs, and we haven't found one yet."). With this argument the claim that all stop signs are red is provisionally true, but can be made false if the defeater is ever activated by spotting even one non-red stop sign. For an AV safety case, there would be an obligation to report any non-red stop signs to the engineering team if one were to be spotted during operation. In the meantime, the claim that all stop signs in the operational domain are red would be considered true for the purpose of supporting the safety case.

To structure a defeasible safety case in a purely deductive style, one might simply add "and there are no unmitigated defeaters identified" to each claim. In practice all arguments in a safety case have that reasoning, whether or not it is explicit or implicit. The catch is that this claim is not precise enough to match the real world. The correct addendum is "and there are no unmitigated defeaters identified *yet*."

A "no defeaters identified *yet*" attached to each claim in this type of safety case takes care of the "as far as we know" part of the claim. But how do you know how hard to look for defeaters before the "yet" part is reasonable? At one extreme there is willful ignorance, and at the other extreme there is an essentially infinite list of increasingly improbable and implausible defeaters to consider for any claim.

Willful ignorance is clearly wrong. But how might you do due diligence in looking for defeaters to rule out of falsifying the claim before deployment?

Three primary sources of defeaters to consider during design and test are: your own experience, other people's experience, and SPI violations. For your own experience (more broadly that of your design team), use your judgment to add defeaters that seem helpful in building the credibility of the safety case. For other people's experiences look to standards and lists of best practices (with a defeater being failure to follow best practice for example).

---

[429] A paper that describes problems with safety cases by Nancy Leveson is worth reading. See: http://sunnyday.mit.edu/safer-world/safety-case.doc

ANSI/UL 4600 in particular is chock full of potential defeaters that should be addressed by safety cases.

7.2.2. SPIs and defeasible safety cases

Beyond learning from experience and references, a third source of defeaters is SPI violations. SPIs provide instrumentation to point out what has been overlooked as surprises arise during testing and operation of the system.

Ideally you find most SPI violations as part of testing. Think of collecting data during testing and checking it for SPI violations as another type of test instrumentation. You want to test whether the AV passes all its functionality tests at the component and system levels. But you also want to know that the safety case claims have not been violated by testing as well. An SPI violation during testing should be treated as a defect report and test failure, just the same as a functional defect.

Once a system is deployed, SPI monitoring is a way of discovering that an unknown unknown has been encountered. You thought your AV was acceptably safe when you deployed, but an SPI violation during operation begs to differ with you. Root cause analysis will identify the source of the problem and require some changes to the AV design and safety case.

Putting together the concept of an SPI and a defeasible safety case, every SPI acts as a catch-all defeater to a specific claim. It is a metric that, if triggered, falsifies the claim. Informally: "well, your safety case said that this claim can never be false, but here we are – it was just falsified." While it is not necessarily practical to create an SPI for every claim in the entire safety case, at least claims that are easy to create metrics for should be monitored to provide leading indicators of safety case issues before there is a crash. Leading metrics are associated with claims deeper in the safety case, and lagging metrics are associated with claims higher up in the safety case.

The predictive power of an SPI as a leading indicator is inherent in its construction. Rather than simply measuring something that intuitively sounds like it is related to safety, an SPI measures something that you are guaranteed by construction is related to safety. An SPI violation by definition means that part of your safety case has been proven wrong. It is difficult to get more safety relevant than that.

7.3. Summary

In this chapter we covered the concept of a safety case, which is a structured argument supporting a claim of acceptable safety, further supported by evidence.[430] While in a mathematically pure world a safety case would be provably correct and use purely deductive logic, the messy real world means we can only claim AV is acceptably safe based on what is known at the time. That means claims are not proven true unconditionally. Rather, claims are true as far as we know, and part of evaluating a safety case is asking whether enough due diligence has been put in to looking for potential flaws in reasoning, deficiencies in evidence, and other potential issues.

The concept of defeasible reasoning gives us a way to ethically deploy an AV even with imperfect knowledge. We add defeaters to show an absence of disproof of claims within the safety case.[431] This takes the form of: this claim is true because of <reasons>. However, if some defeater – call it X – were the case the claim would be false, <reasons> notwithstanding. But as far as we can tell X does not apply, so the claim is true as far as we know. Moreover, we will need to pay attention during deployment in case X becomes relevant later. Also, we might discover some new reason Y we did not even know about that can also disprove (falsify) the claim.

As a more concrete example of defeasible reasoning: our AV is safe because of <reasons>. Defeater: but what about snow, which is not covered by <reasons>? Response to defeater: we have done a lot of work to determine that it will never snow in this location, so it should still be safe. Result: snow defeater resolved, and claim remains true. Until the day comes, if ever, that it snows at that location.

Sources of defeaters include not only the team's experience, but also lessons learned from others, with ANSI/UL 4600 being a primary source of defeaters for an AV safety case.

To mitigate the risk of missing relevant defeaters, SPIs are used to instrument measurable claims within the safety case. An SPI violation shows that a claim within the safety case has been falsified even though it was otherwise believed to be true, making it a defeater that can be monitored during testing and deployment. In other words, monitoring SPIs provides a general purpose defeater monitoring mechanism to mitigate the risk of dangerous unknowns causing crashes of AVs operating on public roads.

---

[430] For guidance on creating good safety cases, see: Assurance Case Guidance, Challenges, Common Issues and Good Practice, SCSC-159, Ver. 1, ACWG, Aug. 2021, https://scsc.uk/r159:1

[431] "Absence of disproof" is the kind of double-negative structure that makes thinking about these topics tricky. But it's not proof of safety. Absence of disproof is "true as far as we know." This corresponds to failing to reject the null hypothesis in the scientific method. You have done a bunch of experiments, and none has disproved your theory. The more experiments you do the more confidence you gain. But you can never 100% prove you are right – you just build confidence that as far as you know you are not wrong.

8.   Applying SPIs in practice

Now that we have discussed how SPIs fit into a safety case, we can focus on how to create and manage SPIs, as well as the use of SPIs for continuous improvement of the safety case.

This chapter assumes that some sort of safety case has been created that can have SPIs linked to it. Creating a safety case is a substantive discussion well beyond the scope of this book. But in terms of determining if an AV is safe enough to deploy, once you have a safety case you have the basis for an SPI approach to measurement using those steps.

For this discussion we assume that a two-prong approach is taken to determining acceptable safety for the safety case. The first prong is setting a target loss rate based on crash frequency and related metrics. The second prong is identifying leading metrics that will help predict the expected loss rate. The issue of uncertainty is also relevant, and is discussed in section 9.2.

8.1. Creating a metric target for safety

Summary: Determining that an AV is "safe enough" will require establishing a baseline for how safe human drivers are. It turns out that is complicated. The baseline needs to account for severity of harm, which driver, where the vehicle is being driven, and under what conditions.

To establish a "safe enough" target that relates to an expected crash and other loss event frequency, there has to be some notion of a baseline for comparison that serves as an anchoring point for SPI thresholds. We assume that a Positive Risk Balance baseline is used because that seems to be the leading contender, although any comparison will have similar considerations. To create a granular PRB baseline we need to consider the different types of incidents, operational conditions, and victim demographic profiles.[432]

8.1.1. Lagging incident metrics

Metrics included in the baseline should include both loss events and incidents clearly relevant to safety such as:
- Fatal crashes per Vehicle Mile Traveled (VMT)
- Severe injuries per VMT
- Minor injuries per VMT
- Significant property damage only (PDO) events per VMT (for example, with airbag deployment or requiring the vehicle to be towed)

---

[432] This chapter revisits topics in section 5.2 from a different angle.

- Minor PDO events per VMT (for example, repairs without airbag deployment)
- Non-loss crashes per VMT (no mechanical repair necessary, damage within normal wear and tear allowances)
- Significant moving violations per VMT (running red lights, running stop signs, crossing a centerline into opposing traffic, and so on. These would be events that might result in a ticket or police warning for a human driver if a police officer observed the violation.)
- Minor traffic infractions per VMT (partially blocking a crosswalk when stopped, failure to signal for a turn, and so on that did not escalate into more severe incidents, which might still warrant a ticket or police warning, but which are less likely to be associated with a loss event)[433]

For each baseline metric there needs to be a reasonably precise definition of what counts, what does not count, and a defined resolution process for determining how to tally borderline situations.

Just as importantly, there needs to be an SPI threshold set for what is deemed acceptable, likely based on human driver statistics. In keeping with the previous discussion about SPIs, there are two measurements that matter. One measurement categorizes determines if a particular situation passes a threshold to be contribute to the violation of a claim (e.g., an AV runs a red traffic light). The other measurement is a triggering value as to how frequently such an incident is permitted to occur by the safety case while still preserving the overall argument of acceptable safety (e.g., X red light violations per 100M miles is tolerable with acceptable risk, where X is presumably a small number).

8.1.2. Baseline operational conditions

The baseline metrics should not be defined based on broad averages, but rather should be based on measurements with reasonably comparable conditions to the AV's ODD. As discussed in section 5.2, real-world safety outcomes can vary dramatically according to the ODD, so any comparative risk measure is valid only if it accounts for such variations.

The baseline will likely contain multiple different segments of data broken down by relevant combinations of operational conditions, such as one baseline for daytime dry conditions and a different baseline for wet night driving conditions. The baseline operational conditions should consider at least the following:

---

[433] The distinction between significant and minor traffic infractions here is somewhat arbitrary, but we think one is appropriate. There is a significant risk difference between blowing through a red light at full speed and stopping 6 inches past the required stop line at an intersection. In the absence of other criteria, one could look to the points-based demerit system already used to determine license revocation thresholds for repeat offenses to create severity bins for traffic violations.

- Geographic area. This is useful as a proxy for numerous ODD characteristics such as driver aggressiveness, road maintenance condition, and pedestrian behavioral norms. The geographic area might need to be broken into different sub-areas if there is a wide variation of relevant factors across the whole ODD.
- Road type. This includes limited access roadways, arterials, side streets, private property, and so on, as well as travel speed. Likely there will be a mix of such road types to be considered.
- Time of day. This is likely to be an exposure profile in terms of miles driven at various times of day that serves as a proxy for traffic conditions. For example, rush-hour data is likely to differ from 3 AM data, and also differ from mid-day non-rush-hour data.
- Weather: This should include at least wet, dry, snow, and ice to the extent they are relevant to the ODD.
- Lighting: This should consider at least sunny/cloudy; day/night/; sunrise/sunset glare; and street lights/unlit.
- Human driver capability: at least driver age group, driver impairment, and distraction.
- Vehicle features: a newer vehicle equipped with automatic emergency braking (AEB) and in good repair would be expected to have a better safety record than a very old vehicle in bad repair with no active safety features. At least vehicle safety features that are considered in assigning insurance rates should be considered here.
- Any other driver or vehicle considerations that are likely to significantly affect the baseline metric value for comparison.

It is not necessary to explicitly measure every possible operational condition effect on baseline metrics with high precision, because many will not matter much. However, some will matter a lot, and those must be taken into account. Knowing which factors matter will need to be part of testing and maturing the safety case, potentially by observing SPI violations during early testing.

One pragmatic approach could be to measure factors that are considered major, such as: geographic area, road type, weather, presence of AEB, and human driver age, likely setting aside data from impaired drivers. If it is not known what the distribution of actual operating conditions will be, pick a baseline that is on the safer end of the spectrum for human drivers such as an easy-to-drive location with well-maintained roads, dry weather, daylight, with an unimpaired 45-65 year-old experienced human driver in a higher-end vehicle with mainstream active safety features as a baseline. The idea is that any error in the baseline should be conservative, setting the safety threshold for baseline comparison to be in favorable conditions for human driver safety. You will want your AV to be at least that safe. Only invest time in relaxing a very conservative human driver safety baseline if your system is so close to that baseline that the difference matters.

8.1.3. Baseline victim demographic profile

A significant practical concern for AVs is that they have the potential to shift risk from one demographic segment to another. It seems unlikely that AV crash victims will be demographically distributed in exactly the same way as for human drivers, because AVs will make different mistakes than human drivers. However, any egregious risk transfer to vulnerable road users is likely to be seen as a significant issue by a variety of stakeholders.

A concrete, but hypothetical, example of risk transfer would be if traffic deaths were cut in half overall, but the number of pedestrian fatalities increased – and the vast majority of those fatalities were children in marked crosswalks in school zones. While that particular outcome is (hopefully!) very unlikely, it illustrates that simply reducing the absolute number of injuries and fatalities is not enough if the remaining risk is transferred in a way that increases the risk to a particular vulnerable population.

Contributing to the potential risk transfer issue is the well-known propensity of machine learning-based technology to be biased by training data. Some of the biases obviously affect defined demographic segments, such as an ML-based system that has trouble recognizing pedestrians with dark skin coloration.[434] But some outcomes can be less intuitive, such as problems identifying road users dressed in high visibility colors (e.g., hi-viz vests for construction workers, and yellow raincoats for pedestrians). Or the system might be under-trained on uncommon pedestrian configurations such as wheelchair riders, people using walkers, or pedestrians walking while pushing a bicycle.

While it is difficult to know in advance how risk transfer might occur in practice, the following points should be considered when creating metrics for road user involvement in incidents and loss events to help identify and minimize the severity of any such issue:

- Breakdown by age range, gender, ethnicity:
  - Age range might be considered as a proxy for size, agility to evade an AV behavioral mistake, judgment in assessing situational risk, road use rule following, and other factors.
  - Gender might be considered a proxy for appearance (hair styles, head gear, fashion choices), and to some degree size.
  - Skin color should be considered because that is a known issue for machine learning-based technology. Hair color might also be considered, especially uncommon fashion hair hues.
  - Ethnicity might be considered as an additional factor to account for situations in which ethnic clothing choices differ from the

---

[434] Results from a 2019 study on skin color and AV safety by Wilson et al. are widely mischaracterized. That study posits that skin color is a *potential* issue for AVs rather than identifying it as an actual issue in any particular AV. Nonetheless, the concern raised is a reasonable one that should be considered, even if speculative. Reference: https://arxiv.org/pdf/1902.11097.pdf

surrounding population. For example, bare heads and bare legs are unusual in some locations, while covered heads and legs might be unusual in others.

    o   Different categorizations might well be considered, tailored to the needs of the deployment location. Some of these considerations might matter, while others do not. Some considerations might start mattering suddenly due to a shift in how a machine learning algorithm processes training data, or an otherwise subtle shift in the environment. The goal here is to determine if there are patterns of appearance, behavior, and perhaps even cultural norms that make a particular demographic more vulnerable to AV harm.

- Identification of road users at special risk, including:
  - Pedestrians (free walking, with shopping packages, with children, with rolling suitcases, etc.)
  - Light mobility users (bicycles, scooters, pedestrians dismounted pushing or holding a mobility device, etc.)
  - Ability-impaired users (wheelchair riders, walking assistance devices, vision impaired, hearing impaired, etc.)
  - Road workers (road construction, traffic flow, school crossing guards, etc.)
  - Participants in special activity scenes (police traffic stops, disabled vehicle situations, clearing debris from the road, building construction zones, etc.)
  - Riders in different vehicle types (extra-light vehicles, older vehicles, farm equipment, construction equipment, horse-drawn vehicles, etc.).

The different potential risk transfer categories should be considered at engineering design time to make sure that no identifiable demographic is exposed to substantively increased risk due to oversights in system design, biased training data, and so on. Moreover, field data should be analyzed to detect if some unforeseen identifiable pattern in incidents or loss events involves risk transfer beyond normal random variations onto an identifiable demographic segment of the population.

8.1.4. Overall baseline metrics

It is essential to consider safety metrics in the context of what, where, who, and how: a set of metrics for different possible occurrences of undesirable events, a set of different operational conditions, and a set of different types of victims that might be affected in different ways. Considering these factors lessens the potential issue of an unreasonably risky AV looking acceptable because it is being compared against a baseline that is not representative of the intended real-world use. Considering these factors also helps avoid risk transfer that puts specific demographic segments at unacceptable risk in specific situations. Special attention should be paid to risk presented to vulnerable road users and populations that are already exposed to increased risks from other sources (for example, populations that are economically disadvantaged).

In principle, this approach means there is a separate SPI for every point in the cross product of what, where, who, and how.[435] Beyond that, it would be good practice to continually analyze incident and mishap data reports to look for outlier clusters of elevated risk associated with a specific situation or demographic group that might not have been anticipated by the initial SPI selections.

The result of this process is that lagging metric targets have been identified to judge how an AV deployment is doing after it has been deployed compared to the baseline risk it is supposed to improve upon.

8.1.5. Confusing performance metrics with safety metrics

It is all too common to see performance metrics portrayed as safety metrics. The distinction can be slippery, and there might well be overlap between the two types of metrics. The tricky bit is that some performance metrics can intuitively seem to be safety metrics at first glance, but in reality have little or no predictive power for safety outcomes.

A Key Performance Indicator (KPI) is a metric regarding whether the system or an engineering process is behaving desirably. For example, a KPI might be the average distance between an AV's center line and the center of a road lane to measure how well lane tracking is working. It is easy to believe that a system with poor KPIs is likely to be unsafe, because an AV that cannot keep itself in its own lane is at some point just not a competent driver. That can be especially true if the KPIs extend into other aspects of roadmanship.

However, KPIs are not necessarily predictive of safety outcomes. For example, a KPI having to do with avoiding inducing motion sickness in passengers might be essential for market acceptance, but might have nothing at all to do with mitigating crash risks. And a KPI value for lane centerline tracking that is 1 inch on average away from the lane center rather than 2 inches might sound twice as good, but seems unlikely to be twice as safe given how small that is compared to overall vehicle widths.

An excessively bad KPI value certainly gives cause for concern. And a KPI might be good enough for use in estimating insurance risk in some cases. But a KPI that is not linked in some causal way to the vehicle's design or operational practices can easily give an overly optimistic (or pessimistic) prediction as to safety. Even a seemingly predictive KPI can become less useful if something in the AV design or the external world changes in a way

---

[435] In practice there will be large regions of evaluation spaces that are considered to be equivalent, with each region having an aggregate SPI. The point is to not collapse differentiation of risk across different groups into one giant equivalence class that loses the important special cases.

that breaks a serendipitous correlation that previously gave the KPI some predictive power over safety outcomes.

Only some metrics having to do with vehicle performance are truly related to safety, while others might be related to ride quality or other aspects of functionality that are not as directly predictive of safety. Metrics that are not SPIs might be important to determine if a product is ready to go to market, but should not be included in the safety baseline.

8.2. Identifying leading SPIs

Summary: Leading SPIs are used to predict AV safety issues before loss events are likely to happen. They encompass not only system behaviors, but also component functionality, engineering process maturity, and operational process maturity.

Identifying leading SPIs emphasizes finding ways to detect potential problems before they become system-level loss events. While intuitively it might seem that leading safety metrics should be about measuring how often things fail or work incorrectly, that is only part of the story. The failure of one particular function might not materially affect safety, while the failure of some other function might result in a catastrophic crash the majority of the time. Some SPIs measure process failures that set the conditions for a loss event rather than equipment failures. What matters is not the frequency of failure, nor whether any failure seems dramatic from the point of view of the function itself. What matters is the effect of a given rate and type of failure on net vehicle-level safety. Moreover, it is better to have the metric relate directly to a reason the system is considered to be safe rather than a statistical correlation with no evident causal relationship between the metric and system-level safety. This means that the leading metrics should be SPIs that detect situations in which a claim within the safety case has been shown to be false.

The precise leading SPIs that are relevant will depend on the safety case that applies to any specific AV. Therefore, our discussions of leading SPIs should be considered examples that convey a general idea, and not necessarily exact metrics that are guaranteed to apply to all safety cases.

We somewhat arbitrarily divide leading SPIs up into four categories: system level, component level, process, and operations. Ultimately, violating any SPI means that the system is not living up to its safety case regardless of classification. However, it is conceptually convenient to divide leading SPIs up into categories because they tend to have different properties and might be measured in different ways.

It is important to remember that, by definition, an SPI needs to trace to a specific claim in a safety case. Without that traceability to a safety case claim, it is not truly an SPI.[436]

8.2.1. System-level leading SPIs

System-level leading SPIs are based on measuring risky behaviors and other properties of the entire AV and its supporting infrastructure. A system-level leading SPI should be rooted in vehicle behavior as well as tied directly to a claim in the safety case.

Traffic rule violations that do not result in crashes can be considered in some ways to be a leading SPI because no actual loss event has occurred. However, we take the view that they should be treated as lagging indicators. By the time an AV has run through a red traffic signal, whether or not a collision occurs is more a matter of circumstance than good design. Such incidents should be treated with urgency based on potential harm regardless of luck.

While behavioral anomalies such as panic stops might be correlated with safety outcomes, they do not necessarily tie to the safety case, and so are not necessarily SPIs.[437] Similarly, behaviors that a human driver might find a bit sloppy or aggressive might or might not be SPIs. It all depends on the safety case.

8.2.1.1. Inherently risky vehicle behavior

If traffic rule violations are lagging SPIs, and aggressive driving is not necessarily an SPI, where does that leave us on leading SPIs at the vehicle behavior level?

An intuitive type of leading vehicle-level SPI is risky vehicle behavior. Panic stopping might be a reasonable SPI after all, but for a somewhat different reason than it is for human drivers. For human drivers, panic braking might be seen as a proxy for either driver inattention (distracted human driver jams on brakes at the last second to avoid impact) or driver immaturity (young human driver jams on brakes as part of a pattern of overly aggressive and risk-taking driving behavior). Both of those relationships might well be valid for typical human drivers. But there is no reason to believe those relationships will exist for an AV which is supposed to be neither prone to distraction nor prone to emotional outbursts while driving.

---

[436] It is conceivable that some leading metrics that have nothing to do with a safety case will be good predictors of eventual system-level safety. However, metrics that are not associated with a safety case are at risk of being gamed (even unintentionally) or invalided due to some change in the system design. Thus, we concentrate on SPIs tied to a safety case here rather than correlative KPIs.

[437] For example, if panic stops are only performed when the system is confident there is no closely trailing traffic, the relevant SPI measurement would not be panic stops, but rather panic stops while closely followed.

On the other hand, an AV that decelerates with maximum braking force might still be prone to more crashes. Some crashes might be due to failing to leave engineering margin for environmental uncertainty. Braking full force to stop only one centimeter before hitting a leading vehicle is asking for trouble. Even a slight miscalculation due to unforeseen slick spots or sandy patches on a road surface can convert such an aggressive stop into a collision. Other crashes might be due to being rear-ended by tailgating vehicles (AVs or human-driven) that do not react quickly or forcefully enough to avoid impact. While being rear-ended during a hard braking event might be blamed on the following vehicle, an elevated crash rate is still a problem.

There might well be more subtle driving behaviors that are also associated with increased risk. Behaviors such as tailgating, motions that tend to confuse other motorists as to near-term intentions, and driving styles that in practice provoke other drivers to make dangerous driving decisions[438] might all be considered as vehicle-level safety metrics, and be formulated as SPIs to the degree that they contribute to overall system risk of a crash. Whether those SPIs are said to be leading or lagging is a matter of taste. Either way, disentangling effects caused by operating in a naturally high risk environment vs. an AV driving style contributing to mishap rates will be important.

8.2.1.2. Loss of confidence in vehicle design

A different sort of vehicle-level SPI that is more clearly a leading metric has to do with detecting safety-relevant misbehaviors and system-level faults.

Consider a vehicle coming to a stop at an intersection with a stop sign but no painted lines. The required location of the stop might well depend on the circumstances. If a pedestrian is to cross, the vehicle should not force the pedestrian to walk out into cross traffic to get around the front of the AV. If there is no pedestrian and no marked crosswalk, rules of the road might permit stopping a bit further toward the intersection to get a good view of cross traffic. Sometimes prudent driving will require one stop for potential pedestrians, and another stop for better visibility before fully committing to entering the intersection. For the design to be assessed for safety, there needs to be a defined set of rules for stopping locations in various situations.[439]

---

[438] The degree to which an AV is at fault when foreseeably provoking another road user to do something dangerous is not an easy thing to resolve. We assume that anything that contributes to overall system risk of a crash is relevant to safety, regardless of assigned blame or whether other road users should or should not behave in certain ways vs. how they actually behave. AVs will need to meet human drivers where they are, not where they wish they were.

[439] Traffic laws might not provide detailed guidance here. Nonetheless, if an AV maker needs to self-certify their vehicle for safety, they need to be able to say where safe stopping locations are to assess whether the vehicle behaves properly at intersections. Otherwise, any road testing would be performed without a grading rubric beyond "didn't happen to crash this time," yielding results of unclear value.

Now consider a vehicle that consistently stops three or even six inches closer to the intersection than it should. Is that likely to cause a dramatic increase in crashes? Perhaps there is no measurable change in crash rates, and perhaps pedestrians slightly blocked by the vehicle are annoyed, but not annoyed enough to complain to anyone. Nonetheless, this type of misbehavior should be considered an SPI violation.

Think about a hypothetical safety case in which one claim is "AV obeys traffic laws" and a sub-claim is "AV stops at the correct position for stop signs." Under that stop sign claim there might be two cases: pedestrians present, and no pedestrians present. Traffic laws might leave considerable room for interpretation on correct stopping distance, but to conduct testing the designers and testers have agreed on specific locations at intersections beyond which the AV should fail the test.

If the AV is frequently failing its stop sign location test that should be an indication that something is wrong with the AV's design for safety – even if the location is strictly speaking legal because of a wide range of ambiguity in the relevant traffic law.[440] This would not qualify as a lagging metric because the behavior is not in itself immediately dangerous. Rather, stopping at a slightly wrong place is an indication that the vehicle behavior does not match the design intent, which bodes poorly for a safety-critical system.

The important thing to understand about these types of SPIs for vehicle-level behavior is that they are intended not to flag vehicle behaviors that are obviously and immediately dangerous. Rather, they are intended to flag situations in which the vehicle does not behave as expected, even if it is unclear what the exact numerical contribution will be to system-level risk. Any time a safety-critical system does not behave as expected, that is a red flag indicating a potential weakness in safety analysis. Not even having behavioral expectations is an even bigger red flag.

8.2.2. Component-level leading SPIs

Component-level leading SPIs measure whether safety case claims being made about components, subsystems, or other parts of the system are being met. Typically that will have to do with whether the component behavior contributes to safety as expected. A component SPI might be violated even if other aspects of the system render overall AV behavior safe from a practical perspective. As with other SPIs, the emphasis is not on whether the AV's overall behavior is dangerous, but rather whether the safety case accurately reflects what is going on in the system.

As an example, a leading SPI might be the false negative rate for detecting pedestrians with a camera. Each false negative would be a situation in which relevant pedestrians are missed that could have and should have been

---

[440] While this might be "fixed" by loosening the test criteria, at some point the vehicle needs to behave as intended by designers, so there are limits to how far such a "fix" can, or at least should, be abused.

detected.[441] This is a statistical measure, so occasionally missing pedestrians might be fine so long as they are comparatively rare and likely to be detected by other sensors in use. However, when too many pedestrians are being missed, the SPI threshold is violated. The type of safety case this would apply to might be an argument that while any one sensor type might miss a pedestrian, it is extremely unlikely that two different sensors would miss a pedestrian, so two-out-of-three voting can be used across three sensor types to avoid both false positives and false negatives from the sensor array.[442] That argument in turn would likely boil down to a calculation of probabilities and an assertion that there are vanishingly few situations in which failures are correlated for the same type of object across two sensor types. If one sensor type has inaccurate results too often, the probability math falls apart along with the safety case claims based upon that math.

Some other component-level leading SPIs might have to do with combinations of components. For example, there might be a design requirement that at most one out of three cameras will completely stop working during a single drive cycle (with an assumption that any failed component will be repaired before the AV is used again). There might be two SPIs associated with this: one to measure the single camera failure rate, and another to measure the double camera failure rate. The single camera failure rate is likely a factor in a calculation that shows the probability of two cameras failing within a maximum length drive cycle is sufficiently small. Even if two cameras have not failed together yet, a higher-than-expected single-camera failure rate predicts getting unlucky and having two cameras fail one after the other during a single future drive. The two-camera failure SPI might have its threshold set at zero because it is never supposed to happen. Nonetheless, it is important not to simply assume it will never happen because it is thought impossible, but rather to be able to detect when it did happen, revealing a defect in the safety case. (If a double camera failure makes the vehicle unsafe it should also trigger a reaction from the vehicle such as a safety shutdown, but our emphasis here is on SPI feedback to the safety case.[443])

---

[441] There are all sorts of distractions in discussions like this. For example, a person on the horizon that is only half a pixel tall in the camera field of view might be missed, but not be relevant, and so not a false negative. In these sorts of examples the reader should assume that something sensible and meaningful for safety claims is being measured even if we do not recite a long and tedious list of constraints and caveats such as minimum pixel height, occlusion, framing, lighting, and so on.

[442] This is an extension of the redundant camera detection claims sketched in section 7.1.2.

[443] The alert reader might ask about a vehicle that uses both design strategies. If an AV with two-out-of-three voting for sensors keeps operating after one sensor fails, what does it do when the remaining two sensors disagree? It will likely need to cease operations a short time after the first sensor fails to avoid too much exposure to the possibility of a two-sensor disagreement caused by a second sensor failure. Or it

The general idea of a component-level leading SPI is to monitor the behavior and other characteristics of components to see if they are operating in a way that supports the claims made about them in the safety case. That means these leading SPIs are a way to measure and monitor whether the safety case corresponds to real-world operation of various components, even if vehicle-level behavior appears normal. Knowing the safety case is being violated is important even in the absence of a crash or other operational issue (yet).

8.2.3. Leading SPIs for process

A large part of creating safe systems is executing a rigorous design process. Testing will not somehow transform an unsafe AV into a safe one.[444] Safety has to be built in from the start. Doing that requires engineering rigor and other application of design processes, operational processes, and so on. If those processes are broken, the safety case is likely to be unsound, and the system is likely to be unsafe in practice.

SPIs should be created to monitor whether the engineering processes required for safety are being followed rigorously. At least some SPIs are likely to reflect traditional Software Quality Assurance (SQA)[445] metrics such as whether peer reviews are being conducted effectively and whether compiler warnings are being resolved according to defined engineering processes.

The way a process SPI fits into a safety case depends on the specific development approach. However, we would expect it to go something like this. Safety is in part based on a sufficiently small risk of software defect being activated in a way that causes a loss event. Having high software quality (often in the form of having a high safety integrity level) is an approach used to mitigate the risk of such a bug existing. Strong software quality practices are established by following a good engineering process. If you fail to follow a good engineering process, you have undermined the credibility of any claim in the safety case that the software will have a low activated bug rate in operation. Poor SQA does not guarantee bug-riddled software, but it means that is a possibility. Strong SQA helps reduce the risk of software defect escapes into production systems by ensuring higher software quality.

---

might have a fourth sensor in the design to tolerate one permanent sensor fault as well as a second sensor with a transient detection failure.

[444] Testing and fixing issues found might make a really unsafe AV into a somewhat less unsafe one. But a testing-only approach cannot build acceptable confidence in safety due to issues of scale unless it is additionally supported by some sort of safety case that addresses engineering rigor. See sections 4.3 and 4.4.

[445] SQA is not about the quality of the code itself, but rather about the effectiveness of the processes used to create and validate the software.
See: https://en.wikipedia.org/wiki/Software_quality_assurance

There are at least two types of SPIs that can be associated with process claims: process conformance assessment and results of root case traceability.

Process conformance assessment SPIs are likely to be associated with a claim that some engineering process has been completed in an acceptable manner. For example, a design team might claim that compiler warnings and other static analysis issues have been eliminated to the extent practicable, and that any remaining warnings from a static analysis tool have been approved via a defined deviation process.[446] The SQA team might check the claim of clean static analysis by a combination of running a conformance tool on the code itself to look for warnings as well as checking that the approval paperwork is in order for any deviations.

The claims in an example safety case fragment will involve a parent claim along the lines of "suitable engineering rigor has been applied to software design" and a subclaim for this activity of something like "code conforms to MISRA C." That subclaim SPI would have a metric of "non-conformance of MISRA C issues found by SQA" and probably a threshold of zero.[447] In other words, the claim of MISRA C conformance is supported by design team processes and activities, but the SPI independently checking conformance uses data supplied by SQA.

A root cause traceability SPI could also be associated with that same claim of conformance to MISRA C. This SPI would not be a direct examination, but rather a data feed from root cause analysis done on software defects found during testing and deployment. For each software defect found, part of the root cause analysis checklist would include the question: "did non-conformance to MISRA C contribute to the occurrence of this defect?" If so, then the claim that conformance to MISRA C has been falsified. If a design team were foolish enough to make a claim that conformance to MISRA C will prevent all software defects,[448] discovering a software implementation defect that did not violate MISRA C rules would falsify any such claim.

Some engineering processes involved in AVs are novel compared to more traditional software development practices. This is especially true in areas

---

[446] For those not steeped in software quality methods: a static analysis tool looks over software source code and issues warnings for things it thinks look like dodgy code. The code might rely on non-standard compiler behavior, or be the type of thing that is very prone to error. Safety-critical software typically follows a set of rules that outlaw those types of practices. If there is a rare situation in which there is no practical choice but to bend the rules, a formal approval process must be executed for any such deviation from the rules, leaving a paper trail. One popular approach for this type of process involves the use of the MISRA C coding guidelines: See: https://www.misra.org.uk/misra-c/

[447] A deviation process is included as part of MISRA C guidelines, so any approved deviation is still within conformance to those guidelines.

[448] Sadly, we have heard of teams who claim that conformance to MISRA C means that the safety box has been checked and no further efforts are required for safety. That is akin to saying that because you buckled your seatbelt (which is an excellent safety practice), there is no need to worry about injury from a car crash.

dealing with data collection, data cleaning, and the machine learning training process. In these areas there might not yet be mature industry standards, but there should still be best practice conformance that should be tracked via SQA and monitored via SPIs. Additionally, any testing failure or road incident should be checked to feed an SPI that is tracking whether the claim of conformance to best practices is mitigating risk to the degree required by the safety case.

8.2.4. Leading SPIs for operations

How operations are conducted can dramatically affect safety. An AV is a complicated piece of machinery. It must be used, maintained, and otherwise supported in accordance with the requirements established by the engineering process to achieve safety in operations. For example, maintenance of safety-relevant components must be completed correctly and as scheduled. Wear items such as tires and brake pads must be replaced as needed. And any safety-related software updates must be made in a timely and accurate fashion.[449]

Examples of leading SPIs for operations that are likely to be relevant to an AV safety case include: fraction of scheduled maintenance/inspections completed on time, how often operational failures occur due to improper maintenance, whether maintenance is being performed by properly trained personnel, how often counterfeit spare parts are detected in inventories, frequency of failure of a wear part before its scheduled replacement, and so on.

8.2.5. System-level leading KPIs

Some metrics sound like they ought to be important or are directed to properties that AV passengers and other road users attribute to safety – but might not be predictive of safety outcomes. As a hypothetical example beyond the hard braking one previously discussed, consider an AV that consistently enters intersections well into the yellow phase of a traffic light. The pushing of the yellow light phase makes passengers uncomfortable. You might argue that squeezing out a few more seconds of traffic flow during a yellow light increases road use efficiency and reduces trip time. You might also argue it is safe to do this because you only do so when the intersection is clear, and you have sensors that can do a better job than human drivers at making sure that no pedestrians or other vehicles are anticipating the cross-direction green and entering the intersection early. Presumably you also have

---

[449] This generally corresponds to the aviation use of Safety Performance Indicators, with numerous examples given in this document:
https://www4.icao.int/demo/SMI/9.5.4%20SM%20ICG%20Measuring%20Safety%20Performance%20Guidance%20for%20Service%20Providers.pdf

checked that the degree to which you push yellow lights is not increasing crash risk, and that such behavior is legal in your ODD.[450]

Such an approach to pushing the limits of yellow traffic signal lights might well make passengers nervous if they associate aggressive yellow light behavior with reckless driving – even if road data shows that the crash rate is unaffected by such AV behavior. Measuring how much yellow light time is left after entering an intersection might be a relevant customer-facing KPI, but might not be associated with safety outcomes.

It is completely reasonable to define and monitor KPIs as part of an AV development effort. Areas such as ride quality, perceived politeness to other road users, and behaving in ways that passengers find more natural can be essential for product success. But if a KPI is not tied to a claim in the safety case, then by definition it is not an SPI.

8.3. Monitoring SPIs

Summary: Monitoring SPIs requires observing a source of data to see if a claim in the safety case corresponds with what is actually happening. Many SPI monitors will need to be statistical in that there is a very low – but non-zero – acceptable rate for a measurement threshold being violated while still achieving acceptable safety. There is a subtle but somewhat tricky safety case notation choice to be made as to whether that low threshold violation rate is itself included as a secondary threshold in the SPI, or kept as part of the SPI monitoring mechanism itself.

Once SPIs have been defined, data needs to be collected and monitored over the system lifecycle. SPIs will need to go far beyond the constraints of data available in real time from only a single vehicle. Because of that, SPIs can have more flexibility in how and what they measure to provide a big-picture look at safety across a fleet of AVs.

8.3.1. Sources of SPI data

SPI data can come from wherever an activity is being performed or a system is operating if a way can be found to measure results and tie them to a safety case claim. Some SPI data will be based on vehicle behavior at runtime. However, other sources of SPI data can and should include sources

---

[450] The law might be that it is forbidden to enter when the signal is red, and yellow is just there to help drivers comply with the red signal law. If an AV has a high-definition map annotated with the length of every yellow light cycle, it might be able to avoid a red light infraction while routinely entering intersections during the last fraction of a second during a yellow light. Regardless of legality, how often such a yellow accelerator experiences a sudden meeting with a green anticipator mid-intersection will also have an effect on safety outcomes, and needs to be accounted for in any safety case. We recommend not cutting it too close.

beyond vehicle operational sensor data. Some ideas for SPI data sources include:

- On-board vehicle data recorder
- Operational logs (e.g., safety driver observations)
- Test track instrumentation
- Simulator logs and instrumentation
- Software Quality Assurance (SQA) data
- Independent verification and validation reports
- Maintenance logs
- Infrastructure road sensors (traffic cameras, speed sensors)
- One AV monitoring another AV's road behavior
- Third-party reports from emergency responders at crash scenes
- Crash reconstructions

The important thing to realize is that SPIs span much more than just in-the-moment vehicle behaviors, so there are many potential data sources to detect issues with a safety case beyond automated vehicle data logs.

8.3.2. How to measure

After a source of data has been identified, the more difficult question can often be how to formulate a measurement that is relevant to a safety claim. Some measurements are relatively straightforward based on the claim. However, any measurement that requires comparing AV functionality to a goal based on perfect knowledge of the external environment is tricky. For example, consider how to measure false negative rates. If a sensor fails to detect an object, how are you going to know that something was missed if the sensor did not see it?

Claims of coverage across sets of things that can include unknowns are also tricky. For example, how do you know a claim that you have tested all possible scenarios is true if you might be missing scenarios from your list?

There is no one-size-fits-all answer, but there are some techniques that can be useful for creating SPIs described in the following subsections.

8.3.2.1. Temporal consistency

Look for temporal consistency. Consider a sequence of five images, #1 - #5, with each image taken $1/30^{th}$ of a second apart. If an object appears in images #1, #2, #4, and #5 but not in #3, it is a fair bet that it was there in #3 as well. It is possible that a small or fast-moving object might have been occluded by a foreground object for only one frame, so #3 is only a potential detection failure. But this type of sequence is a good place to start looking for detection algorithm failures.

It is common for an AV to use an object tracker to predict where an object will be even if an occasional frame detection fails. In practical operation the missing frame #3 will not cause a control system problem, because other logic in the AV will likely automatically drop in an estimated #3 position into the data stream. But rather than simply say that such smoothing of data means there is no problem, an SPI data accumulator should record the fact that the interpolated position was used to make sure it is not happening too often. Additionally, the number of multi-frame object detection dropouts (e.g., both frames #3 and #4) should be monitored.

Using tracker-based estimation to ride through an occasional false negative detection is fine within limits, and in practice will be essential for reasonable performance. The safety case issue comes in when a higher-level system dependability analysis ignores the fact that the tracker is compensating for sensor faults and takes credit for the sensor operating perfectly when it is not. The relevant SPI does not trigger when a single object disappears for just one frame, but rather it triggers when such disappearances are happening too often or there are too many runs of many frames in a row with disappearances that are not explained by occlusion.

For example, consider using a 3 out of 5 detection heuristic: any object in 3 out of 5 frames at nearby locations is declared to be there for all 5. If an object is missing for 1 out of 5 once in a while, no big deal. However, if some object types are missed 1 out of 5 on a consistent basis, then that calls into question the capabilities of the object detector.[451]

Using that same 3 out of 5 approach, having an object missed for 2 out of 5 frames is a more significant concern. Yes, the system will be safe with 3 detections and 2 misses in 5 frames. However, if the system is seeing a lot of 2 misses out of 5, it is reasonable to assume it is also prone to seeing 3 misses out of 5, resulting in a false negative such as not seeing a pedestrian in front of the vehicle.

An SPI approach would be to instrument how often 1 miss out of 5 was happening as well as 2 misses out of 5. Some probability math should be done to determine the expected ratio of 1 vs. 2 misses out of 5 and consider the implications for the probability of a safety-critical 3 out of 5 miss situation. An elevated rate of 2 misses out of 5 likely means a weakness in the system for detecting some types of images that predicts a 3 misses out of 5 situation will happen with higher than acceptable probability.

On the topic of runtime vs. SPI data collection, even a few events of missing 2 out of 5 frames might be enough to generate an urgent issue regarding the safety case. But a runtime monitor might not shut down vehicle operation for 2 out of 5 on a particular mission because the system is designed to still work properly. With this type of approach, every 2 out of 5 miss situation should be reported as SPI data and fed into statistical checks that consider the entire set of AVs. A runtime monitor might not trigger a shutdown until it has seen a cluster of multiple 2 out of 5 misses in a short time interval.

---

[451] For this and other parts of the example we assume that checking is done to ensure that the misses are not due to occlusions or other legitimate environmental situations.

8.3.2.2. Cross-function consistency

Look for consistency across both similar and dis-similar functions. For similar functions, see if they come up with the same answer. If they differ by too much (more than a reasonable threshold), instances of mismatches should be fed into an SPI metric to keep track of how often mismatches are occurring. "Too much" is highly context dependent, but should be based on providing a useful signal of which circumstances are worth more investigation without too many false alarms.

As an example, consider an AV with overlapped fields of view for cameras. Any time there is an object that is in the field of view of two cameras, it is worth checking to see whether one camera missed it. That can give some information about the false negative/false positive rates of individual cameras. Similarly, if a lidar and a radar put an object at a significantly different location from each other, that mismatch can provide information about sensor issues.

There is a pitfall here in that some functions have poor determinism or high sensitivity to minor variations in sensor data values and timing. Some types of path planners are notorious for both of these issues. Two redundant path planners that use pseudorandom algorithms will likely produce two different paths, and those paths might not be close at all even though both are safe.

Even if a path planner is constrained to be highly repeatable, small timing variations in delivery of sensor data and subtle data variations across different sensors can produce dramatically different results across replicas of the same software function that are otherwise deterministic. As a simple example, an AV that is precisely pointed at the center of mass of an obstacle might have one planner decide to go around it to the left while another decides to go around it to the right based on the smallest variations on sensor data and timing arrival of data samples from shared sensors. Both paths might be safe, but the difference could register as a software failure in any architecture that compares outputs to look for similar results from redundant components. Any redundancy management plan that assumes redundant algorithms will always reach the same answer will struggle with such situations, especially if the algorithms are intentionally dissimilar in an attempt to mitigate potential algorithmic common cause failures.

Another type of cross-function consistency is comparing map data to sensor data. If you think of a map as a virtual sensor, consistency checks can be done to see if vehicle sensors are correctly detecting buildings, road furniture, and signage by checking the sensed world against the map. Sometimes it will be the map that has gone stale and not a physical sensor failure, but any disagreement is worth monitoring and likely useful as an SPI.

There will be some objects or circumstances in which a given type of sensor performs poorly. In those cases, using a dissimilar sensor can help determine there has been a sensing failure. For example, if no cameras see a particular object that is seen by lidar, the lidar information can be used to infer a false negative for the cameras (or, possibly, a false positive for the lidars). Whether such a false negative is reasonable or not will depend upon the type of object, the operating conditions, and the false negative budget for the cameras in the safety case. But the approach here is to use a different type of sensing to provide better information about whether any given type of sensor is suffering from false negatives or false positives.[452]

8.3.2.3. Sanity checks

In some cases, SPIs can be associated with so-called sanity checks, otherwise known as plausibility checks. These are frequently used in conventional automotive applications and can detect some occurrences of the unexpected, whether caused by a hardware fault, a software fault, or an unexpected input.

Typical sanity checks include: range limits (a value too high or too low compared to expectations), rate of change limits (changing faster than physical inertia permits), large variations across multiple samples of the same data source, and disagreements among multiple data sources. This is a generic concept that includes consistency checks we've already discussed as a special case.

It is important to realize that sanity checks do not provide complete fault coverage. Saying "we have a sanity check" is a much weaker statement than "we are able detect all relevant failures." Computations can be incorrect and even dangerous while still passing all sanity checks. Nonetheless, failing a sanity check indicates something is wrong, so sanity checks should be used as a source of SPI metrics that provides partial detection of issues.

8.3.2.4. Safety envelopes

A specific sanity check that is especially useful for SPIs is a safety envelope. A traditional *safety envelope* is a boundary on the system state space outside of which the system behaves dangerously. For example, an AV is likely to be unsafe when making too tight a turn too fast, with the safe turn curvature depending on the vehicle speed among other factors (very tight turns are only safe at low speeds). The safety envelope for this situation would be defined by the boundary of the tightest possible turn that maintains vehicle stability for each vehicle speed. Inside the safety envelope is safe.[453]

While safety envelopes are a useful concept in principle, they can be difficult to apply in practice for a very complex system. That is because defining a highly accurate safety envelope for a complex system can sometimes end up being as complex as designing the system itself. To address that limitation in practice, system designers can use looser definitions

---

[452] The logic of what a failure means might get a bit complex, but remains centered on whether observed sensor failures violate expectations. If weather conditions predict that cameras will fail but lidars will succeed, then the outcome is as expected and there is no problem from an SPI point of view.

[453] Safety envelope ideas discussed here are generally useful for runtime monitors as well. However, we limit the discussion scope to SPIs. For a brief video explaining safety envelopes, see: https://youtu.be/_wxlgbl4s-g

of safety envelopes including underapproximations, overapproximations, and partial safety envelopes.

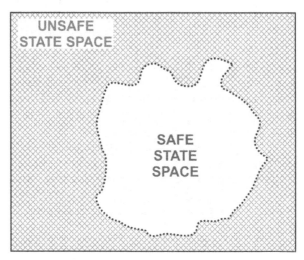

Figure 8.1 A hypothetical two-dimensional safe state space.

It is not necessary for an SPI to be a perfect expression of what safe behavior is. It is sufficient if an SPI alerts when there is potentially unsafe behavior so that offline analysis can occur. Additionally, it is sufficient if multiple safety envelopes work together as a set to monitor potential safety issues rather than requiring that a single safety envelope take into account all possible safety factors. Even an SPI arrangement that only detects some unsafe situations can provide value.

Figure 8.1 shows a hypothetical two-dimensional operational region for an AV in which operating inside the region is safe, while outside the region is unsafe. In real life, the safety envelope might well have three or more dimensions. A perfect safety envelope would exactly follow the boundary of the safe operating region. For practical reasons creating a perfect safety envelope might be too difficult on an engineering basis, or sensors with accurate enough information to do so might be unavailable. That means the idea is to find ways to approximate the boundary of the safe state space with one or more safety envelopes in a way that is feasible with available sensor data.

For this discussion we will use a hypothetical vehicle stability example in addition to an abstract graphic.[454] Any vehicle has limits to how fast it can safely take a turn without losing traction and skidding or spinning – or in

---

[454] The conceptual figure is not intended to match the example. The figure is about very abstract state spaces that should appeal to those who think about safety envelopes as literal enveloping boundaries in n-dimensional state space. The example is simplistic, but hopefully more accessible to those who think in terms of very concrete systems.

some cases completely rolling over. In general, the faster the speed and the tighter the turn, the more prone the vehicle will be to having a problem. However, other factors matter such as the banking (superelevation) of the curve, road surface slipperiness, vehicle suspension, height of the vehicle's center of gravity above the road, and so on. Precisely specifying the absolute maximum speed for each turn radius would be a complex computation, but the boundary obtained by performing that computation for every possible combination of speed and every other factor would form an exact safety envelope.

An underapproximated safety envelope, shown by the circle in figure 8.2 would be more conservative than the true safety boundary, but might be easier to implement.[455] Whenever the AV is inside an underapproximated safety envelope, the system is known to be safe. Outside the circle the system might or might not be safe, depending on exactly where it is on the 2-D graph. Because the envelope computation might not have the ability to determine what is safe vs. unsafe outside the envelope, all that can be said is that safety outside the envelope is unknown, and therefore is presumed to be unsafe. Such an approach can guarantee safety so long as the system always operates inside the circle. However, that restricts operation of the system by excluding some potentially safe parts of the operational space in exchange for keeping things simple in the safety envelope monitoring function.

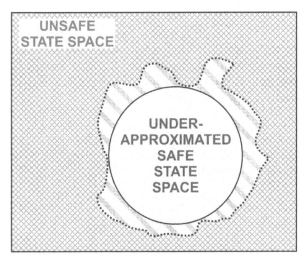

Figure 8.2 An under-approximated safety envelope

---

[455] The circular shape in figure 8.2 is conceptual – it does not literally need to be a circle, sphere, or hypersphere in n-dimensional system state space. The idea is that it is some comparatively easy to compute function with the property that no point inside the computed envelope is unsafe, and at least some points outside the envelope are unsafe.

For our example, a very simple underapproximation might be that any speed under 3 mph is safe for the tightest turn the vehicle can perform on any road surface within the ODD, and the safety envelope is therefore a maximum speed of 3 mph. Simple, but not very useful for most vehicles.

A more sophisticated underapproximation for vehicle turning might be precomputing a tightest safe turning radius for 5 mph, 10 mph, 15, mph, and so on under worst-case environmental conditions. The turning radius permitted for any speed is limited by the precomputed radius for the next higher multiple of 5 mph. Attempts by the vehicle control system to turn more sharply than permitted would generate SPI violations.

This approach based on 5 mph speed bins restricts vehicle motion limits more than a theoretical maximum size envelope because of worst-case assumptions within each 5 mph speed bin. However, it is better than limiting speed in even the slightest of gentle turns to 3 mph overall.

Contrasting a fixed speed limit vs. speed/turning radius precomputation also illustrates the inherent tradeoff between permissiveness of an SPI to permit a greater range of motion conditions without generating SPI violations vs. complexity in the SPI computation. More complex computations might provide more permissiveness, but the point is that the tradeoff of complexity vs. permissiveness is there.

One way to overcome the limits to an underapproximation while still staying simple is to switch to an overapproximation approach as shown in figure 8.3. With an overapproximation, a simple safety envelope (circular in figure 8.3) is set up for which anything outside the envelope is known to be unsafe. However, things inside the envelope are possibly unsafe or possibly safe. The envelope enforcement system is not able to ensure that operation inside the envelope is always safe, but it is sure that anything outside the envelope is unsafe.

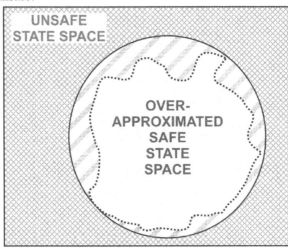

Figure 8.3 An over-approximated safety envelope

The use of an overapproximation envelope is a bit counter-intuitive for safety. After all, usually what you want is to be able to prove something is safe, and this does not quite do that. However, especially for an SPI, overapproximation has the virtue of keeping things simple while yielding no false alarms. If an SPI violation is triggered by an overapproximation, you can be sure that indeed the system was operating in an unsafe manner.

For the sharp curve running example, an overapproximation might be a set of values for how sharp a curve is too sharp, precomputed for every speed at 5 mph intervals for best case conditions. For example, if there is no road condition in which a certain tight curvature would be safe at 10 mph, then that curvature (and anything that is an even tighter curve) is an overapproximation safety envelope for that speed.

In practice, it might well be the case that the design team does not know the exact placement of a safe state space boundary. While this might seem odd at first, it has to do with the common situation that a great many different factors combine to determine which operational states are safe, and the team does not have resources to build a high fidelity model. This situation can be dealt with using a sandwich-style approach to safety envelopes.

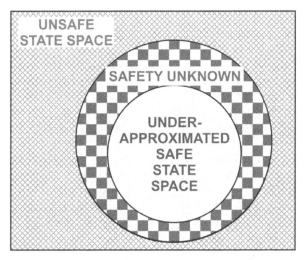

Figure 8.4 The sandwich area between under- and overapproximated safety envelopes has unknown safety.

Figure 8.4 shows a safety envelope sandwich. The outer circular envelope is an overapproximation. Anything outside the outer envelope is known to be unsafe. The inner circular envelope is an underapproximation, within which the system is known to be safe.

The space between the circular envelopes in a safety envelope sandwich is a region of uncertainty. Some parts might be safe, and some parts might be unsafe, but either the design team does not know, or creating a thinner safety envelope sandwich is too complex to be practical.

A possible instrumentation approach would be to use any violation of the outer safety envelope as hard evidence that the system has operated unsafely, likely generating both SPI data and a runtime monitor alarm. Every time the system operates outside the outer envelope, that event consumes part of the system risk budget, which should occur only rarely.

Operating in the safety unknown sandwich area is quite different. It means that the system is potentially at increased risk because it is operating in an unknown area. Maybe it is violating the safety case claims, but maybe not. In that unknown region the SPIs are not sophisticated enough to distinguish false positives (really everything is OK even though the SPI metrics show a problem) from true positives (a situation counter to the associated claim is taking place).

If rare, operation in the sandwich area can be further analyzed to weed out false positives. For example, a manual process might determine what was really going on. Clearly that is not scalable in production. Alternately there might be a baseline established for inner safety envelope violations during system validation that shows the system operates in that area infrequently enough that the risk is acceptably low. In that case an elevated rate of operation in the sandwich area should provoke attention to find out what has changed.

The inner envelope also has value during initial system development. It is common for designers to not be very sure where the safety envelope boundary should be placed for a novel system. One way to proceed is to create a sandwich arrangement even if the area between the two safety envelopes is excessively large. During initial testing, clusters of underapproximation envelope violations are analyzed to determine why such a pattern might be taking place, improving understanding of system operation. The inner and/or outer envelopes are then adjusted in response to that improved understanding. Over time, the sandwich area between the envelopes shrinks as the design team improves their understanding.

In terms of the sharp turn running example, before doing track testing there might be a very crude estimate of speeds and turning radius situations that are obviously unsafe (tight turns at high speeds), as well as situations that are obviously safe (wide turns at low speeds). As computer simulation and track testing progress, the sandwich can be tightened based on available test data, with the inner envelope permitting not-quite-so-wide turns at higher speeds as sure to be safe, and the outer envelope accounting for very tight turns at moderate speeds being unsafe. As the envelopes are tightened, control system permissiveness can be improved to exploit the newly available safe operating state space.

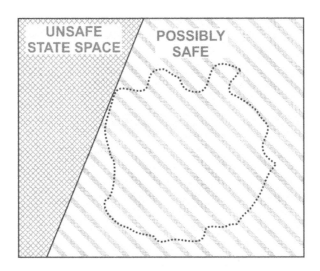

Figure 8.5 A partial approximation that divides the state space into a known unsafe region and a region of uncertain safety.

The final way to use safety envelopes that we will discuss is the use of partial safety envelopes. Sometimes the design team simply does not have enough information to create a complete safety envelope, but has information to say something useful about safety. That insight can be used to create one or more partial safety envelopes. Figure 8.5 shows this conceptually. In that figure everything to the upper left is known to be unsafe. However, things to the lower right are unknown in that they fail to violate the SPI threshold boundary, but might or might not be unsafe due to the partial nature of the envelope. Again, the envelope computation simply knows the boundary and has no way to know where the optimal safety envelope location is.

More than one partial SPI might be identified. Sometimes multiple SPIs might work together to fully enclose an area in the state space, converting that set of SPIs into an aggregated underapproximation or overapproximation safety envelope.

8.3.2.5. Latent redundancy failures

A somewhat different type of SPI data source has to do with detecting when redundancy that is supposed to be available in case of a failure is not there. For example, if an AV has a primary computer and also a backup computer, the backup computer must be ready to take over when needed. What happens if the primary computer fails but the backup computer is not there when you need it? A relevant SPI would involve measuring the uptime of the backup computer, for example with health checks, to ensure it is ready to take over a very high fraction of the time.

Latent redundancy SPI failure sources can include results of built-in self-test for backup units, how often backup components fail to activate when called upon, and diagnostic coverage of self-test (usually less than 100%, but still helpful for predicting potential backup computer failures).

The important thing for a latent redundancy failure SPI is to find a test to see if the redundant component is able to function. That can be more difficult than it sounds. Simply pinging the component for a response (a heartbeat monitor) is a start, but is prone to false optimism. A common naïve heartbeat implementation is that an interrupt service routine responds to the heartbeat request. That routine will work even if all the other software in the computer has crashed, so life critical systems need to do better.[456]

Determining backup health can become quite involved, but ultimately you need a way to quantify the real-world probability the backup computer will be there when you need it. An SPI should be used to monitor whether the probability calculation reflects real-world performance.[457]

8.3.2.6. Coverage

Measuring engineering process coverage or validation coverage is a different take on SPI metric sources. Coverage generally considers how thoroughly some task has been performed, or what fraction of multiple instances of a potential problem has been addressed. The idea is that 100% coverage means that the entire set of all possible things of interest has been addressed. These tend to relate to engineering processes (did you do all the engineering tasks on everything you should have) and validation (did you test everything that should have been tested).

---

[456] A simplistic analogy is calling to check on a neighbor's health and determining that everything is fine if the neighbor's answering machine takes a message. Really, it is pretty much that bad. But we have seen this in real live products so often!

With more detail: an interrupt service routine is a piece of software that runs directly in response to an external request without involving any of the other software running on a computer. Using an interrupt service routine to respond to a heartbeat request amounts to creating a health monitor that does little more than checking the health of the monitor itself – even if the main software is severely malfunctioning. This is an incredibly common type of mistake we have found across a wide range of embedded systems. Rules for good heartbeat practices parallel those of watchdog timer practices, with a discussion here:

https://betterembsw.blogspot.com/2014/05/proper-watchdog-timer-use.html

[457] Another simplistic example: A major reason for the impressive safety record of passenger aircraft is that they have two or more engines. If one engine fails, there is another one to take over. That sounds pretty obvious, but imagine flying in an aircraft if one engine ran and the other was always turned off to save fuel – and you were not sure if the second engine were actually working until you needed it. What if it had never been run since the aircraft was manufactured – would you still trust it to be there when you needed it for an in-flight emergency? Might it be like that flashlight you kept for a power outage that, when you needed it, turned out to have the batteries rotted into a goopy mess inside it? You would want a metric to tell you the probability any redundant backup will work when needed was extremely high.

Examples of coverage SPIs include: fraction of code that has been peer reviewed, fraction of code that has been unit tested, fraction of system-level requirements that have a system-level test, fraction of hazards that have been mitigated, fraction of scenarios tested in simulation, fraction of scenarios tested in road test, and fraction of components that can have configuration automatically self-reported for configuration management audits.

Perhaps surprisingly, there are some aspects of the system such as built-in self-test for which high coverage (90-99%) is important, but perfect 100% coverage is elusive. This makes it important to carefully consider the threshold part of the SPI {metric, threshold} pair so that the threshold is not too lax even if it cannot be 100%.

Coverage metrics tend to come from engineering analysis of the product or support processes rather than automated monitoring of the vehicle itself. An SPI violation here might be only indirectly related to the probability of an operational AV crash. However, coverage metrics are essential for supporting claims of engineering rigor. A hypothetical argument claim chain goes something like: our vehicle is safe because (in part) it is well engineered; it is well engineered (in part) because we have tested it thoroughly; thorough testing includes testing 100% of scenarios and simulation, and validating simulation accuracy via road testing for at least 94% of scenario types with the remainder of scenario types validated via other means including closed track testing (or something like this – numbers are entirely hypothetical). In that example, if fewer than 94% of scenario types had indeed been validated via road testing, that would generate an SPI violation.[458]

8.3.2.7. Failure rates

Failure rates measure how often something goes wrong. The perfect software plus computer hardware system that never fails has yet to be invented, and failures involving any human process are sure to occur. Safe AVs will compensate for failures, but can only do so much. It is important to make sure that things going wrong do not exceed the ability of the AV and supporting processes to compensate. That means that SPIs should be established to make sure that failure rates are not worse than anticipated.

Failure rates can address different parts of the lifecycle. Equipment examples include: software crashes, transient failure rate (rebooting fixes it), permanent failure rate (component needs to be replaced), communications interruptions, and whether components wear out or need maintenance sooner than expected.

Process examples include: fraction of software defects that are missed by peer review, fraction of software defects that escape simulation validation to be found in road testing, and fault reinjection ratio (how often fixing one bug causes another bug as a side effect).

---

[458] The number 94% is purely hypothetical for the purposes of the example.

Lifecycle examples include: missed maintenance, incorrect maintenance, and root cause analysis that found inspection failed to identify a problem that should have been detected via inspection.

Data on failure rates can sometimes come from equipment logs, software quality metrics, and diagnosis of field failures.

8.3.2.8. Requirement violations and temporal logic

It is common for safety requirements to encompass some aspect of time. For example, saying that there is a requirement for an AV to stop moving after a certain kind of fault leaves open the question of how long that stopping process can take.

Including the temporal relationship and allowing for delays between activities is essential in checking the behavior of any real-world system that includes moving parts, inertia, and control loops that need time to settle after a change in command. That is why a requirement such as "the vehicle shall stop when brakes are applied" is too simplistic to be checked accurately. It takes time to physically start braking, and more time for the braking to absorb vehicle energy to come to a stop. But how long is too long to start braking, and what is the maximum stopping distance permissible for safety in a particular situation?[459]

We have found it helpful to express requirements violations and monitors in terms of a simplified temporal logic that combines Boolean logic operations with time-constrained operators that can be used to represent notions such as "until," "before," "after," "longer than," and "shorter than." As a simple example: "the vehicle shall start reducing speed within 350 msec after a braking command is issued." And: "the vehicle shall come to a stop no longer than 30 seconds after a failure of this type."

We prefer metric temporal logic,[460] and have found it to be convenient for AV runtime safety monitoring.[461] MTL can be just as useful for SPIs. Such an approach permits SPIs to express concepts such as the maximum length of time two different measurements are permitted to disagree due to timing skew, or how long after a command has been sent to wait for confirmation that the command has been carried out. In any real system there will be synchronization, ordering, and inexact timing considerations.[462] An MTL approach can conveniently specify the maximum bounds on measurements that are delayed or are allowed to temporarily disagree.

---

[459] The situation definitely matters here. The stopping distance for a heavy vehicle on a steep hill in slippery conditions can easily be however far it is to the bottom of the hill and/or the first other car that can be hit, and then some. For a selection of videos see: https://www.youtube.com/results?search_query=car+sliding+hill+ice

[460] Metric temporal logic (MTL) uses constructions such as "until, next, since, previous" and seems a good fit for many AV requirements. More here: https://en.wikipedia.org/wiki/Metric_temporal_logic

[461] See Kane et al. 2015 at: https://users.ece.cmu.edu/~koopman/pubs/kane15_monitoring.pdf

[462] See: https://en.wikipedia.org/wiki/Synchronization_(computer_science)

One way that data consistency can become difficult is when samples arrive out of order compared to when they are collected. This can easily occur if sensors transfer data via internal data networks or otherwise use shared resources. Time stamping sensor data samples can help, but introduces the thorny problem of synchronized distributed time bases.[463]

Another practical problem is dealing with data sampled at different frequencies. Combining a slowly sampled piece of data with a metric sampled at a higher frequency typically forces a choice of whether to check the threshold at every high-frequency sample, or only when the low-frequency sample is taken. Checking only with new low-frequency samples might miss threshold violations due to transient glitches in the high-frequency data. But threshold checking for every high-frequency sample means that stale data will be used for the low-frequency data, potentially leading to inconsistent system states being checked.

Getting things right when checking multi-frequency data samples requires paying attention to both synchronizing data samples and deciding what to do with data sampled at different rates. There is no single right answer, and likely there will need to be a variety of techniques even within a single system depending on the exact nature of the SPI being checked.[464]

8.3.2.9. Process hygiene

In practice, any safety case will need to include process considerations such as whether the design process has been followed, whether maintenance procedures have been followed, and so on. Process hygiene SPIs measure whether processes are clearly defined and are being executed effectively.

Some key forms of process SPIs are: coverage SPIs for processes having been defined in writing, how often processes are followed, whether field incidents are traced to a root cause of a process failure, and audits revealing noncompliance with required processes. SQA activities are likely to provide data for this type of SPI.

We call this area process hygiene because routinely following processes as a way to support safety is analogous to routinely washing hands to prevent the transmission of relevant infectious diseases. Any one instance of a hygiene fault might or might not result in a problem, but routinely skipping hygiene steps predicts bad outcomes eventually.

---

[463] See: https://en.wikipedia.org/wiki/Clock_synchronization regarding clock synchronization in general. Within a distributed system such as an AV the problem gets worse because each computing unit inside the system cannot necessarily afford a high-quality independent clock. An alternative approach for safety critical systems is the use of time triggered design. See:
https://www.microsoft.com/en-us/research/video/the-time-triggered-architecture/
[464] This topic turned out to be much trickier than we had expected. You can read about these adventures in Kane et al. 2014:
https://users.ece.cmu.edu/~koopman/pubs/kane14_dsn_cpsmonitor.pdf as well as the associated dissertation by Kane here:
https://users.ece.cmu.edu/~koopman/thesis/kane.pdf

8.3.2.10. Root cause analysis

There should be an implicit SPI data feed linking every claim with the outputs of root cause analysis.[465] Ideally, each SPI violation regardless of position within the safety case undergoes a root cause analysis to determine not only the technical cause of the problem, but also the safety case implications of the problem. That means the result of a root cause analysis can, in principle, propagate beyond the claim being monitored to also determine that other claims are likely to have been falsified, even if no direct measurements of those other claims are available.

An SPI violation on one claim establishes that the claim has been falsified. But how did that happen? Perhaps one or more child sub-claims are also false – even if their SPIs reflect everything is OK. If so, an analysis should dig down into the false claims as many levels as required to find the source of the problem and fix it.

It will be common for a single SPI violation to implicate multiple claims in a safety case, especially including claims above and below the particular SPI violation. If the parent and child claims also have direct measurement SPIs, those SPIs might or might not also be violated depending on the nature of their approximation to claim conformance measurement. Other claims might be too difficult to measure and not have any explicit SPIs associated with them.

If a claim has been falsified by an SPI violation but all its sub-claims are legitimately true, that points to a flaw in the argument supporting the falsified claim. Maybe a new sub-claim needs to be added to address the SPI violation. Perhaps the threshold needs to be adjusted for the SPI, while ensuring that overall parent claims remain sound.[466] Perhaps that portion of the safety case needs to be completely rethought. Regardless of the approach, any SPI violation, by definition, means either that the safety case has been rendered unsound or that an SPI threshold has been set in a way that triggered a false alarm.

In addition to exploring the implications for child sub-claims, the effect of an SPI violation and associated claim falsification should be examined with regard to parent claims. If any particular child claim is false, that does not necessarily mean a parent claim is false. The effects of a false sub-claim depend on the structure of the parent claim. For example, a parent claim of "all of the below sub-claims are true" has a problem if any sub-claim is

---

[465] See: https://en.wikipedia.org/wiki/Root_cause_analysis#General_principles

[466] Caution must be exercised in adjusting thresholds to resolve SPI violations. If an original threshold was set conservatively to avoid the need to spend time on detailed analysis, then the first SPI violation is a good justification to do the analysis and adjust the threshold accordingly. However, adjusting the threshold just to get rid of the violation is akin to removing the battery from an annoying smoke alarm in your house to make it stop beeping – and a really bad idea in case later on there is a real fire. Any time an SPI threshold is adjusted there should be a written justification of the decision permanently added to the safety case. Section 7.1.4.4 discusses this further including managing a reserve risk pool.

falsified. However, a parent claim of "at least one of the below sub-claims is true" could be perfectly fine with sub-claims that are occasionally false.[467]

8.3.3. Computing SPI violations

Once SPIs have been defined, you need to gather data to support them as well as perform computations to check for threshold violations. This might sound straightforward, but can end up being more complicated than expected because of the statistical nature of most SPI violations. The fact that many SPIs require data aggregation well beyond a single vehicle's operational data adds to the complexity.

As we have discussed in section 7.1.4.3, SPIs are different than runtime monitors. Runtime monitors are designed to respond to a risky situation on an individual vehicle in the moment. In contrast, SPIs are intended to aggregate data across multiple vehicles for engineering feedback and do not have any immediate effect on vehicle operation.

Because SPI violations are more of a statistical fleet-wide approach than runtime monitoring, event reporting need not be strictly in real time to be reasonably effective. It might suffice to have event reporting from individual vehicles include just the number of events recorded and the operational exposure (e.g., 2 relevant events in 600 miles for a specific SPI since the last report from that vehicle). That type of information can be reported when the vehicle has access to an inexpensive uplink as part of routine health checks and software updates, such as when an electric vehicle is being recharged. The timeliness requirement is that any data that reveals an SPI violation will be processed and provoke risk mitigation before it is likely that a loss event will occur due to the underlying issue. It might well be that some SPI violations are assigned a high priority (transmit SPI violation event data immediately even if cost to transmit is high) while others are more routine (transmit as part of a bulk data upload when the vehicle is not in use).

We divide SPI data collection approaches into a variety of flavors in the following subsections. The boundaries between different types of SPI approaches overlap, so the point here is to explain there are different approaches rather than present a complete, precise categorization of all possible approaches.

---

[467] Some sub-claims might be true only sometimes, and an aggregate set of sub-claims works together to support a parent claim (e.g., At least one of A or B or C is always true). Associating an SPI with a sub-claim that is only occasionally true might not be useful. However, reformulating the safety case might be productive in such situations. For example, for a three-color traffic light claims that each of the three colors is illuminated will be false on a regular basis. However, a claim that exactly one of the three lights is always illuminated (accounting for gaps or overlaps permitted by local traffic rules) is likely to be a lot more useful for a safety case.

8.3.3.1. On-vehicle discrete events

An obvious way to collect SPI information is using on-vehicle monitoring to compare real-time vehicle state to claims made about what vehicle states are potentially unsafe. Many such claims will have to do with specific events or conditions being very rare. For example, un-commanded airbag deployments, component failures, having the vehicle be forcibly ejected from the ODD (e.g., rain squall for a desert-only vehicle), and so on are generally assumed to be quite rare. From a vehicle point of view, any occurrence of such a discrete event should be reported to the engineering team because the fact that it happened at all is likely to be highly relevant to SPI processing.

An individual vehicle is unlikely to have the context to determine if a rare SPI-related discrete event is an SPI violation. Extending the use of a previously discussed example of a buffer space around a pedestrian, let us assume that the acceptable buffer for a particular AV in a particular set of conditions is 1 meter. Consider if for one AV the vehicle passes half that distance to a pedestrian just one time during a trip. Does that falsify a claim of "less than 1 meter no more frequently than 100,000 miles?" For an individual vehicle we could wait for a million miles for statistical significance. But that is a long time to wait (likely longer than the life of the vehicle) to see if this AV happened to get unlucky or there is a larger problem. We would like to do better.

Assuming we have a large fleet, the answer is we do not know if a single safety event on a single vehicle is a problem unless we combine it with data from a much bigger fleet.[468] If the fleet is driving 100,000 miles per day overall (say 500 vehicles each driving 200 miles per day) on average such an event will happen to one vehicle per day. That one vehicle has no way of knowing whether it was the unlucky vehicle that day, or if the problem is happening to every vehicle in the fleet that day. So rather than assuming that a too-close approach to a pedestrian means the vehicle is unreasonably dangerous, any vehicle seeing such a situation should report it to the engineering team for further analysis.

The implication of this is that if an SPI calls for recognizing events (e.g., "closer than 1 meter") each such event should be reported to the engineering organization. The engineering organization should continually monitor such events and flag an SPI violation if the statistical arrival rate is too frequent.

There are two special cases for discrete events that should be considered: small fleets and multiple violations.

For a small fleet the total fleet exposure might well be small compared to the permissible arrival rate of SPI violations. This is especially true during road testing and pilot deployments. An SPI violation that is supposed to occur only once every 10 million miles should not occur at all on a 1 million mile road testing campaign.[469] For such situations every single event should be considered as a *likely* SPI violation regardless of the exposure for the

---

[468] For our purposes a "fleet" is a set of monitored vehicles of a similar type, regardless of ownership and operational model.

[469] Strictly speaking it might occur, but with low probability.

purposes of root cause analysis. That is because you do not expect to get enough data to determine the actual arrival rate with statistical significance. As a simple illustration: if you see a once per 10 million mile SPI violation in the first hundred miles of testing, it is a good bet you have a problem that needs to be fixed. There is no point waiting millions of miles more to figure that out.

Another special case is multiple SPI-related discrete events in one drive cycle. Consider driving 100 miles and seeing two distinct violations of an SPI measurement threshold (e.g., you pass closer than 1 meter to pedestrians in two separate incidents assuming a 1 meter buffer zone). If the budget is one such event every 100,000 miles, then it is just barely possible this is still OK – but that is not the smart bet. Instead, the AV should assume that an SPI violation has likely occurred and report the situation immediately, without waiting for fleetwide data analysis. A conservative safety action would be to cease operation of that one vehicle and send a high-priority message to the fleet manager to investigate. Perhaps it is a statistical fluke. But more likely is that there has been some malfunction or some unforeseen operational environment change that is breaking the safety case. It is important to note that the measurement system itself might have a failure in such a situation and be falsely reporting SPI violations that are not actually occurring. Nonetheless, a cautious approach should be taken if something that is supposed to happen only very rarely across a fleet happens repeatedly on a single vehicle.

8.3.3.2. Fleet-wide vehicle trends

Some SPI thresholds will not be counting specific problematic events, but rather an expected rate of arrival of some otherwise ordinary event, or an expected distribution of values over a fleet of vehicles.[470] One example might be an SPI associated with credit taken for low exposure to adverse conditions. As an example, an AV might have moderately increased risk when operating in icy conditions, although still compare favorably with a human driver in the same conditions. In terms of net acceptable overall risk, the claim will be that road ice, and in particular difficult-to-detect black ice is very rare. Such a safety argument might be appropriate for a warm weather climate. However, if a cold snap takes place there might extensive road icing that falsifies an "ice is rare and only in small patches" assumption that was made in a safety case. Timely detection and reporting of this SPI violation might or might not prevent the first crash, but could lead to a quick stand-down of a fleet to reduce the total number of crashes, followed by revisiting the safety case to fix an incorrect assumption that such weather will not happen in that geographic area of operations.

A potential mitigation might be adding an additional weather forecast data feed to predict periods of ice to ensure that the AV fleet does not attempt to operate during extensive icing conditions. In terms of ODD enforcement, this

---

[470] As a terminology note, by "fleet" we mean deployed vehicles of similar type, whether individually owned or operated by a "fleet operator."

amounts to replacing an assumption that ice is irrelevant to ODD enforcement because it never happens (i.e., the OD never has ice, so the ODD model does not need to account for it explicitly), to requiring weather monitoring to detect an ODD exit when icing is likely to occur.

Other examples might include: maximum observed braking force of lead vehicles for determining safe following distance, frequency of other vehicles making unsafe maneuvers (e.g., cut-in with insufficient following clearance for own vehicle), pedestrian density in specific urban locations, and correlated failure rates for sensors that are expected to have common mode failures (e.g., two cameras both miss the same object, which can happen due to an algorithmic error, but also would be expected to happen due to adverse weather conditions).

These types of SPIs are likely to be reported as statistical averages or statistical distributions over an operational period rather than as a huge set of discrete occurrences. As a simple example, the fraction of the time that pavement is dry, wet, and icy might be reported on a percentage basis after each trip to feed a fleet-wide SPI related to representativeness of weather. If an SPI checking that wet roads are rare is violated, simulations used for validation might need to be updated to account for weather experience being different than the weather model used when validating software.

8.3.3.3. Simulation and test SPIs

While it is essential to monitor some SPIs based on real-world vehicle experience, it is also important to create SPIs related to simulation and testing.

Simulated vehicles should be instrumented to report SPI data that is also anticipated to be reported by real vehicles. Doing so can give a preview of SPI performance to help set realistic SPI thresholds, adjusting the safety case as necessary to accommodate any net vehicle safety implications. In a sense this can be thought of as co-development of the system, the simulation models, and the SPI monitoring capability. If a simulated vehicle produces SPI violations, there might be little reason to expect things will improve in the real world. Therefore, much time can be saved by fixing problems found by SPI violations in simulation before deployment.

A significant advantage of simulation is that it is much easier to determine ground truth. For fully synthetic test environments, the simulator knows exactly what is supposed to be happening in the environment. This provides ground truth data for SPIs that measure the AV's ability to create an accurate world model.[471] It also makes it easy to generate SPI metrics that might be difficult to capture in the real world. For example, determining the percentage of pedestrians not detected by any sensor in the vehicle tends to

---

[471] Or at least this will validate the AV software's ability to recreate the world simulation that the simulator is feeding into the AV. That is a start, but validation still requires ensuring that differences between the simulated world and the real world do not cause problems here.

be a lot easier if you have a simulator giving your SPI data feed a precise count and location of pedestrians in the simulated world.

A similar approach applies to closed-course testing, instrumented test ranges, tests for which data has been annotated by analysts to provide ground truth information, [472] and in general any situation in which there is an independent source of ground truth to check against the AV's world model. Any external information that can be used to provide data to SPIs makes it easier to detect problems compared to relying on just the AV's own sensors. In addition to feeding SPIs with external ground truth data to monitor the performance of AV functionality, validation should also include checking that in-vehicle data feeds to those same SPIs are sufficiently accurate for the purpose.

From this point of view, the measurement regime should be viewed as a smooth, continuous evolution from subsystem simulation to vehicle simulation to vehicle testing to deployment. SPIs should be monitored at every step. SPI measurement capability for later steps should be checked by comparing to ground truth when available in earlier steps. From an SPI point of view, the last day of crewed road testing should be a seamless transition to initial deployment that simply continues SPI monitoring without interruption.

8.3.3.4. Process trends

Not all SPIs have to do with data collected in real time on vehicles. An important contributing factor in assuring safety is checking on the health of the processes used to design, validate, and operate AVs. For example, if software developers take shortcuts in design reviews or safety analysis, that is likely to (eventually) lead to real-world loss events. A safety case needs to argue that, in part, safety is acceptable because a suitably rigorous design and validation process was used. SPIs should be associated with process rigor claims.

A wide variety among process SPIs approaches will help create a robust safety case. Process SPIs will often take the form of coverage metrics, incident rates for failure to follow process, incident rates for defects traced to a process problem, and so on.

Design process SPIs tend to be settled before production release. That means the data for these SPIs is coming from a Software Quality Assurance (SQA) database rather than vehicle operation. Nonetheless, such SPIs are crucial to provide confidence in claims of design rigor that support a top-level safety claim. An important pitfall to avoid is waiting to collect design process SPIs at the end of development. If the design process SPIs are

---

[472] A significant issue in machine learning is that labeled data can have shockingly high error rates. One study showed a 3.4% error rate on benchmark test sets, which are supposed to be pristine. In practice, labeling error rates can be much higher on everyday operational data that is not a polished benchmark data set. It might be argued that this is less of a problem for common objects, but it can significantly degrade performance when rare objects that are already under-represented in data are also mislabeled. See: https://l7.curtisnorthcutt.com/label-errors

unsatisfactory, no amount of testing and bug fixing will correct that. Instead, there might be a major need for rework. Worse, many software quality techniques are ineffective if done in a hurry.[473]

For the likely case that an AV has continual software updates, design process SPIs should be re-evaluated at least before every software release. Some process SPIs will be updates of existing SPI values related to modifications and defect fixes. Other SPIs will deal with the integrity of the software update process itself.

There will also need to be extra-vehicular operational SPIs related to maintenance, inspection, repair part supply chains, and so on. Operational SPI data is likely to originate from business operations rather than from individual vehicles.

The SQA group should probably own design process SPIs and include SPI tracking in their other quality management tasks. The group responsible for the Safety Management System (SMS) should own SPIs related to post-deployment processes.

8.3.3.5. Adding SPIs

Sometimes the answer to investigating an SPI violation is that it is difficult to know what has gone wrong, especially if the SPI violation occurs in a region of the safety case that has sparse instrumentation. A response to an SPI violation to understand what happened might be to add more SPIs near and especially below the claim falsified to see if there are associated violations of other claims that can be detected.

While it is always better to figure out what is wrong with a safety case in response to an SPI violation, sometimes the only feasible response will be "we don't know." In that case adding more instrumentation in supporting claims might help pin down the problem based on more experience, or based on analysis of historical data if available. Simulations or other approaches might be able to generate or play back data for a newly identified SPI to help with diagnosis efforts. It is important not to give up too easily on analysis and become dependent on just adding more instrumentation – but ultimately it might be the only option left.[474]

8.3.3.6. Multiple measurements for an SPI threshold

While each SPI is associated with a metric threshold pair, in practice most SPI metrics will have a complex threshold computation with at least two stages. The first threshold stage is some sort of safety envelope violation or other acceptance test of some value directed toward the substance of the

---

[473] Peer reviewers can only review so many lines of code per day before their brains turn into mush. Ineffective marathon peer review sessions won't fix a process problem either.

[474] Software developers will recognize this as the safety case equivalent of adding "print" statements during debugging. While not ideal, sometimes that is the best you can do. However, this analogy does raise the intriguing question of what a debugging tool that incorporates SPIs for a safety case would be like.

claim. The second threshold stage has to do with the permissible frequency of claim violations – which will end up being greater than zero in many practical situations.

As an example, consider a claim of "the AV does not pass closer than 1 meter to a pedestrian." The first threshold computation stage is whether the AV in fact passed closer than 1 meter to the pedestrian based on best available distance information. It is unrealistic to expect that such a requirement will be met 100% of the time, especially if the overall risk budget is greater than zero (which it almost certainly will be). The fully stated SPI is more likely to be: "the AV passes closer than 1 meter to a pedestrian less frequently than once every 10,000 hours."[475]

The important thing to note is that there are two different measurements associated with a threshold violation for this type of SPI: a first metric that indicates some measurement is unacceptable (1 meter in this case), and a second metric that involves the permissible frequency of violations of the first metric (once per 10,000 hours for this example).

Whether both thresholds are part of the claim, the SPI, or split across them is perhaps a matter of taste. The safety case should be consistent about this on a stylistic basis, but what matters in the end is the SPI detecting claim falsification.

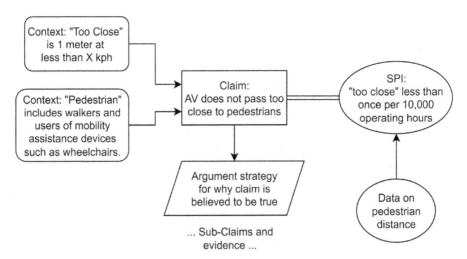

Figure 8.6 A safety case claim showing supporting context and an associated SPI.

---

[475] In reality there is likely to be a more nuanced definition of buffer zones around pedestrians based on operational situation and vehicle speed. And there might well be a set of buffer limits of increasing severity and decreasing permissible frequency. Additionally, 10,000 hours is a completely hypothetical number. We use this example to keep the discussion simple.

We favor splitting the data measurement threshold as part of the claim and the statistical threshold as part of the SPI, as illustrated in figure 8.6. In this example, the claim is "no closer than 1 meter" and the SPI defines "once per 10,000 hours" as the permissible claim falsification rate. At some point an acceptable risk decision might need to take into account how often the "no closer than 1 meter" part of the claim is violated. Also, the argument itself might have a statistical aspect that takes advantage of the once every 10,000 hours falsification budget. For these reasons, the cluster of the claim, the claim's context, and the claim's SPI should be thought of as a single combined node for safety case analysis purposes.

Nonetheless, splitting the two thresholds this way makes it clearer what is going to be monitored directly at the data source (the claim acceptance test) and what will be monitored more centrally as a statistical value (the SPI threshold). There is no hard-and-fast rule about this division, and the reader is encouraged to do something sensible, keeping in mind how the SPI data will be processed and any implications for clarity in the safety case.

For the rest of the SPI discussion, we will assume the issue of where thresholds are associated (with the SPI vs. with the claim threshold itself) is a stylistic issue that has been resolved and just talk about different types of SPI threshold functions more generically.

8.3.3.7. Data computation and transmission

The mechanics of collecting data on potential SPI violations must account for the difference between safety envelope measurement thresholds and statistical claim violation thresholds as discussed in the previous subsection. For many SPIs there will need to be a split between computations performed in the AV or other local situations versus computations performed by a central engineering location or other cross-fleet computing facility.

Data collection in practice will be limited by a combination of on-vehicle data storage size limits, on-vehicle computation resources, and each vehicle's external communication bandwidth. For deployed vehicles, data relevant to SPI calculations will be transmitted back to a centralized facility for analysis. For many SPIs there will be too much raw data to transmit in real time, too much data to store until a high bandwidth network connection is available, and in many cases too much data to send even with a high bandwidth connection when the vehicle is done with its mission.[476] We expect most AV designs beyond the first few engineering prototypes will take a hybrid approach in which some data is processed locally on the AV and some SPI processing happens to data sent to a more centralized facility. In general, the

---

[476] AV test vehicles tend to solve the data size and communication bandwidth problems by installing huge data drives in each vehicle and physically swapping them for blank drives daily. As fleets get larger this is likely to change to a local processing model with highly selective communication of data back to the engineering organization as we propose. The perennial question is what data to send back. SPIs give an answer to how to trigger data collection and what types of data might be most relevant for safety.

more local computation that can be performed, the better. However, there are limits.

The starting point for deciding what data to process locally vs. centrally is likely to divide along the lines of SPI acceptance tests being computed locally (if computationally feasible) and statistical calculations being performed centrally.

Consider the example from the previous subsection about passing within 1 meter of a pedestrian no more frequently than once every 10,000 hours. Sending all pedestrian distances for an entire drive is going to be too much data to be practical for a production vehicle. Even sending the closest point of approach for each pedestrian is a lot of data, and unnecessary for SPI monitoring.[477] Rather, SPI monitoring just needs to know when a 1 meter buffer around a pedestrian has been breached. For this example, the 1 meter threshold computation should be done locally on the AV based on the best information available.[478]

On the other hand, the once every 10,000 hours part of the threshold should be computed in a centralized facility. Attaining statistical significance as to whether a single 1 meter threshold violation is an SPI violation could take longer than the operational life of any individual consumer vehicle. Holding a potential SPI violation inside a vehicle to wait to see how things turn out tens of thousands of operational hours later defeats the point of having SPIs. Instead, each event that is subject to statistical analysis should be reported to a centralized facility as an event to be considered along with the accumulated operational hours (or other appropriate statistical denominator) of that vehicle and comparable events from other vehicles.

What about reporting urgency? The reporting urgency will be a matter of engineering tradeoffs. Likely, high consequence events that are expected infrequently should be reported most urgently, with more routine events reported less urgently. It might sound counter-intuitive to report the least frequent events most urgently. But the most important safety issues could show up as dangerous events that are supposed to be infrequent, but suddenly show up much more frequently. Eventually something catastrophic will happen to some vehicle in the fleet, but that might be within acceptable safety limits if it is the one rare time it happens. If it happens three times the same day to different vehicles, that is a potentially huge safety issue that is

---

[477] This type of data might be very useful for investigating a problem, but routinely sending huge amounts of data when no problem is suspected might be too expensive for production vehicles. A middle ground would be computing statistical distributions of pedestrian distances over each mission, with special emphasis on data for approaches near the 1 meter buffer distance.

[478] During simulation, the simulator might perform this distance computation because it has a better source of ground truth than the AV. The AV should also run this computation based on its own (simulated) sensor data so that the simulation can cross-check AV SPI calculation accuracy. After deployment the AV can only rely on its own sensor data.

likely to need an immediate response such as grounding the fleet. Noticing that type of pattern requires urgent reporting of the relevant SPI violations.[479]

As a concrete example, if a high consequence safety envelope is only supposed to be violated every 100 million miles, any violation occurrence should likely be reported immediately using an allotment of limited bandwidth cell phone connection data. If multiple cars in the fleet are seeing such events on the same day, that could be a huge problem that needs immediate attention.

On the other hand, if an excursion from a safety envelope is permissible once every 10 miles, then there is no point in making a big deal about excursions that are happening less than about every 10 miles. A tally of such events can be sent when the vehicle has reached a high bandwidth data connection at the end of its mission. This is much more of checking to make sure there are no clusters of violations or changes in violation rate, and not a four-alarm firefighting exercise for each violation.

Between the extremes are shades of gray in terms of reporting urgency that should be considered in light of the likely consequence of a claim falsification and the permitted number of failed claim acceptance tests before the statistical aspect of the SPI has been violated. For many SPIs a daily report is likely to be fine, especially if the report is an accumulation of operational experience with no SPI violations that is simply building confidence in the safety case.

A similar approach should be taken for process-based SPIs. For example, the number of defects found in a particular peer review session along with the number of lines of source code reviewed should be logged as a data annotation for that source code peer review record. Similarly, data from all testing should be annotated with the number of tests passed and tests failed. A centralized SPI computation should gather data from all peer review records and all test records to compute metrics such as fraction of defects found in testing vs. peer reviews.

8.3.3.8. Statistical confidence for online measurements

An important consideration for determining whether an SPI violation has occurred for statistically based SPIs is taking into account statistical confidence. Consider an SPI that permits a claim measurement threshold to be violated infrequently, such as once every million hours of operation. If you are examining a batch of data with tens of millions of hours of exposure, you can apply statistical math to determine if a certain number of failures is likely to violate the SPI statistical threshold with a given statistical confidence.

However, periodically processing a batch of newly arrived SPI data makes the problem more difficult, especially if the new batch of data is

---

[479] In some situations the fleet might be grounded after only one severe event. Urgent reporting of high severity SPI violations makes it harder to make the mistake of dismissing that one event as a fluke, and forces recognition of any systematic issue that might be occurring across the fleet.

comparatively small compared to the amount of data required for statistical significance. As an example, consider a fleet that operates 1 million hours per day in which leading SPIs are processed daily.[480] If the SPI threshold is about the same as the amount of daily exposure (say 1 million hours between SPI acceptance test failures for 1 million hours per day of exposure), some days might see no SPI violations, but there might be two SPI violations on other days, even while the safety case remains sound. Something needs to be done to smooth out the arriving data across potentially long time intervals.

It might be tempting to just use a moving average to smooth out such data. However, there are pitfalls for the unwary that suggest augmenting a moving average with detection of some special cases.

Any moving average should emphasize more recent data instead of historical data, possibly via use of a weighting system that weights more recent data heavily. A system that has behaved perfectly for a year should not be permitted to have months of zero events outweigh a recent large cluster of SPI violations that all happen on the same day. Such a cluster is highly suggestive of something having changed or something new going wrong.[481]

Any change to the system should prompt de-weighting SPI data from before the change, especially for SPIs in claims that impact analysis shows are likely to be affected by the change. This also argues for a weighting system that is aware of when changes have been made, perhaps resetting running average integrators to discard older, pre-change data.

A spike of SPI violations in a comparatively short length of time should be considered a cause for concern even if averages still look good. A cluster might simply be a statistically insignificant fluctuation. But it might also indicate something in the operational environment has changed that has invalidated claims in the safety case, even if averages over longer time intervals are still within bounds.

All these considerations push for considering the most recent SPI data in favor of older data, with "recent" vs. "old" depending on the ratio of permissible SPI threshold violation frequency to the amount of data included in each newly arrived data batch. While it is true that any cluster of recent SPI violations might be just random chance, any such anomalous cluster should be examined to determine whether it is instead an early warning of a bigger safety problem.

A related issue is that a confidence interval should be assigned to statistical SPI violation calculations.[482] That confidence interval will put a limit on how much leeway can be afforded a cluster of SPI violations before

---

[480] Some critically urgent SPI-relevant events with essentially a statistical threshold of zero might be processed immediately, especially if related to high-severity loss events. For this discussion we are talking SPI data that takes a while to accumulate to see if a statistical threshold is being violated.

[481] It might just be a fluke event, but a strong safety culture is reluctant to dismiss suspicious data without investigation.

[482] For example, 95% confidence, although some in the automotive industry might argue for a lower confidence of more like 70%.

declaring that there are too many to dismiss as a statistical fluke. The important part is that you need a defined line beyond which the arrival of some amount of SPI relevant events over some length of time constitutes an SPI violation with no further wiggle room.

If software changes are happening frequently, SPIs with a very small budget for violations might never get enough data for averaging to help. For example, if major software updates are deployed every 10 million operating hours and an SPI has a statistical threshold of 100 million hours, there will never be enough statistical data on the current version to permit a non-zero number of SPI violations. In that type of situation, the SPI statistical falsification budget should be treated as effectively zero, meaning that every SPI acceptance test failure should be treated as an SPI violation. This effect will be relevant even for relatively generous statistical thresholds with a small fleet that is updated continually, because the exposure will simply not be there for statistics to even out.

In practice, early versions of safety cases might just as well set a statistical threshold of zero falsifications before declaring a violation for most low-statistical-threshold SPIs, at least until the technology matures and the fleet has a chance to scale up. A pragmatic approach is to set the statistical budget to zero permissible acceptance test failures for most SPIs initially, and then refine the numbers to something more suitable based on experience and deeper analysis in response to any potential SPI violation.

8.3.4. Responding to a leading SPI violation

Given that SPI monitors have been installed in an AV and its associated lifecycle processes, what happens when an SPI is violated? Does an SPI violation mean a particular AV that you thought was safe a day ago is suddenly unsafe?[483] Well .... maybe.

8.3.4.1. The meaning of an SPI violation

The important thing to keep in mind for a leading SPI violation is that it does not *necessarily* mean that the system is unsafe. An SPI violation means that the associated safety case claim has been falsified. You previously had reason to believe that claim was true based on both the underlying argument and previous lack of falsification via its associated SPI. But now you know it is false because some data just arrived that disproved the claim.

The implications of having a claim disproved depend on the claim. If it is a system-level lagging indicator directly tied to your safety goal, yes, an SPI violation means your AV is unsafe. This especially applies to primary

---

[483] This already happens with conventional vehicles. One day you think your vehicle is safe. The next you get a recall notice from the manufacturer that it has been declared unsafe until a remedy is conducted. In reality it has been unsafe since the time it was manufactured for most recalls. It is just that nobody figured it out until the recall investigation process started – and you didn't know until months later when the customer notification part of the recall process was carried out.

lagging SPIs such as crash rates and injury rates. In those cases, the best option is likely to be immediately pausing operations until the root cause of the problem can be assessed. Operations might resume with limited service if a pattern can be found in the SPI violations, such temporarily limiting the ODD to only in fair weather if SPI violations are only associated with rain.

For leading SPI violations the meaning is well defined, but the implications are less clear. An SPI violation of a leading indicator means that the entire safety argument above the SPI violation has potentially been falsified, all the way up to the top claim of safety. This is true even if SPIs associated with those higher level claims have not been violated, because SPIs in general are only an approximately of safety constraints. It is also true no matter how deep the falsified claim might be in the safety argument tree.[484]

However, a falsified safety case does not quite mean the system is unsafe. What it means is that the safety case has been shown to be unsound, and we no longer know if the system is safe or not. The consequences might range from the risk of a nearly immediate crash to some long-term fluctuation in safety outcomes that in the end will still turn out to be acceptably safe. Without further analysis we simply do not know.

Nonetheless, in life-critical safety if you are not sure if a system is safe, then it should be considered provisionally unsafe. So any SPI violation needs to be taken seriously.

8.3.4.2. SPI violation response plan

Every organization should have an SPI management and response plan. That includes policies for how to collect SPIs and how often to evaluate them on a rolling basis. It also includes what to do when an SPI is violated.

The SPI violation response plan should at a minimum include:

- A named individual or defined group responsible for monitoring SPI violations and determining SPI violation responses.
- Stand-down policies on fleet operation in response to an SPI violation. This might include pre-categorizing the severity of violating each SPI to trigger different immediate responses for violations depending on severity.
- A defined time window for an initial analysis as to root cause. If that window is missed the stand-down posture should be made more aggressive, because any stand-down posture less than an entire fleet operational suspension is based on an assumption of a timely response and rectification of the SPI violation.

---

[484] There is one important exception for a claim that requires only some of its sub-claims to be true. That type of claim might be able to tolerate a falsified sub-claim. For example: "at least one of the below three sub-claims is true" can survive one sub-claim being false. There is also the possibility of a false alarm SPI violation that will need to be managed appropriately.

- Statistical confidence levels, averaging approaches, and triggering policies for clumps of events when determining when triggering of statistical SPI thresholds has occurred.

As mentioned in section 7.1.4.3, one technique to manage the effect of an SPI violation on operations is to set aside a reserve risk budget in the overall safety case.[485] Doing so means that the safety case argues that the AV is safer than it needs to be, but sets aside the difference between the net risk requirement and the argued system design risk as a reserve. Once that has been done, SPI violations with minor effect on overall risk might be resolved simply by relaxing their SPI threshold and allocating some of the risk reserve to cover that new, slightly more risky threshold. This will work only with relatively minor risk issues, and eventually that loan from the risk reserve budget needs to be repaid. Nonetheless, it is a way to continue operations unaffected while the safety case and/or implementation is sharpened to repay the risk engineering debt back to the risk reserve pool.

8.3.5. Root cause contributing factors

When interpreting SPI violations, it is critical to go beyond a superficial analysis. You should ask "why" more deeply than the first reason.[486] You should also assume that in general there are multiple contributing root causes that should be addressed.[487]

From a safety case point of view, treating a root cause analysis as an exercise in blame is counterproductive. Finding the place where a fault was injected into the system is to some degree not the main goal, but rather simply a point of departure for improving the conditions that let the fault escape into a production product. The emphasis should be on identifying opportunities to have avoided the conditions that caused the fault to be injected, as well as finding out why opportunities to have detected and corrected the fault missed their chance to do so. If one fault makes it into a fielded safety critical system, it must be assumed that any process weakness also let other similar faults escape that have not been encountered yet.

Consider what happens if you treat every SPI violation analysis as an exercise in assigning blame. In such an exercise one finds something that can be blamed for an SPI violation and fixes it. Such an approach tends to identify a shallow, singular thing to "fix." Too often the fix is the thing seen as easiest from a dysfunctional organizational point of view, such as blaming

---

[485] A reserve risk budget is described in UL 4600 section 17.4.1.3.b

[486] Techniques along these lines include "Five Why" analysis (see: https://en.wikipedia.org/wiki/Five_whys) and "Why-Because" analysis (see: https://en.wikipedia.org/wiki/Why%E2%80%93because_analysis)

[487] A number of approaches to root cause analysis are listed here: https://en.wikipedia.org/wiki/Root_cause_analysis

the bearer of bad news.[488] Focusing on shallow fixes can miss opportunities to improve support structures and processes to avoid future bad outcomes.

Rather than focus on blame (whether personal or technical), every SPI violation should provoke consideration of factors that could have avoided the SPI violation, even if not directly "blamed" for the issue. This includes not only technical improvements to the vehicle and corresponding safety case changes, but also improvements to support processes. As a simple example, if a software defect results in an SPI violation, the result should not just be fixing the defect, nor should it be blaming the programmer for making the mistake or blaming the tester for not catching the mistake. None of those things are likely to affect the probability of future SPI violations due to other issues.

Responses to SPI violations should first look at the soundness of the argument underlying the claim, including both arguments being made and evidence supplied to support the arguments in a broad sense. For example, if a software defect makes it into deployment, this calls into question claims such as "software process is rigorous," "software testing is thorough," "peer reviews are effective" and possibly "requirements are complete" among others. Rather than pick one of these claims as having missed something, you should consider it possible that confidence is undermined in all these claims by a software defect that results in an SPI violation.

Put another way, an SPI violation is not simply a bug that needs to be fixed. Rather, it indicates that the engineering process that is described by the safety case has failed. Sure, the product and even the safety case itself need to be fixed. But you also need to improve the engineering process that let this happen if you want to avoid bigger problems downstream.

8.4. SPIs and bootstrap safety arguments

Summary: Bootstrapped arguments of safety involve doing a little driving and then saying that because no crash happened there is an acceptable risk of doing a little more driving. The usual approaches to such arguments are deeply flawed from a safety point of view even if the math is impeccable. However, an approach based on SPIs might work.

There is extreme pressure in the AV industry to deploy as soon as possible, even if there is insufficient statistical evidence to support a notion that the AV will be acceptably safe when initially deployed. The usual clever approach suggested is some sort of bootstrap [489] argument that builds confidence in safety via using incrementally larger fleet sizes.

---

[488] For example, by firing or transferring the person bringing the bad news that something needs to be fixed. Even if the fix is a software bug patch, a shallow patch to resolve symptoms might not fix a deeper underlying problem.

[489] Bootstrapping originally referred to the fanciful notion of lifting oneself up by pulling on one's own bootstraps. Back when more people wore boots, and boots had

8.4.1. Bootstrapping starting with a pilot deployment

A bootstrapping approach to safety assurance based on system-level safety outcomes starts with a small pilot fleet and grows confidence in safety over time to permit the operation of larger fleets.[490] While the reasoning that exposure increases over time can be seductive, such a process does not assure acceptable safety during the bootstrapping process itself the way one might think.[491] Rather, it amounts to a strategy to plan to get lucky, with the day of reckoning delayed until the first severe crash.[492]

Here is the general idea and why it is problematic.[493] We use an intuitive approach based on simple probability rather than a sophisticated mathematical analysis. We also assume a safety approach that is exclusively testing on public roads rather than a more sophisticated safety engineering approach, again for simplicity.

The seductive way to think about bootstrapped safety is as follows, illustrated with a concrete but arbitrary hypothetical example. Say you have run 100K (100,000) miles with a safety driver and had no reason for the safety driver to intervene. At this point you know there is a reasonable

---

straps instead of zippers. More recently it has come to mean parlaying meager resources into a much larger pool of resources. See:
https://en.wikipedia.org/wiki/Bootstrapping

[490] Others have worked out the math for a bootstrapped approach based on miles tested. See: Bishop et al. 2021 at https://arxiv.org/abs/2110.10718

[491] Bishop et al.'s paper referenced in the preceding footnote is a mathematical analysis rather than a deeper inquiry to the safety and ethical implications of such an approach. While we know from personal communications that it was written with the best of intentions, we believe a pure bootstrap approach should not be used for a road testing campaign for reasons described in this subsection. The issue is not with the math itself, but rather with the accumulated risk presented to road users in the case that the AV is significantly less safe than required. The paper does, however, yield an important safety result if read a slightly different way. If an AV test program has even one crash during road testing or pilot deployment, proving it is safe via continued road testing is essentially hopeless. Nothing in this writeup should be interpreted as saying anything negative about the paper or authors, who have worked for decades to promote safety. Rather, they have codified the bootstrap idea in a way that allowed us to figure out why we should stop recommending it as we previously had ourselves – and instead recommend against it. It was not until we read their paper that we could articulate the argument in this section. We thank those authors for their paper, follow-up discussions, and continued dedication to improving safety.

[492] This might be seen as a viable strategy for a startup company solely focused on a near-term lucrative exit such as being bought early in the pilot phase. They can just plan to get lucky until their exit before The Big Crash is likely to have happened. Or it might be used by a company that has not carefully thought through the implications. But we provide an argument in this section that such an approach presents undue risk and is unethical if pursued after having seen this analysis.

[493] Wow, with a footnote sequence buildup like that this better be good! We hope we do not let you down...

chance that if you pull out the safety driver, all things being equal, your AV will be able to run at 33K miles or more between crashes (at 95% confidence interval[494]). But if your target is 100M (100 million) miles between crashes, you really have no idea if you will be that good or not, because your testing is a thousand times shorter than your target. Your expectation, for now, is no worse than 33K+ miles between crashes, and possibly better. How much better is a complete guess based on this data.

You start the bootstrap process by driving one additional mile with no safety driver. You have confidence that there is less than about a 1 in 33K chance of a crash driving just one mile, which is pretty small, especially for just that one car. You reason that this chance is minuscule compared to all the other risks for a startup company, so you roll the dice, and your car has no crash. You now have 100,001 miles with no crash. You observe that the risk of a crash has gone down by a tiny amount. Emboldened by those improved odds you drive another mile. And so on, working your way mile by mile towards your validation goal. Every 3 miles you drive without a crash improves your confident mean time between crashes by 1 mile. So every mile you drive reduces the risk even further. You are on quite the roll here!

Your plan is to drive about 300M miles without a crash, thereby proving your AV is safe with confidence for 100M miles between crashes. You will get there by, for each additional mile, arguing that because you had no crash yet, the actual time between crashes is growing larger than you could prove previously and the risk of doing one more mile is even lower than it was for the previous mile. And that previous mile turned out OK, so the next one will be fine too.[495]

By the time you have worked the risk even lower, you start driving ten vehicles instead of just one, then 100 vehicles, with the fleet expanding in vehicles and/or miles on a regular basis. The miles add up ever more quickly. Eventually you decide that risk has been driven down low enough that you can deploy with paying passengers while you accumulate the final miles, and you continue. Every mile you drive increases your confidence and reduces your calculated risk for the next mile. Eventually you scale up the fleet to the point you have driven a billion miles with only a couple crashes perhaps, and you have proven your point that your vehicle is safer than a human driver. Bootstrapping is now completed.

If your AV is acceptably safe, bootstrapping is an efficient way to prove that. If ramped properly it can help with risk management. All things being equal, the probability that multiple high severity crashes will happen on any given day might be (incorrectly) seen as quite low.[496] The plan would be to

---

[494] See: https://reliabilityanalyticstoolkit.appspot.com/mtbf_test_calculator

[495] The reader is encouraged to ask what differences – other than the trappings of math – there are between this argument and the process of normalization of deviance that can undermine safety culture.
See: https://en.wikipedia.org/wiki/Normalization_of_deviance

[496] The comfort provided by an insufficient number of testing miles is illusory. If a software defect on a new version causes one crash, it might well cause multiple

suspend operation for all vehicles after just one severe crash, hoping to avoid an even worse problem of a second high severity crash before there is time to stand down the whole fleet.

This approach might make risk managers happy,[497] but not those engineers who primarily worry about safety. It is not that the math is wrong, but rather that the implications of the math lead to a superficial sort of risk management without providing any tangible improvement in safety assurance compared to simply launching a full-size fleet on the first day.[498]

To see the issue, we need to look at the argument in a different way. Consider a conceptual dice game played with a single die.[499] The number of sides of the die is unknown, but potentially quite large. Exactly one side of the die has the number "1" on it, and the other sides have other numbers. For each mile the AV is driven the die is rolled once. If it comes up with a "1" then a fatal crash occurs. Any other number results in no crash. If a competent safety driver is present when a "1" occurs the crash is avoided. You are not told the number that comes up on a roll if it is not a 1, so there are no other hints as to the number of sides on the die.

From a safety point of view, you need this to be at least a 100M-sided die to achieve an average of one fatality per 100M miles or better. You have no idea of the number of sides on the die when you start driving. However, as you accumulate miles with a safety driver you can glean probabilistic information about the minimum size of the die. If you can go 100 miles in a row without a "1" then the chance of it being a common six-sided die is

---

crashes on the same day even if previous software versions had a very large number of expected miles per crash. Even if there has been no software update, the world of software safety failures often does not conform to the convenient statistical assumptions of being random and independent.

[497] The argument that only one severe crash has time to happen assumes that fatal crashes will happen independently and that there will be no situations that correlate crashes of multiple vehicles in a short period of time. Only risk managers who believe black swan events never happen should be happy with this argument. To recalibrate any such belief, see:
https://en.wikipedia.org/wiki/The_Black_Swan:_The_Impact_of_the_Highly_Impro bable

[498] Bootstrap arguments tend to ignore the issue that every software update in principle resets the odometer to zero miles and invalidates previous bootstrapping evidence. For a large fleet, avoiding a sudden large-scale common cause failure might be done by slow-rolling software updates. However, a slow rollout is in fact a bootstrap argument subject to the same safety problems.

[499] For those who wish to quibble about the viable numbers of sides on a fair die you can substitute some other game of chance with the same odds. Those who are so minded can instead consider this a game of Russian Roulette with a single bullet and an unknown but very large number of chambers in the revolver. It ends up in the same place. See: https://en.wikipedia.org/wiki/Russian_roulette

vanishingly small.[500] But there is still a better than 18% chance of this outcome with only a 60-sided die despite getting lucky 100 times in a row.[501] Or it might be a billion-sided die. You do not know – all you can do is calculate the smallest number of sides for the die that is likely to explain this outcome. Your risk on the next roll has a probability based on the number of sides of the actual die, *not how many miles you have successfully driven.*[502]

The key thing here is you do not actually know the chance you are taking on the next mile for sure because it is a probability distribution based on the unknown safety of the system. Yes, you are ruling out a nearly certain crash in the next mile, but the risk taken for each mile is still significantly higher than for an average human driver until you exceed at least 100M miles driven.

Looked at in this light, after 100K safety driving test miles, your probability is as before – 1 in 33K of a crash or better. But if your safety target is 1 in 100M miles (which is "average" human drivers including the drunks), your testing might be more than *3000 times more dangerous than a human driver* for that next mile! The statistical bound on how much more dangerous you are than a human improves over time. But it starts out quite low, and even after 10 million miles of bootstrapping the best you can likely say is that you might be no worse than 30 times more dangerous than an average human driver even if there has been no crash whatsoever.[503]

The insidious nature of the problem is not simply that the first mile after 100K miles is 3000 times more dangerous than a human driver, but also that the metaphorical die is rolled for every single mile after that. Someone could work some math to express the risk over time, but it is the implications that matter, not the actual equations. Put another way, yes you are very likely to get lucky on each additional mile. But getting lucky is not the same as being safe, and if you roll the die enough times the odds are likely to catch up with you with a fatality.

The implication of bootstrap math stems from the practical application of the math to practice. Say that an AV company tests with a test driver until they go as long as they can afford to (but less than 100M miles), and have

---

[500] The probability of this outcome with a six-sided die is about one in 83 million. See: https://www.wolframalpha.com/input?i=1%2F%28%281-%281%2F6%29%29**100%29

[501] The probability on each roll of avoiding a 1 is (59/60) raised to the 100th power for 100 rolls.
See: https://www.wolframalpha.com/input?i=%281-%281%2F60%29%29**100

[502] From this point of view, a bootstrap safety argument falls into a classic probability thinking pitfall. If you flip a fair coin 99 times in a row and get 99 heads, the probability of heads on the 100th flip is still 50%. Coin flips are memoryless, and the history does not affect the odds on the next flip.

[503] This is the math. For those who want to justify this math as being acceptable for some utilitarian reason such as the prevention of future deaths or the fact that other deaths are occurring on public roads from human drivers please see the chapter on ethics. But please do not pretend that this is not the math.

test driver intervention. In our example we say it is 100K miles to make it seem like a large number, but the math applies whether it is 10 miles or a million. Once that feat has been accomplished via good engineering or luck (the point is we won't know which until later), the safety driver is removed.

Now uncrewed testing or deployment continues, with the bootstrapping math relentlessly driving down the risk expectation for each mile. If the AV is safer than a human driver then all is well.

But what if it is not?

In the absence of engineering rigor or other ways of ensuring safety beyond brute force testing, we have no way of knowing if the AV is 1000 times safer than a human driver or 1000 more dangerous until the big crash occurs.[504] If the big crash occurs well before about 100M miles then the answer is the AV was probably not safe after all – but the cost of finding this out was a severe crash. If bootstrapping ends after 100M to 300M miles or so, then we might consider the AV safe.

The appeal of a bootstrap argument is seductive, especially because it can be wrapped up in a mathematical expression. But the implication of how this approach works in practice is a problem unless there is a very strong prior belief in acceptable safety before the bootstrapping starts.

There is a profound difference between a strong, engineering-based belief that an AV is acceptably safe before testing even begins vs. testing to see how safe it turns out to be. If there is weak engineering and no safety case, the situation devolves into every AV company getting a free pass to operate without actually knowing whether its vehicle is remotely close to human driver safety until that catastrophic crash happens. Or does not happen.

The main difference between a huge initial deployment and a limited-scale pilot deployment that ramps to a larger deployment via bootstrapping is, at best, a risk management approach. If the ramping is done with the right slope of increasing number of vehicles over time, bootstrapping reduces the probability of _multiple_ severe crashes in a short period of time before the fleet can be grounded. It does not, however, change the number of miles before the first fatality is likely to occur. Bootstrapping also does not affect safety on a per-mile or other exposure basis such as is required by a PRB framework.

Trying to bootstrap safety based solely on test mileage accumulation amounts to putting an AV on the road and seeing how long it takes to kill someone. If it takes a long time, it turns out the AV was safe. If not, then it was not safe. But we will not know the answer until after the fatality has

---

[504] A more subtle argument might try to predict big crashes based on small ones. But in practice small crashes tend to be excused away or blamed on other drivers. Moreover, there is no data supporting the proposition that AVs will have the same ratio of fatal crashes to fender benders as human drivers. In practice even this approach will require some sort of supporting safety case beyond brute force road testing.

occurred or the AV fleet has operated well over 100 million miles without a fatality. If the AV is not safe enough, we find out by killing someone.[505]

> Approving a pure bootstrap testing program in essence awards the test organization a voucher good for one kill.

We already know from decades of experience that it is unlikely a system will be made acceptably safe in the absence of engineering rigor. More recently, engineering rigor approaches have been codified into safety standards. Any organization not following industry safety standards cannot expect to have acceptably safe systems.[506]

In the absence of engineering rigor that sets an expectation of acceptable safety before deployment, bootstrapping based on test miles alone presents undue risk to the general public. For that reason, it has significant ethical issues. No amount of bootstrap deployment math will fix this reality. However, we *might* be able to do better if we set a strong prior expectation of safety. The approach then would be not to prove safety via bootstrapping, but rather confirm a strong prior belief in safety[507] via a modified approach.

8.4.2. Bootstrapping a safety case with SPIs

Regardless of the severe issues with pure mileage-based bootstrapping just discussed, bootstrapping remains a *potentially* appealing approach if based on SPI improvement rather than mileage.[508]

The real issue with bootstrapping based on miles alone is the weakness of the prior belief in safety before the bootstrapping begins. Mileage accumulation alone will not provide a sufficient basis for safe bootstrapping, because there is no knowledge of whether the AV will be acceptably safe during the bootstrapping process itself. Mileage-based bootstrapping is exploring whether the AV is safe (testing to see if it is safe with no reason to believe that it is other than hope), not confirming a prior strong belief based on engineering that it is safe (testing to be sure safety engineering did not

---

[505] Perhaps we will be lucky and avoid the fatality in a near-hit. But one of the lessons from the Uber ATG fatality in Tempe Arizona in 2018 is that with anything less than a very robust safety culture, it is more likely the organization will ignore near hits and continue attempting to bootstrap until the fatality occurs.

[506] There is a possibility that equivalent internal safety practices will achieve the same effect. However, there is ample reason to be skeptical if such a situation is claimed with no transparency as to what those practices might be.

[507] Paging Thomas Bayes and Pierre-Simon Laplace. Do we have any Bayesians in the house? See: https://en.wikipedia.org/wiki/Bayesian_probability

[508] If you lose the thread during this subsection have a look at section 9.2.2 where we revisit the idea without as much gory detail. This proposal is both academic and speculative. People's lives should not be put at risk based solely on this section without further confirmation and detailed analysis by others qualified to do so.

miss something). Even if a rigorous engineering process has been followed, it might well be that the amount of testing needed to ensure safety via traditional approaches (e.g., conforming to ISO 26262) is too much to be practical.

However, it might be possible to use a more indirect approach of not bootstrapping confidence in the safety of the system itself, but rather bootstrapping confidence in the soundness of the safety case. If the safety case starts with high initial confidence due to the use of engineering best practices, that gives us a reason to have strong prior belief in safety before bootstrapping even begins.[509]

It is important to note that this is a speculative idea that might not work out in practice. But it is presented here in the hope that it provides a starting point for a viable hybrid approach to establishing a reasonable belief in safety up front, followed by using a bootstrapping approach based on real-world experience to build confidence in the safety case over time. How much crewed testing will need to be part of building the prior belief in safety is something that will have to be decided, and we express no opinion on that here.

The idea of bootstrapping the safety case involves tracking SPI violations rather than crashes. Additionally, the approach takes credit for the ratio of benign SPI violations to vehicle-level safety misbehavior.

A general SPI-based bootstrap argument goes like this:

- Build a safety case and instrument as many claims as practical with SPIs.
- Improve the safety case to the point that it is sound as far as the design team and independent assessors can tell, including the use of best practices for engineering rigor. That likely means it still has some unknown deficiencies. For example, in a SOTIF procedure this would be the point in which the design adequately deals with known situations, while the remaining effort switches to searching for unknown unsafe triggering conditions.
- Monitor SPIs for violations during simulation and crewed testing. Record each SPI violated, the degree of hazardous vehicle-level behavior displayed by the system at the time of the SPI violation, and any data needed to support diagnosis of the incident.
- For each SPI violation encountered, record the incident, and fix any issues broadly implicated by the SPI violation.[510] This is likely to require concurrent improvements to areas such as: source code defects, training

---

[509] This might be seen as an exercise in building a stronger Bayesian prior belief as an initial basis for bootstrapping. In that context someone might still argue for mileage-based bootstrapping, but we believe that an SPI-based bootstrapping approach will provide a much stronger basis for safety during the bootstrapping process.

[510] A conservative approach is to set the SPI thresholds tighter than they would normally be during deployment to catch borderline cases, providing some engineering margin.

data gaps, engineering procedure issues, validation procedure issues, testing scenario gaps, and so on.

- Do trend analysis on how often SPI violations are occurring and the ratio of severe incidents.[511] There is an assumption that crashes and other loss events will have triggered SPI violations, so every incident will be recorded.

The initial bootstrapping phase occurs during simulation and road testing supervised by safety drivers. As the design matures one would expect that SPI violations occur less frequently. Eventually the AV design should get to a point at which there have been no SPI violations in a respectable amount of testing. That means that not only have there been few or no crashes (based on the amount of testing vs. acceptable crash rates), but also the safety case has held up during road testing as well. So, it is not simply an absence of crashes, but also no near hits, no subsystem SPI violations, and in general no hints that there is anything wrong with the safety case in the last stretch of road testing.

In parallel to the maturation of the system and safety case that drives down SPI violation rates, data is collected about the nature and severity of every SPI violation during the process. The ratio of directly dangerous SPI violation incidents to benign-in-the-moment SPI violations is tracked. Dangerous SPI violations are associated with the AV doing something actively dangerous at the time of the SPI violation, such as requiring a safety driver intervention to avoid a crash, or otherwise violating vehicle-level safety envelopes.

A benign-in-the-moment SPI violation is associated with a safety case claim falsification that does not present immediate danger, but rather pushes the safety case into the unknown realm regarding overall safety. A concrete example might be that a false negative rate for a sensor detection algorithm slips from past its limit of 4% to 5%. It is likely (although not guaranteed) that engineering margin and other factors mean a crash did not occur immediately. Nonetheless, the safety case has been falsified and something needs to be corrected to deal with the one percentage point overrun past the 4% limit.

We then use the ratio of benign to total SPI violations to compute a safe failure fraction.[512] This lets us take credit for only some SPI violations causing immediate danger to the AV and other road users while others are benign from an immediate operational safety point of view.

The bootstrap argument then gives us a reasonable basis for multiplying the benefits of road testing to predict safety well beyond the actual road testing amount. This is feasible because measuring SPI violations is a much more thorough instrumentation regime than just measuring crashes. Near-

---

[511] This amounts to a surprise metric analogous to software reliability growth modeling as discussed in section 6.3.5.

[512] This notion is inspired by that term as used in the IEC 61508 safety standard historically used by the process industry.

zero SPI violations should be a more difficult goal to achieve than simply crash-free driving, but that difficulty reflects higher confidence in the safety engineering effort that has been applied. Recall that each SPI violation means the safety case is unsound, and we presume that the goal is to deploy with a sound safety case, so a near-zero SPI violation goal should be the target before deployment.

The bootstrapping argument goes like this for a hypothetical 100K mile testing phase and a hypothetical safe failure fraction:

- Simulation and road testing were conducted with all SPIs monitored.
- Over time, SPI violations consistently reduced in frequency, to the point that no SPI violations occurred in the last 100K mile road testing phase.[513]
- Over time, including simulation and testing before the final 100K test phase, the safe failure fraction ratio for SPI violations stabilized to 99%. That means that the next SPI violation has only a 1% chance of being dangerous. (Any SPI violation should still be addressed, but probably it will not cause a crash at the time it occurs.)
- All things being equal, that last 100K test phase demonstrated that the SPI violation rate is lower than approximately one per 33K miles, and that the safe failure fraction ratio of 99% from the development phase holds, which means we can expect a dangerous crash no more often than once every 3.3M miles.

The idea is to combine the experimental estimate of SPI violation distance with the safe failure fraction, giving a much larger estimate of distance between likely severe crashes. For this example, the AV would still be at least 30 times more dangerous than a human driver – but not 3000 times more dangerous as would be the case measuring crash data alone. This example shows that what you would really need to prime the bootstrapping cycle is no SPI violations in 3M miles demonstrated with a safety driver, assuming the same 99% safe failure fraction holds. After that it might be defensible to remove the safety driver and continue to gain experience. (Again, a more rigorous analysis of this approach should be undertaken before using it in a safety critical application in the real world.)

A requirement for this approach is that by the end of crewed testing the safe failure fraction for SPIs is known. Somewhat paradoxically, an expectation of safety is built based on previous safety case failures. There needs to be a track record of maturing the safety case to support this approach. But that is precisely what SPI violation rates might provide.

One of the questions that will arise is whether a benign-in-the-moment SPI violation during testing resets the testing odometer to zero. If an SPI violation results in a change to the AV implementation itself, impact analysis might force a reset of the testing odometer since a new system is being

---

[513] Again, this uses ideas from software reliability growth modeling. SPI violation trends and rates seen in testing or recent operations are treated as predictive of likely SPI violation rates in later operation.

tested. If the SPI violation is resolved with a minor safety case change such as risk allocation from the risk reserve budget, that might not cause any problem and the bootstrapping can continue. That having been said, the role of impact analysis and changes on the bootstrapping process will need to be scrutinized carefully to ensure that safety is not compromised.

This argument hinges on supposing that good SPI coverage will result in SPI violations that are a good predictive metric of safety. In particular, the assumption is that good SPI instrumentation will find problems early, netting a high safe failure fraction. Our experience indicates this is likely to be the case,[514] although to date there is no conclusive research of which we are aware that proves the point.

We believe that naturally robust designs will display SPI violations at more detailed levels of the safety case even while compensating for such issues at higher levels of the safety case. As a simple but concrete illustration of this idea, consider flying a two-engine jet aircraft. You have done some parallel reliability math[515] that shows that with random independent failure rates it is just sufficiently unlikely that any aircraft will lose both engines on the same flight.[516] Say SPI violations show individual engine failures are happening about ten times more often than they are supposed to. You do not need to wait for both jet engines to fail to know you are less safe than you thought.

We believe that there will be natural pressure to improve SPI coverage over time due to the use of the ratio of operationally benign to dangerous SPI violations as the safe failure fraction. Instrumenting the safety case in more detail is likely to provide more lower-level, operationally benign SPI violations compared to higher level SPI violations associated with loss events. That could provide earlier warning of system problems while giving a better safe failure fraction.

There will be some incentive to water down the SPIs by instrumenting seemingly benign claims. However, at some point this effect will be limited by the fact that SPIs have to be associated with claims in the safety case. To counteract potential metric gaming we further suggest that: (1) peer reviews be used to prune fluff safety case claims, (2) duplicative SPI violations that involve multiple violations of a single claim or multiple SPIs on the same claim only be singled-counted to avoid artificially driving up benign violations, and (3) each set of related SPI violations be counted only as a single event so that a benign event that violates 100 different SPIs concurrently does not get to out-vote severe issue crash that only happens to violate one SPI.

---

[514] See especially section 4.4 in the work of Hutchison 2016: https://users.ece.cmu.edu/~koopman/thesis/hutchison.pdf

[515] See https://youtu.be/g9wOyuiPuBI

[516] It is a bit more complicated than that. This video on Extended Twin Engine Operations (ETOPS) is a nice treatment. Any safety video that starts with "It will be a cold day in Hell before…" about something you the reader might well have done personally is worth a watch: https://www.youtube.com/watch?v=HSxSgbNQi-g

No doubt this proposal can be improved and could benefit from a more rigorously stated mathematical framework. The objective here is to propose this as a potential solution to the bootstrapping problem that might be both practical and useful in ensuring safe AV deployment.

8.5. Summary

In this chapter we discussed applying SPIs in practice. There needs to be a baseline lagging metric target for overall risk that takes into account the specifics of the operational conditions and other factors. Leading metrics need to include not only system-level SPIs, but also SPIs that cover safety case claims associated with components, processes, and operations.

Monitoring SPIs breaks down into two somewhat different aspects: monitoring a behavioral envelope for the data being measured via an acceptance test (e.g., passing too close to a pedestrian, or a source code review that finds too small a fraction of defects in a piece of code), and a statistical measurement that any such acceptance test failures are sufficiently rare. The statistical budget for how often a claim can be falsified without compromising overall safety is likely to be a very low frequency. Due to bandwidth and data storage constraints, most acceptance tests should be run locally on each vehicle while statistical analysis for frequency should be done centrally across an entire organization and its fleet of AVs.

A bootstrap approach of using an initial set of mishap-free miles to justify iteratively driving a few more miles is seductive. But, ultimately a classical bootstrap argument is problematic because it presents undue risk to other road users. The problem boils down to one of mistaking risk management (there are likely to be very few fatalities in the next few miles, and probably no fatality) for safety (the risk to other road users should be less than that presented by human drivers, which might not be the case for bootstrap safety approaches). Bootstrapping purely on miles should not be done. It is possible that bootstrapping based on a combination of SPIs and a measured safe failure fraction of SPI violations is possible, although that is still a speculative approach.

9.   Deciding when to deploy

At some point, the design team needs to decide that it is time to deploy their AV. This type of decision will need to be made repeatedly during the lifecycle, including deciding when it is time to advance to the next phase of testing, when it is safe to expand the ODD, and when each software update is safe to deploy.

Because human lives are on the line, the decision to deploy should be made in an intentional, structured way based on a technically substantive assessment and the team's understanding of system safety. To avoid making questionable decisions under pressure, the method and criteria for a deployment decision should be defined early and not changed in the heat of the moment under a looming deadline. This means that a written deployment procedure containing pre-set decision criteria should be used.

In this chapter we can provide guidance on how to go about making a deployment decision. The procedure, organizational approach, and criteria will depend on the system being deployed, the operational context, and the organizational context.

9.1. An approach to setting deployment criteria

Summary: Deployment decisions should consider at least: the governance model, a safety case, a definition of acceptable risk, any additional safety constraints, management of inevitable uncertainty, a defined decision process, security, safety culture, and ethical issues. Public road testing is also a deployment, although of a different nature.

The decision to deploy should be based on reasonable confidence that the AV is acceptably safe and that the risk from unknowns is acceptably low. This confidence should be based on a safety case that spans at least the areas of engineering rigor, validation, and process health including safety culture.

A path for responsible deployment of an AV should address at least the following considerations:

- Governance: Who makes the decision to deploy using what criteria must be fixed in writing, transparent, and acceptable to all stakeholders. Section 10.3 discusses this topic in more detail.

- Safety Case: A safety case is constructed that soundly supports a claim that the AV and supporting infrastructure are fit for purpose, including a specific claim that the AV is acceptably safe. The safety case explicitly addresses the other criteria in this list. The safety case includes and is updated to keep pace with the system lifecycle including data collection, design, simulation, testing, deployment, operation, maintenance, and retirement. We strongly urge AV design teams to create a safety case that conforms to ANSI/UL 4600.

- Determine Acceptable Risk: Define a system-level risk acceptability threshold. The most likely approach will be to ensure expected AV risk is better than unimpaired human driver abilities for comparable operating conditions, accounting for different aspects of harm including both injuries and fatalities.
- Determine Additional Safety Constraints: Meeting a defined "average" risk target is just the starting point. There are additional considerations that must be addressed for stakeholders to find safety acceptable. Likely candidates include:
  - No identified demographic group is projected to be at increased risk compared to conventional vehicles. For example, pedestrians should not be at higher risk from AVs than they are from conventional vehicles.
  - Best practices for engineering, operations, and other aspects of system design and lifecycle are followed to ensure software integrity and system safety. This is true even if there is room for debate as to whether those best practices are directly linked to risk reduction. For example, relevant industry safety standards must be followed even if it is difficult to put a numeric value on the risk reduction obtained from doing so.
- Uncertainty Management: Uncertainty must be accounted for in initial deployment and managed throughout the life cycle:
  - An initial safety factor is added into risk evaluation to account for pre-deployment uncertainty. For example, the expected risk presented by an AV might need to be ten times better than for a human driver in comparable conditions to leave room for uncertainty in that estimate. To be clear, this safety factor does not mean the AV will be ten times better, but rather gives a safety margin in case the initial safety estimate is ten times too optimistic. This will reduce the chance that the deployed AV fails to meet its safety objective if surprises result in worse than expected safety performance.
  - Safety performance indicators are continually monitored and updated during the design cycle as well as the deployment life cycle. The rate of SPI violations during simulation and road testing can help predict the maturity of the safety case, with a mature safety case indicating a reduction in uncertainty for expected system safety. Over time, leading indicators for safety become validated as having predictive power, permitting more accurate predictions of expected safety for system updates and revisions, potentially permitting a less aggressive safety factor.
- Deployment Decision Process: In support of the governance model already mentioned, a detailed deployment decision process should be in

place to identify roles and responsibilities for deciding when an initial deployment can be permitted.

- o This process should ensure that the safety case is sound, that the safety case addresses the other identified criteria in other bullet points in this list, that any other deployment considerations such as regulatory requirements have been met, and that there is a documented paper trail to justify the decision based on these criteria. Other factors affecting the deployment decision may be relevant and should be included in the documented justification.
- o A related process should determine approval of software or other system updates to ensure that system updates do not degrade safety.
- o A related process should also address procedures and situations in which AV operation for the fleet of deployed vehicles should be restricted (for example reducing the scope of the ODD) or a stand-down order issued to halt vehicle operations due to discovering a safety problem, especially considering responses to SPI violations.
- o Neither an initial AV deployment nor an update should be performed in a situation involving an unsound safety case.[517]

- Security: Although cybersecurity is generally out of scope for this book, it is nonetheless an essential topic for safety. Any security attack that impairs the operation of the vehicle or undermines the integrity of data used for operation will have safety consequences. Issues such as privacy of passenger information can also affect personal safety of occupants. There is much ground to cover here, but we leave that task to other authors.[518]

- Safety Culture: A generic term for an organization's commitment and follow-through to ensure safety is generally called its *safety culture*. This term is prevalent in the chemical process industry and aerospace, and applies to any safety-critical activity. One way of summing up safety culture is that anyone in an organization is encouraged to speak up about a potential safety issue, and when that happens management will both support that individual and take corrective action. Without a robust safety culture, it is all too likely that all the other aspects of safety will simply be performance art instead of reality.

- Testing Safety: Safety for the testing of AVs on public roads must be addressed, including ensuring that testing does not present undue public risk. This should include following industry best practices for testing

---

[517] Keep in mind that a reserve risk budget might be used to temporarily cure an SPI violation pending a more thorough fix.
[518] ANSI/UL 4600 clause 10.8 covers cybersecurity as it relates to an AV safety case.

safety and use of a Safety Management System to assure operational safety for testing. [519]

- Ethical considerations: Ethical considerations must be considered in deciding when, where, and how to operate AVs. Chapter 10 in general applies, but the very specific considerations in section 10.7 on ethical regulatory approaches should be addressed by the safety plan even if not required by regulators.

There should be a safety plan that addresses all these areas. There should also be a sufficiently independent named individual who is responsible for the safety plan having been met before any release can take place. That person should not be under undue pressure to say "yes" when doing so is not supported by the considerations just listed.

While it is tempting to smear responsibility across some diffuse organizational roles, the reality is that if safety release authority is treated as a collective responsibility, that means nobody is responsible – and exercise of that authority will not be done in an acceptable manner. One potential role of an external safety advisory committee is to render an independent opinion as to whether it is indeed time to deploy, especially for initial deployments and major system changes.

9.2. Addressing uncertainty

Summary: Deployment decisions will be complicated by having to address significant amounts of uncertainty. A purely risk management approach can too easily sacrifice safety. Using SPIs to manage uncertainty can help.

A significant concern for ensuring that an AV deployment is safe will be dealing with uncertainty. Despite best efforts, the most that can ever be said about deploying something like an AV is not "it is safe" but rather "it is safe as far as we know." The "as far as we know" part is an expression of uncertainty.

It is essential not to evade responsibility via arguing that since perfect knowledge is impossible there is no point even trying. Rather, effort should be made to reduce uncertainty to the extent that doing so is practical. Deployment should additionally require that uncertainty about safety is reduced enough to provide good confidence that the AV will be acceptably safe.

Uncertainty means justifying deployment might amount to a credible statement of the form: "Our AV is acceptably safe as far as we know. We have used industry best practices to reduce our uncertainty regarding safety, and we will continue to monitor and address any safety-related issues that arise after deployment in a proactive and transparent manner."

The uncertainty in being able to predict safety before deploying an AV amounts to a residual risk inherent in deployment. Traditional risk

---

[519] See section 9.5.

management might be employed to deal with residual risk, but can run into problems. We recommend also addressing risks via tracking SPI violations.

9.2.1. Risk management

Actuarial analysis forms the basis for the insurance industry, and is a primary tool of risk management.[520] If there is a body of experiential data, one can build a model of the data and make useful statistical predictions of risk.

The trouble with applying this approach to AV safety is that AVs use novel technology for which we do not have the experiential data for at-scale deployment. Moreover, even when we do have enough experience with AVs, the models are unlikely to be predictive in the face of continual software updates if software quality practices are chaotic and safety engineering best practices are not being followed. Predicting software quality is – at best – an immature practice in most software industries, with the novel software technology used in AVs making things even more challenging.

Insurance-style approaches can be helpful for managing risk, and especially spreading financial risk via the reinsurance process.[521] However, the bigger problem we face is not the risk itself, but rather the uncertainty about the model that can be used to predict risk. Insurance-type approaches might be able to take some of the edges off the consequences of the uncertainty problem, but they will not address uncertainty completely until we have proven risk prediction models for AVs. Getting there will take a long time.

Probabilistic Risk Assessment (PRA) is an engineering analysis approach related to safety engineering used for especially complex engineered systems.[522] It amounts to using the risk equation:

risk = probability * consequence

summed across all identified risks. It works best when both probability and consequence are well understood.

PRA has historically struggled with accurate probability estimates for low probability catastrophic events that are, in essence, "never" supposed to happen. "Never" somehow finds a way to occur a lot sooner than expected. Every nuclear power plant disaster is a practical demonstration of the limitations of PRA.[523] Since we would be guessing at probability for AVs, and to some degree even the consequence of a large common cause AV safety failure, PRA will not really solve the AV risk prediction problem.

At a higher level, the issue with risk management approaches is that they assume we have some accurate estimate of the risk up front so that we can manage it. The uncertainty being dealt with in such approaches is aleatoric

---

[520] This section revisits the topic of risk management discussed in section 4.6.1.
[521] See: https://en.wikipedia.org/wiki/Reinsurance
[522] See: https://en.wikipedia.org/wiki/Probabilistic_risk_assessment
[523] For example, see: https://en.wikipedia.org/wiki/Fukushima_nuclear_disaster

uncertainty[524] – the uncertainty of chance such as the roll of dice. While the specific outcome in each case is random, the overall statistical distributions need to be understood for such approaches so that expected values and likely statistical distributions can be accounted for.

The primary issue with AV safety uncertainty is, in contrast, epistemic uncertainty – the uncertainty of not knowing what the risk model even is.[525] As a simple example, aleatory uncertainty is not knowing which side a die will land on for the next roll. In contrast, epistemic uncertainty might be not knowing how many sides the die even has. Guessing the probability of a "1" showing on a fair six-sided die is easy. Guessing the probability of rolling a "1" gets more difficult if you are also guessing at whether the die has 4, 6, 8, 10, 12, 20, 60, or even 120 sides.[526] You could always make the conservative bet by applying a safety margin and assuming the odds are 1 in 4 for a bad outcome – but you are pessimistic by a factor of 30 if what you really have is a 120-sided die.

By way of analogy, as we discussed previously in section 8.4.1, the uncertainty inherent in predicting AV safety is like predicting what the probability of rolling a specific number on a die with an unknown number of sides, potentially in the billions. It is not an easy problem.

A straightforward way to address epistemic uncertainty for AV safety is to build in a safety factor so large that stakeholders agree there is no reasonable basis for concern. And likely that is part of the solution. But if we couldn't afford to get enough data to get statistical significance for the baseline safety target, setting a safety target 100 or 1000 times higher is going to make that problem 100 or 1000 times worse instead of better.

Safety issues that happen often enough to be estimated based on road testing might well be handled via insurance and in general subject to traditional risk management approaches. However, what should keep risk managers (and insurance executives) awake at night is the potential for catastrophic common cause losses that affect a large number of AVs nearly simultaneously. In effect, there could be a software-induced AV equivalent of a hurricane disaster. There are examples of small software defects that induce outsize consequences on the Internet and other computer-based systems.[527] There is no reason to believe that AVs will be exempt from such problems.

---

[524] The term aleatoric stems from "alea" – the Latin word for a die used in games of chance. As in: https://en.wikipedia.org/wiki/Alea_iacta_est

[525] See: https://en.wikipedia.org/wiki/Uncertainty_quantification

[526] There are even more possible die configurations than that! See: https://commons.wikimedia.org/wiki/Dice_by_number_of_sides

[527] One particularly instructive example is the Fastly outage of June 8, 2021. A software defect activated by one customer doing an otherwise innocuous operation caused the failure of numerous web services such as newspapers, social media, and even the British government's home page. Imagine if that had also disabled cloud services that stranded AVs in the middle of the road across the world. See:

9.2.2. Uncertainty estimation via SPIs

The most difficult part of dealing with deployment uncertainty will be addressing the area in which PRA falls down: low probability events that have high consequence. Because they are low probability they likely will not be seen during development and testing. Such low probability events might have inaccurate analysis or even still be unknowns.[528] Nonetheless, the high consequence means that if they happen more often than expected the results can be potentially catastrophic.[529]

The only way we know to mitigate rare catastrophic event risks is via the application of engineering rigor. For our approach, the safety case tells the story of engineering rigor, which is why it is so essential to managing uncertainty. If the probability is uncertain, we should assume that the catastrophic event will happen more often than we can afford, and mitigate it accordingly.

To be sure, there is epistemic uncertainty in terms of the safety case potentially missing aspects of safety. We also have uncertainty as to how much epistemic uncertainty there is. While we can never resolve an infinite recursion of meta-uncertainty issues,[530] we can at least recognize that uncertainty will always be there and plan to deal with it in a responsible way.

If we want to deploy with uncertainty, we are going to need to model that uncertainty. This subsection sketches a simple way to do this. No doubt there can be much more sophisticated approaches, so this should be considered a proof of concept for saying that epistemic uncertainty can be modeled rather than the final word on how to do that modeling.

To start, assume that the aleatory sources of risk are understood. Some combination of design methodology rigor, simulation, road testing, and so on have given us an indication that the AV has acceptable risk if deployed – so far as we know. For example, simulations show that even in known high-risk scenarios the AV does well enough, all high-risk software defects identified have been fixed, and everything else is in order. Additionally, we have a safety case instrumented with SPIs that convinces all stakeholders that due diligence on engineering design and validation has been completed – except for whatever risk is presented by the unknown unknowns.

The issue is that without some way of modeling the unknown unknowns we do not know what additional risk they present. But how do we build a model of the unknown?

---

https://www.npr.org/2021/06/09/1004684932/fastly-tuesday-internet-outage-down-was-caused-by-one-customer-changing-setting

[528] Our colleague Roy Maxion is fond of variations on this aphorism: "You might forget the unknowns, but they won't forget you."

[529] The usual PRA failure mode is summed up as "that would be terrible, but it will never happen" followed a few years later by a 3 AM phone call that starts "so hey, guess what just happened…"

[530] To paraphrase the old punch-line: it is *uncertainty* all the way down. See: https://en.wikipedia.org/wiki/Turtles_all_the_way_down

We recommend addressing this problem via tracking the trend of new SPI violations.[531] Here is why that might make sense. For simplicity consider the decision to remove the driver from the vehicle on public roads.

During design, a safety case has been constructed and instrumented with SPIs. During the final validation cycle those SPIs were used to collect data during simulations and road testing in addition to any process-based SPIs that also involve engineering activities and so on.

At the time of deployment there should be no unresolved SPI violations. The reason this needs to be the case is that the deployment decision is based on a safety case, and an unresolved SPI violation means, by definition, that one or more claims in the safety case have been shown to be false via some type of measurement evidence. A falsified claim makes the safety case unsound, so deployment cannot happen until that situation is rectified.[532]

In the context of this discussion, an SPI violation after the design team thought the safety case was mature amounts to a "surprise." We say this because as far as you know the safety case is sound when you deploy, and you will be surprised if a later SPI violation proves you wrong.

Even if we strongly suspect our safety case is missing something (we have epistemic uncertainty), if we do not know what that something is, we cannot fix it. But what we can do is model the risk presented by a stream of previously encountered unknowns even if we do not know which unknowns to expect in the future. To do this, we can look at the history of SPI violations during the development and validation cycle.

As a practical matter the likelihood that an AV design and safety case will be perfect on the first try is essentially zero. Perfect on the first try is just not going to happen in the real world. This is especially true given the iterated training and model-building approaches used for the machine learning part of the system. However, this is good news, because it presents an opportunity to build an SPI violation arrival rate model.

Consider the first time that an AV is tested against a full set of scenarios in a software simulator and does not crash into anything. Or perhaps it only crashes in scenarios in which it is physically impossible to avoid crashes, so one could say it only crashes when it is supposed to.

Even though no unavoidable crashes occur during a simulation test, there might be SPI violations that indicate the safety case is not suitable for deployment. Later, behavior on the road might differ from simulations, violating SPIs associated with claims that simulation results predict road behavior. Also, new scenarios might be discovered during public road

---

[531] A different spin on this idea is given in section 8.4.2 via bootstrapping a safety case with SPIs. We give a different presentation of that same idea here. If that previous section made perfect sense, then you can skip ahead here to avoid the chance of this explanation making it more confusing instead of less. If that section left you confused, here is another bite at that same apple.

[532] A small risk reserve budget can be used to defer small SPI violations until later. So this is not a demand for perfection, but rather a way of making sure nothing major is wrong while avoiding simply sweeping small but legitimate issues under the rug.

testing, violating SPIs associated with claims that the scenario database and simulator give a complete representation of public road testing conditions. And so on.

Any significant safety issue should be fixed. But along with the fixes the design team should track SPI violation data. Think of this data as a bug report database, except with the bugs reported against the safety case as opposed to the software itself. For each SPI bug report there should be a resolution recorded, as well as whether the SPI violation was directly associated with overtly dangerous vehicle behavior when it occurred. Over time, one hopes that the arrival rate of SPI violations (i.e., arrival rate of surprises) slows down, and is relatively smooth over time.

When it comes time to deploy, the SPI data is analyzed to help quantify the risk presented by unknowns. One looks at how often surprises are arriving, and what fraction of them occurred during situations that also presented dangerous vehicle behavior.

With this approach, if very scary surprises are happening every day, then it is too early to deploy. If, however, the arrival rate of surprises (SPI violations) has trended smoothly downward *and* the vast majority of surprises have presented little risk of a loss event, then there is a case to be made that the risk from residual uncertainty is low. The next surprise will no doubt happen, but it will take a while and will be unlikely to be deadly.

Put another way, the trend of SPI violations provides a measure of the maturity of the safety case. Having a mature safety case reflects that engineering rigor has been applied successfully in that the analysis reflected by the safety case is matching real-world operation. That in turn means we have more confidence that the safety predicted by the safety case will be reflected in real-world operation.

Such an argument is not an absolute guarantee against a catastrophic surprise the day after deployment. However, it can build confidence that the additional risk presented by uncertainty is reasonably low if used in conjunction with other best practices for safety engineering, software quality practices, and other safe system design practices as reflected in a robust safety case. This discussion also assumes that the safety case is populated with a reasonable number of SPIs at all levels of claims rather than solely at the topmost vehicle level of claims.

9.3. Conformance to standards

Summary: Any AV testing and deployment should conform to the industry's own safety standards. This should be a given – but sadly too many AV companies appear to be cutting corners here.

Another essential aspect of acceptable safety is conforming to relevant safety standards. Safety-critical industries routinely conform to relevant safety standards, such as IEC 61508 (historically used in the chemical process industry), and EN 50126/50128/50129 (rail). Automotive is the most important industry which does not have a track record of conforming to its own safety standards.[533]

While the standards landscape, especially for AVs, is continually evolving, at least the following safety standards should be conformed to: ISO 26262, ISO 21448, ANSI/UL 4600, ISO/SAE 21434. SAE J3018 should be conformed to for public road testing. Additionally, a best practice Safety Management System should be put into place. (Section 4.5 describes these standards and more.)

Responsible deployment of life-critical AV technology should conform to safety standards and best practices issued by the automotive and AV industries themselves. There is no excuse for dodging standards conformance when putting life-critical technology on public roads.

9.4. Safe updates

Summary: Software updates will need to happen throughout the life of the AV. They need to be done safely and securely.

It is inevitable that software updates will need to be sent to operational AVs. This will be required to correct safety-relevant defects, address emergent security issues, and update AV behavior to deal with changes in the environment.

From a security point of view, the update process will itself need to be secure to avoid malicious actors planting malware inside the AV. The details of this are beyond the scope of this discussion, but at the very least a combination of integrity and authentication for any updated software image and new data sets will be needed. That combination will ensure that only updates from the manufacturer are installed, and that the updates have not been tampered with by malicious actors. In addition, a secure boot capability will be required to make sure that malicious software is not able to bypass integrity and authentication measures.

From the safety point of view, the question is how safety will be assured for a new software image. A brute force approach would be to re-evaluate everything. And for major changes that might be required. But it will be too expensive and time consuming to do a complete start-from-scratch safety certification for every single update.[534]

---

[533] To be fair some companies are said to conform, especially first-tier suppliers when customers pay for such conformance. But even for those companies it is difficult to find public statements that this is the case.

[534] It is irresponsible to say that validation is too much bother in an attempt to justify deploying a software update while skipping safety assurance. Rather, the challenge is to practical find ways to make updates having acceptable safety.

For "minor" changes[535] perhaps we can do better. For any change there will be ripple effects to other parts of the system. Even if one line of code is changed, it might interact with other software throughout the AV. Determining the scope of the interactions is done via a process known as impact analysis.[536]

With impact analysis a change is not only considered with regard to lines of software source code, but also considering the corresponding designs, requirements, test plans, lifecycle impact, and so on. Often there will need to be an update to the safety case to incorporate the effects of the change. These changes might provoke other changes, causing a ripple effect throughout the AV's design. If the ripples are small, it is a minor change, with the distinction between minor and major being a matter of degree rather than a crisp threshold.

After any change the AV design will need to be validated again, potentially including design analysis, simulation, and road testing. Everything that was updated or otherwise potentially affected by the change needs to be revisited. For a very minor change this might just be a handful of tests and a quick road test to make sure there were no big disturbances to the system. For a larger change it might end up being that substantially all the engineering needs to be re-checked and completely revalidated. The answer to how big the ripple effect is will depend on the specifics of the change and the engineering processes being used.

The hardware and software configurations of the AV and any support infrastructure will need to be considered as part of the impact analysis. Any software change must work on every combination of deployed hardware and software in existence – or something in the safety case must argue that any incompatible versions of the AV both do not need the change and do not get the change.

After any changes have stabilized, the soundness of the safety case must be revisited. Questions to ask include why the safety case did not catch the problem before release, how the safety case and underlying processes have been changed to ensure this problem is truly fixed, and how the safety case helps ensure that any ripple effects from the change did not introduce new safety issues.

Independent assessment of the safety case will be required after any change. As with software validation this might be done incrementally on any changed part of the safety case if that change is "small." Or it might require that substantially the entire safety case be reassessed if the change is large.

Regardless of the size of any changes, a safe update must address at least the following concerns:

• The change fixes the relevant problem in the AV.

---

[535] In this case a "minor" change refers not to how many lines of code are changed, but rather to how big the effect is on the rest of the system.
[536] See: https://en.wikipedia.org/wiki/Change_impact_analysis

- Any relevant ripple effects from the change, including process changes to avoid future similar issues, have been taken care of.
- The new design, processes, safety case, lifecycle support, and everything else have been validated, as informed by impact analysis.
- The AV design and the safety case have been independently reassessed, for example to ensure standards conformance.
- Everything changed has been placed under configuration management both in terms of development materials (including the associated safety case) and also in terms of deployed vehicle configurations.[537]
- All AVs have been updated as required with any new software images in a secure manner.
- The AV update is only deployed to vehicles that are compatible with the update, considering configurations of hardware, software, and infrastructure support.
- Infrastructure has been updated as required, taking into account the need to support multiple deployed configurations concurrently.
- Safety concerns related to update timing and failed updates (e.g., stranded passengers) have been addressed.

9.5. Road testing safety

Summary: Road testing safety is fundamentally different than deployment because the safety case for testing rests primarily on the skills of a human safety driver rather than the automation technology. Anything other than testing with a qualified, monitored, in-vehicle driver with full controls is likely to be asking for trouble.

Safety during road testing is a crucial concern for AVs. Road testing safety will not only matter during initial development of the technology, but also during the continual cycles of software updates. Regardless of the degree to which validation of software updates is performed in simulation, ultimately there will need to be real-world validation before release on public roads, and the safety of that public road testing will matter.[538]

---

[537] The critical importance of rigorous configuration management in life critical systems might not yet be as widely appreciated in the AV business as it should be. See: https://en.wikipedia.org/wiki/Configuration_management
See also EIA 649C: https://www.sae.org/standards/content/eia649c

[538] Safety of participants in closed-course testing and end-of-line manufacturing tests also matters. However, both of those permit safety practices more rigorous than those available for public road testing, including both controlling the environment and isolating operation from the general public via the use of access controlled facilities.

9.5.1. Safety driver effectiveness

The most important point to keep in mind about road testing safety is that it is more about the role of the human safety driver, and less about the safety of the automated driving functions. The key assumption during road testing is that the safety of the automation technology itself is unproven, and therefore possibly contains a life-critical defect. The primary role of the human safety driver is to intervene as necessary to prevent any automation defect from causing harm to other road users.

This means that the safety of the automation itself is only a part of the total safety picture. A much larger part of the picture is the ability of the human safety driver to detect an automation malfunction and intervene in a timely and safe manner to prevent a loss event.

The ability to remain alert and situationally aware is a significant challenge, because supervising automation is a more difficult task than driving due to the inevitability of driver automation complacency.[539] It is appropriate to build a safety case for public road testing. However, that safety case is quite different than the safety case for AV deployment. The majority of the claims in a public road testing safety case have to do with the safety driver's ability to detect and react to safety issues with a presumption that the safety driver will be able to compensate for any safety-relevant automation defects. The safety of the takeover mechanism is crucial, but the safety requirements of the automation itself are lower because the primary safety argument is that the driver will intervene as needed.

Due to automation complacency, there is reason to believe that as automation capability improves testing will actually become *less* safe, at least to a point. The probability of a crash involves both the probability that the automation will fail and the probability that a complacent safety driver will fail to react to prevent the crash. The issue is that people become complacent to automation capabilities much sooner than they should in terms of minimizing total risk.

---

[539] The National Transportation Safety Board (NSTB) has written on this topic extensively as part of crash investigations involving AV testing and autopilot-style driver assistance features. See:
https://www.ntsb.gov/Advocacy/safety-topics/Pages/automated-vehicles-investigative-outcomes.aspx

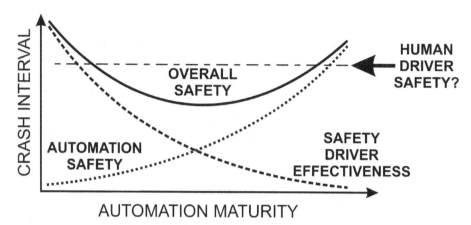

Figure 9.1. Overall safety will tend to decrease due to reduced safety driver effectiveness while automation safety is still improving.[540]

Figure 9.1 shows an illustrative diagram of the effect in action. Perhaps counter-intuitively, fairly poor automation is likely to have fewer crashes than moderately good automation. If the automation is poor enough that it fails on a regular basis, the safety driver is more likely to remain alert and responsive out of a general desire for self-preservation, if nothing else. However, when a crisis response is required only once in a while, the driver will struggle to remain alert while the automation remains nowhere near as safe as a human driver. As the vehicle misbehaves less often, the driver will struggle to respond well enough to ensure safety. With poor driver monitoring it would be no surprise if net safety ends up worse than a comparable vehicle with no automation.

Proponents of highly capable supervised automation modes believe improved safety driver effectiveness can push the total safety above the human driver safety line. A similar argument must be made for safe testing, taking into account that test vehicles are prone to malfunction in more egregious ways than fully validated supervised automation production vehicles. While selecting experienced, capable safety drivers and training them is essential, we believe that additional methods are needed to ensure effective safety driver attention management.

The leading contender for helping safety drivers remain engaged with the supervision task is using an effective Driver Monitoring System (DMS). However, it is not sufficient to have just any old DMS such as a sensor that hands are on the steering wheel. An effective DMS must be able to determine that the safety driver is actually paying attention, has good situational awareness, and has the mental focus to react when called upon to ensure

---

[540] Based on Koopman & Osyk 2019. That paper also contains a reference safety case for public road testing. See:
https://users.ece.cmu.edu/~koopman/pubs/koopman19_TestingSafetyCase_SAEWC X.pdf

testing crashes are avoided. Current thinking is that this requires at least a camera-based DMS that includes eye tracking abilities. However, this is still an evolving area of technology.[541]

9.5.2. In-vehicle safety drivers

Road testing organizations will sometimes claim that their testing is safe because they use "trained" or "professional" safety drivers. Government regulators have historically been satisfied by such statements accompanied by a relatively low bar of safety drivers having a driver's license, clean background check, and insurance. However, more is needed.

Just because someone is qualified to drive a conventional vehicle does not mean that they have the skills needed to safely supervise road testing. Safety drivers need to pay continuous attention to a vehicle that might suddenly do something dramatically wrong, and be able to grab control instantly to correct the situation. Not everyone is cut out to do this, driver's license or not.

Fortunately, there is a starting point for acceptable road testing safety: SAE J3018:2020 Safety-Relevant Guidance for On-Road Testing of Prototype Automated Driving System (ADS)-Operated Vehicles.[542] (We will call this J3018 for short.)

J3018 covers safety driver credentials, driver training, test route selection, pre- and post-trip operational protocols, safety driver performance monitoring, and incident response. While it is somewhat high level, it does provide a starting point for a process much more robust than simply exhorting a test driver to pay attention.

Training is important, but so is continual evaluation of real-world safety driver effectiveness at the ability to maintain vigilance despite the grind of a long testing campaign. It is also important to ensure that the safety driver can be effective in the role in practice. This can be supported with a Safety Management System (SMS) that tracks driver training and effectiveness.[543]

---

[541] For a discussion of some aspects of DMS technology, see Barnden 2021: https://www.eetimes.com/busting-myths-of-driver-monitoring-systems/
And also by Barnden 2021:
https://www.embedded.com/automotive-focus-shifts-to-driver-monitoring-systems/
[542] There are different versions of this standard, so be sure to get the 2020 version. https://www.sae.org/standards/content/j3018_202012/
A free document that is a predecessor of J3018 and has similar content can be found in: AVSC Best Practice for In-Vehicle Fallback Test Driver Selection, Training, and Oversight Procedures for Automated Vehicles Under Test AVSC00001201911: https://www.sae.org/standards/content/avsc00001201911/
[543] A best practice document for AV testing SMS approaches is: AVSC Information Report for Adapting a Safety Management System (SMS) for Automated Driving System (ADS) SAE Level 4 and 5 Testing and Evaluation AVSC00007202107: https://www.sae.org/standards/content/avsc00007202107/

Even with a proficient safety driver, vehicle behaviors need to be conservative enough to allow for adequate safety driver reaction time. If an AV tailgates a leading vehicle because the automation has a lightning-fast response time, what happens if a software defect causes the AV to not brake instantly? Will the human safety driver have time to intervene to prevent a crash? Probably not.

There are limits to any human safety driver's reaction time regardless of how fast the AV can react. The issue is that in testing, the AV will not always react properly, or might even do something overtly dangerous for no apparent reason. The point of testing is to find out whether such a malfunction will happen, so the human safety driver must have enough time to react if things go wrong. The limits to human reaction capability and timing need to be accounted for in setting driving policies for the autonomous driving system under test.

As a simplified example, consider an AV being tested that has been designed to wait until the last split-second to brake at a stop sign, using full braking capability when it does so to make best possible travel time. If the AV fails to brake at the correct location, it will enter the intersection, potentially causing a collision with cross traffic or a vulnerable road user. The human safety driver's job in such a situation is to ensure that the AV stops at the stop sign. The safety driver will have been told not to intervene until it is clear that the AV has malfunctioned. However, because the AV waits until the last possible second to brake, it is not possible to know if the AV has malfunctioned until it is too late to stop at the stop sign. A crash due to over-running a stop sign in that type of vehicle might be blamed on the safety driver to deflect criticism from the AV. But the reality is that a significant contributing cause to any such crash is that the design was inherently unsafe for supervised testing because it did not afford the safety driver sufficient time to react to prevent a crash.

This sets up a bit of a dilemma for AV testers. An AV cannot be tested with maximum driving efficiency because to do so would squeeze out the extra time necessary for a safety driver to intervene during road testing. Testing that affords extra slack in vehicle maneuvers to give testers time to react does not confirm operation at maximum efficiency. This means that it is not possible to conduct safe road testing of a maximum-efficiency AV with human safety drivers. Mild inefficiency is essential to ensure that human safety drivers have the extra time they need to intervene if something goes wrong in testing.

Perhaps someday simulations will be good enough at predicting road testing safety that the awkward issue of accommodating human safety driver reaction time for road testing can be overcome by testing with extra safety margins and closing any efficiency gaps based just on simulation results. But for the near- and intermediate-term future, AVs will need to leave extra slack in their following distances, braking profiles, and other performance parameters to account for this issue. The best that can be done is to hire safety drivers with exceptionally fast and accurate reaction times to minimize the extra timing padding on AV behaviors required for safe testing.

AV testing should never put a human safety driver in the position of requiring super-human reaction times to assure safety. Such an approach will not accomplish safety. Rather, it will simply transfer blame for a crash onto a hapless safety driver who has been put in a no-win moral crumple zone situation.[544]

9.5.3. Road testing with a telepresent safety operator

Sometimes testing is performed with a telepresent driver or safety operator, typically located at a remote operating base, although sometimes closely following the AV test platform in a chase vehicle for cargo-only AV configurations.

Beyond the considerations for an in-vehicle safety driver, telepresent safety operators have to additionally contend with at least:

- Restricted sensory information such as potentially limited visual coverage, lack of audio information, lack of road feel, and lack of other vehicle physical cues depending on the particular vehicle involved. This could cause problems with reacting to emergency vehicle sirens and reacting to physical vehicle damage that might be detected by a physically present driver such as a tire blow-out, unusual vibration, or strange vehicle noise. Lack of road feel might also degrade the driver's ability to remotely drive the vehicle to perform a fallback operation in an extreme situation.

- Delayed reaction time due to the round-trip transmission lag. In some situations, tenths or even hundredths of seconds of additional lag time in transmissions might make the difference between a crash and a recovery from a risky situation.

- The possibility of wireless connectivity loss. Radio frequency interference or loss of a cell tower might interrupt an otherwise reliable connection to the vehicle. Using two different cell phone providers can easily have redundancy limitations due to shared infrastructure such as cell phone towers,[545] cell tower machine rooms (for some providers), and disruption of shared backhaul fiber bundles.[546] A single infrastructure failure or localized interference can disrupt multiple different connectivity providers to one or multiple AVs.

---

[544] See section 10.2.2 regarding the moral crumple zone.

[545] For example, a cell tower fire video shows the collapse of a tower with three antenna rows, suggesting it was hosting three different providers. See: https://www.youtube.com/watch?v=0cT5cXuyiYY

[546] While it is difficult to get public admissions of the mistake of routing both a primary and backup critical telecom service in the same fiber bundle, it does happen. See: https://www.postindependent.com/news/local/the-goof-behind-losing-911-service-in-mays-big-outage/

9.5.3.1. Role of remote safety operator

Achieving acceptable safety with remote operators depends heavily on the duties of the remote operator. Having human operators provide high-level guidance with soft deadlines is one thing: "Vehicle: I think that flag holder at the construction site is telling me to go, but my confidence is too low; did I get that right? Operator: Yes, that is a correct interpretation." However, depending on a person to take full control of remotely driving a vehicle in real time with a remote steering wheel at speed is quite another, and makes ensuring safety quite difficult.

A further challenge is the inexorable economic pressure to have remote operators monitoring more than one vehicle. Beyond being bad at boring automation supervision tasks, humans are also inefficient at multitasking. Expecting a human supervisor to notice when an AV is getting itself into a tricky situation is made harder by monitoring multiple vehicles. Additionally, there will inevitably be a situation in which two vehicles under control of a single supervisor will need concurrent attention when the operator can only handle one AV in a crisis at a time.[547]

There are additional legal issues to consider for remote operators. For example, how does an on-scene police officer give a field sobriety test to a remote operator after a crash if that operator is hundreds of miles away – possibly in a different country? These issues must be addressed to ensure that remote safety driver arrangements can be managed effectively.

Any claim of testing safety with a telepresent operator needs to address the issues of restricted sensory information, reaction time delays, and the inevitability of an eventual connectivity loss at the worst possible time. There are also hard questions to be asked about the accountability issues and law enforcement implications of such an approach.

9.5.3.2. Active vs. passive remote monitoring

A special remote monitoring concern is a safety argument that amounts to the vehicle will notify a human operator when it needs help, so there is no need for any human remote operator to continuously monitor driving safety. Potentially the most difficult part of AV safety is ensuring that the AV actually knows when it is in trouble and needs help. Any argument that the AV will call for help is unpersuasive unless it squarely addresses the issue of how it will know it is in a situation it has not been trained to handle.

The source of this concern is that machine learning-based systems are notorious for false confidence. In other words, saying an ML-based system will ask for help when it needs it assumes that the most difficult part to get

---

[547] In the limit for at-scale operations this ends up being a customer service call center model. Submitted for your consideration as a dystopic story idea: "We're sorry, but our remote operator is busy handling a different crash at the moment. Your impending crash will be handled in the order in which it was received. Your estimated wait time is ...... four ...... minutes. We value your business. Please stay on the line to complete a brief customer service survey after your crash experience is completed."

right – knowing the system is encountering an unknown unsafe condition – is working perfectly during the testing being performed to see if, in fact, that most difficult part is working. That type of circular dependency is a problem for ensuring safety.

Even if such a system were completely reliable at asking for help when needed, the ability of a remote operator to acquire situational awareness and react to a crisis situation quickly is questionable. It is better for the AV to have a validated capable of performing Fallback operations entirely on its own rather than relying on a remote operator to jump in to save the day. Before autonomous Fallback capabilities are trustworthy, a human safety supervisor should continuously monitor and ensure safety.

Any remote operator road testing that claims the AV will inform the remote operator when attention is needed should be treated as an uncrewed road testing operation as discussed in section 9.5.7. Any such AV should be fully capable of handling a Fallback operation completely on its own, and only ask a remote operator for help with recovery after the situation has been stabilized.

9.5.4. Road testing with a Big Red Button

Some road testing uses an emergency stop or other similarly named control colloquially called a "Big Red Button" (BRB) to disable automation during testing. [548] Traditionally, such buttons are used on mechanical equipment to immediately de-energize electrical circuits and apply brakes to stop motion on systems ranging from factory machinery to escalators. The name comes from the historical large red mushroom press-to-stop buttons used for that purpose, although in some domains the term kill switch is used more often.[549] The BRB might be augmented with additional actions such as human driver movement of brakes, steering, or other vehicle controls triggering a human driver takeover and disabling automation. The BRB is typically designed as a higher-integrity last-ditch cutoff capability in case the usual user control interventions do not work properly.

More advanced systems do something more sophisticated than de-energize power. For example, removing power and locking the brakes on a vehicle moving at 100 kph is more likely to put the car into an uncontrolled spin and crash than it is to result in a safe in-lane stop. For that type of situation, the effect of the BRB needs to be more nuanced than slamming on the brakes. However, the idea of the BRB is that a human operator activates a simple emergency switch that triggers a pre-programmed safety shutdown response from the automation. That shutdown response might bring the vehicle to a safe stop, or might forcibly transfer control to the human driver, depending on the system design and operational safety concept.

---

[548] Sometimes these buttons are not actually red, but they are often still called a BRB regardless of color.

[549] To be clear, it is the equipment power that is to be killed.
See: https://en.wikipedia.org/wiki/Kill_switch

Creating a safe BRB approach is more complex than it might seem at first glance. One key issue is that BRB activation must bypass any component that might be responsible for creating the safety issue in the first place. For example, consider hooking the BRB up as an input to the primary autonomy computer. If a safety risk involves that autonomy computer freezing up, it will not only stop controlling vehicle motion – it will also ignore the BRB.[550] There are more subtle issues in the same vein that end up in similar places. The BRB intervention mechanism must have suitable safety integrity (typically in the form of appropriate ISO 26262 ASIL conformance) and operate completely independently of any features being tested.

Another issue with the BRB is how to reset the system to normal operation. Pulling the BRB back to the "normal" operating position can cause the AV to execute a pending command that was suppressed by the BRB, such as accelerating as fast as possible to highway speed even though it is in the middle of a crash scene.[551] This can be handled with suitable design, but the point here is that providing a BRB is more complex than just cutting power and restoring it based on whether the button has been pressed.

A well-designed BRB can provide an extra level of safety for an AV that also has manual takeover controls for the safety driver. For a very slow-moving vehicle in a benign environment simply slamming on the brakes might be a viable BRB action. But for AVs that operate faster, some serious consideration needs to be given as to what the BRB function really is. It might not be a complete vehicle stop, but instead be a way to force isolation of the automation computers from the vehicle so that a safety driver can force a switchover to manual control.

A significant abuse of the BRB approach can be when a human safety driver is held responsible for vehicle operational safety but is only given a BRB instead of full driver controls to be able to take over. For example, simply stopping the vehicle might not be the safe thing to do in some situations. Consider the BRB stopping a vehicle on the proverbial train tracks at a grade crossing when the automation attempts an unsafe crossing, or a BRB that stops a vehicle halfway through a left turn in front of oncoming high-speed traffic. You want the AV to keep moving to reduce risk rather than staying stopped on train tracks. But the BRB forces an all-or-nothing choice between being stranded in a high-risk situation or re-enabling malfunctioning driving automation.

A BRB makes sense as a backup mechanism to force automation to turn off at the command of a safety driver who is then able to take full control and

---

[550] You might think that this is too obvious an issue for any design team putting an AV on public roads to get wrong. Nonetheless, we have found it worthwhile to emphasize this point more than once.

[551] A similar issue was said to cause the crash of an AV test truck that started executing a left turn command enqueued minutes earlier that was suppressed but not deleted during automation disengagement. See O'Keeffe & Somerville 2022: https://www.wsj.com/articles/self-driving-truck-accident-draws-attention-to-safety-at-tusimple-11659346202

responsibility for vehicle motion. A BRB that stops a vehicle with no safety driver ability to regain control might make sense for benign low-speed applications, but needs to take into consideration the possibility that some stop locations might be unreasonably risky.

9.5.5. Road testing with a conductor

Some road testing operations have a human attendant who is less of a safety driver and more of a conductor. A conductor is someone inside the AV who helps passengers load and unload, and might have a Big Red Button available as a defense in depth approach in case the vehicle tries to do something weird. But the conductor is not tasked with (and often not able to) taking over vehicle motion instantly in case of an automation malfunction.

The distinction between a safety driver and a conductor is important. A safety driver must have a set of full takeover controls available the entire time the vehicle is in operation,[552] as well as the availability of undivided attention to monitor and intervene for safety any time the vehicle is or could be in motion. Anything less makes that person a conductor.

A conductor should not be held responsible for driving safety. Partly this is due to the limitations of a BRB safety switch, and partly because the conductor's attention is distracted between vehicle operation and interacting with passengers. A conductor can still, however, play an essential role in operational safety by performing non-driving safety tasks such as ensuring passengers are properly wearing seat belts, managing the safety of any cargo brought on board by passengers, assisting with any post-crash vehicle evacuation, and the like.

In some cases, especially low-speed shuttles, conductors were said to be safety drivers in public messaging, but were turned into conductors in practical operations, leading to potential safety issues. For example, in a 2017 Las Vegas crash[553] a low-speed shuttle was stopped using a BRB and was then hit at slow speed by a large truck. In practice, for that scenario activating the BRB did not improve safety, but rather ensured that the backing truck would hit the shuttle.[554] The vehicle had operator controls, but those controls were in a storage space at the time of the crash. The operator in charge of the vehicle was a conductor at the time of the crash, not a safety driver. This means that an experimental AV was operating without a credible

---

[552] Some companies have deployed test vehicles in which a vehicle occupant or remote supervisor is said to be a safety driver, but is only given a BRB instead of a full set of vehicle controls. We have never seen anything to convince us that this is a safe testing practice. However, it is often plausible that the plan is to blame that "safety driver" for not avoiding a crash, effectively forming a moral crumple zone.

[553] The NTSB report on this crash is at:
https://www.ntsb.gov/investigations/AccidentReports/Reports/HAB1906.pdf

[554] This is not intended to fault the attendant who presumably was following procedure. Rather, it is an illustration of the pitfalls involved in having a BRB as the only available driver control for a test vehicle.

safety driver capability at the time of the crash when it clearly needed a real safety driver. Simply calling someone a "safety driver" does not make it so.

9.5.6. Beta testing

Among some AV vendors it is fashionable to deploy "beta" versions of automation technology, either embedded in whole vehicles or as add-on kits to conventional vehicles. The classical idea of a "beta" version of software is that it is supposed to be fully functional, but might have a few requirements gaps that will be exposed when a carefully selected initial set of users exercise the software in ways that the designers did not think of. However, in practice the designation "beta" is sometimes applied to software that is nowhere near ready for production deployment as a sort of a "do not blame us if this does not really work – it's beta" disclaimer. All bets are off, and the vehicle might do the wrong thing at the worst time.[555]

Deployment of "beta" AV features makes the vehicle operator a de facto safety driver conducting testing on public roads. As a practical matter, it is not possible to assure the safety of that operation if the driver has not undergone specialized safety driver training and the road testing operations are not according to an SMS managed by the AV vendor. AV beta testing with civilian drivers is not responsible road testing, but rather simply deploying immature software that should be presumed to be dangerously flawed and using the operator as a moral crumple zone.[556]

A responsible approach to beta testing would be to manage civilian test drivers as if they were professional testers, including at the very least requiring formal training, requiring that they operate under a company-managed SMS, and only permitting drivers who have met and continue to meet safety driver qualification requirements to perform testing.[557] In other words, as a practical matter, vehicle owner "beta testers" should be indistinguishable from any other qualified road tester used by the AV company other than, arguably, payroll status.

---

[555] See: https://www.edmunds.com/car-news/the-wrong-thing-at-the-wrong-time-tesla-full-self-driving-disclaimer.html

[556] The concept of a moral crumple zone is discussed in section 10.2.2. In short, it is setting up a system in which the consequences of any technological failures are blamed on the nearest convenient human instead of the technology.

[557] The Tesla practice of using a risk-based "safety score" to qualify drivers as beta testers falls short because it does not involve assessing testing skills, but rather only some limited aspects of normal driving skills. Additionally, as implemented, it permits drivers other than the one who earned the score to operate the vehicle as a tester. It also does not involve a driving records check, or even a check that the driver has a valid driver's license as far as has been disclosed publicly. A more detailed discussion of the issues involved with Tesla's Full Self Driving public road testing can be found in Widen & Koopman 2021:
https://papers.ssrn.com/sol3/papers.cfm?abstract_id=3931341

A different approach to beta testing and phased deployment would be to ensure that no AV occupant is responsible for safety. In such a situation the beta tester would be there to resume vehicle operations using manual vehicle controls if an automation failure results in the vehicle safely shutting itself down (e.g., pulling onto a road shoulder). In other words, a "beta" product should be unquestionably safe, but might have higher than desirable outage rates due to performance limitations. Human backup drivers would be more in the nature of valets to move any car stranded in an inconvenient position while not being on the hook for real-time driving safety.

9.5.7. Uncrewed road testing

Some companies and regulators have promoted the concept of uncrewed road testing, in which an AV that is not yet ready for deployment is operated on public roads without a safety driver. To the degree that this testing is performed with a vehicle that is not already thought to be safe enough to deploy, this is an unreasonably risky activity that should not be permitted on public roads. There are some nuances at play, so here is a breakdown.

There are various possible approaches to testing on public roads without a full-fledged safety driver in the vehicle. Many we have already discussed, including the Big Red Button approach and teleoperation approaches. This section considers only situations in which there is truly no human with continuous real-time responsibility to monitor and respond to dangerous situations while the vehicle is driving. No teleoperation until after a Fallback maneuver has been completed under autonomous operation, and no person with hand poised to slam the BRB.

The usual justification for deploying an uncrewed test vehicle is to "build confidence" in the system. If the system is already safe enough to deploy and the uncrewed testing is to demonstrate availability or improve customer experience, then building confidence in availability, ride comfort, and so on can be OK. But driving safety must be assured before any uncrewed testing can take place.

Before any uncrewed testing can take place on public roads there needs to be an acceptable safety case in place just as for a deployment. The only difference should be – at most – that the vehicle is expected to engage its failsafe behaviors more often than would be desirable in production. Even so, there must be a plan to deal with the risk of a stopped test AV being hit by other traffic in a travel lane, impeding the progress of emergency vehicles, and so on.[558]

---

[558] An in-vehicle backup driver should be in the vehicle until confidence has been attained that risks involving a stopped AV have been acceptably mitigated. This might not be a safety driver, but rather simply a valet who can operate the vehicle manually if a safety shutdown has already occurred and the vehicle has been stranded in an awkward spot, presents a public nuisance, or otherwise is left in a bad situation. Over time the valet function might be performed remotely, but due to the likelihood of unanticipated scenarios it should be performed by a physically present

There are two prevalent types of dysfunctional reasoning used in an improper attempt to justify uncrewed testing: investor milestones and building trust. The investor milestone reason is based on taking out the safety driver to appease investors who are demanding signs of progress. We explore that issue in section 10.3.1.

The building trust argument tends to go something like this: the vehicle works fine, and the only way to prove it is safe enough is to do uncrewed testing, because anything else is not realistic enough to provide proof. This building trust argument is faulty for at least two reasons.

First, you do not need uncrewed road testing to establish a reasonable expectation of acceptable safety. Safety standards and safety case approaches build trust without uncrewed road testing. Often what AV companies really mean when they want to use uncrewed road testing is they want to such testing as a substitute for following best safety engineering practices.

Uncrewed testing should only come after designers have done their safety homework, including comprehensive and successful crewed testing, rather than being used as an expedient way to cut corners on safety engineering. If any company says that frequent safety problems after the start of uncrewed testing are to be expected as the price of making progress, then that company is cutting corners on crewed testing. Uncrewed testing that does not have a safety case and crewed testing experience supporting at least a PRB safety expectation should be considered to present unreasonable risk to other road users.

Second, a "build trust" operation can be done without compromising on safety. Simply put a physical telltale on the safety driver controls that does not impede safety driver takeover.[559] If no driver intervention occurs, take credit for (simulated) uncrewed testing. If the telltale indicates the safety driver has used vehicle controls, that means your safety driver prevented a crash you would have had with uncrewed testing. False alarm interventions mean that either the safety drivers are inadequately trained or that the AV is operating in an overly-aggressive manner that would have similarly prompted false alarm interventions during crewed testing. Telling safety drivers not to intervene when they feel they should amounts to rolling the dice on safety during this type of testing.

The real agenda behind a "build trust" argument often seems to be more about appeasing investor expectations and getting positive press. While there is no doubt that press releases and ride videos by executives and personalities showing a driver removed from a vehicle generate a splash, doing so on public roads before safety engineering has been completed is irresponsible.[560] Uncrewed AV testing before safety has been assured amounts to taking a

---

driver initially. Cruise has notably had issues with the lack of an in-person valet in their San Francisco operations. See: https://techcrunch.com/2022/06/30/cruise-robotaxis-blocked-traffic-for-hours-on-this-san-francisco-street/

[559] Data logs showing no safety driver interventions should suffice.

[560] These companies should keep in mind that fatal crash videos also generate a social media splash of the wrong sort.

gamble that you will get lucky and not have a crash, even though your AV is probably not even as safe as a human driver.

At some point there needs to be the first drive without a safety driver on public roads. But that testing should only be done after safety has been firmly established, not as a part of proving safety. Uncrewed testing while still proving safety is simply a different form of the bootstrapping safety argument approach shown to be problematic in section 8.4.1.

Regardless of the motivation for uncrewed testing, if it is done before the vehicle is ready to deploy with regard to safety, the net result is putting other road users at increased risk for the sake of the AV company's business interests. For anyone who thinks that an AV company will self-moderate its risk-taking behavior to achieve short-term goals in the interest of long-term success … well, there is a reason the next chapter covers ethics.

9.6. Summary

In this chapter we get to the main question of this book – how do we know it is time to deploy an AV? Section 9.1 sets forth a high-level deployment decision strategy including a variety of factors. The decision criteria must go well beyond some expectation of Positive Risk Balance. We will argue in chapter 10 that having the right governance model is the most important ethical aspect of a decision to deploy, because it drives the selection and enforcement of all the other criteria.

The biggest technical challenge to deployment will be managing uncertainty as to how safe the AV will really be when deployed due to lack of extensive experience with the predictive ability of SPIs. This might be overcome to a degree by tracking SPI violation rates to judge the maturity of the safety case. Additional considerations for deployment include conformance to standards and an ability to make software updates that are both safe and secure.

Deciding when and how to deploy vehicles for road testing safety is a significant issue, and will remain so as the technology continues to mature over the coming years and decades. Anything less than a professional, trained in-vehicle safety driver raises substantive concerns about the safety of other public road users. In particular, uncrewed testing should not be undertaken until after acceptable AV safety has been firmly established.

10. Ethical AV deployment

No discussion of "how safe is safe enough" is complete without touching on the subject of ethics. Whole books can be written on this topic, so we do not attempt an exhaustive treatment here. Rather we touch on some of the common topics that are often misunderstood and other topics that do not get the attention they deserve.

10.1. The Trolley Problem

Summary: The Trolley Problem is a distraction from much more important ethical issues when it comes to AV deployment.

This section is here because far, far too many people think that AV ethics exactly equals the Trolly Problem. That is simply not the case. But let us dispense with this topic up front so we can move on to things that matter in practical application.[561]

An incredible amount of effort has been spent on the so-called Trolley Problem and its variants. The classical formulation recast for AVs as the following no-win situation: on its current course the AV will hit and kill five people, but changing course means it will only hit and kill one person who would not otherwise be harmed.[562] Should the AV kill five – or should the AV swerve and sacrifice one otherwise bystander to save the five? The Trolley Problem name comes from a thought experiment in which a trolley is approaching a switch that can change tracks from running over five unfortunates instead of only one if the trolley driver throws the switch.

10.1.1. Problems with the Trolley Problem

Variants of the kill one or kill five dilemma involve ascribing various social attributes to the potential victims such as age, gender, and profession. Should the AV kill the young nurse getting off shift from a hospital helping

---

[561] While you're here, have a look at our favorite comic strip on the topic of why autonomous trucks will win in the marketplace vs. cars, and moral philosophy. See: https://www.smbc-comics.com/comic/self-driving-car-ethics

[562] The origins and variations of the Trolley Problem as well as other AV ethics topics are discussed in the Koopman, Kuipers, Widen & Wolf round table discussion from 2021 here: https://ieeexplore.ieee.org/document/9622307
The origin of the Trolley Problem is not kill one vs. kill five, but rather why people tend to think that killing one to save five using a trolley track switch is acceptable while deliberately executing one innocent person to save five hostages is unacceptable. See: https://en.wikipedia.org/wiki/Trolley_problem#Original_dilemma

sick people, or the grandmother about to check in to that same hospital for testing who will be told tomorrow that she only has a few weeks to live? How about the philanthropist who just got pardoned on a technicality from a high-profile banking fraud criminal trial? And so it goes. As an experiment in social values placed on various aspects of the human experience, it can be fascinating. But ascribing different values to different people's lives is not relevant to AV safety in any actionable way.

An AV deployed on the roads any time soon has no way to know the demographic details of potential victims. How would an AV know the age, gender, profession, societal contribution, parental status, medical situation, criminal record, race, ethnicity, immigration status, social credit rating, and whatever other factors might be deemed relevant by a survey in valuing a life?[563] There are other issues such as attempting to accurately predict the severity of injuries that will occur in a specific situation, to a pedestrian with a particular medical history (including undiagnosed medical problems), potential control instability issues with sudden maneuvers, secondary harm caused by debris such as a wheel detached during a crash, and so on. And all this would have to be figured out in a fraction of a second.

Expecting an AV to do nuanced, game theoretic real-time decisions according to highly nonlinear social norms, involving crash physics based on information of all actors that it is unlikely to have, accounting for difficult-to-predict harm, according to an ethical framework that might not even be agreed to by all stakeholders in that specific event – well, that sounds like an unreasonable expectation.

But, even if we were to decide that detailed tradeoff calculations were worth doing, the technology is nowhere near ready to perform such a process. The problem we have with AV safety now is not deciding whether to hit grandma or the child. The problem is knowing if the thing it is looking at is a person at all, much less how many people of what description are standing in a clump of pedestrians. Or maybe it is a clump of bushes – hard to be 100% sure. Any experiment in kill-one-to-save-five seems likely to end with some really bad press for the AV industry the first time five person-looking bushes are heroically saved at the cost of killing one real, formerly live person minding their own business at a sidewalk café.

Exercises in who and how many people of various classification bins "should" die can reveal insights into social norms, individual ethical frameworks, and so on. But for the foreseeable future they are not relevant to the technology of safe AVs.

---

[563] Adding identification and "value of this person's life" information to cell phone beacons has been proposed as a solution. Even if morally acceptable, which we do not concede, this is likely unworkable on a technical basis. In any event, such an approach would create an instant market for falsified beacon information. It would also engender equity issues regarding people who do not carry a cell phone due to poverty, personal beliefs, children having a phone taken away by a parent due to misuse, or being too young to carry one.

10.1.2. The solution to the Trolley Problem

The real answer is to design AVs to drive so conservatively that they are unlikely to get into Trolley Problem situations in the first place. The vast majority of deaths and injuries do not involve such no-win tradeoffs. Assuming that AVs get safe enough that Trolley Problem situations start forming a non-negligible fraction of harm we can (1) congratulate ourselves on having made roadways incredibly safe, and (2) decide what to do about it then.[564] In other words, our best case outcome is that the Trolley Problem is the biggest safety problem left to solve.

Some ethical framework is useful, but in practice it needs to be simple enough to be actionable by a real-world AV. For example, a German Ethics Commission report[565] imposes rules that include: protection of individuals takes precedence over other utilitarian considerations including damage to property and harm to animals; AVs should be designed to avoid no-win Trolley Problem situations; personal features *cannot* be used in planning responses to unavoidable crash situations; and reducing total number of casualties *may* be justifiable, but parties involved in the generation of mobility risks must not sacrifice non-involved parties.[566] A close reading of those principles is likely to result in more questions than answers, but it is an important starting point for the AV industry.

A nuanced, detailed solution to the Trolley Problem is unreasonable to expect as a blocking condition for deploying otherwise acceptably safe AVs. A few general principles might suffice at first, such as valuing life over property and considering an AV that gets itself involved in Trolleyesque situations with a non-negligible frequency is too dangerous to be operating on public roads in the first place.

There are some very selective subsets of this topic that are relevant that can and should be addressed at least within an AV design team, such as:

- Should an AV hit what it thinks is a pedestrian (causing harm to the pedestrian) or hit some other object such as a tree (causing more harm to passengers)? One can argue that hitting the tree is the better choice because passengers have significant passive safety protection whereas pedestrians do not. And, arguably, the passengers opted into the risks attendant to riding in an AV. But people who spend a lot of time in vehicles do not necessarily like that answer, and might prefer a switch that permits them to prioritize their lives over pedestrians, which raises ethical issues. Whether the pedestrian would have been hit anyway or the

---

[564] And even then, a viable solution is more likely to be something like either do not change course if it will change the victim, or only change paths if it results in a significantly slower predicted collision speed.

[565] BMVI 2017: https://www.bmvi.de/SharedDocs/EN/publications/report-ethics-commission.html

[566] Apparent implication: it is forbidden to change vehicle trajectory to intentionally kill another road user in order to save the AV occupants.

AV maneuvers to intentionally hit a pedestrian in response to the AV hitting a tree on its default trajectory likely factors into this issue.

- How sure should an AV be in deciding that something is not a pedestrian and can be run over? There is a practical tradeoff between an AV being afraid of its own shadow and running over everything that does not look exactly like the (likely biased) training images it has seen. We would prefer to err on the side of caution and avoid hitting might-be-pedestrians until the technology matures. But is it OK to hit a few thousand 1% pedestrians and eventually get unlucky?[567]

While these special cases should be folded into AV safety considerations,[568] at a high level, the generalized Trolley Problem is a distraction from things that matter much more to the immediate deployment of the technology.

Time spent on the Trolley Problem distracts earnest people interested in the effect of AVs on public safety away from other urgent safety topics. It might also serve as a useful distraction to stall public policy decisions in a quagmire of debate while the industry continues to press forward with inadequate regulatory scrutiny.

We feel that topics that are practical and are likely to affect many more road users are what matter to AV safety for the foreseeable future. These topics include who gets to make the decision as to how much risk an AV can present to the general public at deployment. And how much oversight for-profit companies chasing a trillion-dollar market should have when testing immature autonomous vehicle technology on public roads.

10.2. Skin in the game

Summary: A major source of ethical issues for AVs is that the people financing, designing, and deploying them are not the ones who are going to be physically harmed in crashes. Despite best intentions, the misalignment of incentives cannot help but be a problem.

---

[567] To be fair, that "1% pedestrian" might not have the obvious everyday meaning if the probability value came from a machine learning classifier. But ultimately the probability of false negatives in which a pedestrian is not detected needs to come into play, and will ultimately involve ethical decision making. Likely this will be resolved by claiming net PRB for pedestrians compared to human-driven vehicles.

[568] The reader is left to ponder why it seems that turning AVs loose in a city with immature automation technology because eventually that technology might save lives seems to be acceptable, while (at least some think) purposefully using live children on public roads to test immature crash avoidance technology would be unacceptable. This is the case even though the argument for both is that live road testing is more realistic than simulations and consequent earlier deployment would save lives in the long run. See:
https://www.theverge.com/2022/8/20/23314117/youtube-tesla-removes-video-full-self-driving-beta-real-kids

A central ethical issue for AVs is that the people who are responsible for ensuring safe driving are distanced from actual events on the road. If there is a fatal crash, a remote safety supervisor or design engineer is at no risk of death. If a manager decides to deploy a vehicle that is not as safe as it should be, it seems very unlikely they would serve jail time. And so on. The people most at risk are other road users who are uninvolved in the AV design and deployment decisions.[569]

Moreover, a computer driving a car will not be deterred from unethical or illegal driving behavior by the prospect of fines, license points, or jail time. A computer simply has no capacity for worrying about personal consequences.[570] Insurance premiums similarly present small incentive for safety, as they are a minuscule fraction of the operating costs for an AV development company. A few tens of thousands of dollars in insurance premiums pale in comparison to a million or more dollars per day running such a company. For that matter, paying a few million dollars of settlement money to the family of a victim can be treated by such companies as merely the cost of doing business while chasing a trillion dollar market.[571]

A significant problem with AV safety now is that the people in charge of making sure AVs are safe (the AV companies themselves) have insufficient skin in the game to be threatened with direct personal harm if their AV operations are unsafe.[572]

---

[569] Those riding in the AV might be considered to have voluntarily consented to the risk associated with riding, although we argue it is largely uninformed consent due to rampant disinformation. Regardless, they have seat belts and airbags available to protect them. Vulnerable road users such as pedestrians are also placed at risk by this technology without such protections. Non-passenger road users did not personally opt into the human subject experiment that is AV testing on public roads.

[570] See section 10.4.7 for a continuation of this thread of discussion.

[571] While there are many caring and conscientious people involved in the industry, it is all too easy for tremendous piles of money and investor pressure to cloud the judgment of even well-intentioned senior players. Workers can too easily be captured by management messaging on saving lives with technology and deadline pressure if they are disconnected from personal risk exposure. Moreover, the specialists who do much of the difficult technical work often have little training in the area of software safety. It is too easy for everything to seem like a complex video game until confronted with the reality of a pedestrian death. It is also too easy for non-safety-specialist designers to honestly think they are doing well enough on safety, when in fact they are not, due to benign ignorance of the principles and practicalities of safety engineering. It seems likely that all these factors were at play in the Uber ATG fatality to some degree.

[572] The distancing of AV developers and operators from the risk born by vulnerable road users during testing is even more problematic than is the risk distance from human drivers in their highly protected driving cocoons to other more vulnerable road users. Yet worse is the even further distancing of those making financial and project management decisions regarding hitting deployment milestones and resource allocation. Anything that enables such distancing seems likely to put negative pressure on safety culture.

10.2.1. The Moral Crumple Zone

The Moral Crumple Zone is a concept from a 2016 paper by Madeleine Clare Elish.[573] Briefly, the moral crumple zone comes into play when a human actor bears the brunt of the moral or legal responsibilities for the failure of an automated or autonomous system despite having only limited control of the actions of that system. In more direct terms, the plan of the system designers to avoid responsibility for bad automation behavior is to blame the most conveniently available human instead, even when it is unreasonable to expect the human to have prevented the loss.

While the term is comparatively new, the concept comes from a well-worn automotive industry playbook. Drivers are told they are responsible for safety, including compensating for design flaws and technical malfunctions that might occur.[574] The car companies might then stick the drivers with blame even if it was unreasonable to do so, thereby evading liability.

As a classic example, if a car suddenly applies full throttle acceleration due to an unquestionably defective design, the driver is blamed for not pressing the brake at all or not pressing the brake hard enough to stop a crash. Drivers usually press the brake and avoid a crash. But sometimes a panicked driver accidentally presses the wrong pedal when startled and does not have time to correct the error by pressing the brake hard enough before crashing in a parking lot.[575] Nonetheless, the *cause* of the crashes is said to be a driver error of pressing the wrong pedal, even though that only happened after the "tried" to crash by accelerating without any driver command to do so. This is not hypothetical – this is literally the story of the infamous Audi 5000 "pedal confusion" narrative that birthed the tactic of blaming human drivers for uncommanded acceleration problems.[576]

---

[573] See Elish 2016: https://papers.ssrn.com/sol3/papers.cfm?abstract_id=2757236

[574] This potential problem is baked deep into the automotive safety engineering culture, with the concept of "controllability" that is a factor in determining ASILs in ISO 26262. If used properly, ASILs can be a reasonable engineering approach. But if drivers are given more controllability credit than is appropriate given limits to human driver performance across the demographic spectrum, that can creep into a moral crumple zone approach deep in the engineering process. Due to a lack of safety transparency in the industry, it is difficult to know how much an issue this is, but it is not just a hypothetical problem.

[575] Data we've seen demonstrated convincingly that drivers are very good at pressing the brake pedal instead of accelerator pedal in a panic situation, and quickly self-correct in the rare case that they make a mistake. But in a parking lot there might not be time for those few to self-correct before impact, potentially explaining why such crashes are more common.

[576] Koopman 2018 explains the history of the pedal misapplication narrative. Reference 24 in that paper is to a government report that documents the Audi uncommanded acceleration situation as initiating due to an engine controller design defect, not pedal misapplication.
https://users.ece.cmu.edu/~koopman/pubs/koopman18_safecomp.pdf

The 94% human error narrative debunked in section 4.10.1 is a descendent of a long-term industry strategy of blaming human driver frailties rather than acknowledging the much more complex nature of car crashes and in particular the role of technical design faults.

The deployment of a moral crumple zone allows people making decisions regarding AV safety to avoid being criticized for fast and loose approaches to safety. Rather than taking responsibility for hitting a pedestrian, they can try to blame a pedestrian for jaywalking,[577] or another driver for not acting perfectly when a crash occurs. Pretty much anything that can be blamed other than the AV will be blamed. We have already seen this dynamic in action in AV testing, especially with regard to attributing "blame" for crashes. There is every reason to expect it will continue as aggressively as the AV industry can manage. Expect to see the Moral Crumple Zone deployed in various ingenious, potentially subtle ways as the industry scales up.

10.2.2. Moral Crumple Zones as a design strategy

If a Moral Crumple Zone is intentionally built into an AV's design or operational concept, this amounts to setting up a situation in which the plan is to scapegoat a human to avoid blame and liability for the technology. Examples include the following, some of which have at the time of this writing progressed to criminal charges having been filed against the driver involved, and most of which have either been deployed or proposed at one time or another:

- Expecting a testing safety driver to remain alert without a second support occupant, with operationally ineffective driver monitoring, and apparently while being tasked with text communications that require taking eyes off the road.[578]
- Expecting a driver of an automated but not autonomous system to remain engaged without effective driver monitoring despite personal experience that the car can "drive itself" reliably in some situations and extensive public messaging to that same effect. This applies to numerous Tesla crashes investigated by the US National Transportation Safety Board (NTSB), and seems likely to figure in a case involving a driver facing criminal charges.[579]
- Telling everyday drivers that it is their responsibility to maintain continuous vigilance and compensate for technical malfunctions in not-

---

[577] The invention of the crime of jaywalking is an early example of inventing a moral crumple zone by the car industry. Pedestrians were being harmed by cars, so the industry solution was to deflect blame onto the victims. See Lewis 2014: https://www.bbc.com/news/magazine-26073797

[578] Smiley 2022 tells the story of the safety driver involved in the 2018 Uber ATG crash: https://www.wired.com/story/uber-self-driving-car-fatal-crash/

[579] See AP 2022: https://www.npr.org/2022/01/18/1073857310/tesla-autopilot-crash-charges

ready-for-production "beta" software and equipment. It is well known that people are bad at monitoring automation. This is in essence asking human drivers to do the impossible, and then blaming them for the results.

- Expecting drivers without comprehensive training to operate test vehicles safely on public roads, even in situations in which the manufacturer knew (or should have known) the software has dangerous deficiencies. Not all people have the skills to do this safely even with training. Moreover, it is irresponsible to "test" behaviors that are already known to be defective or otherwise dangerous on public roads. Nonetheless, legal fine print is often used to hold the safety driver responsible when failing to compensate for a technical malfunction.

- Using test drivers as disposable blame absorption devices during a testing campaign. When an incident happens, the test driver can be fired and – so the reasoning goes – the problem has been solved because that particular test driver has been fired. While it is possible there is a bad actor tester who caused a problem, it is much more likely the case that the equipment, test procedures, and/or working conditions set the driver up for failure. Firing the driver is merely used as a way to avoid fixing other, more systemic problems.

- Blaming crashes on pedestrians and other road users for not following traffic rules perfectly, or whatever other reason can be found to deflect blame from the technology or company deploying and operating the technology.

- Installing safety controls more for the purpose of shedding blame than for operational safety. Example: installing a red emergency stop button accessible to a civilian robotaxi passenger sitting in the back seat that, if not pressed, results in blaming the passenger for failing to avoid a crash.

- Installing crash recording data that asymmetrically monitors the behavior of other road actors. Example: post-crash data has extensive video of other road actors but omits key data as to whether AV software was working properly. Any contribution to a loss event by another party is captured, but whether the AV was malfunctioning might not be.

- Post-crash procedures and company behavior emphasizing blame of other road actors without critical analysis of the AV's potential role in causing or failing to reasonably avoid a crash.

- Legal and regulatory approaches that place significant burden on passengers or other road actors to prove they were not at fault before the potential for an AV design defect is addressable or recovery for losses is possible.

- Public safety procedures that do not account for the involvement in vehicle automation in crash reports. For example, a crash report form that does not have check-off boxes for possible involvement of automated vehicle features. [580] As a result, involvement of vehicle automation features in crashes is systematically under-reported and drivers are often solely blamed for crashes.

There are no doubt other dark patterns for moral crumple zones that will emerge as the industry continues to grow. But all of them have the characteristic of finding someone to blame to avoid fixing issues with the AV equipment, operational procedures, or other problems that should be fixed.

The most important takeaway for the concept of the moral crumple zone is quite simple. Expecting humans to display super-human ability without adequate support and training is unreasonable, especially when their task is to not only monitor automation but also to compensate for design defects.

From a safety point of view, it is not assigning blame that matters. Firing, blaming, or otherwise finding a way to blame a person simply enables continuing unsafe AV deployment and operational practices via use of a Moral Crumple Zone. Such a strategy will not stop the next similar crash.

> Blaming a safety driver will not stop the next AV crash.

10.2.3. Insurance as ethical insulation

A supplement to deploying Moral Crumple Zones is setting up a framework in which nobody is to blame when an AV harms someone. This might be done in a fairly straightforward way by casting the discussion topic as insurable risk instead of safety. This approach to non-accountable safety theater might involve:

- Step 1: Convince stakeholders that AVs will be safer than human drivers via whatever arguments seem to work. This is typically a propaganda exercise, not a legitimate safety case approach. See section 4.10.

- Step 2: Further convince stakeholders that a comparatively small amount of insurance paid out under something that amounts to a "no fault" plan is fine, given that it can be taken for granted that AVs will be safer than human drivers. Ensure that state laws are written in an obtuse manner that will make insurance claims difficult and lengthy. Make regulatory statements of accountability so confused and ambiguous that exceeding a low required insurance payout requires appeals to the relevant state supreme court to determine who is financially responsible for a loss. Victims attempting to collect judgments will need to do so proportionally from every different entity involved in the AV deployment rather than from one source. Bonus points for making it opaque who those

---

[580] The complexities in updating historical police procedures and practices to address vehicle automation technology is acknowledged, but it is past time to take action on this point. NHTSA AV crash reporting requirements only somewhat help with this issue, but are a start.

proportional parties might even be for any particular loss event without extensive discovery.

- Step 3: Deploy using a Moral Crumple Zone strategy to the extent practical.
- Step 4: When a mishap occurs, tie up any claim in the court system for as many years as possible, then confidentially settle at the optimum time to keep the true facts of fatalities and major injuries from becoming public. This buys time to grow the market and the company valuation. With any luck initial investors will have exited before a significant, public court loss has a chance to occur.

Sadly, this playbook of maximizing the transaction cost for any potential victim to collect more than a small insurance amount is a common situation in the US at the state level. This is made worse by the many state laws that provide incredibly permissive oversight of AV safety with little accountability for mishaps that will inevitably occur.

A major problem with using an insurance narrative is that no party (other than the victim) has much skin in the game for any particular mishap. The computer driver of a completely automated delivery vehicle has no fear of being hospitalized due to a crash, nor is the threat of jail time for a computer[581] a real deterrent for driving recklessly.

Rather, if risk is treated as an insurance payout proposition, reckless driving that increases profitable use of the equipment is incentivized so long as the payouts to harmed victims stay lower than the increased profit. If laws limiting the required payout can be passed via aggressive lobbying, so much the better – for profits, not for public safety. The risk of eventual regulatory backlash is high, but does not seem to be of concern to the industry at the current time.[582]

The deeper issue with this approach is that accountability is lost in the process of dressing up safety as just a manifestation of ordinary, insurable risk. The feedback loop between cutting safety corners and the day of reckoning on paying out on a loss event due to poor safety can easily be stretched to years – at which time either the company has failed (so the payout is zero) or the company expects to be valued in the hundreds of

---

[581] In at least some states the "computer" is considered the driver of the AV. There is literally nobody to blame for driving that would count as a reckless fatality if it were performed by a human driver, because the automated driving computer does not count as a person in the eyes of the law. In some situations the "owner" or "operator" of the vehicle is on the hook to at least get a ticket. Even if that comes with criminal responsibility (which is unclear), it is uncertain whether an otherwise uninvolved investor asleep at home at 3 am when a fatal crash occurs will be held criminally responsible and sent to jail by a jury if an AV drives recklessly due to a software defect written by someone completely different.

[582] The reader is invited to consider the cautionary tale of the rail industry's rise and fall as it relates to overly aggressive legal strategies to minimize safety liability – and the subsequent regulatory backlash. See Conclusions part A of Widen & Koopman 2022: https://papers.ssrn.com/sol3/papers.cfm?abstract_id=3969214

billions of dollars (so buying off a victim's family for a few million dollars is in effect chump change).

The risk is that insurance used as insulation can help turn an ethical obligation to mind safety into a venture capital financial gamble by those making the risk decisions. Only the victims are left bearing meaningful consequences of harmful events. Sadly, this scenario is in essence what is playing out in the US right now for the industry as a whole.

10.3. Deployment governance

Summary: The most pressing AV ethical issue is whether the people who are in charge of a company – and who stand to profit enormously from "winning" the race to autonomy – should be able to decide when an AV is safe enough to deploy without substantive, informed input from other stakeholders.[583]

When evaluating the ethical component of an AV company's plan it is essential to understand its true business model and incentives. People will feel pressure to act the way they are incentivized to act. Therefore, incentives that guide actions away from safety are an ethical issue due to the pressure they exert, even if the people involved have the best of intentions to act in other ways more supportive of safety.

AV companies that have incentives for near-term demonstrations of functionality can come under considerable pressure to take shortcuts on safety if they perceive that the odds are in their favor.

The question of incentives leads to the most pressing ethical issue for AV safety. The question of deployment decision governance is: who gets to decide when AVs are safe enough to deploy, based on what criteria, and under what oversight.

The most pressing AV ethical issue is deployment governance.

10.3.1. Thought experiment: do you deploy under pressure?

Let us consider a thought experiment. You, the reader, are in charge of a company that needs to do a public road demonstration with no driver in an AV. You know that safety is not where you would like it to be. In fact, you have no safety case at all. You might not even have any real safety engineers on staff. But you have a smart, super-capable team. You have done a lot of test driving and it is going pretty well.

You intuitively figure it is more likely than not that you can pull off a one-time demo without a crash, and even less likely that a crash will kill

---

[583] Well, when we put it that way it does sound like a problem. Yes, that is the point.

someone. You figure you have something like 5 chances out of 6 of pulling off the demo with nobody getting hurt, and it is, in your mind, near certainty due to low-speed urban driving that any crash would avoid a fatality. For good measure maybe you plan to station employees near the demo site to shoo away any pedestrians and light mobility users who would be at increased risk of harm, and do the demo very late at night when roads are usually empty of other road users. Regulators are not in a position to influence your decision.

Your investors have told you they will pull the plug on your entire company if you do not demo by December 31st. Right now, it is the first week of December, and it is time to decide what to do. If the investors pull the plug at the end of the month, you lose perhaps $1B in personal equity you hope to net in next year's public offering. And all your employees will lose their equity as well as their jobs. This will also end a journey you have spent your life on to build and deploy a truly self-driving car.

Further negotiations with the investors are not possible. It is time to decide. That leaves you three main options:

- Case 1: The AV company does not do the demo because it cannot assure a PRB level of safety. The company runs out of money and folds. This option kills the company.

- Case 2: The AV company does the demo and harms a road user. This might or might not result in termination of funding depending on the optics of the crash (perhaps a pedestrian victim can be blamed for jaywalking, being impaired, or having low societal status; maybe all three). You think minor harm is more likely than a fatality, and you will have lots of money available to pay off a potential victim to keep quiet. You will not pre-announce the demo, so you feel able to control the narrative if something goes wrong. The company and the mission go on unless there is a truly unlucky break during that one demo/test session that cannot be cleaned up. Even Uber ATG kept going for a while after a really bad crash, and you know in your heart that your team is better.

- Case 3: The AV company does the demo and gets lucky, not harming any other road users. The company meets its milestone and gets more funding. This the most likely case, and it would be a perfect victory.

Given this setup doing the demo is clearly the best financial bet for the company. Probably you will get lucky with a positive outcome. No harm will be done, and the demo can be said to be safe [584] under the culturally dominant no harm/no foul principle.[585] But if the demo is skipped due to safety, the company is sure to die, and the decision maker is out a billion dollars.

---

[584] We would argue that the demo is in fact not safe – it is unreasonably risky. There is an important difference between attributing good luck to safety after the fact versus actually being safe. A reader wanting to delve further into the nuances of this line of thought might reflect on the implication of having chosen 5 out of 6 odds of success for this example. Hint: the analogy is not a 6-sided die.

[585] See: https://idioms.thefreedictionary.com/no+harm%2c+no+foul

Even if you get unlucky, the cost of a few million dollar settlement pales in comparison with the billions of dollars on the table. Really – you might think – a payout is just the cost of doing business. And even if the crash optics get out of control and the startup company folds, the investors have hedged their bets and the team can simply move to another company and try again. Pretty much everyone will do fine. Except for the victim, if there is one.

This is how demo milestones incentivize deploying systems when the calendar and funding flow says it is time for a demo rather than when the demo is known to be acceptably safe.[586] After all, it is someone else who is injured or dies, not the decision maker. And a billion dollars is a ton of money. And probably it will be fine. Only other companies kill pedestrians.

10.3.2. Real-world AV deployment governance

As of this writing, in the US the situation is that AV deployment governance is, for all practical purposes, in the hands of the companies making the AVs. That boils down to the top decision maker in the AV company and any decision support structure that might be in place. That decision maker can be expected to have a duty to shareholders to optimize for the best financial valuation of the company, even if at times that might conflict with personal views.

Some states have laws requiring AV testing and deployment permits. However, there is little more than cursory technical oversight over safety, commonly in the form of the AV company attesting to their vehicles' safety with no sharing of detailed technical information. Generally the conversation runs that the AV company says they have had no testing crashes, testing crashes are all due to dangerous human drivers hitting their AV (someone else's fault), or that any causes of testing crashes have been fixed, and any regulatory approval (if there is any) for the vehicle equipment has granted.[587]

There are some requirements for insurance, and some states require a disclosure of high-level operational safety procedures for emergency responders and the like. But there is no engineering oversight, and no requirement to follow engineering design safety standards. In a few places there is a requirement or strong request for companies to attest that they

---

[586] To be clear, we do not argue a demo should never be done. We simply argue that demoing without having done due diligence on ensuring acceptable safety is unethical. Additionally, the risk of a decision maker's ethics being unwittingly compromised or even corrupted by a billion dollar payout must be considered by the reader, regardless of the moral fiber of the person involved. It is simply that much money. Nonetheless, we do not believe such compromise to be inevitable if the decision maker has set up a robust safety culture and accompanying decision support process before it comes time to make the final decision.

[587] Recall that the regulatory approval for equipment has nothing to do with the vehicle's AV capabilities per FMVSS.

follow the SAE J3018 testing safety standard, but even that is rare and has no effect on uncrewed deployment decisions.

For practical purposes, the car companies themselves are deciding whether their vehicle will present acceptable risk to the public. There is little, if any, transparency to other stakeholders. To a large extent this has always been the case for car companies releasing conventional vehicles in the US, especially when it comes to the topic of computer-based system safety. However, the AV situation changes things dramatically.

The technical demands of AV safety are much higher than for traditional vehicles because there is no human driver to intervene (and blame) when something goes wrong. But beyond that, the corporate incentives to get safety right are arguably much weaker in an AV company that is not also a traditional car company. A traditional car company (Original Equipment Manufacturer – OEM) has a lot of reputation and existing product sales to lose if they deploy a car that turns out to be unsafe, as some companies have found out the hard way with conventional vehicles. While imperfect, the threat of brand damage moderates their behavior to a degree. However, a new AV company that has no existing sales has much less to lose.[588] They can see deploying an AV of unknown safety as a gamble that pays off huge or does not. But the worst-case downside for a new AV company is the loss of high-risk venture capital, not the destruction of an existing car manufacturing brand and business, with attendant shareholder lawsuits.

The AV companies have huge amounts of investment and potential return on that investment at stake – easily over a hundred billion dollars in aggregate. They also can have demanding financial backers who want to see scheduled milestones met. Funders and management can put enormous pressure on a design team to hit milestones such as public road demos even when they might not be as safe as they would like, or when they have too high an uncertainty as to safety. This is especially a problem if there are weak safety evaluation processes in place. It is all too easy under pressure to flip a reasonable "demo only if it is safe" discussion to a broken safety culture situation of "demo unless you can prove it is unsafe."[589]

A way to manage the immense pressure to demonstrate functionality and deploy while cutting corners on safety is to put a robust safety support structure in place. This should at least include a high-level head of safety who has credible authority to veto any deployment. Backing that person with an independent safety advisory board who is both technically qualified and incentivized to speak truth to power is even better. It should also include a written safety plan and – most importantly – objective safety deployment criteria that are committed to well in advance of any deployment decision. A

---

[588] One can speculate whether this was a contributing factor to the decision for most OEMs to spin off their AV development to separate arms-length companies with different branding, although there are other reasons for having done so as well.

[589] A decision of this type to override a no-launch engineering decision due to management considerations was a key event in the loss of the Space Shuttle Challenger. See: https://onlineethics.org/cases/telecon-meeting

safety support structure also needs to include a commitment to funders that deployment will happen when it is safe to do so rather than on an arbitrarily selected calendar date. Such a setup still does not guarantee things will work out, but it would be a strong start.

10.4. Other ethical issues for AVs

Summary: There are numerous ethical issues beyond deployment governance that need attention. They include equity, bending the rules, how foreseeable misuse should be managed, and more. This section is a catch-all for some of the conversations that will have to happen before AV technology can be scaled in the real world.

There are other real, very pressing issues for the ethical design and deployment of AVs – none of which are the Trolley Problem.

Readers can likely think of other ethical issues beyond what is discussed here, so this section should be considered the start of a more global conversation rather than a final answer. At the very least, we hope to preempt the Trolley Problem from sucking all the air out of the room for AV ethics discussions as it has happened too often in the past.

10.4.1. Occupant vs. pedestrian safety

The balance between occupant and pedestrian safety has been changing in recent years, with both the number and proportion of fatalities born by pedestrians (and light mobility road users such as bicyclists) increasing.[590] Active and passive safety systems have been making crashes more avoidable and survivable for vehicles and their occupants, but safety improvements for mishaps involving vulnerable road users have not kept pace.

AVs have the potential to accelerate this dangerous trend if care is not taken to do otherwise. Consider a hypothetical (but plausible) outcome: AVs get good at avoiding collisions with other easy-to-detect and easy-to-predict large vehicles, but have trouble detecting and predicting the motions of pedestrians and bicyclists. The deployment case that wins is AV local delivery vans, with lower operational costs driving demand for an increase in vehicle miles. Due to having no occupants, such AVs by definition can only harm people outside the vehicle if they crash. They cannot harm a driver, because there is no driver in the vehicle. In such a world it is quite plausible that pedestrian harm will continue to increase while vehicle occupant harm

---

[590] Road safety in general has been degrading since the start of the COVID-19 pandemic in the US, with the trend much worse than in many other highly developed countries. This has accentuated an increase in vulnerable road user fatalities that had started years earlier. A representative discussion of this issue is Kuntzman 2022: https://usa.streetsblog.org/2022/04/07/road-deaths-rise-again-as-post-pandemic-period-proves-particularly-perilous-to-pedestrians/

decreases, even if the total number of people harmed is reduced. A similar shift in harm could occur for uncrewed AV heavy trucks sharing highways with conventional vehicles.

Spending resources on protecting pedestrians vs. vehicle occupants is difficult for several reasons. The most obvious concern is that vehicle buyers will likely prefer to buy a vehicle that – if forced to choose – will save the occupant (themselves) rather than another road user (a stranger). However, this is a bit of a false dilemma akin to the Trolley Problem in that such situations are both rare and fail to take into account the vastly superior protection afforded occupants. Passengers ensconced in multi-ton vehicles with passive safety features are in a much less vulnerable position than pedestrians and light mobility users to begin with.

More subtle issues are likely to come into play regarding the ability of AVs to avoid putting vulnerable road users at elevated risk. The main issue is cost. Building an AV that has the sensor and processing capability to successfully detect and react to unusual road user presentations and difficult-to-predict behavior can be expected to be more expensive than one that does a poor job at that. And, that cost is born by the vehicle owner, who is not seeing a personal safety benefit from that extra expense. Similarly, installing pedestrian passive safety devices such as pedestrian airbags will be an up-front purchase expense born by all vehicles that does not increase safety for occupants.

Making matters worse, any increase in insurance premium from a somewhat elevated risk of harming pedestrians is paid over the life of the vehicle as part of operating costs. On the other hand, the cost of pedestrian protection is built into the up-front vehicle purchase price. There might not even be any insurance savings if repair costs for pedestrian protection sensors and airbags are high due to damage from other, non-pedestrian crashes. So it is more expensive up front to install the protection even if there is longer term reduction in the cost of risk (lower insurance payments).

While a situation in which vulnerable road user harm increases is not guaranteed to happen, there are economic headwinds to a good outcome here.

10.4.2. Risk transfer and demographic groups

Even if the overall risk of deploying an AV is acceptable, it is possible that the risk for some portions of the public road user demographic profile will get worse. This was discussed in the context of baseline risks in section 5.2.1 in terms of characteristics of the people themselves. But it also applies to situations and other identifiable clusters of loss events as well.

Risk transfer between groups can occur if one group experiences a reduction in risk while another group experiences an increase in risk. Whether the risk transfer is intentional or not is a bit beside the point. If some identifiable group has a higher risk from AVs than from human-driven vehicles, eventually that tendency will be discovered and portrayed as a way in which AVs are unacceptable.

The idea is that if some situations have increased risk for an AV compared to a human driver, risk transfer might be taking place. A few illustrative examples include:

- Harm to emergency responders on highways[591]
- Harm to occupants of broken-down vehicles, especially if occupants are attempting roadside repairs (this is a reason why even heavy trucks that operate on non-pedestrian highways will need to deal with pedestrians in a limited fashion)
- Harm to pedestrians under-represented in training data that are not detected accurately due to skin coloration, clothing style, or other characteristics
- Harm to people with readily identifiable demographic characteristics that exceeds harm to other groups such as children or the elderly
- Harm to users of mobility assistance devices
- Harm to users of light mobility devices
- Harm to pedestrians crossing the street in other than marked crosswalks
- Harm to pedestrians in especially high-risk situations due to AV failing to exercise more caution than otherwise required by road markings, such as chaotic pedestrian scenes near a large social event, busy playground or an emergency response scene
- Harm to occupants of unusual vehicle configurations such as farm equipment, construction equipment, or horse-drawn vehicles being operated on public roadways
- Harm to road users in economically disadvantaged areas due to, for example, emphasizing such areas for road testing

The general idea with risk transfer is that there is some type of object class or situation that the AV is less proficient at handling safely. That weakness in turn exposes people involved to an elevated level of risk compared to more typical object classes or situations. Even though an argument might be made that overall risk presented by the AV is lower, if there are identifiable patterns in poor AV behavior, those will be seen as a safety problem, better average risk notwithstanding.

A purely utilitarian approach might try to discount such issues in light of improved average safety. However, consider a purely hypothetical situation to illustrate the problem: what if the total number of fatalities is improved by a factor of 100 compared to human-driven vehicles, but every single fatality is a child crossing in a marked school zone crosswalk? Or what if the number of pedestrian fatalities goes down dramatically for people with some colors of skin, but does not improve at all for people with other skin tones? Imagine

---

[591] Tesla Autopilot crashes at emergency responder scenes are the subject of a NHTSA investigation, singling out the possibility of elevated risk for this specific type of crash.
See: https://static.nhtsa.gov/odi/inv/2021/INOA-PE21020-1893.PDF

the public response to a company saying they saw no need to address such problems because their AV was already the safest car on the road.

While these specific examples should not be allowed to happen and are purely hypothetical, they point out the potential issues with a marked increase in risk for some road users even if overall safety is improved compared to human drivers.

10.4.3. Bending the rules and breaking the law

Inevitably there will be pressure on AVs to bend the rules a bit, potentially breaking some traffic laws or abusing gray areas of driving courtesy and conventions. After all, who wants to be stuck in an AV doing exactly 55 mph when human-driven vehicles are blasting past at higher speeds, getting their passengers to their destinations more quickly?[592]

10.4.3.1. Ambiguities and doing the right thing

Some regulatory practices reward rule-breaking, such as the infamous 85% rule: if more than 15% of traffic exceeds the speed limit, the relevant authority is incentivized to raise the speed limit to match what is happening regardless of potential safety.[593] At least in principle, if AVs exceed 15% of the traffic on a particular road, they can collude to set whatever speed limit they want.

Add to the situation that regulations are designed to be interpreted and enforced by people who are judged by a standard of reasonable behavior, and are customarily permitted to break or bend rules if doing so makes sense. Typically, it is OK to bend a rule if doing so keeps traffic moving in an unusual situation as long as doing so is not unreasonably dangerous. As a simple example consider a two-lane road with a no passing centerline ("double yellow" painted centerlines on many roads). If a tree falls down and completely blocks one direction, most drivers would consider it reasonable to cross into the opposing traffic lane to get past the tree so long as there is no oncoming traffic. More aggressive drivers might even push their way into opposing traffic on a busy but low-speed road to force an alternation to keep traffic flowing in both directions. As long as these procedures are done in a reasonable way such behavior is pretty normal. However, someone exercising poor judgment in breaking the centerline traffic rule might well be held responsible for a crash due to having crossed the centerline in an unreasonable way. The catch here is that "reasonable" is pretty subjective and not well suited to representation as a machine interpretable behavioral rule.

---

[592] This is a long-standing cultural sore spot.
See: https://en.wikipedia.org/wiki/I_Can't_Drive_55
[593] This is codified in the US Federal Highway Administration's Manual on Uniform Traffic Control Devices as the 85th percentile rule.
See Miller 2017: https://usa.streetsblog.org/2017/07/27/ntsb-speed-kills-and-were-not-doing-enough-to-stop-it/

A particular challenge to traffic rules designed for human drivers is that rules are sometimes vague and do not specifically enumerate all possible exceptions. Rather, the rules and their enforcement rely heavily upon reasonable behavior by drivers and reasonable enforcement by police and the court system. "Do The Right Thing" weighs heavily in dealing with ambiguous traffic rule situations. The catch is that the computers in AVs have no way to reason about what "The Right Thing" might be in a novel situation for which they have no specific guidance.

10.4.3.2. The Tesla FSD rolling stop recall

Other traffic rule violations are done less of necessity and more due to a sense of urgency combined with erosion of respect for rule following. A classic example of scofflaw behavior is rolling through stop signs rather than coming to a full and complete stop at a stop sign before proceeding. The frequency and aggressiveness of this driving technique vary by driver and location, with some drivers barely slowing down if they think an intersection is clear. However, to be clear, such drivers can be and often are given traffic citations by police for breaking the law. Such drivers are in a difficult position to defend their actions if they end up in a crash because they were violating an important traffic law. Nonetheless, many human drivers defend rolling stops because they believe them to be safe if performed with care and see them as an accepted road behavior custom.

The question is what AVs should do. Possibly they should be allowed to bend ambiguous traffic rules in situations that would otherwise preclude them from making progress so long as they accept full responsibility for the consequences of their actions.[594] But what if AVs break road rules not out of practical necessity, but merely for convenience to slightly speed up trips? Where is the line drawn between getting a little more speed vs. bending rules to avoid a major impairment of functionality? And what does it mean for an AV to take responsibility for its actions in bending or breaking rules?

Tesla's public road testing of their so-called Full Self Driving (FSD) beta software put this question to the test. Some versions of the FSD beta feature were intentionally programmed to perform rolling stops for a specific set of conditions at all-way stop sign intersections. These would happen if the vehicle thought the intersection was clear and if any operational mode but the most timid behavior profile for FSD had been selected. Users were told that "rolling stops" would be enabled but were not informed of the decision criteria or behavioral parameters for such behavior at the time of making the profile choice.[595] Once this became widely known, NHTSA discovered that rolling stops were indeed programmed to occur at stop signs with speeds up

---

[594] This leaves open exactly who would be accountable. If the answer is that no person will be held accountable, rule-bending should not be permitted.

[595] Rolling stops at sidewalks and similar situations are legal in some places, but not rolling stops at actual stop signs. Social media posts at the time indicated confusion on this point and there was no accurate public statement of vehicle behavior available at the time.

to 9 kph/5.6 mph involving no slowing down nor stop if the vehicle sensed a low-speed (30 mph or less) intersection was clear. NHTSA required Tesla to perform a safety recall to disable the feature.[596]

Proponents of the FSD rolling stop feature tended to argue that human drivers commonly performed rolling stops (which was said to be prevalent in California where many Tesla owners live) and that the vehicle only did it at empty intersections. However, the fact remained that software with control over vehicle behavior had intentionally been programmed to break a traffic rule when doing so was not required to avoid halting progress on a trip. Even the owners were unaware of the extent of the behavior involved until the recall information was posted, so they did not make an informed consent to whatever personal and legal risks they were taking by enabling the behavior.

We believe that the Tesla decision to build rolling stops into FSD beta was highly problematic for many reasons:

- The behavior was illegal, and apparently added as part of a break the rules now and ask forgiveness later strategy. Ignoring the law until you get caught is untrustworthy behavior. Tesla could have and should have worked this out with NHTSA in advance, and state regulators if and as required. Such behavior is not required to deal with exceptional road conditions, but rather is purely for customer convenience. Tesla could have lobbied for regulatory change if needed. Instead, Tesla unilaterally decided to deploy illegal driving behavior without asking for permission.

- Even if this were justifiable rule-bending (which it was not) any rule-bending behavior needs to adjust to local conditions and context to be acceptable, which was not done here. Local customs are relevant, but so are immediate conditions that affect risk. Potentially relevant risk factors such as whether the intersection was near a school or playground with elevated risk of undetected pedestrians in an intersection was not taken into account.

- The vehicles involved are in "beta test" and at the time were clearly nowhere near having a fully competent autonomous driving feature. Any statement that FSD would proceed only when conditions are clear ignores the severe issue of the system not having an assured ability to judge when the road is clear. Moreover, given contemporaneous videos of owners letting their FSD system run through stop signs and even red traffic lights at higher speeds without stopping, it was clear that those same drivers could not be counted on to intervene accurately via purely passive monitoring in case of vehicle automation malfunction. That means that even if rolling stops were OK (they are not), the vehicle should not proceed until the driver could signal affirmative confirmation to the vehicle that the intersection is clear.

- The top end of 9 kph of speed permitted for rolling stops is jogging speed, which is more like a yield sign than a stop sign. It is far different

---

[596]Source: NHTSA Part 573 Safety Recall Report 22V-037
https://static.nhtsa.gov/odi/rcl/2022/RCLRPT-22V037-4462.PDF

than some ultra-slow 1 kph crawl that might be portrayed as a not-quite-complete stop, but perhaps close enough compromise.

- Arguing that AVs will be safer because they will not make bad human driver choices, and then emulating human drivers who make a bad choice by bending traffic rules, is not a particularly convincing approach to building trust.[597]
- Rolling stop traffic rule violations differ in kind from crossing a centerline to go around a disabled vehicle. Shaving a few seconds off a trip by not stopping does not justify breaking traffic laws. There is no pressing mission completion issue as there is for a complete lane obstruction.
- Saying "people break that law too" is whataboutism.[598] There is a huge difference between setting a law-breaking policy as an enduring operational mode as was done in FSD versus instance-by-instance human choices to direct a machine to violate the speed limit.
- The approach degrades human agency in a decision that could in principle result in criminal justice consequences. Human drivers are directly involved in evaluating the context while weighing risks as they make such decisions, whereas FSD simply took a blanket approach of violating a traffic law in a set circumstance regardless of the larger context. Saying that the human driver remained in charge ignores the issue of automation complacency and the lack of involvement of the human driver bearing responsibility at the moment of breaking a traffic law.
- NHTSA has better things to do with its limited resources than play Whac-a-mole[599] with Tesla. Tesla can flout rules faster than NHTSA has resources to enforce them, making this part of a larger ethically problematic pattern of Tesla behavior. This appears to be just one incident in a larger campaign of that sort by Tesla.[600]

Perhaps the most problematic ethical issue with the Tesla rolling stop fiasco is that the policy removed agency from the human driver in deciding when to break the law. Tesla has made it exceedingly clear that they intend to make the driver completely responsible for anything bad that happens during FSD operation. Nonetheless, they programmed in relatively opaque law breaking behavior. If a Tesla had hit or killed a pedestrian in such a

---

[597] See also section 4.10.1. While Tesla and its supporters argue that FSD beta is an SAE Level 2 driver assistance to regulators when it is expedient to do so, in reality it is a test platform for full automation, which makes it a Level 3 or 4 AV. See: https://www.jurist.org/commentary/2021/09/william-widen-philip-koopman-autonomous-vehicles/

[598] See: https://en.wikipedia.org/wiki/Whataboutism

[599] See: https://en.wikipedia.org/wiki/Whac-A-Mole

[600] For example, Tesla had previously enabled video game play while driving on the main driver console display. https://www.npr.org/2022/02/01/1077274384/tesla-recalls-autos-over-software-that-allows-them-to-roll-through-stop-signs

circumstance the driver could easily have found themself facing criminal charges for a fatality due to reckless driving of a sort they had no way of really knowing the vehicle would perform.

Any time an AV behavior breaks a traffic law it is essential that the responsible party make an explicit decision with full awareness of the context, risks, and benefits involved. If the driver is responsible for safety, that should be the driver explicitly commanding such behavior at the time it is performed. If it is not the driver who is responsible, then some legal framework should be provided to hold someone else with both responsibility and authority over having broken the traffic law accountable if harm results from the decision to perform a law-breaking action.

At a higher level, it is clear that something needs to be done about determining how AVs can and should be given flexibility to "Do The Right Thing" when interpreting traffic laws designed to be applied and enforced by humans with a degree of discretion. This should be worked out in a dialog between AV designers and regulators rather than treated as a unilateral exercise in seeing what an AV design team can get away with before regulators happen to notice and intervene.

10.4.4. Passenger overrides and urgent egress

In any automated system there will be times when an occupant wants to override the automation, and especially when they want to exit a moving automated vehicle. Reasons might include: wanting to re-open transit vehicle doors if a passenger was unable to exit in time at their stop; an attack of claustrophobia; wanting to get away from another passenger due to personal safety concerns; or even needing to escape a cabin fire. Some egress requests might constitute misuse or abuse, such as stopping a vehicle to intentionally block traffic, or intentionally accessing an off-limits area such as a bridge with no pedestrian infrastructure.

Creating a complete list of all possible motivations is difficult, and weighing the merits of all such egress attempts in advance seems intractable. Nonetheless, there are times when a passenger desire to exit a moving vehicle should be honored, although the vehicle should likely at least stop before permitting an exit.

In still other situations passengers might want to force an otherwise stopped vehicle to move. One reason might be fear for personal safety if threatened by malicious actors while stopped at a traffic light. Another reason might be overriding a police stop if the vehicle occupant suspects a stopping officer is instead a criminal imposter, at least until legitimacy of the police stop can be confirmed via contact with an emergency dispatcher.[601]

Another special situation is one in which a passenger has a compelling reason to order an AV to operate outside its ODD or with degraded equipment in an emergency, even if doing so will result in a reduced safety

---

[601] Yes, this is a thing. Report of an accused police imposter pulling over a van full of legitimate police detectives: https://www.youtube.com/watch?v=ogGBwrrkKY4

margin. For example, an AV might be programmed not to drive through heavy smoke, but doing so might be required to escape a burning town in a wildfire situation. The AV occupant might want to take the chance of driving rather than remaining in the burning town.[602]

Human drivers have the authority to deal with these situations so long as they are willing to accept the responsibility. Do you start driving when someone is trying to forcibly break into your car at a traffic light even if you might injure that malicious actor by doing so? The choice – and responsibility for consequences – falls upon the person driving a manually driven car.

The question is: to what degree should an AV support operator overrides of safety-relevant behaviors? A complication is that there might not be a responsible individual in a vehicle to exercise control. What if a passenger is allowed to override some behaviors of the vehicle, but that passenger is impaired, or not capable of exercising mature judgment? Should an 8 year old riding solo be able to command vehicle safety overrides?[603]

Answers as to how much control a passenger should have over AV operation will depend on how stringent qualifications are for a passenger to be capable of mature decision making. It is easy to say there must be one qualified driver if there are any passengers in an AV and that manual controls must be available if needed. However, requiring a qualified driver undermines the potential benefits that AVs might provide for those who are not capable of driving or should not be driving at a particular time.

If other than unimpaired licensed drivers are permitted to override AV behaviors, there will be difficult tradeoffs as to what overrides might be permitted. Likely an 8 year old child should not be permitted to exit a school vehicle in the middle of a highway to avoid going to school. On the other hand, a 14 year old[604] might be considered mature enough to demand an emergency stop if the vehicle tries to drive into flood waters, or initiate an emergency exit with their younger sibling if the cabin fills with smoke from a vehicle battery fire.

Even if a passenger is an adult licensed to drive, should that adult be permitted to override vehicle behavior if drunk or otherwise impaired? If not, should the vehicle disable override capability if the passenger is drunk? Or should it be illegal to enter an AV with override capability when drunk?

---

[602] This consideration has become especially relevant for residents of California. See: https://www.insideedition.com/how-drive-through-fire-48422

[603] One might say that no 8 year old should ride in an AV solo. But if that is the case, what exactly is the cut-off age? Some public high school systems rely on public mass transit instead of dedicated school buses, so any AV public transit vehicle will have under-age ridership. Is training or perhaps even a "rider license" required to ride in an AV and use the override controls? This topic gets complex quickly.

[604] Some states issue driver licenses to 14 year-olds in special cases. Would such a driver license be required in this case?
See: https://www.thedrive.com/news/39184/americas-rarest-drivers-license-lets-14-year-olds-hit-the-road-legally

While it can be an interesting exercise to conjure extreme situations, the issue of passenger overrides and egress can also be as simple as a passenger saying "I want to get out now" when the vehicle is stopped at a red traffic light but not at the end of the scheduled trip. Should the passenger be able to unlock doors and exit? Or should the passenger be kept locked inside the vehicle until the end of the trip? Should there be a workaround available such as changing the destination? If so, should the passenger have permission to do this if some authority figure such as a parent input the original destination? Where should the threshold be drawn at which such a passenger request is denied both in context (speeding down a highway vs. stopped) or passenger maturity (a passenger one day before turning 18 years old but with no driver's license vs. grade school age child)?

There is the possibility that remote operators will need to mediate requests for overriding AV behavior either routinely or if there is doubt as to the competence of passengers to make reasonable decisions. However, any such remote operators can be expensive, will have problems scaling, and might result in wait times long enough to impair safety by delaying decisions in urgent situations.[605]

For AVs to be deployed at scale, designers will need to decide how much authority passengers have to override vehicle behavior, and whether emergency manual vehicle controls will be required even in vehicles that are intended to be completely automated. There will be no perfect policy choice, but not setting a consistent policy is also a policy choice.

10.4.5. Foreseeable misuse and abuse

A tricky part of setting and measuring safety expectations is whether and how to account for incidents of abuse and foreseeable misuse.

While it is easy to just blame people for being stupid when something bad happens, digging a bit deeper into the situation can often reveal that the situation was not so clear-cut. Moreover, even when people are acting in ways that seem to be irresponsible, attempting to deny or outlaw human nature is counterproductive to achieving safety in the real world.

AVs and the operational systems they are part of should be designed to account for likely patterns of misuse and abuse. Doing so is not straightforward, and will involve dealing with a moving target in terms of behavioral issues and consequences for passengers and other road users. However, ignoring the inevitability of foreseeable abuse and misuse will simply lead to loss events that could have been avoided and accompanying

---

[605] The usual solution proposed is remote customer service operators that intervene when needed. Those proposing that passengers need have no control because remote operators can solve all safety problems need to spend more time waiting in customer service phone waiting queues. An additional consideration is the likely disruption to emergency response services during a natural disaster that will also require simultaneous attention to numerous AV passenger distress situations. New Year's Eve screening of requests from potentially drunk passengers will also be challenging.

reputational tarnish for AV technology and the companies who make them. In the final analysis it is the number of crashes that will matter to safety outcomes, not the reasons or blames attached to those crashes.

Dealing comprehensively with this topic would likely require a book of its own due to the complexities of human behavior and the likely adversarial nature between people incentivized to abuse or misuse an AV and any countermeasures developed in response. Countermeasures to misuse and abuse likely require broad social and legal mechanisms in addition to technical measures. The mix of such approaches must be sufficient to mitigate misuse and abuse to sustainable levels for overall safety.

Here are some example problematic scenarios that come to mind. Many of them have to do with the lack of a human driver being available to exercise supervision over the vehicle state, passengers, cargo, and operations:

- Failure of AV passengers to perform required safety hygiene practices such as buckling seat belts, not extending body parts through open vehicle windows, or loading more people than the vehicle is configured to handle.[606]

- Transporting hazardous cargo without proper safety precautions, including improperly secured cargo that breaks loose mid-trip and hazardous liquids in open containers.

- Dangerous activation of any vehicle control behavioral overrides.

- Abusive behavior by other road users such as aggressive pedestrians or aggressive operators of other vehicles.

- Attempting to operate the AV outside its intended ODD or with impaired equipment in a way that presents unreasonable risk.[607]

- Use of "cheat codes" or secret operational modes to override AV safety mechanisms such as by entering factory access passwords leaked onto the Internet.[608]

For many (or perhaps all) of the scenarios just described some will simply say "people shouldn't do that" with an accompanying escalation of responses along the lines of: increased warning intensity, education, more warnings, more education, public shaming, statements that the driver knew the risks (questionable in general, but not applicable to other road users who did not choose to board the AV), and an argument that any fatalities amount to Darwinian selection in action.[609] Another reaction might be "human drivers make those mistakes too" which might be true, but is not a productive approach to improving AV safety, especially in situations in which there is

---

[606] See: https://guinnessworldrecords.com/world-records/most-people-crammed-into-an-old-vw-beetle/

[607] There is an inherent tension between this concern and the desire to let responsible passengers override AV safety settings in extenuating circumstances.

[608] Also a thing. For a non-AV automotive example, See:
https://www.motortrend.com/reviews/2022-rivian-r1t-secret-software-mode-yearlong-review/

[609] See the Darwin Awards: https://darwinawards.com/darwin/

not even a nominally responsible adult involved as there would be in a human-driven vehicle. There are also legal dimensions to this problem such as where the line is drawn between incorrect occupant actions and product defects that are beyond the scope of our discussion.

History shows us that warnings and education have very limited ability to stop misuse and abuse, especially when there are short-term incentivizes to misuse equipment such as shorter travel time or an exhilarating ride. And there is the counterpoint that responsible adults should be allowed to make their own choices – with the caveats that not every AV rider will qualify as a fully responsible adult, and other road user crash victims had no say making the relevant risky choice.

If AVs are to deliver on their promise of improved road safety, more will need to be done about abuse and misuse beyond reiterating warnings and blaming people for being "stupid." It is likely that a combination of approaches will be required. However, failing to respond to obvious trends in avoidable harm will simply ensure that the harm continues.

10.4.6. Fatalities vs. time to market

Arguments that insurance and related risk management approaches bestow safety are debunked in sections 4.6.3 and 9.2.1. Here we return to that topic with an emphasis more directly on ethics.

Arguing that financial risk management incentives will necessarily drive safety ignores at least two real-world pressures on the behavior of AV companies.

The first issue is a fundamental difference between reducing harm and optimizing profits. Assume for the moment that a purely financial point of view is taken for the cost of harm (for example USD $12 million per human life[610]). But the cost of development is far from free. Assume you are spending USD $2 million per day on development,[611] and will not see any profits until the day you are able to deploy. Now set up a hypothetical situation in which you spend money on engineering to improve safety with the expectation of reducing harm, but doing so costs engineering effort and increases time to deployment.

The hypothetical situation is that you are less than a year away from deployment, and cash is tight. You hope to deploy without needing another investment round. Consider which hypothetical scenario you choose, with

---

[610] In 2021 the US Department of Transportation set the valuation of a statistical life at $11.8M. See: https://www.transportation.gov/office-policy/transportation-policy/revised-departmental-guidance-on-valuation-of-a-statistical-life-in-economic-analysis

In practice settlements and court awards in some states might well be less.

[611] This is cheaper than some such efforts. In the second quarter of 2022, the Cruise autonomous vehicle program was costing about $5.5 million per day. See: https://carbuzz.com/news/gm-loses-a-staggering-5-5-million-per-day-on-robotaxis

deaths spanning both the road testing program and an initial deployment period:

- Option 1: Expected deaths = 1 ; Engineering development 200 days
  - Cost = $400 million labor + $12 million harm = $412 million
- Option 2: Expected deaths = 4 ; Engineering development 100 days
  - Cost = $200 million labor + $48 million harm = $248 million

From a purely financial point of view, Option #2 is a clear winner. Yes, insurance will be four times more expensive for that option (assuming insurance cost ultimately tracks the payouts for harm), but from a strictly financial point of view for the company in this case killing extra people is dramatically more profitable. Whether option #2 is ethically viable might be largely driven by whether the number of deaths for similar exposure for human-driven vehicles would be higher or lower than 4 within the total time period considered, among other considerations.[612]

The real-world analysis is more complex, and must address the time value of money, the value of being faster to market, and so on. But those effects merely accentuate the pressure to take the quicker path that is likely to do more harm. The issue is the absence of specific consideration of acceptable limits on harm regardless of the monetary angle.

The factor driving potential ethical concerns is that the scale of the money involved with development costs and lost time to market is high compared to the assigned value of a human life. This dynamic is one reason why there needs to be a specific effort on safety, and why safety regulatory agencies need to exist, especially in industries in which the profit potential for cutting corners on safety far exceeds the economic cost of fatalities. The temptation to cut corners on safety engineering is often just too high to get a good outcome without independent checks and balances.[613]

Another issue is that the hypothetical example assumes purely rational actions optimized for the overall financial good of the company by the AV company management. While there are motivations and pressures to act this way, there are also motivations to act in other ways that are likely to be suboptimal (but perhaps not outright neglectful) with regard to company objectives. Factors such as pursuing bragging rights for being the first to

---

[612] We emphasize that these numbers are completely hypothetical, with a purpose of illustrating in a concrete way that the cost of killing someone is comparatively cheap in light of the cost of running an AV development program. That presents a concerning moral hazard for decision makers who are obligated to achieve the largest financial return possible to investors. While there is theoretical downside from a newsworthy crash, in practice we have seen it is common for companies to neglect reputational risk when making return on investment decisions on crashes they subjectively think won't happen.

[613] A poster child for cost-cutting on safety engineering that went wrong is the total loss of the Petrobras P-36 oil rig. See: https://sma.nasa.gov/docs/default-source/safety-messages/safetymessage-2008-10-01-lossofpetrobrasp36-vits.pdf

deploy, winning a race against competitors, chasing personal glory in news headlines, and the satisfaction of achieving a personal vision to deploy AVs can motivate risk taking beyond what would be prudent from a purely risk management point of view.

For AVs the insurance picture is further muddled by the effects of the insurance market itself. While the deployed AV fleets are small, insurance companies are incentivized to artificially lower insurance premiums as a loss leader to obtain market share, further reducing the financial pressure on companies to invest in safety.

10.4.7. Blaming the computer

A technique being used by the AV industry in pursuing state regulation is attempting to blame the computer for any crashes by saying that the Automated Driving System (the computer) is considered to be the driver of any AV operating on public roads. That way there is no person at fault for any harm to road users. Yes, really, that is what is going on.[614]

The general AV industry tactic when lobbying for such rules is to argue that when fully automated driving is engaged the "driver" is the driving computer (the ADS). Any remote safety supervisor is just there to lend a hand. In some states a remote human support team member need not have an appropriate driver license, because it is said that the ADS that is the driver. Superficially this seems to make sense. After all, if you are a passenger who has paid for a retail robotaxi ride and the AV breaks a traffic law due to some flaw in the design, you as the passenger should not be the one to receive a ticket or go to jail.

But the tricky bit is that ADS computers are not afforded the legal status of being a "person" – nor should they be.[615] Corporations are held to be fictitious people in some legal circumstances, but a piece of equipment itself is not even a fictitious person.[616]

If a software defect or improper machine learning training procedures result in AV behavior that would count as criminally reckless driving if a human were driving, what happens for an AV? Perhaps nothing. If the ADS is the "driver" then there is nobody to put on trial or throw into jail. If you take away the driver's license for the ADS, does it get its license back with the next software update?[617] Where are the repercussions for an ADS being a bad actor? Where are the consequences?

---

[614] For a compilation of US state laws and legislative hearing materials see:
https://safeautonomy.blogspot.com/2022/02/kansas-av-regulation-bill-hearings.html

[615] Despite occasional hype to the contrary, machine learning-based systems are nowhere near achieving sentience, let alone being reasonably qualified to be a "person."

[616] I am not a lawyer (IANAL/TINLA), so this is a lay understanding of the rules that apply and nothing in this book should be considered as legal advice.

[617] In several states an ADS is automatically granted a driver's license even though it is not a person. It might not even be possible to take that license away.

Blaming the ADS computer for a bad outcome removes a substantial amount of deterrence due to negative consequences because the ADS does not fear being harmed, destroyed, locked up in jail, fined, or having its driver's license revoked. It does not feel anything at all.

A related tactic is to blame the "operator" or "owner" for any crash. In the early days of AV technology these roles tended to be either the technology developer or a support contractor, but that will change over time. Contractors perform testing operations for AV developers. Individual vehicle owners are operators for some AV technology road tests. Other AV operators might work through a transportation network service. Someone might buy an AV in the manner of a rental condo and let it run as a robotaxi while they sleep.

Imagine an arrangement in which an investor buys a share in a group of robotaxis as might be done for a timeshare condo. A coordinator lines up independent contractors to manage investment money, negotiate vehicle purchases, arrange maintenance contracts, and participate in a ride-hailing network. Each AV is the sole asset of a series LLC to act as a liability firewall between vehicles. The initial investor later sells their partial ownership shares to an investment bank. The investment bank puts those shares into a basket of AV ownership shares. Various municipal retirement funds buy shares of the basket. At this point, who owns the AV has gotten pretty complicated, and there is no substantive accountability link between the AV "owner" and its operation beyond the value of the shares.

Then a change to the underlying vehicle (which was not sold as an AV platform originally, but rather was adapted by an upfitter contractor) impairs functionality of the aftermarket add-on ADS manufactured by a company that is no longer in business. If there is a crash who is the "operator?" Who is the "owner?" Who should pay compensation for any harm done by the AV? If the resultant ADS behavior qualifies as criminally negligent reckless driving, who should go to jail? If the answer is that nobody goes to jail and that only the state minimum insurance of, say, $25K pays out, what is the incentive to ensure that such an arrangement is acceptably safe so long as the insurance is affordable compared to the profits being made?

While the usual reply to concerns about accountability is that insurance will take care of things, recall that we have taken some passes at discussing insurance and risk management can be insufficient incentive to ensure acceptable safety, especially when it only meets a low state minimum insurance requirement[618] originally set for human drivers that have skin in the game for any crashes.

---

[618] IIHS/HLDI keeps a list of autonomous vehicle laws including required insurance minimums. The $1M to $5M numbers fall short of the $12M statistical value of human life, and are typically per incident (so multiple victims split that maximum). In other states the normal state insurance requirement can apply, which can be something like a maximum of $50,000 per incident and might permit self-insurance by the AV company, such as is the case in Kansas: https://insurance.kansas.gov/auto-insurance/ This insurance maximum payout requirement is less than the cost of a typical AV. In practice it might be the case that victims are limited to recovering

10.4.8. The blame game

The blame game is played by AV companies when they find some reason – any reason will do – for an AV crash that is not the fault of the AV itself. As discussed in section 10.2, candidates for blame include the safety driver, drivers of other vehicles, jaywalking pedestrians, and possibly unexpected conditions. A cousin of the blame game is claiming that the AV acted in a lawful manner even if doing so was clearly inappropriate for the situation. At a deeper level, the blame game is an extension of the tactic of blaming human drivers for being imperfect to deflect attention away from operational flaws with AVs.

The reality is that placing blame does not make streets safer. Driving involves a continual stream of social interactions with other drivers in which, hopefully, most drivers follow most of the rules most of the time. Importantly, drivers are expected to compensate for mistakes and any lack of rule following by other drivers to the degree they can.[619]

For every AV crash in which the AV design team insists some other party should be blamed, an essential follow-up question is whether the AV could have done something to avoid the crash, even if that something is not strictly required by the rules of the road. Any generally useful response that might have avoided the crash should be added to the AV behavioral repertoire even if not strictly required by law.

As a hypothetical example, when encountering a wrong-way driver it is likely better for an AV to pull to the side of the road than to continue driving in-lane until impact. This is the case even though the AV has right of way, and might be fully justified by the rules of the road in continuing to drive in its lane right into the impending crash. At worst, pulling to the side of the road reduces the relative impact speed. At best an impact is avoided as the other vehicle continues driving the wrong way in the travel lane. And who knows – it is possible that the AV itself was the vehicle going in the wrong direction due to a mapping error or other issue.[620] Blaming the other vehicle for wrong-way driving post-crash provides cold comfort to the families of the victims.

At a higher level, blame is irrelevant for determining AV safety. The crash rate is what it is, regardless of blame. Consider an AV that has twice as many crashes as human-driven vehicles, but would theoretically be able to prove in a court of law that every single crash was someone else's fault. Such a perfectly blameless vehicle would nonetheless have a track record of being

---

insurance plus the scrap value of whatever is left of the AV after a crash, with everyone else being judgement-proof.

[619] As an example, pedestrians are not supposed to cross mid-block, but if they do so vehicles have an obligation to make best efforts to stop to avoid a collision. In states with this rule an AV that does not make a reasonable attempt to stop to avoid hitting a jaywalking pedestrian is failing to abide by the rules of the road.

[620] Yes, AV tests traveling the wrong way is a thing. See: https://qz.com/798092/a-self-driving-uber-car-went-the-wrong-way-on-a-one-way-street-in-pittsburgh/

twice as dangerous as a human-driven vehicle. That type of approach should not be how AV designers claim that they are safe.

10.4.9. Harm now, benefits later

It is common to see utilitarian arguments to the effect that some deaths early on from AVs are a regrettable but necessary price to pay for eventual safety benefits later. This is another spin on the argument that delaying AVs is tantamount to murder discussed in section 4.10.10, and a cousin of the idea that testing deaths are regrettable necessity discussed in section 4.10.13. Those types of arguments tend to be supported by a variety of tricks that are both rhetorically and statistically invalid.

At this point in the book, we will avoid rehashing these discussions and simply point out that a significant ethical issue hinges on the lack of proof that AVs will ever be safer than human drivers with currently available technology. It is unknown how long it will take to be safer than human drivers – if ever.

If society collectively determines that it is OK to sacrifice randomly unlucky road users at the alter of AV development, with a harm now, benefits later rationale, so be it. However, that situation should be (a) communicated clearly to all stakeholders rather than hidden behind a wall of safety theater, (b) involve all relevant stakeholders, including the voices of potential victims, and (c) be done within a framework of ethical regulatory approaches as discussed in section 10.6.

This does not mean we should abandon hope that AVs will make roads safer. Hope springs eternal and is justifiable. However, intentionally sacrificing lives now (even if they are just statistically expected lives) for the aspirational hope of possible lives saved in the future is highly problematic on an ethical basis, because we are just guessing as to whether lives will ever be saved with the currently available or near-term expected technology.

10.4.10. Transportation system interactions

Indirect negative safety consequences might be associated with a large-scale deployment of AVs. AVs might benefit society if they can, for example, provide reliable first and last mile service linked to mass transit.

However, there is reason to believe that AVs, and in particular single-passenger lower-cost AVs, might end up as replacements for mass transit. In those cases an AV that is safer than a human driver might still increase overall transportation harm if it displaces the use of even safer transportation modes such as buses and rail.[621] If AVs cost less than crewed hired vehicles, they might serve as a replacement for mass transit by those for whom the incremental cost of a robotaxi is affordable compared to a mass transit fare. That in turn could lead to reductions in mass transit service due to decreased

---

[621] See Schmitt 2014: https://usa.streetsblog.org/2014/12/19/heres-how-much-safer-transit-is-compared-to-driving/

demand and a spiral of less safe, more congested roadways. There is every reason to believe that simply replacing rideshare human drivers with computers will only exacerbate existing rideshare transit problems.[622]

The societal safety implications of an ill-considered AV technology deployment can go much further than per-mile fatality rates for the AVs themselves. At worst, they might significantly increase overall transportation fatalities while degrading the viability of mass transit by stealing ridership. A fleet of AVs that is somewhat safer per mile could increase total harm if miles travelled in AVs increase dramatically due to more convenient, cheaper vehicle service.[623] Managing that issue will require an enlightened overall transit policy that goes far beyond per-mile AV safety.

A related topic is that there are other ways to improve road safety that do not involve AVs. It is possible that the tremendous resources poured into AV development could improve transportation safety by being deployed in other ways. However, to the degree that AV investment is done by private organizations, how they invest is their business. The ethical consideration here is to avoid having government transportation infrastructure money chasing AV investments in the name of safety if government investment in other alternatives might provide higher safety benefits in the public interest.[624]

10.5. The effect of AV company business model

Summary: The business model and exit plan for an AV company can powerfully incentivize behavior that is at odds with public safety and transparency. This is probably not news regarding any private company, but it is especially a problem for AV safety.

The business model of the AV development company will influence how safety plays a role, for better or worse.

An AV developer with a plan to develop, deploy, and long-term sustain their technology should be incentivized to reach at least some level of safety subject to all the ethical issues discussed already in this chapter. If they do not, they will probably not have a viable long-term business. Arguments for a light regulatory touch often make this argument that companies will act in

---

[622] See Wilson 2020: https://usa.streetsblog.org/2020/03/02/the-broken-promises-of-the-ride-share-revolution/

[623] Consider a hypothetical situation in which total vehicle miles doubled due to increased ease and comfort of travel in AVs. If AVs were 10% safer than human vehicles per mile, that would still increase total fatalities by a factor of 1.8 because of the increased miles. It is difficult to know how this will really work out. The point is that such effects on net transportation harm might be significant even with AVs that are safer than human-driven vehicles.

[624] The National Safety Council has started an activity to understand this topic. See: https://www.nsc.org/road/future-of-mobility

their own long-term best interest. But what if the business incentive model is optimized for something shorter than the "long-term" outcomes?

Short-term aspects of the business objectives and the business structure itself can add pressure that might tend to erode any commitment to acceptable safety. Factors include at least the following, several of which can interact with each other:

- Accepting money from traditional venture capital sources can commit a company to a five-year timeline to produce products. Thus far we have seen that five-year timelines are far too aggressive to develop and deploy an AV at scale. Re-planning and raising more funding can lengthen the timeline, but there remains risk that funding incentivizes aggressive milestones to show increased functionality and, in particular, remove safety drivers rather than core efforts on safety. Some companies will likely be better at resisting this pressure than others.

- A business exit plan of an Initial Public Offering (IPO), going public via a Special Purpose Acquisition Company (SPAC), or being bought out by a competitor historically emphasize perceived progress on functionality rather than safety. If the exit plan is to make safety someone else's problem post-exit, it is more difficult to justify spending resources on safety rather than functionality until the company goes public.[625]

- The AV industry as a whole takes an aggressively non-regulatory posture, with that policy approach historically enabled by US DOT.[626] This situation forces little, if any, accountability for safety until crashes happen on public roads. There is a tendency for at least some companies seem to treat safety more as a public relations and risk management function than a substantive safety engineering function. Short-term incentives can align with a dysfunctional approach.

- Founders of AV companies with a primarily research, consumer software, or other non-automotive background might not appreciate what is involved in safety at scale for such systems. They might earnestly – but incorrectly – believe that when bugs are removed that automatically bestows safety, or otherwise have a limited view of the different factors of safety discussed in chapter 4. They might also earnestly believe some of the incorrect talking points discussed in section 4.10 regarding safety myths promoted by the AV industry.

---

[625] Safety theater money spent to impart an aura of safety is a different matter, and spending on this area can bring good return on investment. But we are talking about real safety here. In the absence of a commitment to conform to industry safety standards it can be difficult to tell the difference without a deep dive into company practices and culture.

[626] The official US Department of Transportation policy still in effect at the time of this writing states: "In this document, NHTSA offers a nonregulatory approach to automated vehicle technology safety." See page ii of:
https://www.nhtsa.gov/document/automated-driving-systems-20-voluntary-guidance

- The mind-boggling amount of money at stake and potential winnings for participants in this industry would make it difficult for anyone to stay the course in ensuring safety in the face of rich rewards for expediency and ethical compromise. No matter how pure of spirit and well intentioned.

It is impossible to know the motivations, ethical framework, and sincerity of every important player in the AV industry. Many participants, especially rank and file engineers, are sincere in their desire to build AVs and believe they are helping to build a better, safer world. Regardless of that sincerity, it is important to have checks and balances in place to ensure that those good intentions translate into good outcomes for society.

One has to assume that outcomes will align with incentives. Without checks and balances, dangerous incentives can be expected to lead to dangerous outcomes. Checks and balances need to be a combination of internal corporate controls and government regulatory oversight. A profit incentive is insufficient to ensure acceptable safety, especially if it is associated with a relatively short-term business plan.

10.6. Ethical regulatory approaches

Summary: We present a set of ethical regulatory principles broken into the topics of safety, compensation, transparency, inclusion, and non-discrimination. Any regulatory framework should address all these topics.

We have observed that legislators making decisions about AV regulatory laws are often motivated by AV industry promises of jobs, economic opportunities, and high-tech reputation. They promise safety too, but that is not their motivation for supporting industry-leaning bills. These priorities can be reflected in legislation establishing regulatory approaches and authority.

What is not considered enough in most state legislation is that deployment and especially testing of AVs on public roadways exposes other road users to novel and ill-quantified risks. The regulatory approach used should ensure that in exchange for the opportunity to use public facilities and put the public at potentially elevated risk, the AV companies need to both act responsibly and provide ready access to fair compensation for any potential adverse outcomes.

We have identified some important elements of a regulatory approach to AV testing and deployment organized along five principles: Safety, Compensation, Transparency, Inclusion, and Non-Discrimination. [627] Each principle has several elements identified. All elements identified should be addressed by any proposed AV regulations. The reader is encouraged to use this section as a grading rubric for their own state's AV regulatory rules. Expect to be underwhelmed.

---

[627] This section is an update of a brief essay co-authored with Prof. William Widen of the Miami University School of Law. See:
https://safeautonomy.blogspot.com/2022/02/five-principles-for-regulation-of.html

10.6.1. Safety

Operational safety: Commit to a testing and deployment standard for automated driving system (ADS) performance of "substantially better than the average unimpaired human driver" (AUHD) rather than the vague "sufficiently safe" criteria messaged by many AV companies.[628]

Metrics: State the metrics used to make the performance comparison between an ADS and the AUHD, requiring that data be derived from comparable operational scenarios and conditions.

Industry standards: Commit to following published professional industry standards appropriate for the type of AV operation (testing, trials, or deployment) including: SAE J3018, ANSI/UL 4600, ISO 21448, and ISO 26262, as informed by AVSC00001201911 AVSC Best Practice for safety operator selection, training, and oversight procedures for automated vehicles under test and AVSC0007202107 AVSC Information Report for Adapting a Safety Management System (SMS) for Automated Driving System (ADS) SAE Level 4 and 5 Testing and Evaluation. Other standards, including security standards, should also be followed as applicable.

Regulatory time-out: Allow all regulators (federal, state, and local) to temporarily enjoin AV operations (including testing) as a response to events which raise safety concerns, and to revoke testing permits for significant adverse events as well as for patterns of unsafe AV operations or operations that violate law. AV testers and operators should demonstrate safety is acceptable before beginning operation and again to restore operation after a regulatory stand-down.

10.6.2. Responsibility for loss (compensation)

Duty of care: Any company or person operating an AV should, by statute, have a duty of care for safe operation. Any harmed party should not be burdened with having to prove that an AV operator or other responsible party has a duty to avoid harming other road users or passengers. The duty of care should not be delegated to a computer system or other entity that is not a legal person.

Insurance levels: Use a required insurance amount not less than the US DOT's statistical value of a human life ($11.8 million per person in 2021, adjusted annually).[629] Do not allow self-insurance by AV companies which are not cash flow positive, because they might not be around by the time it comes to pay out for a loss. Establish clear single-risk limits and treatment of multiple injuries/fatalities in a single event, with separate treatment for

---

[628] This might not be as robust a bar as Positive Risk Balance, but at the very least testing should not present elevated risk to other road users. Our preference is that AUHD be set as equivalent to a safety case baseline lagging risk indicator per section 8.1.

[629] See: https://www.transportation.gov/office-policy/transportation-policy/revised-departmental-guidance-on-valuation-of-a-statistical-life-in-economic-analysis

special cases, such as truck platooning which might be expected to cause greater harm on a per incident basis.

Owner/occupant liability: Clarify the liability of an owner/occupant of an AV for loss caused when an ADS is properly engaged. May an injured party sue the owner/occupant in the absence of negligence and collect against the owner's insurance policy? Are claims limited to ADS designers, manufacturers, and upfitters for defects? Explain interaction with negligence claims for maintenance, upgrade, and installation failures.

Single collection point for plaintiffs: Allow a plaintiff to collect from a single responsible defendant in full, with joint and several liability and a right of contribution from other responsible parties (regardless of whether the liability is based on negligence or product defect). Doing otherwise burdens harmed parties with a complex and expensive process of determining who should be pursued for collection and then potentially attempting to collect partial sums from numerous parties in potentially international jurisdictions.

Insurance policy with plaintiffs in position of a named insured: Allow plaintiffs to make a claim against AV company insurance policies as if they were a named insured to facilitate prompt payment of medical bills and other amounts so plaintiffs do not face financial pressure to settle quickly for less than full compensation. If the vision of shared autonomous vehicles comes to fruition, far fewer passengers involved in AV crashes will have their own automotive insurance to cover them, and will be in a position of potentially having to sue an AV insurance carrier without the benefit of having their own insurance company acting on their behalf.

Eliminate barriers to collection for full damages: As applicable, lift caps on damage collection by potential plaintiffs with lower cost insurance policies, such as limited tort option policies in Pennsylvania. There is economic incentive to accept limited protection to reduce policy premiums when purchasing automotive insurance, and those limitations might apply even if the covered person is injured as a pedestrian harmed by an AV.

10.6.3. Transparency

Periodic reporting: Require timely publication of AV safety performance, including how actual performance of an AV compares with promised performance relative to the AUHD. It is important to ensure that required public data reporting emphasizes public safety outcomes rather than technology performance.

Crash data: Require timely publication of all crash data and police reports for any incident involving an AV.[630] This should preferably include reporting all substantive traffic law violations such as running red lights even if not cited by a police officer.

---

[630] If an AV company predicably claims that every scrap of original data is proprietary, require them to instead publish an accident reconstruction report and summary of corrective action taken in response to that crash report.

Publicize testing, trials, and deployment plans: Require public dissemination of a testing plan prior to commencement of testing, trials, or deployment. This plan must explain how the AV company addresses safety, responsibility for loss, transparency, inclusion, and non-discrimination. Allow local regulators to review, comment upon, and approve the testing plan to ensure public safety given local events and conditions.

Identification of times, manner, and locations for testing and trials: Require public posting of information about the times and locations for testing and trials so the public understands areas of potentially increased risk and can comment upon potential discriminatory testing practices.

Do not promulgate myths: Advocates for an AV law, rule, or regulation, should not use marketing and outreach materials containing untruthful or misleading statements or material omissions, such as the myth that 94% of serious crashes are primarily caused by human error.

Disclose a harm now, benefits later justification for deployment: If an AV company plans to deploy AVs at scale when the technology does not perform substantially better than an AUHD, or the level of performance cannot be determined with reasonable certainty, disclose this fact in the testing plan so the public can evaluate and react to a policy which exposes them to harms on the promise of future improvements to AV technology.

10.6.4. Inclusion

IEEE 7000: Require AV companies to consider, and preferably conform to the IEEE 7000 standard series,[631] including especially IEEE 7000 itself to identify all interested parties affected by the testing, trials, and deployment of AV technology (including emergency responders, hazardous material transporters, and those in a work zone). Address the concerns of all stakeholders in public plans and concerning testing, trials, and deployments.

Adaptation to local conditions: Give municipalities the power to limit AV operations based on time, manner, and location to account for local conditions (such as preventing truck platooning in certain neighborhoods or driverless trials in school zones; account for local special events; account for recent incidents which present safety concerns); remove any blanket pre-emption by state law so that municipalities are allowed to exercise this power.

Review global approaches to AV regulation: As part of approving any bill, review the recommended approaches to AV regulation taken in other jurisdictions, such as the joint report of the UK law commissions on automated vehicles,[632] and the EU's ethics guidelines for the development of trustworthy artificial intelligence.[633]

---

[631] See: https://ethicsinaction.ieee.org/p7000/
[632] See: https://www.lawcom.gov.uk/project/automated-vehicles/
[633] See: https://digital-strategy.ec.europa.eu/en/library/ethics-guidelines-trustworthy-ai

10.6.5. Non-Discrimination

No concentrated operations in areas of concern: Provide for municipal review of both public testing and trial plans and the time, manner, and locations for testing and trials. Ensure that at-risk communities, such as low-income neighborhoods, do not experience a disproportionately increased risk of loss from AV operations (without mitigating the identified risk) as opposed to other communities not deemed to be at special risk.

Mitigation strategies: If a need arises to concentrate certain types of testing and trials in an at-risk community, use other means to mitigate the adverse impact of the concentration. For example, restrict time of day and environmental conditions during which testing occurs to reduce risk.

Special review of related laws: Review applicable existing state and local laws to identify situations in which AV operations (including crashes) might adversely impact low-income and other at-risk persons, such as limited damage collection for low-cost policies, and the difficulty and expense of pursuing a product defect claim given legal complexity and number of possible defendants.

Justice40: Situate and harmonize non-discrimination efforts within the broader framework of social justice and equity values, including those contained in the Federal Government's Justice40 initiative.[634]

10.7. Summary

Ethical issues for AVs are both plentiful and pervasive. The situation is complicated by the fact that the people building the automated driving system are not personally exposed to crashes that might occur due to design defects. This lack of direct skin in the game fundamentally changes assumptions about driving rules and laws that are implicitly based on a human driver's desire for self-preservation and consideration of potential criminal consequences for unsafe driving practices.

Computers don't care if they are destroyed in a crash, nor do they care that they might go to prison for a reckless driving mistake. Anything that allows the people behind the computers to distance and insulate themselves from any personal consequences of a crash creates challenges to safety.

The most pressing ethical issue is not the infamous Trolley Problem, but rather the governance question for AV deployment: who decides it is time to deploy, based on what? Potential incentives to deploy using strategies that exploit the moral crumple zone and short-term business model incentives create pressure to skew deployment decisions away from public safety.

Many ethical issues should be considered in deploying an AV, ranging from risk transfer to bending traffic rules to how AVs will affect overall transportation system safety. The considerations are complex, and go far

---

[634] See: https://www.whitehouse.gov/environmentaljustice/justice40/

beyond trying to build an AV that does not crash into things on a typical drive.

We finish the chapter with a set of regulatory principles that should (but mostly do not) apply to state and federal regulations. Ethical AV companies should do their best to follow those principles even if governments do not force them to do so.

11. Conclusions

11.1. Wrap-up

We started Chapter 1 with:

"Just make sure the autonomous vehicle is at least as safe as a human driver." Really, how hard can it be to figure that out?

It turned out that there is a lot to consider, especially what we mean by "at least as safe as" and also what we mean by "a human driver." Chapter 9 builds on previous chapters to give the answer to most of the question of when to deploy, with Chapter 10 noting ethical issues that should be addressed during that process.

At a higher level, knowing when an AV is "safe enough" is difficult because it touches on numerous areas that are not only technical, but also psychological, social, regulatory, political, legal, and even philosophical. Add to this that the exceedingly low failure rates permissible for life-critical systems are beyond people's normal experience, and you have a complex issue indeed. The pressure of huge sums of money being bet as venture capital pushing to get a product on the road now and deal with the fine points of safety later does not help either.

We hope that this book serves as an educational resource[635] and, even better, imparts insight into the complex socio-technical machinery that comes into play when considering AV safety. For the long-term success of the AV industry, all the various stakeholders involved must participate in making AV safety decisions with full awareness of the complexities and consequences involved.

11.2. Resources

The following are resources that might be useful. This is not intended to be an exhaustive list, but rather is a starting point.

11.2.1. "Safe enough" resources

- Blumenthal et al., Safe Enough, 2020:
  https://www.rand.org/pubs/research_reports/RRA569-1.html

---

[635]   Judge: I've listened to you for an hour and I'm none the wiser.
         Smith: None the wiser, perhaps, my lord but certainly better informed.
See: https://en.wikiquote.org/wiki/F._E._Smith,_1st_Earl_of_Birkenhead

- o Free download of e-book version with a different set of voices on the topic of ensuring acceptable AV safety.
- European Commission, Ethics of connected and automated vehicles, June 2020: https://data.europa.eu/doi/10.2777/035239
  - o An "AI safety" take on the topic emphasizing data ethics and responsibility.
- UK Law Commission report on Automated Vehicles, 2022: https://www.lawcom.gov.uk/project/automated-vehicles/
- UK Centre for Data Ethics and Innovation policy paper, 2022: https://www.gov.uk/government/publications/responsible-innovation-in-self-driving-vehicles/responsible-innovation-in-self-driving-vehicles
- NHTSA Framework for Automated Driving System Safety, 2020: https://www.federalregister.gov/documents/2020/12/03/2020-25930/framework-for-automated-driving-system-safety
  - o Also see the NHTSA Advanced Notice of Proposed Rulemaking (ANPRM) that would among other things require following industry standards for AVs. Public comments can be seen here: https://www.regulations.gov/docket/NHTSA-2020-0106/comments

11.2.2. Educational resources

- Author's lectures on AV safety and related materials: https://users.ece.cmu.edu/~koopman/lectures/index.html
  - o Short course on Autonomous Vehicle Safety
  - o Course material on dependable embedded systems
  - o Various recorded keynote and other talks
  - o Podcasts
  - o AV safety overview from 2022: https://youtu.be/oE_2rBxNrfc
  - o SPI lecture from 2022: https://youtu.be/mRXotHN0Z6I
  - o Trust & Governance from 2022: https://youtu.be/hZQyFc9ETCE
  - o Alternate source for lectures: https://archive.org/details/@pkoopman
- IFIP WG 10.4 workshop on Intelligent Vehicle Dependability and Security (IVDS) https://ivds2021.dependability.org/program.html
  - o Talks including slides and video regarding AV safety.
- NTSB hearing on the pedestrian fatality in Tempe AZ: https://youtu.be/mSC4Fr3wf0k
  - o The first five minutes of this hearing should be required viewing for everyone working on AV technology. It emphasizes the need for a robust SMS and reminds us that companies do not have to wait for a fatality to get their safety house in order.

- o The crash investigation report is here: https://www.ntsb.gov/investigations/AccidentReports/Reports/HAR1903.pdf

11.2.3. Other resources

- Safe Autonomy Blog: https://safeautonomy.blogspot.com/
  - o Computer-based system safety essential reading list with many pointers to additional materials: https://safeautonomy.blogspot.com/p/safe-autonomy.html
  - o State legislation case study materials from 2022: https://safeautonomy.blogspot.com/2022/02/kansas-av-regulation-bill-hearings.html
  - o AV regulatory launch page: https://safeautonomy.blogspot.com/2021/12/automated-vehicle-regulator-launch-page.html
- Compendium of selected automotive software defects involving safety recalls: https://betterembsw.blogspot.com/p/potentially-deadly-automotive-software.html
- Web resources on assurance cases:
  - o City University of London: https://researchcentres.city.ac.uk/software-reliability/research/diversity
  - o John Rushby, SRI: http://www.csl.sri.com/users/rushby/assurance-cases.html
- ANSI/UL 4600 launch page: https://users.ece.cmu.edu/~koopman/ul4600/index.html
- Other general resources:
  - o System Engineering Body of Knowledge (SEBoK) https://sebokwiki.org/
- Topical sites and events:
  - o SAFECOMP conference series: 2022 edition: https://safecomp22.iks.fraunhofer.de/
  - o Fraunhofer IKS Institute for Cognitive Systems: https://www.iks.fraunhofer.de/
  - o University of York Institute for Safe Autonomy: https://www.york.ac.uk/safe-autonomy/
  - o Safety-Critical Systems Club: https://scsc.uk/
  - o Workshop on Artificial Intelligence Safety Engineering: https://www.waise.org/
  - o International System Safety Society https://system-safety.org/

Sadly, it is common for Web resources to go stale. If one of the cited references becomes unavailable, try accessing via entering the URL into the archive server here: https://archive.org/

11.3. About the author

Prof. Philip Koopman is an internationally recognized expert on Autonomous Vehicle (AV) safety whose work in that area spans over 25 years. He is also actively involved with AV policy and standards as well as more general embedded system design and software quality. His pioneering research work includes software robustness testing and run time monitoring of autonomous systems to identify how they break and how to fix them. He has extensive experience in software safety and software quality across numerous transportation, industrial, and defense application domains including conventional automotive software and hardware systems. He was the principal technical contributor to the UL 4600 standard for autonomous system safety issued in 2020. He is a faculty member of the Carnegie Mellon University ECE department where he teaches software skills for mission-critical systems. In 2018 he was awarded the highly selective IEEE-SSIT Carl Barus Award for outstanding service in the public interest for his work in promoting automotive computer-based system safety. In 2022 he was named to the National Safety Council's Mobility Safety Advisory Group.

Web link: https://users.ece.cmu.edu/~koopman/

www.ingramcontent.com/pod-product-compliance
Lightning Source LLC
LaVergne TN
LVHW051427050326
832903LV00030BD/2955